THE DRAMA OF DICTATORSHIP

THE DRAMA OF DICTATORSHIP

MARTIAL LAW AND THE COMMUNIST PARTIES OF THE PHILIPPINES

JOSEPH SCALICE

SOUTHEAST ASIA PROGRAM PUBLICATIONS
AN IMPRINT OF
CORNELL UNIVERSITY PRESS
ITHACA AND LONDON

Publication of this book was made possible, in part, by a
grant from the Association for Asian Studies First Book
Subvention Program.

First published 2023 by Cornell University Press

Library of Congress Cataloging-in-Publication Data

Names: Scalice, Joseph, 1976– author.
Title: The drama of dictatorship : martial law and the
    communist parties of the Philippines / Joseph Scalice.
Description: Ithaca : Southeast Asia Program Publica-
    tions, an imprint of Cornell University Press, 2023. |
    Includes bibliographical references and index.
Identifiers: LCCN 2022044174 (print) | LCCN 2022044175
    (ebook) | ISBN 9781501770463 (hardcover) |
    ISBN 9781501770470 (paperback) |
    ISBN 9781501770487 (pdf) | ISBN 9781501770494 (epub)
Subjects: LCSH: Marcos, Ferdinand E. (Ferdinand Edralin),
    1917–1989. | Communist Party of the Philippines
    (1930–) | Communist Party of the Philippines (1967–) |
    Dictatorship—Philippines—History—20th century. |
    Martial law—Philippines—History—20th century. |
    Communism—Philippines—History—20th century. |
    Philippines—Politics and government—1946–1973.
Classification: LCC DS686.5 .S353 2023 (print) |
    LCC DS686.5 (ebook) | DDC 324.2599/075—dc23/
    eng/20230105
LC record available at https://lccn.loc.gov/2022044174
LC ebook record available at https://lccn.loc.
    gov/2022044175

All talk to the effect that historical conditions have not yet "ripened" for socialism is the product of ignorance or conscious deception. The objective prerequisites for the proletarian revolution have not only "ripened"; they have begun to get somewhat rotten. Without a socialist revolution, in the next historical period at that, a catastrophe threatens the whole culture of mankind. The turn is now to the proletariat, i.e., chiefly to its revolutionary vanguard. *The historical crisis of mankind is reduced to the crisis of the revolutionary leadership.*

—Leon Trotsky, *The Death Agony of Capitalism and the Tasks of the Fourth International*

CONTENTS

ACKNOWLEDGMENTS

This book begins and ends in the vast city of Greater Manila; my conscious life began here as well.

The hand-painted billboard skyline of Cubao, the treasure hunt Quiapo bookshops, a stagnant estero in the semana santa sun and a precarious coco lumber walkway over eskinita silt, the waterfront at sunset, the giggling slap at a wandering hand on Luneta's grassy shoulder, tumbang preso and patintero, rice field pilapil receding in Cainta, the hoarse morning cries of hasa and taho, water buffalo carts still plying down Kamuning—these are the inscape of home. My childhood was filled out by this extraordinary metropolis and its haphazard sense of history. More than anything else it was love of Manila that impelled my scholarship.

This story is set in the streets of Manila, but it was found in archives. To be a historian is to live with ghosts. It is to sense in newsprint, letters, and leaflets the particulate heartache and longing and toil of the past—the immensity of what was and the frayed, burned-out ends of what might have been—and assemble this in lines of thought, reconstructing its inner logic without losing its sensibility. No one can do this alone. There are a great many people to whom I owe a debt of thanks.

Pride of place in a work so intimately tied to archival materials must go to librarians. Throughout my work I was assisted greatly by the marvelous staff of librarians at UC Berkeley. In particular, I am grateful to the tireless and friendly help I received from Rebecca Darby in the Newspaper and Microforms Library, the entire staff at both the Interlibrary Services and the Northern Regional Library Facility, and Virginia Shih of the South/Southeast Asia Library. A scholar could not ask for better help than that which they provided.

Even more, I am grateful to the staff of unnamed librarians at the University of the Philippines, Diliman, who courageously and conscientiously collected and filed all of the political journals, manifestos, and ephemera of the late 1960s and 1970s. When martial law was declared, most radicals burned all their political documents. Were it not for the trove carefully preserved in two steel cabinets in the Diliman library, a great deal of history would have been lost. This collection eventually became the Philippine Radical Papers. I could not have written this book without this collection, and I extend my heartfelt thanks to everyone involved in the preservation of this material.

Beyond these were the wonderful collections in the ISEAS-Yusof Ishak Institute, the National Library of Singapore, Tamiment Library at NYU, Hoover Institution at Stanford, the New York Public Library, the University of Hawai'i Library, the National Library of Scotland, the International Institute of Social History in Amsterdam, and the Leiden University Library. The initial stages of my research were made possible by a Fulbright IIE fellowship, and publication of the book was aided by funding from the Association for Asian Studies.

My home at UC Berkeley was in the Department of South and Southeast Asian Studies, tucked away in the uppermost regions of the labyrinthine Dwinelle. The camaraderie of the faculty, staff, and students of SSEAS buoyed my time there. I extend sincere thanks in particular to Jake Dalton, Penny Edwards, Munis Faruqui, Bob Goldman, Alex von Rospatt, and Paula Varano for their generous declaration of support for me during difficult circumstances. Kat Gutierrez, once my student, has outpaced me; I can only cheer. Leloy Claudio is both friend and interlocutor, and I have gained much from his company and ideas. On the wider Berkeley campus, I benefited from working with Andrew Barshay and Dick Walker. Mark Allison was an ideal weekly discussion partner in our careful study of Marx's economic corpus, and I owe him lifelong thanks for introducing me to George Eliot. Kumi Hadler is both an inspiration and a friend, and Maia and Noe were my theatrical partners in crime for weekly performances of Shakespeare. Above all, I am grateful to Peter Zinoman, who took on the role of mentor with the passing of Jeff Hadler. Peter's assistance and advice were irreplaceable.

There are a number of scholars whose ideas and support proved personally valuable; some may not agree with my conclusions, but all have enriched this book. Carol Hau, Bomen Guillermo, and Mike Montesano each contributed to my arguments and my enjoyment of the world. Vicente Rafael is both an intellectual inspiration and a friend. John Sidel supported me continually, put up with my last-minute requests for help, and gave me a world of friendly and vital counsel.

Life both underpins and punctuates all our endeavors. I wrote portions of this while working as an ethnic studies teacher at Castlemont High School in Oakland. I read *The Autobiography of Malcolm X* out loud to my students; they bought me Takis and ice cream, kicked and protested, and left an indelible mark on my soul. When the teachers went on strike, I told my students we were fighting for public education and asked them what they thought our schools needed. In the wealthiest state in the wealthiest country in the world, my students' top requests were fresh pencils in class and toilet paper in the goddamned bathrooms. My fellow teachers and roommates David Brown and Evan Blake are the embodiment of true friendship. They filled a very difficult period in my life with blitz chess and serious-minded conversation and belly laughs and road trips. They are the two best surrogate uncles my children could ever have. Fred Choate, a humane and knowledgeable traveling companion, repeatedly drove me to and from the archives at Hoover. Bleacher seats in the Coliseum—Go A's!—and Tom Waits and John dos Passos; part of me will never leave East Oakland.

A postdoc at Nanyang Technological University, delightfully unexpected, took me to Singapore in late 2019. A scholar could not ask for a better home than NTU. The pandemic locked me in the island nation with the abruptness of exile. The windows of my room in a 1970s-era HDB opened over Boon Lay; Ding and Zi Yan were the best of company in our little flat throughout the pandemic circuit breaker. Taomo Zhou was warmly supportive in friendship and wonderfully sharp in her scholarly contributions. Ang Cheng Guan regularly met with me to discuss, over kopi o kosong, the progress of my writing and helpfully advised me in many regards. Chien-Wen Kung and Wen-Qing Ngoei were like brothers to me during my stay. The gathering of Beer and Books brightened each month—Simon Creak, Gerard Sasges, Samson Lim, James Warren, brave souls who read an early version of this work. Gerard and Shiwen Ng were the quintessence of conviviality. Florence Mok, Yun Zhang, Ameem Lufti, Serkan Yolacan, Nisha Mathew—I was fortunate in the quality of my friends and colleagues. David Brotherson, Michael Goodman, and I were the Athos, Porthos, and Aramis of hand-pressed coffee. In particular I am grateful to David, my companion in laughter and absurdity on more hikes, bike treks, and expeditions than I can count.

My budget a raveled shoestring, I holed up in a garret in Edinburgh to complete this book. My housemates—Alex, Chris, Tracie, Frankie, Thomas—were ebullient with friendship and whisky. If you strain after it you may find shades of fuscous gray, the haar over St. Giles, and trackless miles of the Pentland Hills in the connective fibers of my prose.

Through all my wanderings I was fortunate to have a global set of cothinkers, who with singleness of purpose, grapple with the great questions of history: Eric London, Peter Symonds, Cheryl Crisp, Nick Beams, Max Boddy, Tom Peters, and Dante Pastrana. Joseph Kishore is the sort of friend that you meet once in a lifetime—if you are lucky. I have learned more about history and politics from David North than anyone else I have ever met. It is an honor to be his friend. To sit at table with such companions is to bind together the stuff of the past, the questions of the present, and the prospects of the future in conversations in equal measures intense and humane and good-natured.

North of Manila lies Paniqui, Tarlac, my adopted home. The vast heaving breath of this rural world conspires still to a cyclic conformity and lives measured by inundation and harvest. The faint quickening at its center and the increasingly audible rasp at its fringes are muffled in the timelessness hanging over the town like an immense blanket. Here amid the rice field silences and polyglot market chatter—the laughing, haggling life struggle over peso and kiloweight—is an entire community of my cousins and drinking partners and acquaintances and friends. This book is theirs as well.

I could not have written this book without the unfailing support of Jeff Hadler. Jeff was my intellectual mentor on the Berkeley campus, a humane and honest scholar and a marvelous teacher. I was fortunate to call Jeff my friend for twelve years. Throughout this period he wisely steered my scholarship, went far out of his way to support my work and nurture my intellectual development, and was the source of much good humor along the way. Jeff was my professor when I was an undergraduate and my mentor and friend as a graduate student. He signed my dissertation less than two weeks before he died, and the world dimmed slightly at his passing. And thus I inscribe this book,

To Jeff Hadler, one of the best men I have had the privilege to know—

To my parents, Roger and Janet, in honor of the courage and integrity of my father, who "even though he did not know where he was going, obeyed and went," and the unfailing compassion of my mother—

To Herminio, *isang tunay na Ama kahit ako'y manugang lamang*, in honor of his kindness and boundless hospitality—

And to my children, River, Elizabeth, and Nathaniel, my greatest delights in life—

I gratefully dedicate this work.

NOTE ON TRANSLATION
AND ORTHOGRAPHY

One of the more difficult tasks of writing this book was dealing with the stilted political Tagalog of the Stalinists. A dishonest idea rarely finds beautiful expression, and a dishonest concept in translation fares even worse. Most of the literature in Tagalog—leaflets, manifestos, articles—produced by the Communist Party in the period leading up to martial law seems to have been first conceived in English. The mixed metaphors and vituperation were then translated into Tagalog without any consideration for the new language—Stalinist English wearing Tagalog clothing. The result was far from pleasant. Trotsky wrote that reading Stalin's *Problems of Leninism* "evokes the sensation of choking on finely-chopped bristles."[1] While I have painstakingly translated the prose of the Communist Party of the Philippines (CPP) as honestly and accurately as possible, I have not made it pleasant.

I have included selections from the original Tagalog where I thought it necessary to be absolutely clear what was being said. In the majority of cases, however, I have included only my translation, as incorporating the Tagalog originals would have resulted in a work of considerably greater length.

I have used Pinyin transliterations of Chinese names and places throughout and have retained the use of Wade-Giles only in the titles of existing works. This involved updating the spelling used in the documents produced by the CPP and its contemporaries. In keeping with widely established scholarly practice, however, I have not transliterated Chiang Kai-shek as Jiang Jieshi.

I have used the place-names of Manila that were current at the time. Isaac Peral, Lepanto, Azcarraga, and the Philippine College of Commerce have all been renamed. The evolution of place-names reflects the political dynamic of the country. The names of politicians were plastered over the older Spanish names, often taking a decade before the new names were accepted by the population. Thus, Azcarraga became Recto.

But while you may now land at Ninoy Aquino International Airport, if you head east you will still arrive in Forbes Park, and north will take you down Taft Avenue, until you arrive in Plaza Lawton. Some names have not changed.

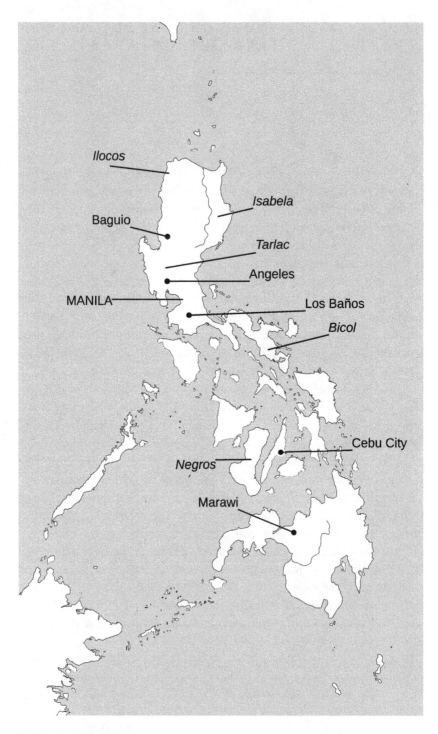

Ilocos

Isabela

Baguio

Tarlac

Angeles

MANILA

Los Baños

Bicol

Cebu City

Negros

Marawi

MAP 1. The Philippines

THE DRAMA OF DICTATORSHIP

Introduction

There is an ominous feeling one gets when reading through Philippine newspapers from the late 1960s and early 1970s. No other period in Philippine journalism quite compares to it. A wide range of dailies and weeklies were in circulation, some of a very high caliber; the quality of their writing and the breadth of their opinions are striking. And then suddenly, abruptly—silence.

The date 22 September 1972 marks the last day of effectively every Filipino newspaper in the archives. Martial law had been declared, and the extraordinary ferment of the preceding period was over. The papers, as well as the radio and television stations, all ceased under executive fiat only to reemerge later, a quiescent media operated by the cronies of the dictator. It was not just the media, however, that were silenced. The streets fell silent as well. On 21 September, fifty thousand people had gathered in Plaza Miranda to denounce the threat of martial law. The day after it was declared, no one assembled and no one rallied; the nation seemingly acquiesced. Alfred McCoy wrote, "In declaring martial law . . . the president would ask the Filipino people to trade their democracy for stability. By their silence and compliance, the majority would tacitly accept his Faustian bargain."[1] That there was silence is irrefutable, but what was its origin? Was it truly tacit consent and the trading of democracy for stability?

Martial law came as a surprise to no one. It was easily the most anticipated event of the decade. People had been warning of it, advocating it, and denouncing it in the daily press and in mass protests since before the First Quarter Storm of January to March 1970, and yet the opposition to martial law, which had a mass following among workers and youths, was utterly unprepared. It was, above all, this lack of political preparation that allowed Ferdinand Marcos to declare martial law. The responsibility for this rests squarely with the Communist parties of the Philippines, which tied the mass opposition to dictatorship to the interests of rival sections of the ruling elite, all of whom were vying to impose military rule.

The historian Donald Berlin details how "the roots of martial law lay in the Philippines' long colonial experience and in the first decades of independence" and describes it as "a natural part of the fabric of the Philippine past."[2] The 1935 Philippine constitution clothed the exigencies of US colonial rule in the gaudy, scanty trappings of democracy. The spirit of the country's democratic traditions, hard-won in mass anticolonial struggles, never touched parchment. The Americans ensured that military dictatorship was written into the legal code and that trial by jury was not. Article VII, Section 10, granted the executive branch the power to "suspend the privilege of the writ of habeas corpus, or place the Philippines or any part thereof under Martial Law." The most basic democratic rights, including that of habeas corpus, the right to challenge unlawful detention, could be stripped away by presidential fiat. Berlin argues that martial law under Marcos was a return to the normal character of civilian-military relations that had been established during the colonial period. In this he errs. While the seed of military rule had been planted by the office of the US governor general, the Marcos dictatorship was not the atavistic re-emergence of a prior mode of rule. Martial law in 1972 was something qualitatively new and was an expression of global developments.

The impulse to impose military rule had existed within the ruling class since the formal granting of independence in 1946. Plots to that end had been drawn up by Elpidio Quirino, Carlos Garcia, and Diosdado Macapagal during their terms of office, but none of them succeeded. What distinguished Marcos's machinations from those of his predecessors was neither his cleverness nor his will to power, but rather the international situation of social and economic crisis. Explosive class struggles erupted around the globe from the middle of the 1960s to the middle of the 1970s, and the First Quarter Storm of Manila was presaged in the streets of Paris and followed in those of Athens. It is in this context that we see the rise of dictatorship as the preferred mode of bourgeois rule. Suharto and Marcos, Pinochet and Park shared a common geopolitical DNA. Washington facilitated and propped up these brutal regimes. Moscow and Beijing, looking to secure advantage against each other, followed suit. Moscow supported Suharto; Beijing, Pinochet.

The postwar order was collapsing. The restabilization of capitalism in the wake of the Second World War, funded by Washington and carried out on terms that it dictated, had established a temporary equilibrium that rested above all on the unprecedented level of global economic dominance exercised by one nation—the United States. This equilibrium could not be sustained. The economies of Europe and Japan, so necessary as buffers against both the Communist bloc and working-class unrest, had to be rebuilt, and the buffers rapidly became rivals. The hegemony of Washington was built on an economic superiority that, as the 1950s aged, eroded and was sustained by the machinations of the Central Intelligence Agency (CIA), which toppled, installed, and propped up leaders around the globe. The massive export of US capital, in conjunction with the establishment of the gold-backed US dollar as the world currency, gave a monetary expression to the relative decline of American capitalism in the early 1960s. Washington's shrinking stake in the global economy could be assayed in gold at the rate of thirty-five dollars to the ounce and measured by its inability to pay. A crisis was in the offing, and the palace intrigues and little wars of US intelligence could no longer sustain its rule. The year 1965 was the tipping point. Economic dominance had eroded under US hegemony, and the entire edifice threatened to collapse. New forms of rule were required, a mass deployment of the military and a vast apparatus of social repression— war and dictatorship, Vietnam and Indonesia.

At stake in this violent rebalancing were not simply US interests. Capitalism around the globe, from the financial speculations in London to the sugar plantations on Negros, had been rebuilt out of the ashes of the war on the scaffolding of Bretton Woods. The sharp balance of payments crisis in Washington expressed the rot pervading the entire structure; the scaffolding groaned ominously. The British pound sterling was devalued in 1967, and in March of the next year, banks closed in the face of the gold crisis. A two-tier fiction was established by an emergency summit of world banks on 17 March: central banks would honor the thirty-five dollar convertibility; all other dealings would follow the free market price of gold. The transoms and braces had been removed. Massive inflation and a mad scramble to secure profits followed; the living standards of the working class around the globe were slashed to the bone. In August 1971, US president Richard Nixon ended dollar convertibility, and the framework of the postwar order collapsed.[3]

A component of the postwar hegemony of Washington was the entirely subservient and dependent economy that it chartered of its former colony, the Philippines. Under the terms established in particular by the Bell Trade Act (1946) and the Laurel-Langley Agreement (1955), the Philippine economy was tied to the United States as a source of cheap raw materials and a market for finished goods. As the undisputed dominance of the US dollar declined and then spiraled into crisis, Filipino capitalists scrambled to secure their interests, seeking new markets and the renegotiation of the Laurel-Langley Agreement.

Crisis entailed unrest. Profits were imperiled and needed to be secured through the increased exploitation of workers. The ghetto uprisings in the United States of 1964–65, brutally suppressed, presaged a threatening future for world capitalism. Antiwar demonstrations followed. By 1968, the French working class had shut down the country in the largest general strike in history. As the new decade opened, these tensions compounded as the cost of basic necessaries soared; the price of rent and food expanded beyond the reach of an average worker's pay.[4] Immense social struggles returned to the fore, and the question of revolution was in the air. This was sharply expressed in the Philippines. Mass anger at the brutality of the US war in Vietnam combined with rapidly worsening living conditions to produce a palpable sense that an explosion was imminent.[5] In August 1967, Marshall Wright of the National Security Council wrote to National Security Advisor Walt Rostow, "It would be nearly impossible to overestimate the gravity of the problems with which our next ambassador to Manila must deal. It has become common-place for people knowledgeable on the Philippines to predict a vast social upheaval in the near future. There is widespread talk that the current president will be the last popularly elected Philippine chief executive. Many high-level American officials consider the Philippines to be the most serious and the most bleak threat that we face in Asia."[6]

The rival sections of the ruling class, and their leading political representatives, agreed on the need for authoritarian rule, but they could not peaceably select the permanent occupant of the presidential palace of Malacañang. As Marcos took office as president in 1966, the quiet measured steps toward dictatorship commenced. The more astute observers, particularly the young opposition senator Benigno "Ninoy" Aquino, noted this and began preparations of their own. By 1967, the imminent end of popular elections was "widespread talk" among the bourgeoisie. In August 1969, the economic crisis broke: an irremediable balance of payments deficit, massive inflation, and a devastating rice shortage. Months later, Marcos secured reelection, trouncing his opponent and becoming the first incumbent president to retain office in the postcolonial period. With their profits and political offices at stake, the opposition turned murderous. Social crisis and political crisis aligned; the curtain lifted on the drama of dictatorship.

Nixon took office deeply concerned that the United States had overextended itself in Vietnam; neither the budget nor public opinion would sustain the United States' current presence in Asia. The Nixon Doctrine, announced in

July 1969, sought to uphold Washington's interests in the region while reducing its overhead by using targeted aid that "deliberately facilitated the construction and consolidation of repressive, exclusionary regimes in Southeast Asia."[7] Thus, when Marcos imposed martial law, the United States tripled its military aid to the Philippines.[8] The mantra of modernization theory that economic development is the foundation of political stability, Camelot's vision for the Third World, was upended. Political stability—authoritarian rule—was the bedrock to which existing economic interests would anchor. The United States boarded up the showcase of democracy in Asia.

Here the tale twists. The Soviet Union and China, in open conflict with each other, shifted policy in the same period in a manner akin to Nixon. Moscow began to promote the Non-Capitalist Path of Development, and Beijing the Three Worlds Theory. These were marketing pitches, theory as ad copy. They touted the geopolitical reorientations of the national bureaucracies in their pursuit of friendly relations with autocrats. The incentives they offered were extended through rival national Communist parties—in the Philippines, the Partido Komunista ng Pilipinas (PKP) and Communist Party of the Philippines (CPP). These parties proved instrumental in the imposition of dictatorship.

It was a profoundly contradictory affair, bitterly ironic in its development and tragic in its denouement. Communist Party leaders and anti-Communist politicos allied; US imperialism and the Soviet bloc aligned, hostile forces drawn together in plots against democracy. The Moscow-oriented PKP terrorized Manila with bombings, secretly coordinated with Marcos's military, to justify the imposition of dictatorship. The Beijing-aligned CPP worked with forces tied to the CIA in an attempt to install a rival faction of the capitalist class—similarly bent on dictatorship—by coup d'état. The central pretext for martial law, cited by both Washington and Marcos, was the danger of Communism, and yet martial law was imposed with the support of a Communist party and with the backing of the Soviet Union. How does one untangle this snarl of contradictions?

The opportunism and duplicity of individual leaders doubtless played a role, but it possessed an accidental character, flotsam on the deeper currents of history. A satisfying explanation must account for why there were two Communist parties and not one. It must be rooted in concrete social developments in the Philippines and yet establish why diverging political tendencies in the country found their interests aligned with the positions articulated in the geopolitical rivalry of Moscow and Beijing. Finally, the explanation must, in a logical, causal fashion, demonstrate why these supposedly Marxist tendencies, when refracted through the prism of social upheaval and dictatorship, illuminated the interests of rival factions of the ruling elite. The answer lies in the program of Stalinism. A historical explanation is necessary.

Stalinism

The 1917 October revolution created the world's first workers state—a transitional form, no longer capitalist but not yet socialist. The questions posed and ideas raised by this revolution gripped the political imagination of the twentieth century. Russian Social Democracy—both its Menshevik and Bolshevik wings—grappled with the relationship between bourgeois-democratic and socialist revolutions.[9] Georgii Plekhanov, head of the Mensheviks, argued as far back as the 1880s that Russian capitalism's belated development would necessarily limit a revolution to measures deemed bourgeois and democratic in character, including the overthrow of the czar, the creation of the institutions of democracy, and the ending of feudal relations in agriculture. The objective economic conditions for a socialist revolution did not yet exist in Russia. Only when capitalism had adequately advanced could this second stage of revolution begin. The historically circumscribed character of the first stage assigned a progressive role to a section of the capitalist class; this was, after all, their revolution. The task of the working class in this first stage was to give critical support to the capitalists in their progressive struggles.[10]

Plekhanov's formulas, for all their clarity of thought, remained of an abstract and schematic character. The defeated revolution of 1905 tested his conceptions and showed them wanting. Confronted by a militant general strike of the working class and the formation of soviets, the bourgeoisie retreated; its right wing (the Oktobrists) supported the government crackdown, and its left wing (the Cadets) abandoned the call for a constituent assembly.[11] That year, in the thick of developments, Vladimir Lenin elaborated what became the guiding principle of the Bolsheviks until April 1917. The agrarian question, to be resolved through the seizure and nationalization of the estates, was the central problem of the democratic revolution. These were bourgeois and not socialist measures, Lenin insisted, and yet the capitalist class, tied to landed property and threatened by the growing force of the working class, would oppose all measures of expropriation. History had moved on; the bourgeoisie would no longer play any progressive role. What was needed was the "democratic dictatorship of the proletariat and peasantry."[12] Lenin's phrase possessed a certain ambivalence, a half step between worlds. The bourgeoisie were excluded, but their separate stage remained.

Leon Trotsky, head of the Petersburg Soviet in 1905, imprisoned in 1906, brought the question to its logical conclusion in his article "The Results of the Revolution and Its Prospects."[13] The insistence on the exclusively democratic character of the revolution artificially constrained the organically developing struggles of the working class within the limits of a historically outmoded schema. How would the "democratic dictatorship" respond to striking workers who demanded control of production? Would it side with the owners and insist that workers limit their demands to the boundaries of capitalism, or would it side with the working class and take socialist measures? The concrete requirements of a developing revolution would tear apart Lenin's formulation along the fault lines of its ambivalence. The fundamental question, Trotsky argued, had been wrongly formulated. It was not a matter of Russia's ripeness for socialist revolution. World capitalism—with its global market, system of production, and division of labor—was ripe for socialism. Individual nation-states, whether economically advanced or semicolonial, were subordinate components of this global whole. To complete the democratic tasks they confronted, workers would be compelled to implement socialist measures. The fate of the revolution would be decided on the world stage in the struggle for international socialism. Trotsky wrote, "The completion of the socialist revolution within national limits is unthinkable. . . . The socialist revolution begins on the national arena, it unfolds on the international arena, and is completed on the world arena. Thus the socialist revolution becomes a permanent revolution in a newer and broader sense of the word; it attains completion only in the final victory of the new society on our entire planet."[14]

Lenin's arrival at the Finland Station in Petrograd in April 1917 "laid down a Rubicon between the tactics of yesterday and today," a dividing line between February and October.[15] He set aside his prior conception of the "democratic dictatorship," ended the Bolsheviks' policy of critical support for the bourgeois provisional government, called for all power to be transferred to the soviets, and oriented the party to socialist revolution.[16] The perspective of permanent revolution thus became the program of the seizure of power led by Lenin and Trotsky in October 1917.[17] The fate of the Russian Revolution rested outside its borders; it would rise or fall with the struggles of the international working class for socialism.

Isolated by the crushing of the 1918 revolution in Germany and building on infrastructure devastated by world war and civil war, the workers' government confronted immense challenges. Its new property forms combined with generalized want, breeding inevitable inequality; socialized production was strained through bourgeois distribution. Crisis weakened the organs of workers democracy and imparted to the bureaucracy the exigent power to administer not merely things but human beings as well. The apparatus grew unchecked, and potbellied functionaries, soon in their millions, displaced the lean-thewed cadre of October. Gendarme of inequality, the bureaucracy increasingly felt itself a privileged minority, a separate social layer.[18] They were absorbed with the Soviet economy, in which their interests rooted; international revolution was but a shibboleth. The nationalist interests of this caste found their most concentrated expression in Joseph Stalin, a man of organization and subterfuge.

David North, an expert on the history of the Fourth International, writes, "Though he did not realize this himself, Stalin was articulating the views of an expanding bureaucracy which saw the Soviet state not as the bastion and staging ground of world socialist revolution, but as the national foundation upon which its revenues and privileges were based."[19] In late 1924, months after the death of Lenin, Stalin and Nikolai Bukharin, at the time a leading accomplice of Stalin, first put forward the idea that it was possible to build socialism within the confines of a single country.[20] This notion—the seminal argument of the bureaucracy—contained in embryo the entirety of the political program of Stalinism. All else was determined by this end. Diplomatic and trade relations with world capitalism, from necessary but temporary measures subordinate to the interests of the international proletariat, became indispensable aids in the construction of the national economy. The young Soviet state, however, could bring little to negotiations. The language of Marxism and the usurped mantle of 1917 gave the Stalinist bureaucracy immense sway over the masses of much of the world. This was its greatest capital.

The two-stage theory, hollowed out of Plekhanov's materialist logic and clarity of thought, was presented, chapter and verse, as Stalinist dogma. Decisively invalidated by the very revolution from which the parvenus drew authority, the schema justified their political alliances, a paint-by-number sketch to be filled in with the preferred colors of the capitalists du jour. There were two stages to the revolution—first the democratic, then the socialist—and there were four progressive classes in the first stage of the revolution: the working class, the peasantry, the petty bourgeoisie, and the national bourgeoisie (figure 0.1). They confronted three great enemies: the imperialists, the landlords, and the comprador bourgeoisie, collaborators with the imperialists. One feels a touch embarrassed reciting this breviary, senses the succulence of history desiccated in its lines. The division between the national and the comprador bourgeoisie, between good and bad capitalists, hinged on their independence from or subservience to international finance capital, but this was, like the rest of the schema, a straw man. There are no national capitalist interests independent of the world market and system of currency, credit, and production. In practice, the national and the comprador in the bourgeoisie proved to be labels applied by Stalinists to their allies and the enemies of their allies; the labels were as interchangeable as their alliances. With these formulations, the bureaucrats brought the political movement of labor as a negotiable instrument to the bargaining table of world capitalism.

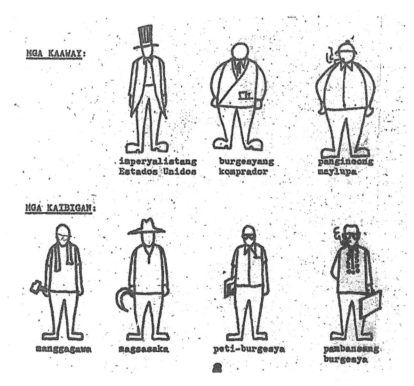

FIGURE 1. Friends and enemies, depicting the basic Stalinist alignment of forces. US imperialism, the comprador bourgeoisie, and the landlords compose the "enemies," while workers, peasants, petty bourgeoisie, and national bourgeoisie make up the "friends." From a 1970s CPP manual on drawing, *Drawing: Tulong sa Pagtuturo* (PRP 06/25.01)

All of the outgrowths and epiphenomena associated with Stalinism—purges, assassinations, mass murder, the cult of the great leader, historical falsification on an industrial scale—emerge organically from this, the political essence of the matter. Bartering the workers movement to secure its national interests, the bureaucracy littered the twentieth century with betrayal upon betrayal. The lurching machinery of Stalinism sought to crush the political opposition this aroused, assassinating Leon Trotsky and murdering the Left Opposition and the old Bolsheviks.[21]

The PKP, founded in 1930, was dragged behind this program. The two-stage revolution and the quest for an alliance with a progressive section of the capitalist class dictated the vicissitudes of its development. The Popular Front alliance of global Stalinism with US imperialism determined the PKP's support for US colonial rule in the Philippines during the Second World War. The PKP placed itself at the head of the Huk peasant rebellion in the early 1950s. Many of the

Central Committee members of the party were arrested, and the rebellion was eventually crushed. The remaining leadership of the PKP adopted the "single-file policy," a mandate that individual cadre would have contact with only two members of the party and that instructions would be disseminated down a chain, a sort of revolutionary game of telephone. The single-file policy was presented as a security measure, but it effectively dissolved the party. At the instigation of the Partai Komunis Indonesia (PKI) in the early 1960s, the PKP attempted to rebuild its organs and reinsert itself into public political life. It was fairly successful in this, and an energetic new party leader, Jose Ma. Sison, was instrumental in the process. The PKP allied with President Diosdado Macapagal, bringing the support of the workers movement behind his administration, and with his support the party founded a youth wing, the Kabataang Makabayan (Nationalist Youth, KM), and a peasant organization, Malayang Samahan ng Magsasaka (Free Federation of Peasants, MASAKA). In 1965, sensing greener pastures, the PKP backed Macapagal's rival, Ferdinand Marcos, for president, proclaiming him representative of the progressive national bourgeoisie. The party remained outlawed, but the mutually agreed on hypocrisy of elite politics in the Philippines supplied its front organizations opportunities for a prominent role. On taking office at the beginning of 1966, Marcos brought a number of party members and supporters into his administration, providing them with salaried government positions.

Crisis gripped the Communist bloc, however, and the PKP reborn confronted a choice of political lines and allegiances: Moscow or Beijing. The Soviet Union and China, both committed to a Stalinist program of constructing socialism within their own borders, never merged their economies. Their divergent national interests inevitably conflicted, giving rise to rivalry, then open split and armed conflict. The uneven economic development of the two countries and their starkly different geopolitical circumstances fueled tensions.

Situated behind the buffer zone of eastern Europe and with a fairly stable industrial base, the Soviet Union followed a policy of peaceful coexistence with the United States and established friendly ties with autocrats. China, in contrast, found itself threatened on all sides by the mid-1960s, facing an imminent threat posed by the US invasion of Vietnam and the loss of its largest international ally, the PKI, after a military coup in 1965 by General Suharto in which hundreds of thousands of party cadres were killed. The Chinese Communist Party (CCP) sought to whip up armed struggle throughout the region to diffuse the threat of US imperialism to China's immense imperiled borders. In September 1965, Lin Biao, head of the People's Liberation Army and one of Mao's most loyal supporters, published a statement, "Long Live the Victory of the People's War!," which extrapolated from the guerrilla tactics of the struggle against the Japanese occupation two and a half decades earlier the principle of surrounding the "capitalist redoubts" from the countryside of the world. The promotion of people's war was a marked shift in Beijing's political line, which had previously pursued relations around the globe in a manner similar to that of Moscow.[22] As Moscow embraced Suharto, the CCP turned to protracted people's war and armed uprisings throughout the "countryside of the world" backed by China, "the Yan'an of world revolution."[23]

This line contained not a shred of opposition to the capitalist class; it was, in fact, mobilized in service to it. Beijing, its historical ties to October 1917 more starkly attenuated and deformed than those of Moscow, made less effort to dress up its line of class collaboration in Marxist garb. It openly hailed capitalism as revolutionary and needful while publicly lauding "progressive" aristocrats and monarchs.[24]

Where Moscow sought the support of dictators to stabilize its peaceful coexistence with Washington, Beijing pursued ties with restive sections of the bourgeoisie, the excluded opposition in a time of unrest, the conspiring understudies in the drama of dictatorship. China could not offer economic blandishments comparable to those of the Soviet Union, but it could supply and orient the barrel of a gun. A peasant army, organized under the leadership of a party loyal to Beijing, would bring tremendous social weight to the bourgeois opposition in a time of uncertainty, unrest, and uprising. Rather than weather the impending storm, parties loyal to the line of Beijing would ride it, channeling its energy behind the rival candidates for dictatorship. Despite being weaker than Moscow, Beijing could thus compel the dispersal of Washington's forces from its borders, spreading them thin throughout the region, and secure ties with potential future rulers. Maoism was thus not something separate from Stalinism. It was a right-wing mutation compelled on the nationalism of Stalinism in countries of catastrophically underdeveloped economy; it was the excrescence of an excrescence.

It was in this context of global social upheaval and conflict within international Stalinism that the PKP tore itself apart. The pressure of the brewing social storm bore down with unbearable intensity on the party responsible for marshaling the nervous energy of the streets through the corridors of state power without disturbing the wall hangings. The party's entire leadership sought national industrialization and the defense of the interests of Filipino capitalists; this was their political lodestar. The gusts of unrest, gathering to gale force on the horizon, however, were headwinds. The dilemma before the party was not its orientation—for Polaris had not moved—but the manner of sailing: tack to center and weather the storm, or yaw sharply to port and belly out the sails. The goal was shared, the means in dispute; the compulsion of choice gripped the PKP.

American money, both its market and investments, represented a relatively diminishing share of the world economy. An important and growing section of Filipino capitalists sought to expand their business interests through ties with Moscow. These views were best articulated in the pages of Tonypet Araneta's *Graphic Weekly*, which in 1966 began running articles in nearly every issue on the benefits of trade relations with the Soviet bloc. The Soviet economy offered a market for Philippine goods and could serve as an alternative source of loans and aid. The Chinese economy was qualitatively weaker and could not fulfill this function.

Marcos, newly elected with the support of both the KM and the Lapiang Manggagawa (Workers' Party), the youth and labor wings of the PKP, was from the beginning of his term receptive to the opening of diplomatic and economic ties with Moscow. In his first statement to the press outlining the foreign policy perspectives of the incoming administration, Marcos's foreign secretary, Narciso Ramos, stated that Manila would give "due consideration" to any "sincere Russian proposal" to establish diplomatic relations. The Marcos government, however, would "remain opposed to any kind of relationship—political or commercial—with the Beijing regime."[25]

Marcos brought leading party members and broad layers of its periphery into his administration, appointing them to comfortable salaried offices from which they could conduct the party's affairs. With its ties to Suharto, Moscow clearly established that it would support and fund dictatorships as a method of securing its geopolitical interests, and these ties, it was reasoned, could build national industry and further the growth of native capitalism. A social explosion was imminent, however, and this choice—to knowingly tread the path to dictatorship in the furtherance of capitalist interests—would place the party outside the barricades. It was a perilous choice, for if the explosion was not contained, the party would lose everything. Those who chose Moscow and Marcos staked their political future on the successful imposition of martial law, and thus, as waves of social struggle washed over Manila, they launched bombing campaigns to justify its imposition and ghostwrote Marcos's apologia for dictatorship.

Broad layers of the PKP bent to this conception. A significant portion of the party's leadership—staid academic and professional elements, many now ensconced in government offices—saw their interests best articulated here. They took with them the party's old established trade unions, but these were not fighting organs of the working class and they carried greater weight on paper than they did on the streets. Above all, the party retained MASAKA, an organization founded on the sole political conception that peasants should appeal to a powerful executive for reforms.[26] The majority of the party's youth, now organized in the KM, were the sons and daughters of MASAKA, and they too followed this line.[27] In sum, as the horizon darkened ominously, a vast majority of the party positioned itself behind Moscow and Marcos.

Jose Ma. Sison, who broke from the leadership of the PKP to lead the founding of the CPP, sought the same ends as the older party. At the beginning of his political career, Sison had written that revolutionary struggles run the risk of becoming "wasteful mobs" and falling into the "pits of anarchy" if they are not marshaled behind the banner of nationalism.[28] His perspective was unaltered, but the means of achieving it needed to be adapted to an epoch of upheaval and unrest.

The narrow layers drawn to the political line of Beijing were largely urban, university-based youth. The global ripples of social explosion bore the acrid smell of gunpowder and the chants of the cultural revolution to the streets of Manila. They were faint at first, but they were unmistakable. Nerves bundled tightly across the body politic. The educated, urban youth around Sison were drawn to this tension; it was electric, charged with an immense destructive capacity. For many who would be won to the ranks of the organizations loyal to the CPP, the lodestar was secondary; what mattered was the explosion. The entire hypocritical social order—corrupt politicians, outmoded mores, wars, poverty—was rotten from top to bottom; it should be blown away. A strong anarchistic streak ran through these layers. The straitlaced and insipid formulations of the old party, a good many of them written by Sison himself, would no longer serve. It was impossible to rouse emotion or constrain and channel outrage behind these lines. The political formulations of Mao were dedicated to audacity and gun barrels. They might suffice.

Young Teodoro Locsin's report in the *Philippines Free Press* of his visit to China in August 1967 is indicative of a growing attitude toward China among radical layers of youth in the year that the PKP split.

Though dictatorial, it was truly a government FOR the people, according to them. The dictatorship of the proletariat, in brief. Certainly it was not a government for landlords or for capitalists or for foreigners. It was a government for the people. The Chinese people. And the people far from being hungry and oppressed by the government, as we had been told they were, were doing well. Much better than they had ever done before. They were far from rich, but they were becoming less poor every day. . . . It is not a dictatorship, of course, for the "foreign devils" that exploited and degraded a great people in a manner that was burnt into their memory. Foreign concessions with extraterritorial rights no longer exist. Chinese now walk in parks where signs once said: "Dogs and Chinese not allowed." The "devils" have been driven out and when they come back to do business, it is on Chinese terms. The Chinese are no longer anybody's dogs.[29]

The contending forces within the PKP expressed the contending interests of rival sections of the ruling class who shared a common goal (martial law) but some of whom required the first waves of unrest to thrust them into office before it was imposed. The attempt to secure rule by yoking the unruly and explosive energy threatening their entire social class was an audacious and dangerous ploy.

Of all the opposition figures, the most audacious and self-assured was Ninoy Aquino, a man both reckless and charming, tied to old money and political prestige. He was thirty-two years old in 1965; the constitution dictated that his age excluded him from Malacañang until 1973. The next eight years of political crisis loomed before him, an eternity to one so young and ambitious. Aquino controlled a significant private army backed by an arsenal of over one hundred guns, but this was a limited, local force. They sufficed to secure for him the governorship of Tarlac, but by 1967 he would run for the Senate, and his eye was already set on Malacañang. He could not wait for the turning of the electoral tide; there would not be a presidential election in 1973, and he, more than anyone other than Marcos himself, knew this. Aquino required the energy of the streets and the backing of a nationwide private army. Lin Biao's protracted people's war and Aquino's private army were the obverse faces of the same political coin. Marcos had a Communist party. Aquino needed one too.

Growing layers of the opposition gathered around Aquino. By 1967, a group of maverick Liberal Party (LP) politicos, known as the Young Turks, were seeking to secure the support of this new Communist party in the making, publicly urging the opening of ties with Beijing, and traveling to China and returning with copies of Mao's Red Book, which they privately passed on to Sison and Dante, who would become head of the New People's Army, and their followers. The catastrophic defeat of the LP and the explosion of social crisis at the end of 1969 brought the majority of the opposition in line with Aquino's ploy. All the names of old-money—Laurel, Osmeña, Lopez—tied their political fate to the storm that broke at the dawn of the decade and to the leadership of the CPP, whose task was to constrain and channel its energy. Aquino funded the CPP, armed it, and defended it, and the CPP in turn ensured that the explosions of the time were safely contained within the pistons of his political machinery.

This was a far riskier choice than that made by the majority of the PKP. Ties with Marcos were already established, salaried positions were on offer, and diplomacy with the Soviet bloc was opening and would facilitate the growth of national industry. Why throw all this away and gamble on Aquino and Beijing?

The theme was audacity—they would "dare to struggle, dare to win"—and the leadership orienting to Beijing and protracted people's war thus expected far more than their Moscow-oriented rivals.[30] Theirs was a sacrificial gambit, but the stakes they sought were far higher. The PKP was content to fill an advisorial role within a cabinet of military rule. A corner office in the dictatorship, ties with Brezhnev, and national industrialization—the thready pulse of the bureaucrat quickened at the thought. The CPP sought joint rule with the capitalist class, modeled on Mao's conception of coalition government; this was an arrangement every bit as dictatorial, but the CPP would secure a decidedly larger slice of the pie.

It was thus that a political organization with a common program, common history, and common orientation split in two. They shared a yearning for national industrialization and the flourishing of native capitalists. The crisis of capitalist rule, however—the imminent social explosion and the drive to dictatorship—split their ranks. Both retained the stamp of Stalinism, but they bound themselves to rival sets of interests: the contending sections of the ruling class and the conflicting national interests of the Stalinist bureaucracies.

When Sison and his cohort were expelled from the PKP, the front organizations of the party and particularly its youth wing, the KM, fragmented. The PKP retained its hold over the majority of the youth organization, most of whom were of peasant background, and organized them in the Malayang Pagkakaisa ng Kabataang Pilipino (Free Unity of Filipino Youth). The PKP also held on to the Bertrand Russell Peace Foundation, a group of university-based youth opposed to the war in Vietnam, and Movement for the Advancement of Nationalism, a collection of businessmen and political figures dedicated to the defense of the interests of Filipino capitalists. Sison managed to retain the KM, but a section of the organization led by Perfecto Tera and Vivencio Jose, drawn to the anarchism of the cultural revolution and opposed to Sison's authoritarian leadership, broke away to found a new youth group, the Samahan ng Demokratikong Kabataan (Federation of Democratic Youth, SDK).[31] Ignacio Lacsina, head of the National Association of Trade Unions (NATU), an influential network of labor unions, was closely tied to the PKP, but he had his own interests at heart and did not fully conform to the political line of either party.

The PKP and the CPP proved instrumental in this mad scramble for martial law. Marcos opened ties with eastern Europe and engaged in trade with Moscow, and the PKP increasingly supported his administration, facilitating his implementation of dictatorship by carrying out terrorist acts throughout the city

to provide a pretext for its declaration. The PKP endorsed his declaration of
martial law and supported his dictatorial regime, murdering members of the
party who opposed this policy. The CPP negotiated ties with Marcos's ruling-
class rivals, mobilizing the vast, angry unrest of the time behind the interests of
Aquino, Fernando and Eugenio Lopez, and Sergio Osmeña Jr. Rather than
building an independent opposition in the working class and peasantry to the
threat of dictatorship, they subordinated these classes to Aquino and his allies
and received in exchange their growing support for Beijing. On declaring martial
law, Marcos arrested a section of the bourgeois opposition, and the majority
either acquiesced to dictatorship or left the country. The few who defied Marcos,
like Aquino, remained in jail. The ruling-class leadership of the opposition vanished, and the CPP was left at a loss. Fifty thousand people had protested the
threat of dictatorship on 21 September 1972; less than a month later, attaching a
piece of paper inscribed with a political slogan to the leg of a chicken and letting
the chicken loose in the market was depicted by the CPP as a revolutionary act.
The party was utterly unprepared. It hailed the declaration of martial law as the
onset of the revolution and directed all residual political dissent to take up arms
in the countryside. And quiet reigned in the streets of Manila.

Sources and Interpretation

Benedict Anderson opened his work *Imagined Communities* with the Vietnam-
ese invasion of Cambodia, which he termed the "first *large-scale conventional
war* waged by one revolutionary Marxist regime against another."[32] Anderson
depicted this as a scholarly quandary, claiming that the persistence of nationalism, particularly in what he termed "revolutionary Marxist regimes," was
"an uncomfortable anomaly for Marxist theory and, precisely for that reason,
has been largely elided, rather than confronted."[33] He wrote this in a book in
which he makes no mention of Stalin and Stalinism and mentions Trotsky only
once and in passing. Anderson should have known better. The dispute over
nationalism was at the core of revolutionary Marxism in the twentieth century,
with Trotsky and the Fourth International defending Marxism's commitment
to international socialism and the working class, and Stalinism fighting for a
nationalist perspective. What Anderson termed "revolutionary Marxist regimes" were in fact Stalinist and had rival national interests and geopolitical
alliances. One cannot account for the persistence of nationalism in these regimes as the modular and resilient imagining of nation without addressing
the political program of Stalinism and its historical roots.

Failure to seriously examine the relationship between Stalinism and nationalism has diminished many otherwise serious scholarly works. As anti-Communist scholarship of the mid-twentieth century churned out volumes, on an almost industrial scale, labeling various leaders as Communists, a range of liberal scholars pushed back. Many of these figures, they argued, were in fact truly nationalists and their Communist allegiance was but a means of achieving nationalist ends. Rather than examining the historical and programmatic roots of Stalinism, these scholars located the roots of "Communist" nationalism in "localization." Where anti-Communist scholarship claimed that local Communists were simply following the dictates of Moscow, liberal scholarship attempted to assert local agency, claiming that the leaders of the local Communist Party adapted and localized Communism to their own ends. The impulse behind this scholarship may have been a healthy one, but the end result was largely parochial.

This scholarly focus on the local and the national failed to take seriously what was being localized and adapted (that is, the program of Stalinism). Stalinism was a global force with a coherently articulated program. It was not the ideas of Marxism, of the *Communist Manifesto*, or even of Lenin that were being localized; it was Socialism in One Country, the two-stage theory of revolution and the bloc of four classes. What is more, undergirding the scholarship on the localization of Communism was a narrow conception that the ambit of local agency was constrained to the boundaries of the nation-state. Local Communist leaders did more than implement and adapt the program of Stalinism to the cultural, linguistic, and political specificities of their country. In the process, they shaped global Stalinism. They were full participants in the implementation and shaping of a fluid, international political movement. The parochial nature of scholarship on localization finds its sharpest expression when dealing with the impact of the Sino-Soviet split. Communist parties in every country split within a few years of each other. This cannot be treated as a national phenomenon, and yet existing scholarship generally treats the split as if it were the product of domestic disputes and local machinations.

Thus, the rather tired chicken-and-egg debate—were the leaders truly Communists or nationalists at heart—finds clear resolution in a historical understanding of Stalinism. Seeking to align the interests of a section of the capitalist class within each country with the interests of the bureaucracy in the Soviet Union or China, Stalinism fed a double dose of nationalism to the working class, promoting the national interests of both local capitalists and the bureaucracies, and coated the pill with phrases of Marxism and the heritage of the Russian Revolution.

This work makes what I believe is a needed revision to the literature on world Communism. It points a way forward. To understand the role played by various Communist parties, it is necessary to grapple seriously with the program of Stalinism. But this cannot be done without dealing with its revolutionary programmatic alternative, Trotskyism and the theory of permanent revolution. Such an approach yields startling new insights not only into the life of the Communist parties themselves but into far broader social developments as well. Stalinism made the CPP and the PKP the interface between developing mass struggles and elite political maneuvers. This role placed the parties, in however hidden a fashion, at the center of every major political development. They were the bellwether of Philippine politics; studying their history places us at the heart of all the major social, political, and geopolitical issues of the day. I believe this book fully vindicates this claim and demonstrates that its methodology promises fruitful results if applied to Communist parties in other nations and periods.

Tracing this role requires careful study of the literature produced by the parties. I define literature here in its most expansive sense: the entire printed records of the parties and their affiliated organizations—pamphlets, leaflets, manifestos, posters, books, articles, editorials, newspapers, fliers, and memos. Every political organization and group brought to each rally and demonstration sheaves of its latest statement, often hastily mimeographed or typewritten. These were circulated, read, and reread. Each was an attempt to sway a developing mass movement. They are not fundamentally the record of the party speaking to itself. Even internal bulletins dealing with internal conflicts grapple with the larger political world. In the contemporary written record produced by the Communist parties—read with eyes turned outward, situating every item in the totality of political developments, in the crisis of elite rule and the geopolitical machinations of the Cold War—we find material for following the molecular changes in the mood and consciousness of the masses of the population in a period of social upheaval. We are not given direct access to the masses in the literature of the parties; the Stalinist parties' engagement with the working class always had a one-sided and contradictory character. For many rallies, however, there may be eight or nine extant pieces of political ephemera, each produced by a different tendency or group. Having reconstructed the social character of each group, we can sense in their conflicting and overlapping attempts to sway the mass movement the living forces with which they were engaged. The literature possesses a hidden polyvalence, for it sought to channel by a variety of means, both direct and indirect, the social struggles it addressed behind the interests of the faction of the elite to which its authors were allied. Working through the literature of the

Communist parties places us not at the periphery, the extremes, but at the very center of political life.

When Marcos declared martial law, most activists burned the political documents in their possession, ridding themselves of the incriminating evidence. Much would have been lost to history were it not for the librarians at the University of the Philippines (UP) Diliman, who over the course of nearly half a decade conscientiously collected tens of thousands of pages of radical material, from one-off leaflets to underground newspapers. They quietly tied these items together in bundles and stored them in two steel cabinets in the library basement. They continued to gather material and grew the collection over the course of the dictatorship. With the overthrow of the Marcos regime in 1986, the collection was brought to light, painstakingly organized into forty-three boxes, and transformed into the Philippine Radical Papers Archive. These papers were housed at UP Diliman and subsequently microfilmed by Cornell University. This material, along with similar collections of smaller scope, provided the core evidence for this book.

The bulk of existing scholarship on the Communist parties of the Philippines rests on interviews conducted from the mid-1980s onward with members, former members, and fellow travelers of the CPP and the PKP.[34] The initial works on the CPP in the 1980s are journalistic accounts based on interviews with members and ex-members.[35] The scholarly works that followed share a number of commonalities; most significantly they are based on interviews and they attempt to cover the history of the CPP from its founding in 1969 up to its fragmentation in the early 1990s. A number of insights can be gained from these overviews, and I have gratefully used these works in writing this one.

Their dependence on interviews and later writings, however, means that while they can be used with caution to reconstruct a basic timeline, they are unreliable in uncovering the political logic of the past. Political tendencies, prominent at the beginning of the 1970s, died or disappeared over the course of the dictatorship. A number of major historical actors are cast as bit characters in these accounts because their representatives no longer occupied the stage in later decades and thus were never interviewed. Histories constructed in this way are constrained to the unintended teleology of subsequent prominence. What is more, interview accounts not grounded in a prior examination of the contemporary written record are necessarily unaware of when the political positions of those interviewed were fundamentally altered or when they were engaged in the falsification of the past. Much had changed in the intervening two or three decades. There were axes to grind and new political alliances to build. When Sison was being interviewed in the late 1980s, for example, he sought to establish relations with Mikhail Gorbachev, and to this end he buried the significance of the Sino-Soviet split, the very struggle that informed all he wrote in the early 1970s.[36]

This is not to argue that while interviews with the leaders of the Communist Party are untrustworthy, somehow the documents they produced are truthful. I show in this work that the leadership lied in their documents and lied repeatedly. The written record is copious, however. Of the documents housed in the Philippine Radical Papers Archive, I digitized every page that was written within this work's time frame and carefully indexed each one. Many items were misdated; others were of obscure origin. By working over this material repeatedly, I was able to reconstruct—to triangulate on the basis of lies, half-truths, and honest accounts—an understanding of what had transpired. Many items were ephemera—for example, single-page fliers announcing a demonstration on a particular issue—and were undated because they were handed out a day before the rally. But by using vocabulary and topical references, I was able to reconstruct the date of almost every item. I found that it was imperative to locate the original documents. Reprinted material was frequently redacted without any indication that it had been revised. Often the redactions articulated a perspective that drastically altered the one put forward previously. The only accounts I found trustworthy were contemporary ones. These might also have been dishonest, but they were the lies that were told at the time, and that in the end is what matters. I have simplified things for the reader where possible. The written record is replete with multiple nicknames for various figures and a specialized internal vocabulary with a vast array of abbreviations in both English and Tagalog for the various organizational structures of the party and its activities. Having waded through this myself, I saw no reason to inflict it on the reader.

There is a culture about the Communist parties of the Philippines simultaneously inflected by amnesia and nostalgia. The leaders of the PKP enthusiastically endorsed Macapagal in 1963, sending the newly formed Workers' Party into a formal coalition with his government, but two years later they fiercely denounced him and allied with Marcos. They did not account for their prior support; they buried it—"Oceania had always been at war with Eastasia." This cultivated amnesia was combined with a nostalgia for an imagined past. Young people joining the CPP or its front organizations learn of the First Quarter Storm and the Diliman Commune—events that are never understood historically but are simply appreciated as the great moral lessons of the past, examples of the revolutionary heroism of their predecessors. This is not baseless. The youths and workers who fought in the battles of the 1960s and early 1970s were often heroic, and I strove to write this work with a tone of sympathy, even admiration, for those who proved so capable of self-sacrifice and endless labor. The best layers of an entire generation fought courageously, and many were tortured and killed by a brutal dictator. But to what end? Here the only honest means of honoring the struggles of this generation is to subject to trenchant criticism the program and machinations of their leaders. The sacrifices made by these youths and workers were first demanded and then dispensed with by Stalinism, which ensured that their lives were no more than grist on the millstone of dictatorship.

Drama underpins this work as an extended metaphor. It is not a theoretical lens but a sustained image holding an exceedingly complex world before the eye of the mind. Like all tragedies, the drama of dictatorship is heavy with fate. The great aims of the age drove forward the interests of the past. For the outcome to be other, masses needed to speak their own lines. They did not; they filled the stage of history, but others spoke in their stead. One reads the words of the Stalinists with a sense of double vision, as the irony between the intended and the said, the contradiction between the interests they articulated and the forces they addressed, is felt in even the most superficial of their lines. Titanic social forces were constrained by these lines to act through surrogates whose motives were antithetical to their own. Assigned by history a central role, theirs remained but a chorus subjectivity. This, more than any other factor, determined the denouement.

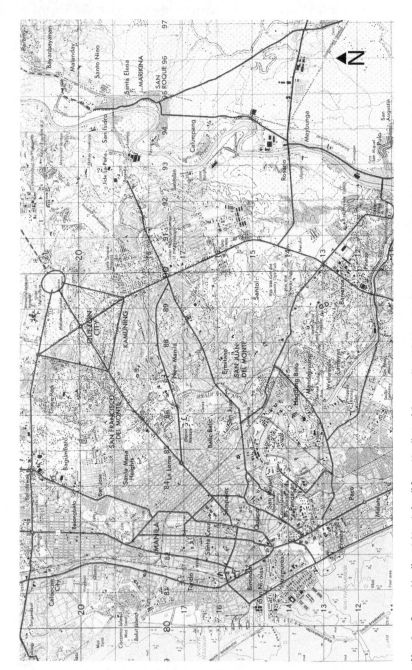

MAP 2. Greater Manila, 1960s. A detail from *Manila and Quezon City*, US Army Map Service Luzon 1:50,000, AMS 5711 (1963). For a detailed view, see https://www.josephscalice.com/assets/images/maps/map2.png.

CHAPTER 1

A Storm on the Horizon

By the late 1950s, political and economic life in the Philippines had achieved a certain equilibrium. Rival families, controlling a vast range of powerful economic interests, established a mutually agreeable mode of political existence organized within two parties: the Liberal Party (LP) and the Nacionalista Party (NP). The spectacle of elections, the horse trading of the primaries, and the party alliances constantly forming and breaking apart—all these combined to provide stability and continuity to the oligarchic politics of the country. The spume of alternating dynastic alliances washed over the archipelago with the regularity of the tides.

Manila had been devastated by the Second World War. Quiapo, Tondo, Binondo, Sampaloc—the entire northern bank of the Pasig—had burned to the ground, and Intramuros, the thickly walled harbor city of the Spaniards at its southern mouth, was largely reduced to rubble. Profit can be minted from catastrophe, and in the haphazard rebuilding of the once-magnificent city, fortunes were to be made. Business empires and political careers were built on the debris of the war. Association with the US-allied guerrilla resistance movement during the Japanese occupation was turned into political capital, and where such ties did not exist, they were often invented. Over the course of decades, Ferdinand Marcos constructed an entire mythology, with fake medals, biographies, and blockbuster movies, on his invented guerrilla past. Yet others worked to remove the stain of collaboration, a cleansing that Washington gladly facilitated.

Leading figures in the Japanese occupation, Jose P. Laurel and Claro M. Recto, "assessing the situation shrewdly, saw the opportunity to lay to rest their Japanese collaborator ghosts by joining forces with Ed Lansdale's American team."[1]

A massive influx of US capital dramatically transformed the postwar Philippines as US citizens were granted parity rights with Filipinos in the ownership of property in the formally independent country. During the Japanese occupation the old landed families, who fashioned themselves as dons and doñas—the barons of sugar in Negros and Tarlac, of coffee in Batangas, or of tobacco in Ilocos—resettled in Manila or left the country entirely. At the end of the war, many did not return to their haciendas. The next generation of hacenderos, many educated in Western universities, ruled their landed holdings through administrators. Capitalist forms of exploitation were implemented throughout the countryside, the traditional patron-client ties of landlord and peasant largely ended and were increasingly supplanted by the cold cash nexus of wage labor and ground rent. The new generation of elite turned its focus to the fashioning of business empires on a national scale, particularly the sugar dynasties, which organized themselves into the powerful political "sugar bloc." "In the 1940s, quite a number of provincial sugar barons made the move to Manila, including the Yulos, the Aranetas and the Cojuangcos."[2]

It was not just the rich who were moving to the capital, however. A vast migration of peasant families over the next two decades populated Manila and its surrounding region, where, from their disembarkation at Tutuban to their settling in the spreading outskirts of the city, they formed the ranks of the rapidly growing working class. As they came, the graceless growth of Greater Manila covered large portions of Bulacan, Cavite, and Rizal.[3] "By the time President Macapagal took office in 1962, Manila had grown far beyond its prewar boundaries to engulf thirteen adjacent towns and its population increased fourfold to 2.4 million."[4]

The swelling metropolis saw a dramatic growth in the number of youth attending the city's universities, most of whom were from working-class and peasant backgrounds. The preponderance of universities in Manila were privately owned, for-profit institutions, and old landed money flooded into the education market as it did everywhere else; the coffee money of the Laurels founded Lyceum, and the sugar of the Aranetas established FEATI.

As with universities, so too newspapers. The wealthy families each bought up or founded a daily paper or a weekly magazine, and in the 1950s and 1960s the Philippines had a flourishing free press. Scores of daily papers, ranging from Tagalog scandal sheets to staid English-language newsprint, were hawked on the Manila streets. Chino Roces operated the *Manila Times*, and Eugenio Lopez the

Manila Chronicle. Teddy Locsin, at the helm of McCulloch Dick's *Philippines Free Press*, produced a remarkably well-written weekly news magazine.

The dense yet sprawling city of Manila was the center of political life. From the end of the Second World War to the declaration of martial law, the country's political battles were largely waged in Manila. The city was marked by the combined and uneven development of global capitalism. Northern Motors, the largest General Motors (GM) assembly plant outside the United States, was based in Manila. The vast factory of US Tobacco produced cigarettes and cigars made from a mixture of Ilocano and Virginia strains. Imported commodities of all sorts were peddled in the glossy pages of the weekly magazines, and their logos filled the massive billboards over Carriedo Street. This frenetic world of global trade and production sat cheek by jowl with the mud and narrow stalls of the wet market and the shanty-lined *esteros* and *eskinitas* that laced the city. Tens of thousands of people, but a few years removed from a life dictated by the rhythms of the rice paddy, now took up inventive forms of informal employment and became barkers for jeepney routes, carried goods in the market, pushed makeshift *kariton* through the streets, and collected and resold scrap.

Over this bustling, disjointed society, political rule was exercised from the Spanish colonial palace of Malacañang, its *azotea* lapped by the waters of the Pasig. Directives arrived routinely from the US embassy, which sat perched on the shore of Manila Bay, pointedly poised between the capital and the rest of the world.

Dramatis Personae

The contending classes, the great, moving forces of history, crowded into Manila. The drama that was to play out was theirs. Its limelit personalities were thrust to the front of the stage by social passions. That the theme of the drama was dictatorship expressed neither Marcos's will to power nor Aquino's reckless subterfuge, but rather a consensus in the elite that the intensity of the social crisis fundamentally jeopardized their interests and could be resolved only through the scrapping of democracy. Personality is of relevance here as a concentrated expression of social forces. In the individual lineaments of Marcos, Aquino, and Sison we find inscribed the particularities of the class roles they were to play.

The political scientist Mark Thompson identified five major ruling-class factions that came into alignment with each other in their opposition to Marcos between 1970 and 1972: Aquino, Laurel, Osmeña, Roxas, and Lopez. Each name represented a dynasty of the landed elite. The leading collaborators during the Japanese occupation, they had been immediately rehabilitated by Washington in the wake of the war and were now the most politically powerful families in the country.[5] The journalist Jose Lacaba perceptively analyzed the character of the elite forces plotting against Marcos in an article published in April 1971: "If a distinction must be made, it must be between natural born oligarchs and self-made oligarchs. Not a coincidence is the fact that the names arrayed against Marcos belong to families with a distinguished lineage: Osmeña, Roxas, Lopez, Laurel. One way of viewing the Nacionalista Party (NP) split and the almost certain emergence of a United Opposition is as a realignment of forces within the oligarchy, as a power struggle between the *ancien* and the *nouveau* within the oligarchy."[6]

In December 1968, on the eve of an economic crisis in which half the population would prove unable to meet their minimum food needs, the *anciens* put their wealth on display at the ruby wedding anniversary of oligarch Eugenio Lopez and Pacita Moreno. International bankers and European nobility filled their glasses with Dom Pérignon, endlessly gushing from three Murano glass fountains crafted for the occasion in Venice. Generalissimo Franco's daughter, her hand on the arm of the Legitimist pretender to the Bourbon dynasty, greeted the celebrating couple. Hans Heinrich Thyssen-Bornemisza, whose industrial concerns had armed the Nazis and who bore the title of baron in Hungary, was present to honor the sugar baron of Negros. Many had been flown on private jets to Manila at Lopez's expense. The gowns of the gathered doñas, each designed for the occasion, were draped with diamonds. The soirée lasted two days, the celebrants bound together in the hubris of hereditary wealth.[7]

Old landed money dominated Philippine politics, and while the oligarchy conducted their affairs with a mannered Castilian flair, they were ruthless in defense of their privileges. Clannish and incestuously intermarried, they did not welcome interlopers and privately sneered at the nouveau riche.

Conspicuously absent from the Lopez anniversary party were Ferdinand and Imelda Marcos; they had snubbed the invitation from the vice president's brother. Marcos was new money, his growing wealth the product of his expanding political power. Mercenary but not venal, Marcos was a talented, grasping, shrewd, and cunning man. Where the *ancien* spoke of their patriliny and of dubious Spanish titles, their patents of nobility in a remote and manufactured past, Marcos, foremost of the *nouveau*, was determined to secure his own in the present. Few historical figures have been as concerned with self-construction as Ferdinand Marcos. He gave concentrated thought to the creation of a historical persona, an end to which he in equal measure labored and lied. His gestures were carefully rehearsed, his actions calculated. With an eye to the public and posterity, Marcos saw himself on the stage of history and was obsessed with expanding his part.

Born in 1917 in Ilocos Norte, the son of a provincial lawyer, Marcos pursued a law degree at the University of the Philippines. He was a remarkable student, but his promising career was derailed when he was convicted of the murder of his father's political rival, Julio Nalundasan, who was shot in the back through a window of his home. Only twenty-one years old, Marcos faced ten to seventeen years in jail, and the solicitor general filed a petition to change the sentence to the death penalty. Imprisoned in a Laoag jail cell, Marcos studied for the bar exam and wrote a three-volume appeal of his conviction to the Supreme Court. He aced the exam, earning the highest score in the nation in 1939. In 1940, the Supreme Court ruled in his favor and threw out the murder conviction. It was a political decision; the nation's top new lawyer should not be facing the death penalty. The Nalundasan affair revealed that the youthful Marcos already possessed what would become his defining traits: determination, talent, and utter ruthlessness. The honored and exonerated Marcos became the subject of national headlines.[8]

He used his notoriety to launch a political career in the wake of the war. He excelled at politics; victory followed victory, and by 1965 he was the NP frontrunner for president. Not content with his own remarkable achievements, Marcos constructed an elaborate personal mythology. He invented a guerrilla past in the Japanese occupation, in which he commanded a large unit, conducted raids, met with General Douglas MacArthur, and was awarded numerous medals. As time went on and the lies became bolder, his unit grew in the recounting to nearly eight thousand troops and he became the recipient of the US Congressional Medal of Honor. The myths entered circulation through popular movies about Marcos's exploits released in the election years of 1965 and 1969, and a melodramatic biography, *For Every Tear a Victory*, written by Hartzell Spence, former editor of the GI magazine *Yank*, who had coined the word "pinup."[9] Marcos cultivated other aspects of his image. He was an intellectual and hired ghostwriters to prove it. Over the next decade and a half, books on politics, philosophy, and history, including a multivolume history of the Philippines, appeared bearing Marcos's name on the title page.[10] The dusty lower shelves of used bookshops in Manila are filled with this "Marcosiana." Even Marcos's personal diary was given over to lies in service to the construction of posterity.[11]

In Imelda Romualdez, Marcos found his counterpart (figure 1.1). Theirs, to use an apt phrase from a flawed work, was a "conjugal dictatorship."[12] Twelve years younger than her husband, she proved his equal in ambition and ruthlessness. Her father was the second son of an established political dynasty

FIGURE 1.1. Ferdinand and Imelda Marcos meet with Lyndon Johnson in Manila, 23 October 1966.

from the Visayan province of Leyte. His wife died at a young age, leaving him with daughters, and his mother selected a replacement wife for him from among the respectably groomed orphan girls of a convent. His marriage to Imelda's mother was not a happy one. By the time Imelda was three, her father had lost his wealth in speculative investment during the early years of the global depression. Imelda and her mother were mistreated and ridiculed by Imelda's stepsisters, who monopolized their father's attention. Imelda grew up on the fringes of wealth and power, the spurned daughter of a dynasty, enviously eyeing her cousins from her home in the garage. She moved to Manila in her early twenties and worked at a music store on Escolta. She traded on her looks and her family name and rose to public attention as a beauty queen, securing the sponsorship of Manila's mayor. Marcos proposed, and they married within weeks.[13] They were ideally suited. Ferdinand was on the brink of a brilliant career that would provide his ambitious wife with opportunities that would otherwise be denied to her; Imelda bore a surname that could serve as their entrée to wider layers of elite politics. History revealed her to be a terrifying but fit counterpart to her ruthless husband: cunning, vindictive, and thoroughly vain.

Despite the patronym Romualdez, the Marcoses remained outsiders to the *ancien*. Ambition in both overflowed into rapacity. They would secure a fortune by theft and a reputation by fraud. The fabled excesses of their dictatorship were imitative, a performative establishment of their superiority to the elite that had excluded them. It lacked refinement, had a tendency to the gauche, but it succeeded in conveying its intent: the apotheosis of the *nouveau*.

It was a younger man that represented old money. Benigno "Ninoy" Aquino Jr. (figure 1.2) was born in 1932 to a landed political dynasty in the Central Luzon province of Tarlac. His father, whose name he bore, was vice president of the Japanese Occupation and director-general of Kalibapi, the fascist party of the Occupation government. At thirteen, Ninoy was gathered among the highest ranks of Japanese militarism in the Nara prefecture as the *Enola Gay* flew over Hiroshima. The stain of his family's collaboration was promptly expunged, and within a decade CIA planes took off from his sugar estate to bomb Sulawesi. He was a quick-witted man, brash, impulsive, and dominant. At age seventeen, he worked as a war correspondent for the *Manila Times* during the Korean War. His familial connections secured him a position as close adviser to Defense Secretary Ramon Magsaysay at the age of twenty-one, which put him well within the orbit of CIA operative Edward Lansdale and US intelligence. Aquino came from money, and at twenty-two he married into yet more; his wife, Corazon, was scion of the Cojuangco sugar dynasty, which ruled much of Tarlac. Political actions had never had negative consequences for Aquino. His rash, precipitate behavior evinced a certain charm. His aspirations, and the coffers of his wife that fed them, were limitless. The nation's youngest mayor at twenty-two, youngest vice governor at twenty-seven, governor at twenty-nine, and youngest senator at thirty-four, he had never known defeat. Where Marcos was methodical, diligent, and calculating, Aquino had political instinct and reckless resolve. He was a flamboyant and talented orator. Marcos memorized his own speeches and would proudly deliver them without notes. Aquino, in contrast, charismatically ad-libbed his way through each performance, confident of his audience's enthusiasm. He was known as the "boy wonder."[14]

Marcos and Aquino were both orators; neither was a writer—despite Aquino's brief foray into journalism. There was, beneath the rhetoric, an inevitable superficiality to both men. In a different period they would have been talented but historically unremarkable figures. The years of their pitched battle, however—1969 to 1972—were years for oratory; the volcanic struggles of the time gave content to the cadence of form and filled out the roles they were to play.

For all their mutual hatred and self-regard, the *ancien* and *nouveau* shared much in their class outlooks. They pursued similar measures to expand their privileges and similar measures to defend them. Nationalism served to dress up these decrepit social layers and their class jealousies as progressive. The concerns expressed by Senator Maria Kalaw Katigbak in December 1966, as tens of thousands protested the US war in Vietnam, were characteristic of this sort of nationalism. "The immediate effect of the influx of American families in any

FIGURE 1.2.   Ninoy Aquino as hacendero, ca. 1970.

neighborhood is the rise in the salary scale for maids, drivers, and such. Filipino families in the vicinity begin to lose their best cooks, only to meet them later dressed in white uniforms marketing for the new American lady inside the walls."[15] For the entire ruling elite, the ancient and the upstarts, politics was something of a dance, a *rigodon de honor*, and everyone knew the choreography and the two-four timed alternation. They would take turns at the center of the floor. The social crisis, however, threatened all this. Dictatorial methods were needed to stabilize the social order and secure their privileges. On this they all agreed. Dictatorship, however, meant an end to the dance, to the alternation. Whoever occupied the stage when the music stopped would rule. And thus, as the social crisis sharpened, the tensions in the ruling class mounted as well.

It is social passions, and not individual personalities, that hang over this drama with a sense of fate. Crowds and classes are often historically faceless, but they are not abstract or impersonal. Through a process of molecular interaction and aggregation, they make up a concrete, coherent whole. In periods of upheaval and revolution, the ideas of classes change rapidly. Trotsky wrote of the Russian Revolution,

> The masses go into a revolution not with a prepared plan of social reconstruction, but with a sharp feeling that they cannot endure the old regime. Only the guiding layers of a class have a political program, and

even this still requires the test of events, and the approval of the masses. The fundamental political process of the revolution thus consists in the gradual comprehension by a class of the problems arising from the social crisis—the active orientation of the masses by a method of successive approximations.[16]

Neither Marcos nor Aquino had any direct relationship to the developing mass consciousness of workers and youths in the struggles of this period. Through demagoguery and bluster they sought to corral it, long enough to crush it. It was the class function of the Partido Komunista ng Pilipinas (PKP) and the Communist Party of the Philippines (CPP) to provide an interface between the machinations of the elite and the developing mass movement. Here a final personality comes to the fore: Jose Maria Sison, founder and leader of the CPP.

Both Marcos and Aquino were talented men, Sison less so. He was not a great orator, nor did he lead by example. He wrote passable prose at the best of times, but painfully stilted jargon when confronted with the immensity of the social forces he sought to direct. There was a cookie-cutter conformity to the elaboration of his ideas, as if precisely repeated phrases were the safeguards of orthodoxy. His Stalinist rivals were thus invariably a "black bourgeois gang," their armed wing a "gangster clique," and Marcos a "shameless fascist puppet."[17] The aspirations and anger and brutality of these years evoked no lyricism from his pen, all fell beneath the stamp of boilerplate. How is it, then, that a mediocrity came to play one of the most significant roles in Philippine politics?

Sison embodied in his person two hostile collectivities: he was born into and intimately connected with the familial networks of the elite, and the derivative lines of Mao gave him a radical cachet that secured influence over mass struggles. Taken in isolation, neither of these factors would have been particularly significant, but conjoined they were decisive. Sison's elite connections gave him the ability to disseminate his program and gain new adherents, while his growing sway over the mass movement added to his influence in the backrooms of political power.

Sison had a certain class affinity with Aquino. Sison came from old money that had recently gone to seed, and his bearing was that of a man convinced he was entitled to lead. His family had been the largest landholder in northern Luzon at the turn of the century. They embodied feudal privilege, with their peasant clients and sprawling landholdings—adjoined and divided up again by intermarriage—and on this basis the Sison clan extended their political power. Sison was part of a pervasive nexus of familial connections that stretched from the National Legislature to the Manila Cathedral: two of his uncles were congressmen; another was the archbishop of Nueva Segovia, which encompassed all of the province of Ilocos Sur; and his great-uncle was the province's governor. At Sunday Mass, the front pews were reserved for Sison's family. The peasant tenants of their estate came each day to his home to "deliver land rent, ask for seeds, do menial tasks around the house or plead for some special consideration."[18]

All of this shaped the psychology of the young Sison. His mother, Florentina, during an interview in 1970, described the child Joma, whom she affectionately called Cheng. "Cheng ordered our maids around—more than any of my other children. Maids had to wait on him constantly. He hardly did things for himself. Even in the bathroom, he would call the servants to hand him his towel, his clothes."[19]

This world, however, had largely disappeared. Commodities that had proved so lucrative for Sison's grandfather—rice, tobacco, indigo, and maguey—fared poorly in the twentieth century. While sugar, processed in centrifugal mills, became a monocropped commodity of immense significance on the world market, the labor-intensive craft manufacture of indigo and maguey died out. The indigo dye was replaced by chemical synthesis, and the fabric of the maguey cactus was displaced by far cheaper industrial goods. The majority of rice production shifted to the fertile region of Nueva Ecija.[20] Tobacco came to dominate the family holdings, but it could not sustain their former wealth, and with the opening of the postwar period, the decline became increasingly marked as the cheaper Virginia tobacco became popular and began displacing older native strains. The dull thud of an ax could be heard in the cherry orchard.

As they reached the age of maturity, Sison and his siblings were less feudal and more urban, and of decidedly more limited means than their forbears. They were, in a word, petty bourgeois. One became a doctor, another a dentist, and yet another a technocrat in the Marcos administration. Sison himself aspired to "become a lawyer, go to Harvard, and be a political leader."[21] The 1960s found him as a graduate student teaching introductory English courses at the University of the Philippines.

Sison became the foremost representative of a social layer that found its interests articulated by Senator Claro M. Recto. The early 1960s saw the emergence of immense excitement among college-educated youth for the nationalist writings and speeches of Recto, and Sison came to stand at the center of efforts to give this energy organizational shape.

At first glance, the senator seems an unlikely figure to have generated so much enthusiasm: an opponent of women's suffrage, a leading collaborator in the Japanese occupation, and a man most comfortable with Spanish, unable to speak passable Tagalog.[22] The basis of the support he received, however, was the perspective of economic nationalism and nationalist industrialization that he came to articulate in the latter half of the 1950s. Recto's speech before the Chamber of Industries in June 1955 was an early and lucid expression of this outlook. The Philippine economy was of an agricultural character rather than an industrial one, and Recto argued that this was the root cause of poverty, for "an agricultural economy is always an economy of poverty," and thus, "nationalism and industrialization are the two faces of the same coin."[23] There was a danger, he warned, in failing to industrialize, for "the more disappointed and disillusioned [the people] become the more prone they will be to listen to offers of radical solutions."[24] By 1957, these ideas had reached their fullest and sharpest articulation. In a speech before the Cavite Jaycees, Recto called for "industrialization of the country by Filipino capitalists, and not simply the prevention of industrialization by foreign capitalists; exploitation of our natural resources by Filipino capital; development and strengthening of Filipino capitalism, not foreign capitalism; increase of the national income, but not allowing it to go mostly for the benefit of non-Filipinos."[25]

Recto's economic nationalism expressed the interests of layers of Filipino capitalists, both industrialists and small businessmen, who sought to secure state intervention to expand their holdings through the deployment of subsidies and the implementation of protective measures against foreign rivals.[26] The Retail Trade Nationalization Law (1954) and the Filipino First policy of the Garcia administration (1957–61) were initial political manifestations of this perspective, transferring segments of the economy from foreign to Filipino ownership. The terms of the Bell Trade Act (1946) and the Laurel-Langley Agreement (1955), however, established parity rights for US business interests in the Philippine economy, and US businesses were thus explicitly exempted from these measures. It was the Chinese business community that bore the brunt of all the nationalization measures, which threatened not only larger retail firms but small corner stores as well.

The limitations in the implementation of Recto's nationalist vision were palpable by the beginning of the 1960s, and the layers of students who were drawn to his perspective sought to overcome these difficulties by mobilizing a mass movement behind this program and putting pressure on the political establishment. At the head of a growing movement of youth (figure 1.3), Sison would prove to be the most capable representative of this conception.

Generating mass support for Recto's vision, however, was not an easy task, for this was a quintessentially petty bourgeois enthusiasm: the demand of support for a set of bosses on the basis of their nationality. Recto's program was effectively a form of trickle-down economics, arguing that Filipino capitalists'

Figure 1.3. The leaders of the KM, soon to be the leadership of the CPP, pose for the press in March 1968. Left to right: Ibarra Tubianosa, Carlos del Rosario, Jose Ma. Sison, Leoncio Co, Art Pangilinan.

control of Philippine industry would improve the Philippine economy, which would, in the end, improve the lives of workers.

Here the program of Stalinism proved instrumental, for it instructed workers, in the name of Marxism and revolution, to form an alliance with the national bourgeoisie in the furtherance of national democratic ends. The Maoist variant of Stalinism gave additional radical cachet to this program. By 1968, Sison sought to achieve Rectonian nationalism through the barrel of a gun.[27] What he lacked was an organized party with an armed wing.

Bernabe Buscayno, who would become head of the New People's Army (NPA), was born to a family that managed the mango groves of a local landlord in Talimundoc, Capas, Tarlac. The hamlet where Buscayno spent his early years was "a cluster of flimsy shacks with a few trees, backyard poultry and a primitive, hand-dug well."[28] The local landlord served as patron to the Buscayno family, and "when Bernabe was old enough to begin his schooling, he and his brother Jose were sent to the landowner's house in Quezon City."[29] Buscayno completed grade school at Burgos Elementary School, and after he finished his second year at Roosevelt High School in Cubao, he and his brother moved to Angeles, Pampanga, to live with their aunt. Bernabe and Jose took up work as waiters. Angeles was the home turf of Commander Sumulong's mafia, the vestiges of the Huk peasant rebellion in the region that now made millions running the organized crime rackets that flourished around Clark Airbase. Within a year, Bernabe had become a runner for Sumulong, adopting the pseudonym Dante. Dante rose through the ranks of Sumulong's organization to become a hit man under Commander Fonting, the head of Sumulong's liquidation squads. The Armed Forces of the Philippines (AFP) rap sheet for Dante listed twenty-five separate murder charges from his time in Angeles. In early 1966, Dante, now a trusted capo of Sumulong, was assigned to head up the region of Tarlac, where he was born. In late 1967 Dante had a falling out with Sumulong over local election endorsements.[30] In opposition to his mobster boss, Dante came to express a type of armed reformism common to much of social banditry: the popular redress of local grievances, a mild redistribution of wealth in combination with support for landlords who were perceived as just, and support for candidates who articulated agrarian reformist goals.

Sumulong was secretly backed by Marcos, who arranged for the military to kill off a number of Sumulong's rivals, while Sumulong secured him the Pampango vote.[31] Dante, meanwhile, operated on the sprawling Hacienda Luisita sugar plantation of the Cojuangco family, and Aquino, husband to Corazon Cojuangco, became his political patron. Dante provided Aquino with an armed base of popular opposition to Sumulong and his men, and therefore to Marcos. Connecting Dante with Sison presented Aquino the possibility of turning his local armed band into a national force. In October 1968, Aquino and Sison met and discussed "how big a problem Marcos was."[32] Two months later Sison founded the CPP, whose programmatic documents spoke of the party's two "magic weapons": the "united front" alliance with the national bourgeoisie and the people's army.[33] Aquino drove Sison to Talimundoc, Capas, where he introduced him to Dante.[34] It was out of this meeting that in March 1969 the NPA was founded. The disgruntled capo of Sumulong joined the Central Committee of the CPP. Sison now had his people's war and Aquino his private army.

Conspiring Understudies

Like much of the rest of world, the Philippines entered the 1970s in the grip of an immense economic crisis. The crisis first manifested itself in the country's plummeting dollar reserves, which began to fall on 17 June 1969. By 1 August the peso was exchanging on the black market at a rate of ₱4.84 to the dollar, while the official rate was ₱3.91.[35] In an attempt to retain its reserve funds, the Central Bank raised its rediscount rate to 10 percent, and a number of smaller financial institutions went bankrupt. Marcos sought an emergency loan to shore up the nation's dollar reserves. US banks deemed his request too risky and refused to extend credit to the Philippine Central Bank, but HSBC and another British bank offered Manila a $10 million emergency loan. Marcos allocated $15 million to the Philippine Deposit Insurance Corporation to cover up to ₱10,000 per depositor with money in defaulting banks. By 18 August the black market exchange rate had reached ₱5.50, prompting the *Manila Bulletin* to run a front-page headline on the dollar reserve crisis that read "Dive, dive, dive."[36]

Inflation skyrocketed and the price of consumer goods more than doubled, as the economic crisis combined with a rice shortage in the latter half of 1969. The recently launched Left newsweekly, *Ang Masa*, ran a cover story by famed author Amado Hernandez on 6 December titled "Biglang Taas ng mga Presyo" (Sudden rise in prices), which opened, "It seems likely that the sudden rise in the price of goods will be the cause of demonstrations."[37] By the end of the year, the Philippines had a balance of payments deficit of $137 million, and by February 1970 the country was confronting the worst economic crisis in decades. On 21 February, Marcos floated the peso; it devalued in a single day by nearly 50 percent. The cost of imports shot upward. "As a result of devaluation, by 1971 nearly half the population, about 16 million people, were not earning enough to buy their minimum food needs. Consumer prices rose 32% by the end of 1971."[38]

The crisis launched the political explosion of the early 1970s. When half of the population cannot afford its minimum food needs, massive social unrest is inevitable. The ruling class was also feeling the pinch; profits were imperiled. Sections of the bourgeoisie with access to political power could use that power to guarantee their profits and shunt the weight of the crisis onto their rivals. When Marcos won reelection and his allies took the majority of the available legislative seats in November 1969, those sections of the ruling class who remained excluded from power saw their business interests jeopardized. Osmeña, Aquino, and their allies began to plot the ouster of Marcos.

In a secret memo to Nixon in June 1970, Henry Kissinger summed up the causes of the social storm that had broken in January of that year and was sweeping over the country. It arose, he argued, "from economic/financial crisis, from the psychological letdown of the elections, from the revulsion against Marcos' manipulation of the elections, and from the long overdue outbreak of student political activism. At least as important, factions of the local Establishment turned against Marcos out of personal animosity and from fear of his growing power reflected in his election victory. Through their control of information media, these factions did an incredible hatchet job on Marcos' reputation within a matter of weeks."[39]

The confluence of the factors of mass unrest and elite conspiracies would, over the course of the next two years, produce a series of political cataclysms, the eruptions of a country gripped by unbearable social tensions, before culminating in the imposition of military dictatorship in September 1972. In January 1971, Henry Byroade, US ambassador to the Philippines, met with Nixon in Washington to brief him on the explosive situation. Byroade gave Marcos worse than even odds of surviving to the end of his term, saying that he felt there was a "60 per cent chance" that Marcos would be assassinated while in office. The top secret memorandum of the presidential conversation continues,

> Ambassador Byroade then declared that he had a very sensitive matter to lay before the President at Marcos' request. At the end of his predeparture conversation with Marcos, Marcos had warned him that he might find it necessary to suspend the writ of habeas corpus and establish martial law in the city of Manila—unprecedented steps which had not been taken by any Philippine president since the late 40's during the Hukbalahap movement. What Marcos wanted to know was: in the event that he found it necessary to declare martial law in Manila, would the United States back him up, or would it work against him? Ambassador Byroade noted that he had promised Marcos he would bring back the President's personal reply.[40]

Nixon's response was unequivocal, declaring that he would "'absolutely' back Marcos up, and 'to the hilt.'" Byroade responded that "he was very happy to hear the President say this. He acknowledged that if Marcos did act he would undoubtedly pick up some of his political enemies among those he arrested, but in general he would be attempting to do the right thing."

Marcos was not alone, however, in aspiring to the imposition of dictatorship in the fraught and perilous years of 1969 to 1972. A majority of Marcos's elite opponents desired martial law as well, for the mass social unrest threatened their interests every bit as much as it did those of the president and his cronies. Plotting to remove the president from office, hiring assassins, funding demonstrations, and destabilizing the administration, they sought to have their hands on the reins of authoritarian rule and not to defend democracy. They were the conspiring understudies in the drama of dictatorship.

The curtain lifted on the first act when the Lopez brothers—Fernando and Eugenio, vice president and business tycoon, respectively—moved to the camp of the opposition at the end of 1969. Like Marcos, Vice President Fernando Lopez was reelected, but in the immediate aftermath of the election, Lopez and Marcos had a falling out with profound political consequences.[41] US diplomat turned historian Lewis Gleeck stated that "the relationship of President Marcos, the political sovereign, and the Lopez brothers, the economic giants, was always an uneasy one. . . . In the beginning, each needed the other, but in the end only one, of course, could be top dog."[42] The Lopezes were not to be taken lightly, as Aquino made clear in his apt description of their political influence:

> The Lopezes are the only family that has consistently stayed on the fringes of power since 1945, when they came to power with Roxas. Consistently they have been the giant-killers. Consistently they have been the manipulators of political balances in this country.
>
> What makes them so deadly? One: their control of media. They have one of the best radio and TV networks in the country. Two: their political base. Having been in power since 1945, they have many people beholden to them, unknown numbers of people in the bureaucracy, in the judiciary, in the political field. Faceless at this moment; but when the chips are down, these people surface. Third: their reckless use of funds. When they fight they put in everything. So groups of politicians gravitate around them. Fourth: the Lopezes are known to fight to the end. Other people you feel inhibited about joining them, for fear they will abandon you in mid-fight. Not the Lopezes.[43]

The rancor between Marcos and Lopez was precipitated by the economic crisis. The business interests of the Lopez family felt the impact of rising prices and they sought relief from the Marcos government; Marcos in turn sought a larger share of ownership in an oil lubricant facility the Lopez brothers were intending to buy. In exchange for approving the deal, Marcos asked for 40 percent ownership, but the Lopez brothers insisted on 15 percent. The haggling turned into open political conflict in the first quarter of 1970 that was followed by a temporary reconciliation. When Marcos raised the import duty on crude oil in December from 10 percent to 15, "to cover the government deficit," the operating costs of Meralco, the Manila Electric company owned by the Lopez brothers, went up significantly.[44] Raul Rodrigo, biographer of the Lopez family, writes,

By 1971, Meralco had incurred a large dollar-denominated debt that it would have a difficult time repaying under its current cost structure and rates. On top of existing debt, it also needed to access an additional ₱1B in financing over the years 1971–77 to finance construction of new plants and the expansion of the distribution network.

The only way for Meralco to survive was to secure a rate increase from the government to keep pace with rising costs. The trouble was, Malacañang held the key to any rate increase.[45]

The Lopez brothers went back into political battle against Marcos at the end of 1970 when he raised the oil import duty. On 5 December, Eugenio Lopez made Renato Constantino a regular columnist of the *Chronicle*, and Constantino used this column to satirize the first couple for their gaucheness and gaudy practices. It was a public humiliation but not a political exposé.[46] A significant portion of the Philippine news media pursued a similar anti-Marcos bent. The historians Patricio Abinales and Donna Amoroso correctly note that

> radical propaganda got a great boost when Marcos's discarded allies, notably the Lopez and Laurel families, sensing that he was faltering, announced their sympathy with "the revolution" and opened their media outlets to student radicals. The television stations and newspapers highlighted demonstrations. . . . Suddenly, a relatively small left-wing group became a major national player, thanks to the political opportunism of anti-Marcos elites. When Marcos warned of an unholy alliance between radicals and 'oligarchs,' therefore, he spoke the truth.[47]

On 8 January 1970, in the lead-up to the explosion that became known as the First Quarter Storm, the *Chronicle* published an editorial, "The Students and the Press," announcing a shift in the paper's policy to provide sympathetic coverage of the students, particularly in the face of police brutality. The paper wrote that the police were "uniformed bullies," "illiterate," and "incapable of understanding the most trivial of sentiment in the student mind," and called for "demonstrators—meaning the student activists—to be dealt with fairly and just in the columns of the press." It called for an end to the "glamorization of police brutality and the denigration of the young."[48] The *Chronicle* was not alone in this editorial shift, for Marcos had alienated a good deal of the remaining press by "cutting dollar allocations for their newsprint."[49] "Freedom of the press without newsprint?" asked an editorial in the *Philippines Free Press*. Protests and demonstrations received overwhelmingly sympathetic press coverage.[50]

The conspiring dynasts did more than provide the protesters with favorable press coverage; they directly and generously funded the front organizations of the CPP, provided salaried positions to some of its leaders, and granted the demonstrators nearly daily access to broadcasting rights on their major radio and television networks. In March 1970, the Kabataang Makabayan (Nationalist Youth, KM) and other front organizations of the CPP had been allocated significant weekly airtime. The Movement for a Democratic Philippines ran a nationwide weekly television program on the Lopez-operated ABS-CBN, and on an episode of the program in early August it broadcast a staging of the play *People's War Is the Answer to Martial Law*.[51] Famed director Behn Cervantes wrote, "Since this was the crest of the First Quarter Storm, it was relatively easy to get contributions [for the KM and Samahan ng Demokratikong Kabataan (Federation of Democratic Youth, SDK)] from big business tycoons."[52] The allied elite opposition helped "plan, pay for, and give favorable press coverage to the rallies."[53] Sergio Osmeña Jr. followed a strategy of leaving the country just ahead of the explosive protests, which he funded, so that he could deny any connection.[54] Owing to the support it cultivated with the CPP, the LP won the 1971 election. While the elite opposition was bankrolling the rallies of the CPP's front organizations, Marcos began funding the protest marches of the Malayang Pagkakaisa ng Kabataang Pilipino (Free Unity of Filipino Youth, MPKP), youth wing of the PKP, which by 1971 was violently clashing with the KM in the streets of Manila.[55] Thus, this heavily funded proxy fight between Moscow and Marcos, on the one hand, and Beijing and Aquino, on the other, began to tally a body count.

The money of Aquino, Lopez, and company was well spent. They not only secured the support of the front organizations of the CPP and the growing protest movement, which they headed, but also acquired the coercive muscle of the NPA as a counterweight to Marcos's increasingly personal hold over the AFP, which he routinely deployed for his own political ends. Each of these elite figures controlled groups of hired armed men; Aquino in particular had a sizable private army supplied with an arsenal of over one hundred guns. These mercenary militias, however, were local and therefore limited in their usefulness. What Aquino and the rest of the opposition needed, and helped build, was an armed force that spanned much of Luzon.[56] Thompson writes, "Anti-Marcos politicians felt they needed the help of new armed groups to survive politically (if not physically). By helping to establish a new communist party . . . traditional leaders were able to add 'muscle' to their local election campaign."[57]

The elite opposition, not content with funding protests to destabilize Marcos, began plotting assassinations and coups d'etát as well. During the 1969 election, Sergio Osmeña Jr. formed a secret organization called the Workshop Group, composed of ex-military and intelligence operatives, under the leadership of the Philippine Military Academy graduate and Magsaysay admin stalwart Terry Adevoso. In the wake of Osmeña's election defeat, the Workshop Group began plotting to assassinate the reelected president and hired foreign hitmen to carry out the job; evidence suggests that the Lopez brothers gave money to assist with these schemes.[58] The hired guns made multiple attempts on Marcos's life, but each was thwarted, owing to a mole in the organization who secretly informed Marcos of the activities and plotting of the Workshop Group.[59]

Aquino, working with his allies Jose Diokno and Raul Manglapus, attempted to organize a military coup to overthrow the president, and the CPP was involved in this as well. Danilo Vizmanos, a captain of the Philippine Navy and secretly a close collaborator of the Communist Party, participated in the plotting sessions.[60] Vizmanos wrote of multiple meetings held in Manglapus's home in Urdaneta village, attended by a "number of generals and colonels, almost all of whom were from the grounds forces," who were plotting "a coup or putsch from within the AFP that would eventually lead to a power sharing between the putschists and the political opposition."[61] In September 1972, weeks before martial law and as coup plotting reached its fever pitch, Sison met with Aquino to discuss the formation of a revolutionary coalition government. Aquino promptly went to the US embassy and told them that he was contemplating taking power with the aid of the CPP but at the same time informed them that if he succeeded he would declare martial law to bring order to the country.[62]

A new political actor emerged out of these plots and machinations: the various right-wing student groups, known collectively as the Social Democrats or SocDems, which were based almost exclusively at elite private universities run by the religious orders, particularly the Jesuits. The Jesuit priest Fr. Jose Blanco, known as "Derps," played a critical instigating role in the emergence of the SocDem movement.[63] Blanco studied at Fordham University in the United States in the late 1950s and worked in Yogyakarta from 1959 to 1967. In 1965, Blanco helped organize Kesatuan Aksi Mahasiswa Indonesia (Indonesian Students Action Front, KAMI), a group that was central to the persecution and hounding of the Partai Komunis Indonesia during the slaughter that commenced that year. They stormed the Chinese consulate and demanded the ouster of Sukarno and transfer of power to Suharto. Suharto routinely and secretly met with KAMI leaders.[64] When Blanco returned to the Philippines he took up work organizing students at the University of Santo Tomas (UST) in a nested series of student organizations, each group kept secret from the others.[65] These groups spread to other campuses and in August 1970 gathered together to form the Kapulungan ng mga Sandigan ng Pilipinas (KASAPI).[66] KASAPI began creating various sectoral front organizations that were parallel to those of the CPP. In February 1970, Jesuit priest Ed Garcia founded a second influential SocDem organization—Lakas ng Diwang Kayumanggi (Strength of the Brown Spirit).[67] These were sharply right-wing organizations that were based among the most elite layers of youth and students enrolled at sectarian private universities. They quickly and deeply integrated themselves into existing Catholic organizations with long-standing anti-Communist credentials, including Student Catholic Action. They focused their energy on organizing urban squatter communities, and these shantytown populations formed the base of political power that the SocDem groups mobilized in their protests. The political scientist Jennifer Franco writes, "Social democratic or 'SD' groups such as *Lakasdiwa* . . . were militantly anti-communist and distinguished themselves from the CPP by an avowed commitment to a non-violent and reformist political strategy."[68] While Franco is correct that these groups were militantly anti-Communist, they were not opposed to the use of violence. During the later martial law period, SocDem organizations would plant bombs throughout Manila to destabilize the Marcos regime.[69]

Emerging in the wake of the 1969 election, the SocDem organizations were allied to Osmeña and Aquino and were an element in their conspiratorial plotting. Their common patrons and shared opposition to Marcos brought the SocDem forces and CPP into close political contact. CPP members joined these groups and sought to win them over to the perspective of the party, national democracy, counterposed to SocDem as NatDem. The alternating struggle and cooperation between the allied forces of NatDem and SocDem in the early 1970s was a critical political factor in the period leading up to martial law.[70] The CPP and its front organizations initially denounced the SocDem groups as "clerico-fascists," but as the alliance with them grew they revised the name to "clerico-reformists." The KM later wrote that "as a result of the extreme barbarism and mendacity of the US-Marcos regime, many of the clerico-reformists veered toward the national-democratic line. The majority of the members of reformist organizations bolted these organizations and became national democrats."[71]

The basic orientation of the SocDem groups, in keeping with their roots in KAMI in Indonesia, was to assist in the instigation and carrying out of a military putsch. At the beginning of 1971, KASAPI published statements addressed to the Armed Forces, calling on them to remove Marcos from power.[72] As the CPP allied with the SocDem forces, it became closely associated with a wide range of CIA assets and former military intelligence figures, all of whom were plotting the ouster of Marcos. By mid-1971, Jaime Ferrer, a key CIA asset, announced his support for the KM-SDK and the "revolution of the youth," and the KM trumpeted his support in *Ang Masa*.[73] A CIA agent and former head of military intelligence, Bonifacio Gillego, who was a leader in the coup plots against Marcos, became a prominent speaker at KM rallies. A little more than a decade earlier he had been interrogating imprisoned Communists for the military. The KM was aware of Gillego's role in military intelligence but claimed that he had been won over to the perspective of national democracy.[74]

Growing Unrest

The storm clouds that burst in 1970 were clearly visible on the horizon. There had been signs that social anger was mounting for several years. A militant demonstration of students and workers against US president Lyndon B. Johnson's visit to Manila in 1966 was brutally suppressed by the police.[75] In 1967 the Philippine Constabulary (PC) opened fire on a march of peasant demonstrators, organized in a politico-religious cult. Thirty-three people were killed, their bloody corpses strewn down Taft Avenue. In a public address delivered that year, Marcos declared that the country "was sitting on top of a seething social volcano."[76] The tremors of unrest quickened as the decade drew to a close.

The year 1969 opened with an eruption of student strikes among the working-class youth of the university belt district who were outraged by exorbitant tuition rates and decrepit facilities. The private institutions of higher education stood clustered along Azcarraga on the northern bank of the Pasig, and within the squat stone walls of Intramuros on its south.[77] Most of the buildings were crowded, multistory affairs to which entrance was afforded by a single roadside gate under the watchful eye of armed security guards, who inspected the entering students' uniforms and identification cards. There were over half a million college students in the Philippines in 1969, one of the highest college enrollment per capita figures in the world.[78] The majority of these students came from working-class and peasant families and were working their way through school as janitors on the night shift, stringers for newspapers, secretarial assistants for the university administration, and sales clerks in the shops on Escolta Street.

From Azcarraga, by traversing the length of Quezon Boulevard past the circumferential Highway 54—now renamed de los Santos, but the name had yet to take—one would arrive in Diliman on the outskirts of Quezon City. There the University of the Philippines (UP) sat in seeming rural isolation, its expansive facilities spreading outward into fields of cogon and *talahib*. At its southern and eastern fringes were the impoverished communities of Cruz na Ligas and Balara, pushing toward Marikina. Twenty-five centavos and a thirty-minute

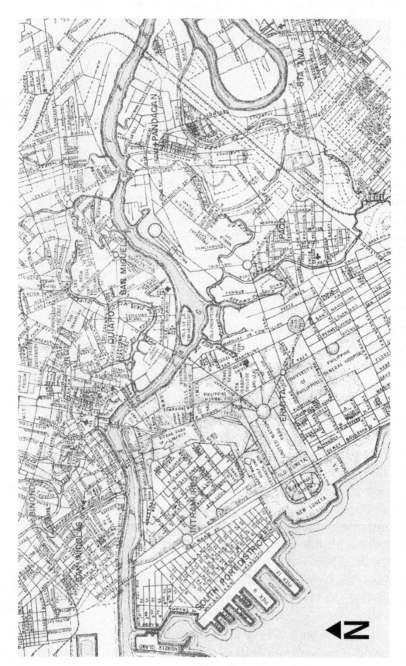

MAP 3. Manila—home to the university belt district, the legislature, and the presidential palace, and the heart of working-class life—was the center of Philippine political life in the postwar period. Based on D. D. de Jesus, *Table and Pocket Map Guide City of Manila* (1960). For a detailed view, see https://www.josephscalice.com/assets/images/maps/map3.png.

jeepney ride could get you from Azcarraga to Diliman, but a lifetime of labor would not have gotten most students in the university belt into the state university. UP provided an education to the children of the elite and the upper-middle class, but also to the most outstanding scholars throughout the nation. The valedictorian of an impoverished provincial high school could be expected to attend the state university, and on a full scholarship. For the rest of the students, they would work their way through school downtown.[79]

Finally, there were the elite religious schools—Ateneo, La Salle, San Beda. These were the enclaves of the extremely wealthy, their corridors of power reserved to cassocks and caciques. They were entirely quiescent in 1969. The majority of the protesters in the period leading up to martial law came from the working-class students of the university belt district; the majority of the leaders, from UP. The dominance of Diliman over Azcarraga expressed the dominance of the petty bourgeoisie over the working class in the national democratic program of the CPP. The events of 1969 revealed this clearly.

The global climate of student unrest in the summer of 1968 provided the initial impetus to the protests that began in the Lyceum and set fire to the fuel of student grievances throughout downtown Manila. Nick Joaquin, writing in the *Philippines Free Press* on 7 September 1968, anticipated that the events in Paris would be emulated by the "anarchs of academe" in the Philippines, but he had his eye on the "groves of Diliman," not the pavement of Azcarraga. The government, too, anticipated a surge of student protests. Aquino, in an attempt to channel and win the support of the emerging unrest, drafted a Magna Carta of Student Rights, which codified a set of limited rights and obligations for students, asserting, for example, the right to free assembly on campus. He did not, however, address the skyrocketing tuition rates and crumbling infrastructure that set off the 1969 demonstrations.

Lyceum student Rene Alejandro wrote a regular column in the campus student paper—*The Lyceum*—during the 1967–68 school year in which he detailed a number of grievances that students were routinely expressing regarding the school, largely having to do with school fees and the general disrepair of the facilities. The Laurel administration responded in the first semester of 1968, suspending Alejandro from the school for one year and suspending publication of *The Lyceum* for the majority of the first semester. The journalism students at Lyceum responded by publishing their own paper, *The Reporter*.[80] Students circulated a petition in defense of Alejandro, calling for his reinstatement, but the school administration refused. In December, at the opening of the second semester, an additional three members of *The Lyceum* staff were expelled and all four students physically barred by security from entering the campus. The cause of the suspended students and their advocacy of improved school facilities and reduced tuition fees found broad sympathy among students throughout the university belt in downtown Manila.

Lacaba wrote, "On January 13 [1969], the *Guilder*, official publication of the College Editors Guild, reported: 'The case of the three dismissed *Lyceum* scribes appears to have stirred a tempest of student unrest as sympathizing students plan to stage a protest demonstration soon if no justice is done them by the proper authorities.'"[81]

On 22 January, striking students formed a picket line at Lyceum but initially drew only about thirty students to their ranks. The picketers formed the Lyceum Student Reform Movement and circulated a leaflet that concluded, "Let us raise the banner of student power!" The Laurel administration responded to the picket by suspending classes at Lyceum for one week, hoping that the protests would disappear in the interim.[82] Far from disappearing, they spread.

The next day, students at Far Eastern University (FEU) formed the FEU Student Reform Movement and likewise went on strike, demanding a "reduction and itemization of tuition fees." They also "objected to the security guards' uniform, which is combat fatigue, and their arms, which include carbines, armalites, and riot guns."[83] On 24 January, three thousand demonstrating students at FEU "broke decorative pots along the streets that border the university, hurled stones at the school buildings and burned placards." Morayta Street was closed to traffic. On the same day, at FEATI, a group calling itself the Movement of Students for Reforms distributed a manifesto demanding improved conditions and academic freedom.[84]

On 27 January the police arrested two of the Lyceum student leaders "for their belligerent attitude." Denouncing the arrests, the striking students attacked the squad car, causing serious damage to the vehicle.[85] Sotero Laurel, head of the Lyceum, refused to meet with the protesters and issued a statement that he was determined to expel the three students. He stated that "a school has the right to defend itself against or rid itself of those who would seek to harm it." The next day the protest at Lyceum again turned violent as striking students were being prevented by security guards from exiting university buildings. A crowd of students gathered, angrily demanding that the guards allow the students to leave. One of the guards fired a warning shot with his shotgun. Students began throwing rocks. The guards beat some of the students, and at least one student was shot. A fire truck arrived and attempted to disperse the students with water; the students stoned the fire truck. Laurel finally agreed that he would meet with the students on the next day, provided they dispersed. Lacaba wrote at the time that "what happened at the Lyceum that night was by far the most vehement expression of dissent in recent history of the Filipino youth."[86]

On 29 January, students at the University of the East walked out of classes to protest "exorbitant and unreasonable fees," and four thousand students from Manila Central University started a boycott of classes, protesting "the deplorable conditions of the university" and demanding a reduction in fees.[87] On 30 January, ten thousand students at FEATI violently demonstrated, hurling rocks and classroom furniture.[88] On the same day, University of Manila students went on strike and classes did not resume until 20 February.[89] On 31 January, the Student Movement for a Better Mapua at the Mapua Institute of Technology led a demonstration of two thousand students demanding a reduction of fees and the improvement of facilities that "turned violent"; no other details are available.[90] Also in the last week of January, students at the Philippine College of Criminology went on strike. On 3 February, a group calling itself the Thomasians for Reforms Movement (TRM) launched protests at the UST, and stones were thrown.[91] On the fourth, the students at Manuel L. Quezon University (MLQU) went on strike.

By the first week of February all the universities in the university belt had been shut down by student strikes, many of which had responded forcefully against violent suppression. These included the Philippine Maritime Institute, 1 February; St. Catherine's School of Nursing, 3 February; Araneta University, 6 February; and Arellano University, 7 February. The strikes began to spread beyond Manila. Students at universities in Bacolod, Cabanatuan, Laguna, Laoag, and Cebu all began to go on strike as well.[92]

In late January or early February 1969, between the founding of the CPP and the founding of the NPA, Joma Sison wrote an article for the Hong Kong–based *Eastern Horizon*, titled "Student Power."[93] Sison was at pains to establish two things: the student strikes in the Philippines were entirely petty bourgeois in origin, and it was imperative for students to take up the "ideology of the working class," which Sison claimed was national democracy.

Sison began, "The social basis of college and high school students is the petty bourgeoisie, although a little minority of them come from exploiting classes."[94] As petty bourgeois, the student is thus "principally concerned with his selfish ambition of pursuing a career within the established system." However, "in time of developing social crisis, the students largely supported by their petty bourgeois parents can easily become agitated when the meager and fixed incomes of their parents can hardly suffice to keep them enrolled in school with the proper board and lodging or with enough allowances." Sison may have been aptly characterizing the student milieu with which he was himself familiar at UP: largely selfish but easily agitated over their declining allowances. His description, however, was grossly incongruous with the character of the majority of the student population. In Sison's depiction none of the students—not even the high school students—were from working-class or peasant backgrounds, and none were working their way through school.

Sison was not alone in this thinking; it characterized the attitudes of the KM and SDK leadership generally. Christine Ebro, a leader of the SDK and a representative of SDK's campus student government party, Partisan, wrote in September 1968 to describe the "situation of almost every college girl in the country":

> Born into a set of conventions, and social restrictions . . . the only activities legitimately open to her, in the traditional viewpoint, are the trivial—cocktail parties, balls, discotheques, picnics, soirées, etc. As a result, she remains isolated from the harsh realities of life; protected from the plight of the "dirty" masses.
>
> Her flighty little brain remains untapped like our rich natural resources, as she attends to petty concerns: confined to the latest dance craze, powdering her pert nose, going to novenas regularly, fingering the rosary, thinking of her next dress and gewgaw to wear.[95]

Sison and his entire cohort had a manifest contempt for the students striking in downtown Manila. Their conception of the students' class background and political goals stands in stark contrast to the actual literature being produced by the striking students themselves. On 17 September 1969, a group calling itself the Progresibong Kabataan ng MLQU (Progressive Youth of MLQU) issued an appeal to the MLQU student body to support its strike, which had begun on 11 September, when students in the College of Business walked out of their classes and were followed by students in the Colleges of Engineering and Education.[96] The striking students stated that they were opposed to University President Leoncio Monzon, who was seeking to turn a profit through exploitation of the students, the staff, and the faculty. The leaflet cited the raising of fees and the cutting of faculty and staff wages and concluded the following:

> If we allow ourselves to be taken advantage of and place our hope in promises, not only will we be victims, not only will our brothers and sisters who will study and follow after us [be victims], but also *our parents who have with great difficulty worked day and night in the fields and factories to pay for our education.* Remember our poor parents . . . rise up!
>
> This fight is not just for students, this is for everyone! Professors, workers, and students.[97]

Sison sought to direct the strikes behind the banner of nationalism and into an alliance with a section of the capitalist class. He wrote, "We have always

advocated the achievement of real national democracy as the goal of our struggle."[98] This could only be achieved, he argued, by "the broad national front
for national democracy among workers, peasants, urban petty bourgeoisie, and
the national bourgeoisie," as "the unifying ideology of the working class," the
"justest [sic] and most progressive class."[99]

Rather than expand the protests of the students to a directly political struggle for free universal public education through the university level, Sison presented national democracy, and not socialism, as the ideology of the working
class and called for an alliance with capitalists. It was this line, dressed up with
armed struggle and the language of Maoism, that Sison would direct to workers and youths over the course of the critical battles of 1970–72.

The student strikes were one expression of a massive growth in working-
class struggles in the country. In 1968, a total of 584,498 worker-days were reported lost owing to strikes and work stoppages. This number nearly doubled
in 1969 to 1,066,642 worker-days lost, and by 1971 it had risen to 1,429,195.[100]
Likewise, the number of striking workers grew from 46,445 in 1968 to 62,138 in
1971. The growth in the number of worker-days lost, however, was grossly
disproportionate to the growth in the number of workers who went on strike.
Where the number of striking workers grew by 34 percent from 1968 to 1971,
the number of worker-days lost to strikes grew 145 percent—an indication that
the strikes were becoming significantly more protracted.

The intensity of the conflict on the picket lines grew alongside the number
and duration of the strikes. In May 1969, workers at Pantranco bus corporation
went on strike, shutting down much of public transportation throughout northern Luzon. The strike started when management attempted to rig a union election. The police and PC repeatedly sought to break up the strike with tear gas
and truncheons, but the workers held their ground. In July, Pantranco management hired members of the notorious Sigue-Sigue Sputnik gang. A busload of
thirty-three strikebreakers, armed with automatic weapons, pistols, bombs, and
knives, drove into the picket lines. They killed four of the striking workers—
three were stabbed, and one was shot in the back. The police covered up the
incident and the strike continued, a bloody battle that lasted months.[101]

The growth of protests in 1969 has been entirely overshadowed in historical recollection by the explosion of the First Quarter Storm. The events of
1970 thus appear to be an abrupt response to an immediate grievance rather
than the cumulative expression of mounting social anger. Large demonstrations and violent suppression had already become an element of public life in
1969. In September, a student protest in front of Malacañang, a continuation
of the strikes from earlier in the year, was violently attacked by Metrocom
agents. UP faculty went on strike in the same month.[102] In October, Manila's

public school teachers went on strike, shutting down ninety-six public schools with 245,000 enrolled students for over a month.[103]

The sharpest expression of political outrage emerged over the acquittal of US petty officer Michael Moomey. On 10 June, Moomey shot and killed a twenty-one-year-old Filipino laborer, Glicerio Amor, on Clark Airbase. US military brass immediately insisted on the extraterritorial sovereignty of their base, and Moomey was tried before a US court-martial. He claimed that he had mistaken Amor for a pig. The charges against him were reduced from murder to "reckless imprudence," and then he was acquitted.[104] Amor's death brought to thirty-three the number of Filipinos killed on US bases in the country, yet not a single American had been convicted of a crime or tried in a Philippine court. Moomey's was the second such acquittal that year.[105] A large demonstration gathered outside the US embassy on 6 October and was brutally dispersed by security forces. A young member of the KM had his teeth bashed out by the butt of an assault rifle.[106]

The 1969 Election

The growing radicalization of youth, the increasingly seething levels of social outrage, and the discontent of the politically excluded layers of the elite all came into sharp focus at the end of the year, as Ferdinand Marcos became the first reelected president in the postcolonial period. The 1969 election was a bloody and expensive affair. Osmeña's famous witticism—"We were outgunned, outgooned, and outgold"—may have been true, but it was not for want of trying; both Marcos and Osmeña spent inordinate sums to purchase Malacañang. Youth played a critical role in the outcome of the election. Sixty-five percent of the electorate in 1969 were below the age of thirty.[107] In the end, Marcos trounced Osmeña and the LP not because he spent more money but because Osmeña was grossly unpopular. Against the strong advice of the younger members of the LP—including Aquino—to court the vote of the youth by posturing in opposition to Washington, Osmeña took the opposite tack, denouncing Marcos for flirting with "the Reds" and for infidelity to the United States. Osmeña's campaign strategy created the remarkable situation in which the incumbent was able to run as the candidate of change and the challenger was seen as that of the status quo.

The LP nominated Sergio Osmeña Jr. as its presidential candidate in June 1969, selecting him over rival candidates Genaro Magsaysay and Antonio Villegas. The LP calculated that his regional Visayan bloc could counter the powerful Ilocano bloc of Marcos. None of the possible candidates for the

LP in 1969 had either the charisma or the political clout of Ferdinand Marcos. The only LP member who did was Ninoy Aquino, the secretary general of the party, but the constitutionally mandated minimum age requirement meant that he could not run for president until 1973. Many leaders of the LP were aware, as early as December 1968, that they could not mount a viable campaign against Marcos in the 1969 election. There was intense discussion within the LP's Executive Committee over the possibility of endorsing Marcos as a coalition candidate and thus securing some of the spoils from the election. Former president Diosdado Macapagal intervened, delivering a speech before the Executive Committee on 22 December rejecting this proposal.[108]

Aquino and a group of first-term LP congressmen known as the Young Turks—Ramon Mitra, Jose Yap, Eddie Ilarde, and Vincenzo Sagun—were thoroughly displeased with the direction of the LP under the candidacy of Osmeña. Aquino, Mitra, and Yap had carefully cultivated ties with the CPP and the KM and were looking to mobilize their support in the 1969 election. They recognized, however, that Osmeña did not have a prayer of getting elected, largely because he was popularly seen as being even more pro-Washington than Marcos himself. At the same time, the Young Turks were looking to secure at least one slot for their group on the senatorial slate of the LP, and thus they could not directly oppose the candidacy of Osmeña.

Osmeña made Genaro Magsaysay his running mate, believing that the Magsaysay name would carry weight with Washington, and then traveled to the

FIGURE 1.4. Ninoy Aquino campaigns for the LP slate in the 1969 election.

United States before launching his campaign, hoping to return with Nixon's support. To his chagrin, Nixon refused to meet with him. Kissinger summed up the thinking of the White House: "We have nothing against him and would not be heartbroken if he won election—odds favor the other guy."[109]

Osmeña's opening salvo in Washington revealed him to be a political operative deaf to the rapidly changing mass sentiment in the Philippines. The regularly published evidence of the brutality of the United States' war in Vietnam and the acquittal of Moomey had created an atmosphere in which ties with the United States were not a selling point. Hoping to salvage some credibility, the Young Turks drafted a foreign policy position statement for the LP that professed the "utmost nationalism" and postured as being nonaligned between Washington, Moscow, and Beijing.[110] Aquino traveled to Japan to personally deliver the statement to Osmeña. Osmeña was in Tokyo en route from Washington to Manila, Aquino en route to Moscow. Aquino sought unsuccessfully to get Osmeña to sign on to the Young Turks' statement and thus to launch his campaign in Manila with the appearance of independence from the United States. Aquino intended to campaign for the Liberal Party on this basis (figure 1.4), and his travel to Moscow was meant to provide weight to this posturing. To the consternation of Aquino and the Young Turks, on his return to Manila, Osmeña did precisely the opposite. He attacked Marcos for having deviated from his allegiance to the United States by opening diplomatic and trade ties with eastern Europe. Osmeña told the press,

> I denounce his administration's two-faced policy vis-a-vis other countries. While professing friendship for the United States, his administration has been shamelessly flirting with Red China and other Communist Countries.
>
> In total disregard of our established national policy against Communism, Mr. Marcos has been threatening to establish diplomatic and trade relations with the Reds, especially when he wants something real bad from the Americans. This is a form of diplomatic blackmail to which I do not subscribe.[111]

Marcos responded, defending the pursuit of trade relations with eastern Europe and Moscow. He stated that "the country must work towards the time when the nation would not be merely a supplier of raw materials but a manufacturer and producer in its own right."[112] Osmeña's anti-Communist bluster ceded to Ferdinand Marcos, the man who had sent Filipino troops to Vietnam, the appearance of independence from Washington. On 12 July, the *Manila Bulletin*—which was both a staunchly anti-Communist and pro-Marcos paper—

ran an editorial responding to Osmeña. It stated that while Marcos was show-
ing a "softening attitude toward red bloc countries," this was selective and
"limited to the Soviet Union and East Europe. There is no known contact with
mainland China." Marcos's moves toward Moscow and eastern Europe were
not mere posturing, however. He saw Moscow as a needed counterweight to
Beijing. In a speech delivered in Guam on 25 July, Nixon announced in outline form what became known as the Nixon Doctrine, the gradual reduction
of US forces throughout the region and the transferring of responsibility for
the "problems of internal security" to "the Asian nations themselves." Speaking with CBS Radio, Marcos declared that if the United States withdrew from
Asia, the Philippines would rely on relations with the Union of Soviet Socialist Republics (USSR) to serve as "a counterfoil against communist China." He
stated that "the Soviet Union will try to neutralize Red China and this is what
we're hoping for in Asia."[113] According to *Pravda*, Marcos stated that "the foreign relations board is now considering the question of establishing diplomatic relations with socialist countries and is to produce its recommendations
towards the end of this year."[114]

Washington assisted Marcos in this nonaligned strategy. The White House
obstructed the investigation conducted by the Symington subcommittee of
the Senate Committee on Foreign Relations, delayed the publication of its final report, and censored its contents.[115] The findings detailed how the Johnson administration had paid Marcos millions of dollars for the deployment of
Filipino "volunteer" troops to Vietnam. Among the material that never saw
print was the revelation that "Marcos and his wife have gone to considerable
lengths to enrich their personal base. [text not declassified] estimate that they
have accumulated approximately $100 million during his term in the presiden-
tial palace."[116] The report, which was published two weeks after Marcos's reelection, exposed the crimes of US empire, of which the corruption of Marcos
was a subordinate component, revealing that the United States was bankrolling counterinsurgency battalions in the Philippines in addition to the Philippine Civic Action Group unit in Vietnam. Senator Stuart Symington balked
not at the injustice of empire but at the cost:

> SYMINGTON: Do you believe the Filipinos, with the rifles we give them,
> are going to shoot other Filipinos to protect US material and people?
> LIEUTENANT GENERAL ROBERT WARREN: I think they probably would,
> at least insofar as the Huk and the insurgent groups go. . . .
> SYMINGTON: How much is the estimated cost, total cost, of each dead
> Huk? Has anybody worked that out?[117]

"Huk"—of which Symington wanted to know the price per corpse—was a holdover term from the peasant rebellion of the 1950s. The label now embraced two rival groups: the mafia of Sumulong and the NPA of Dante. They took opposite sides in the 1969 election and Central Luzon became a war zone. The paramilitary gangster force around Sumulong, with intimate ties to the PC and the Marcos administration, and numerous links to the PKP, was popularly referred to as the "Monkees." Dante's forces, the newly formed NPA, were called the "Beatles."[118] Hidden behind the humorous monikers was a bloodbath. Drive-by shootings, assassinations, and village massacres plagued Central Luzon. Sumulong aggressively campaigned for his political patron, Ferdinand Marcos, disseminating the president's election material throughout the region. His endorsement carried with it the threat of violence against anyone who dared oppose his candidates.[119] The journalist Eduardo Lachica wrote that "Sumulong campaigned for Marcos in 1969. Dante supported Marcos' opponent Sen. Sergio Osmeña, Jr." Territory controlled by the NPA was among the few places where Osmeña won the vote.[120] A great deal of the weight carried by the endorsement of Dante and the NPA came not from their campaigning but simply from the instructions Dante would extend to peasant communities immediately before the election, telling them for whom to vote. Thus, Dante held a meeting with his lieutenants in Pitabunan, Concepcion, Tarlac, a week before the election to determine the broader slate of the NPA's political endorsements. They were torn between endorsing the LP incumbent Jose Yap and endorsing independent candidate Max G. Llorente, for while Yap had close ties to Dante and Sison, the lawyer Llorente had volunteered legal services to defend accused dissidents held in Camp Makabulos. Dante split the NPA's support, instructing certain areas to vote for Yap and others for Llorente. Yap was reelected.[121] The Beatles and the Monkees functioned as armed wings of the political interests of rival sections of the ruling class. There was nothing particularly new about this; it had characterized Philippine politics for decades. The NPA had thrown itself into a very dirty business, and it was the peasant population of Central Luzon that suffered the consequences.

The violence extended beyond the rice bowl of Central Luzon. McCoy writes, "The 1969 campaign also produced incidents of political terror of the sort not seen since the 1951 elections. With the constabulary now under the command of Marcos loyalist Vicente Raval, the PC's Special Forces orchestrated violence in four swing provinces that left forty-six dead."[122]

The PKP, with support from Marcos, launched a terror campaign that it would continue and deepen over the course of the next three years, providing a pretext for the declaration of martial law. This campaign was headed by Pastor Guerrero Tabiñas, who, under the name Commander Soliman, launched the PKP's urban guerrilla forces in 1969.[123] The twenty-two-year-old son of a fisherman, Tabiñas had been orphaned at a young age and dropped out of high school in his third year. He found work in a factory and later became the president of a PKP-aligned union. By 1967 he was working directly with Ruben Torres, Central Committee member of the PKP and salaried employee of the Marcos government, in the Bertrand Russell Peace Foundation (BRPF), a youth front organization of the PKP.[124] Taking the name Soliman in 1969, he established the urban guerrilla forces of the Hukbo Mapagpalaya ng Bayan (People's Liberation Army), known as the People's Revolutionary Front (PRF), in Manila and Angeles, setting up a "laboratory" to create blasting caps and gunpowder from "easily available ingredients."[125] The CPP was taking similar steps. In the same month that Soliman set up his laboratory, Rodolfo Salas, CPP member and head of the KM in Central Luzon, instructed Lualhati Abreu to acquire the necessary supplies to begin the construction of explosives in Angeles.[126] Both the PKP and the CPP discovered from these attempts that it was easier to carry out bombings with grenades pilfered or acquired from the military than it was to make their own.

On 23 July, Soliman's PRF threw a US-manufactured grenade at the Thomas Jefferson Cultural Center of the US Information Service, killing an eighteen-year-old, Rodolfo Carlos, who had been standing in front of the building.[127] Police Chief Gerardo Tamayo used the bombing to justify "a discreet roundup" of "potential troublemakers" before the state visit of Richard Nixon. The next day, the PRF threw another grenade, this time at the Joint US Military Advisory Group. Police Chief Tomas Karingal announced that "a big student organization, led by a former university professor who joined the Huks in Central Luzon recently, is being eyed as behind the incidents."[128] He was referring, of course, to the KM and Sison. Soliman's bombings provided a pretext for the Marcos administration to escalate its security preparations for Nixon's visit and to crack down on the PKP's rival. It would later be revealed that some of the "most active members" carrying out this campaign "were actually agents planted by the military."[129]

The CPP sought to use violence in the lead-up to the election as a means of provoking the Marcos administration into exposing its ties to US militarism. *Ang Bayan* declared that the best way for the NPA to "expose Nixon's lies and call the people's attention to the continuing aggressive presence of US imperialism is to direct fire at its military personnel." US soldiers should be attacked "in their urban haunts and along highways." This would "certainly compel the Philippine reactionary government to use the PC-Army troops as security guards for their foreign masters, thus exposing the real puppetry of the local reactionaries."[130] On 4 July, the NPA shot four US servicemen at their "sin center" in Angeles, killing two and wounding the others. The campaign escalated. In September, *Ang Bayan* reported that it had carried out two bombings near the Balibago gate of Clark on 31 July and 4 August, killing six airmen.[131] The campaign against US servicemen stopped by November; it had been an election tactic.

The rhetoric employed by both incumbent and challenger was a world away from the realities of working-class life. Marcos and Osmeña invested a small fortune in the election, and Marcos's spending in 1969 became the stuff of legend. Imelda Marcos campaigned with a group of well-to-do society women, known as the Blue Ladies; Minnie Osmeña countered with her Pearls. The only thing that was real in the entire god-awful affair was the bloodshed. The response of youth, with their growing sense of political independence and connection with a global spirit of dissent, was disgust.

This disgust found passive expression in a campaign spearheaded by the SDK, an organization that did not begin to join the CPP camp until early 1970. The SDK and its Diliman campus group, the Pagkakaisa-Partisans, issued a call for the boycott of the 1969 elections. Jerry Barican and Antonio Pastelero, the current and former chairs of the UP Student Council, appeared on Lopez's television network, ABS-CBN, on 18 September to launch the boycott campaign, claiming that it "would serve as a protest vote and, at the same time, as a warning against the politicians to reform their ways."[132] The influential Diliman campus paper, the *Collegian*, dedicated an entire issue to promoting the boycott.[133] The SDK enjoined young people, "Be smart, don't vote! [Maging matalino, huwag bumoto!]" The campaign directed the disgusted to simply opt out. There was no alternative presented other than a reformist appeal to the elite: "give us more palatable candidates, or we won't vote."

Neither the CPP nor the PKP sought to build on the disgust and elaborate the need for an independent party of the working class. They were torn between the demands of their patrons and the disgruntlement of their constituents. Uncertain where to place their bets, they played the field—supporting a boycott through some of their front organizations and endorsing candidates for election through others. This strategy, pursued by both parties, was not the result of poor communication or a lack of coordination. It was a calculated and dishonest policy designed to secure the greatest advantage out of the election. It simultaneously cultivated ties with leading bourgeois political figures through endorsement, on the one hand, and attempted to retain mass support by protesting the rotten political system, on the other.

The PKP had a strong incentive to support Marcos in 1969: Marcos openly advocated ties with Moscow and eastern Europe, he had provided salaried government positions to leading members of the party, and he was negotiating the release of the PKP members in prison. The Marcos administration facilitated the international travel of the PKP, and they in turn assisted with his foreign diplomacy with the USSR. The emerging armed wing of the PKP was intimately tied to the military and had just launched a bombing campaign that would later serve as the calculated pretext for military dictatorship. Hernando Abaya, a long-standing intimate ally of the PKP, traveled to Moscow in late 1969 to deliver a lecture to Soviet scholars at the Institute of Oriental Studies. He informed them that "a second Marcos term might augur well for the further easing of contacts between our two peoples since it is under Mr. Marcos that travel to the socialist countries had been permitted."[134]

In August the Central Committee of the PKP discussed and approved the "Thesis on the National Situation."[135] The document laid out the "errors and mistakes" of the organization in the past and established its "strategic aims . . . outlook and perspective" going forward:

> At the present stage of the struggle, the CPP document is in reference to the Moscow-oriented party] sets for itself the strategic aims of achieving complete independence from American imperialist economic exploitation and political domination and the liquidation of the powerful remnants of feudal exploitation and political control, leading to the establishment of a national-democratic state (in which political power is shared by the alliance of the workers, peasants, petty bourgeoisie and the progressive national bourgeoisie) which will proceed to restructure the economy ultimately leading to socialism.

In the pursuit of these strategic aims, the party was "prepared to combine skillfully and flexibly, as the situation dictates, both peaceful and violent, legal and illegal, parliamentary and armed forms and methods of struggle." One of the criticisms leveled by the document was that "the CPP [that is, PKP] has not yet learned to make proper use of the potentialities of the revolutionary students, intellectuals, and other petty bourgeois elements. It is confronted with the phenomenon of intelligent, sincere and dedicated revolutionary students engaged in militant mass actions, following the leadership of the 'Maoist' group or the leadership of the church-led Christian Social Movement [a reference to SocDem]." Nothing in the August thesis distinguished the PKP in its program, strategic aims, or even tactics from the CPP. It was pursuing a national democratic revolution but not yet socialism, was looking to form an alliance with the progressive section of the national bourgeoisie, and was willing to pursue both parliamentary and armed means to achieve this end. The difference between the two flowed from their orientation to rival sections of the bourgeoisie, which expressed in tactical form the rival geopolitical perspectives of Moscow and Beijing. There was thus genuine enthusiasm on the part of the PKP leadership for Marcos and his reelection, but there was also legitimate concern that they were not winning the support of the youth.

To resolve this dilemma, the PKP pursued a fragmentary approach to the 1969 election: Movement for the Advancement of Nationalism (MAN) and Malayang Samahan ng Magsasaka (Free Federation of Peasants, MASAKA), the party organizations expressing the interests of businessmen and peasants, endorsed Marcos, while the MPKP and BRPF joined the boycott campaign, looking to retain support within the youth movement. MAN had been a reliable supporter of Marcos since its founding in the first half of 1967, and at its Second National Congress, held on 15–16 March 1969, it continued and deepened this support. The leadership of the PKP played a central role in the congress, which was cochaired by Central Committee member and Marcos administration employee Ruben Torres, and whose preparatory committee and coordinating committee were in their majority composed of party members.[136] The program of the congress called for a "New Philippine Society," parroting the political slogan of Ferdinand Marcos, who had himself lifted the phrase from LBJ's Great Society. By September, MAN explicitly endorsed Marcos's reelection. In the same month, MASAKA endorsed Marcos in a mass rally staged at Plaza Miranda, spending "a large amount of money (at least ₱30,000) on chartered buses last September 19 to ferry about 5,000 people from the provinces."[137]

The CPP was not yet as closely wed to the LP as the PKP was to Marcos. Those ties came with the First Quarter Storm. Like the PKP, however, the CPP hedged its bets. It campaigned for Osmeña through the NPA, while the KM at least passively backed the SDK boycott campaign.

November saw Marcos win in a landslide (figure 1.5).[138] For the LP, the 1969 election was a devastating defeat. Marcos received five million votes to Osmeña's three million, and Osmeña did not even manage to win his home turf of Cebu. Only one LP senator, Gerry Roxas, managed to secure reelection. The journalist Hermie Rotea wrote that Osmeña, alleging fraud, "petitioned Congress to annul the election. He wanted to stop the proclamation of the first reelected Filipino president. But the NP-dominated legislature through sheer force of number proclaimed him."[139] When his petition failed, Osmeña filed a formal protest before the Presidential Electoral Tribunal, but this ultimately went nowhere. The election was another step in the resistible rise of Ferdinand Marcos.

When Congress opened on 26 January 1970, the number of LP senators had been reduced from nine to five, and its congressmen from thirty to sixteen, and within weeks some of the few remaining Liberals had defected to

Figure 1.5. Ferdinand Marcos and Vice President Fernando Lopez (*left*) campaign in the 1969 presidential election, months before the explosive eruption of their hostilities.

the NP. Surveying the situation in February 1970, *Graphic Weekly* concluded, "Were it not for the students . . . one would indeed be led to believe that Marcos is politically invulnerable."[140] The task of the leadership of the devastated LP—"Roxas, Salonga, Aquino, Montano, and young Rep. Ramon Mitra"—was "to take up the cause of the students, to provide a mode by which the students and those who agree with them can make themselves heard, and make themselves politically potent." The LP, under the leadership of Ninoy Aquino, pursued precisely this course and concluded an alliance with the CPP and the students that it led through the KM and SDK. They would attempt to harness the power of the social storm that was breaking and turn it to their advantage, insinuating themselves into power before the increasingly imminent declaration of martial law. It would be seventeen years before the country would hold another presidential election.

CHAPTER 2

The First Quarter Storm

In response to the dirty election, the University of the Philippines (UP) Student Council sent a fact-finding team to Ilocos, which claimed to find "incontrovertible proof" of military coercion and issued a statement denouncing "election terrorism."[1] The committee formed to investigate electoral fraud took the name Movement for a Democratic Philippines (MDP).[2] On 27 November, the MDP published a declaration of principles in the *Collegian*, which opened "We, citizens of the Philippines, . . . conscious of the need for all progressive Filipinos to consolidate in order to expose and combat all adversaries of a genuine Filipino democratic society, commit ourselves to the principles and objectives of the Movement for a Democratic Philippines." The MDP subscribed to five basic principles: people's democratic rights, civilian supremacy over the military, basic land reform and nationalist industrialization, national self-determination, and a progressive and independent foreign policy. On this basis they committed to "consolidate all progressive sectors of our society into a united front of the nationalist movement."[3]

The UP Student Council (UPSC) ad hoc committee to investigate the rigging of the 1969 election in Ilocos thus established itself as a permanent body. Committed to national democratic goals, but without allegiance to either the Partido Komunista ng Pilipinas (PKP) or the Communist Party of the Philippines (CPP), it spent its initial months working as an organization for student reform. But by February 1970 it had been transformed into an umbrella group of the entire Philippine Left. It played a crucial role in the First Quarter Storm, and through its auspices the Kabataang Makabayan (Nationalist Youth, KM) and the Samahan ng Demokratikong Kabataan (Federation of Democratic Youth, SDK) overcame their split and began working intimately together.

In December the MDP was a small group pursuing student reforms; by January it had been thrust into the maelstrom. On 11 December, for example, the MDP issued a manifesto that addressed specific details of student reforms. "We believe that the Albarracin circular and the similar De La Salle directive were rescinded, not as an admission of error nor a reasonable concession to student protest, but only to diffuse and undercut the projected show of unity by different studentries in a massive demonstration."[4] The manifesto denounced the *Manual of Student Rights and Responsibilities*, published by the Marcos administration, saying that it was "an example of the anti-nationalist position of our neo-colonial educational system," and cited two examples of this antinationalism: the requirement that student demands be submitted through school governance and that school newspapers be subjected to school rules. The manifesto concluded with the demand for the "rescindment of the Manual," stating that "sufficient guidance is already provided in our Constitution, particularly the Bill of Rights." The MDP was a limited organization, and precisely this limited but loosely national democratic character allowed it to serve as the coordinator of the varied interests of all the groups participating in the First Quarter Storm (FQS).

Thunder from the approaching storm rumbled on the horizon on 29 December 1969, when US vice president Spiro T. Agnew visited Manila to attend Marcos's inauguration. The KM and SDK staged a joint rally at the US embassy protesting his visit. Lacaba wrote, "It was the first public manifestation at which the Kabataang Makabayan and Samahang Demokratiko ng Kabataan, the two largest radical youth organizations, which had heretofore been vehemently at odds, acted in concert."[5] Gary Olivar and other leaders of the rally visited the television networks of ABS-CBN, ABC, and IBC earlier in the day to present their perspective and were given airtime.[6] It was the first public hint of Eugenio Lopez and his allies' support for the youth movement. The rally itself was a small one, largely because it was Christmas break and the majority of students had gone home.[7] Someone threw a Molotov cocktail at Agnew's vehicle, and police waded into the protesting crowd, swinging their truncheons.[8]

In keeping with the initial, limited purview of the MDP, both the KM and the SDK narrowly focused on the issue of student reform for the first demonstration of 1970. They envisioned protests proceeding along the same lines as those that had opened the previous year, but this time they sought to be at their head. Assembling in front of Malacañang on 7 January, they described

themselves to the press as the "student reform movement." The KM distributed a leaflet that focused its ire on UP president Salvador Lopez, stating
that "reactionary elements of the like of UP President SP Lopez were quick to
commend the 'rules' even as the order continues to uncover itself as a fascistic maneuver by the reactionary state."[9] The *Collegian* reported that "close to
a thousand students from the University and other schools rallied before
the Malacañang Palace yesterday [7 January]. . . . Workers who were on
strike at Northern Motors joined the students."[10]

The leaflet that the KM produced for the rally turned from the topic of student reform to that of Marcos and fascism, concluding with a formulation
that encapsulated the fundamental political logic of the CPP and its front
organizations in the heady period between the storm and the onset of military dictatorship: "The intensification of the fascistic suppression of the national democratic aspirations of the people by the Marcos military regime only
serves to enlist more adherents to the struggle for genuine emancipation from
US imperialism and local feudalism." Fascism, they argued, only causes the
movement to grow. This cantus firmus, adopted by group after group in counterpoint, emerged as the theme of the political fugue that was the FQS.

Here was the basic logic underpinning all of the mimeographed leaflets circulated by the KM during the FQS. Marcos was a fascist puppet, the main
representative of US imperialism and local feudalism, and as such he should
be the primary target of all protests. The people would rise up to demand national democracy, and they would be violently suppressed. This suppression
would expose the character of the fascist Marcos regime to even more people,
who would then rise up and be suppressed. The people would never be cowed
by fascism. The more "fascist" and violent that Marcos became, the more
people would rise up. But rise up to what end?

At no point were workers and students educated in the need for an independent struggle of the working class for the seizure of power, or that in order to
carry out national democratic tasks, socialist measures must be taken. Rather,
the students were instructed to demand, to request—stridently, but nonetheless
to ask—of the ruling class that national democratic measures be carried out. In
fact, no political program at all was presented. None beyond the need for what
became the clichéd slogan of the movement: "Makibaka, huwag matakot!"
(Struggle, don't be afraid!) The act of struggling, of making demands to the
state, would precipitate state violence, which would, in turn, cause the movement to grow. This was the entire perspective of the KM during this period.

Whose political interests did the FQS serve? Not those of workers or students. They fought courageously and were bloodied in the affair, but the Stalinist leadership worked to ensure that they did not draw independent political

conclusions from the experience and that workers did not organize themselves separately from the bourgeoisie for their own class interests. The PKP lost out as a result of the FQS. It fought a rearguard battle to simultaneously negotiate ties with Marcos and maintain support among the youth. This was an impossible task, and the PKP lost a good deal of its political credibility in the process. The CPP and its front organizations benefited immensely from the FQS. Both the shared barricades of Mendiola Bridge and the exposure of the Malayang Pagkakaisa ng Kabataang Pilipino (Free Unity of Filipino Youth, MPKP) served to heal many of the wounds inflicted during the breach with the SDK. A generation of students were radicalized by the FQS—some only briefly, but for others it was a life-changing experience—and many found their way into the ranks of the CPP. The greatest short-term beneficiaries of the storm sat in the boardrooms of Meralco and the political headquarters of the Liberal Party (LP). For Eugenio Lopez and Aquino and their allies, the protesting students were an ideal proxy in their fight against Marcos. These forces aspired to destabilize and overthrow him, and the blood in the streets served this purpose. They did not succeed in this, however. In the end, the events that began on 26 January 1970 set in motion a countdown to martial law. Marcos recognized in the violent demonstrations a pretext for dictatorship. He fomented violence through agents provocateur and began preparing the architecture of a police state.

Demonstrations followed on 16 and 22 January; the theme of student reform—still audible—was fading, while the staves on fascism augmented. According to the Samahan Pangkaunlaran ng Kaisipan (Federation for the Development of Consciousness, SPK), students gathered outside Malacañang to request from the government the disbursement of funds that had been promised for public education.[11] The placards and slogans of the assembled demonstrators, however, revealed that the political logic of the emerging movement was tending toward a far sharper conclusion. Over a thousand workers and students from different organizations, including KM, SDK, and SPK, rallied on the sixteenth; their signboards read "Justice is a slow process, revolution is faster," "Philippine Constabulary (PC)–Manila Police Department (MPD)–military arm of the ruling class," and "Ibagsak ang pasismo" (Down with fascism).[12] The assembled demonstrators denounced "the alliance between alien capitalists and the armed forces and the rise of fascism under the Marcos administration." Rodolfo del Rosario, vice president of the National Association of Trade Unions (NATU) and a member of KM, addressed the crowd, denouncing the conspiracy of foreign capitalists ("kapitalistang kayuhan" [sic]) and the police in suppressing the ongoing strike at Northern Motors. The demonstrators—workers and students—were violently dispersed by the police.[13]

26 January: "On the Trembling Edge of Revolution"

The forces were all now in place: Marcos, aspiring for a pretext for dictator-ship, his bourgeois opponents for violent destabilization; a restive youth and working class; and two Communist parties, each subordinate to a rival faction of the ruling class.[14]

Anticipating unrest, Metrocom, the unit of the Philippine Constabulary (PC) operating in Metro Manila, made preparations to suppress it.[15] Two organ-izations were granted permits to rally in front of Congress—the National Union of Students of the Philippines (NUSP), headed by Edgar Jopson, and Ang Mag-igiting (The Brave), the political vehicle of radio personality Roger Arienda—while the MPKP was able to secure a permit to stage a protest behind the Congress building. Neither the KM nor the SDK was able to obtain a permit. As late as 22 January, these organizations were still discussing how best to protest during the State of the Nation address. The UPSC under Jerry Barican of the SDK stated that it intended to demonstrate to "clarify its stand on the Constitu-tional Convention and to bid for public support." They weighed holding a sepa-rate rally at Plaza Miranda, where, campus journalist and SDK member Antonio Tagamolila reported, the Kamanyang Players would perform, "reinforcing the issues with dance and drama."[16] This proposal wound up being rejected, and the UPSC, KM, and SDK all decided to join the NUSP rally in front of Congress.

Opening the first session of the Seventh Congress, on Monday, 26 January, Father Pacifico Ortiz, president of Ateneo de Manila University, delivered an invocation. The country was standing, he intoned, "on the trembling edge of revolution." Marcos delivered his State of the Nation speech, titled "National Discipline: The Key to Our Future."[17] His voice, broadcast over four external loudspeakers, resounded over Burgos Drive and echoed on the tree-lined fringes of the Muni golf course, drowning out the "lone amplifier" of the pro-testers.[18] Newspapers estimated that forty thousand people rallied outside the halls of Congress, while "the number of security forces mustered for the occasion was estimated at 7,000."[19] Arienda's group had brought a mock cof-fin that they said symbolized the death of democracy, while a separate group of demonstrators from UP carried a papier-mâché crocodile with a dollar sign on its belly that they set on top of the coffin.[20]

In a manner unintentionally symbolic of its increasing political isolation, the MPKP distributed its leaflet, The Sad State of the Nation, behind the house of Congress. The statement stressed that the organization had no illusion that "Mr. Marcos will take advantage of his position as the first reelected president to pull the country out of the disastrous path of neocolonial development. . . .

Change can only come from the people themselves, particularly those who are most oppressed."[21] The MPKP called for "a mighty wave of mass action to deal with the following problems: The Fascist Menace . . ." In this section the MPKP charged the military with "recruiting student leaders to intelligence agencies and using them to infiltrate progressive youth organizations . . . to push these organizations along a disastrous adventurist line and to sow dissensions in the ranks of the genuine anti-imperialist groups. Just the other day they again circulated a slanderous leaflet against MPKP, charging it of subversion and denigrating its leaders." While denouncing fascism, the MPKP rooted this political danger not in capitalism but in the KM and SDK, which, infiltrated by the military, were pursuing a "disastrous adventurist line." The other problems mass action needed to solve were "Economic Sabotage" on behalf of US imperialism, "Bogus land reform," and the worsening economic conditions of the masses. The group put forward no concrete program to solve any of these problems but simply issued a repeated call for mass action. Action to what end? This was never addressed. The MPKP's call for mass action was subsumed under the slogan "Build Parliament in the Streets!" Given the political line articulated by the MPKP, it was logical to assume that mass action should be mobilized to pressure Marcos to "take advantage of his position."

Arriving at four in the afternoon, just as Marcos was about to speak, "the KM members surged forward through the crowd in a diamond formation until they positioned themselves in the forefront of the demonstration site, their huge red streamer very noticeable and overshadowing all the other placards."[22] They distributed a position paper to the crowd titled "A Neo-colony in Crisis," which began, "As the Seventh Congress of the Philippines opens today, the Kabataang Makabayan presents to the Filipino people the real state of the nation. In the interest of exposing to the people the conditions in the country so that they may act to change them, the KM joins today's demonstration in unity with progressive and national democratic organizations and individuals."[23] The "reactionary Marcos administration," they stated, "has strengthened and deepened its commitments to the neo-colonial schemes of the imperialist United States and Japan and social-imperialist Soviet Union in Asia." The KM denounced Marcos's "plan to open trade relations with pseudo-socialist countries, specifically the Soviet Union." Marcos's plan was "in consonance with the US-Soviet policy of dividing the world between themselves. . . . The Soviet Union has been transformed into a neo-capitalist state that exploits and oppresses not only the Soviet people but also the peoples of its colonies in the same fashion as the United States does" (FQS, 158). The KM warned that "resurging fascism . . . emphatically characterizes the Marcos administration" (FQS, 159). This was evidenced by violence against "the people" carried out by "Hitler-worshippers in the reactionary armed forces" (*FQS*, 161). The KM drew this conclusion: "But one thing is sure. As the ruling class can not rule anymore in the old way, more violent repressions are bound to unfold. Yet, it is a truism that in any society, as the ruling class becomes more violent, the resistance of the oppressed is increased tenfold. The revolutionary movement emerges to destroy the inequities of the old order" (*FQS*, 162).

An array of speakers addressed the crowd, struggling to be heard over Marcos.[24] When former Huk leader Luis Taruc was given the microphone, the demonstrators loudly booed him and shouted, "We want Dante!"[25] Lacaba reported that "there were two mikes, taped together; and this may sound frivolous, but I think the mikes were the immediate cause of the trouble that ensued. . . . Now, at about half past five, Jopson, who was in polo barong and sported a red armband with the inscription 'J26M,' announced that the next speaker would be Gary Olivar of the SDK."[26] Jopson then hesitated, reluctant to give the microphone to Olivar. He led the crowd in singing the national anthem. When the singing finished, he continued to clutch the microphones and then announced that the NUSP rally was over and called on students to disperse. "It was at this point that one of the militants grabbed the mikes from Jopson" and passed them to "a labor union leader"—most likely Rodolfo del Rosario. He "attacked the 'counter-revolutionaries who want to end this demonstration,' going on from there to attack fascists and imperialists in general. By the time he was through his audience had a new, a more insistent chant: 'Rebolusyon! Rebolusyon! Rebolusyon!'"[27]

Shortly thereafter, Marcos emerged from Congress. "No less than Col. Fabian Ver, chief of the presidential security force, and Col. James Barbers, Manila deputy chief of police, personally led the heavy escort. Brig. Gen. Hans Menzi, the inseparable chief presidential aide, trotted behind."[28] The protesters set Marcos's effigy on fire, hurling the crocodile and coffin at his entourage; the police charged the protesters and "flailed away, the demonstrators scattered."[29] The president and his wife safely drove away. The protesters quickly regrouped and began throwing rocks and soft-drink bottles at the police, who arrested some of the demonstrators on the spot. Hermie Rotea wrote that "they continued hitting demonstrators they had just caught even if they were not resisting at all, or were pleading for mercy, or were already down."[30] The police violence was indiscriminate, and a number of reporters were beaten alongside the demonstrators. The police then "retreated into Congress with hostages. The demonstrators re-occupied the area they had vacated in their panic. The majority of NUSP members must have been safe in their buses by then, on their way home, but the militants were still in possession of the mikes."[31]

About two thousand demonstrators remained in front of Congress. They began chanting "Makibaka! Huwag matakot!" (Struggle, don't be afraid!) and then sang "The Internationale." Senator and former vice president Emmanuel Pelaez emerged from the congressional building to address the crowd, and the SDK supplied him with a microphone. The crowd chanted for the arrested protesters to be released, but the KM and SDK leaders silenced the crowd so that Pelaez could speak.[32] Pelaez made a lengthy speech in an attempt to calm the crowd while the police regrouped, moving around to the north side of the building. As Pelaez was finishing his speech, they charged the demonstrators. According to Lacaba,

> The demonstrators fled in all directions. . . . Three cops cornered one demonstrator against a traffic sign and clubbed him until the signpost gave way and fell with a crash. . . . The demonstrators who had fled regrouped, on the Luneta side of Congress, and with holler and whoop, they charged. The cops slowly retreated before this surging mass, then ran, ran for their lives, pursued by rage, rocks and burning placard handles. . . . In the next two hours, the pattern of battle would be set. The cops would charge, the demonstrators would retreat; the demonstrators would regroup and come forward again, the cops would back off to their former position. . . . There were about seven waves of attack and retreat by both sides, each attack preceded by a tense noisy lull, during which there would be sporadic stoning, by both cops and demonstrators.[33]

The demonstrators had hired a jeepney and some crowded into it for shelter (figure 2.1). The police "swooped down on the jeepney with their rattan sticks, striking out at the students who surrounded it until they fled, then venting their rage some more on those inside the jeepney who could not get out to run. The shrill screams of women inside the jeepney rent the air. The driver, bloody all over, managed to stagger out; the cops quickly grabbed him."[34] The police began firing shots in the air and the demonstrators fled.

By eight in the evening, less than two hours after it had started, the battle in front of Congress had ended. Among those injured were members of the NUSP and the KM. Rotea reported that "initial official reports showed that about 300 youths were injured while 72 law enforcers were wounded in the Congress riot."[35] A great many demonstrators were arrested—"thrown into and packed like sardines at the city detention jail." Salvador Laurel and John Osmeña, along with a handful of other politicians, "personally spent the night there and helped expedite their release."[36] Of those arrested, nineteen were charged but were released without bail.

FIGURE 2.1.   Metrocom police beat students huddled for safety in a jeepney, 26 January 1970.

The next three days saw a relentless stream of recriminations and posturing with regard to the violence of 26 January. Nemesio Prudente, president of the PCC, who had been beaten by the police alongside students, told the press, "I will support a nationwide revolutionary movement of students to protest the brutalities of the state."[37] James Barbers, deputy chief of the MPD, issued a statement: "We maintain that the police acted swiftly at a particular time when the life of the President of the Republic—and that of the First Lady—was being endangered by the vicious and unscrupulous elements among the student demonstrators. One can just imagine what would have resulted had something happened to the First Lady!"[38] Mayor Villegas defended "the police action and said they acted on his orders to protect the President."[39] Edgar Jopson published a statement washing his hands of the event, claiming that the riot started when he attempted to end the demonstration. Ruben Torres, chair of the MPKP, issued a brief statement, which concluded, "Police brutality, blatantly displayed in the January 26th demonstration will not dampen the surging activism of the youth. All the more, this even increases the enthusiasm and determination of the youth in their struggle for national democracy."[40] The Bertrand Russell Peace Foundation (BRPF) issued a similar statement denouncing "the use of naked force" by "the power holders."[41] Neither the MPKP nor the BRPF mentioned Marcos at all.

A press statement from the president declared, "Initial reports from police and intelligence indicate that the riot was instigated by non-student provocateurs who had infiltrated the ranks of the legitimate demonstrators. This is being investigated."[42] Marcos sought to blame the riots on CPP infiltrators, yet he was well aware that at least some of the provocateurs of violence were secret police agents among the students, a number of whom played leading roles in the 26 January events and in the subsequent development of the FQS. Lacaba related how a young woman denounced the police during the riot: "Those sons of bitches, their day is coming." (Putangna nila, me araw din sila.) She was Elnora "Babette" Estrada, a member of the National Council of the KM, and an undercover police agent with the rank of sergeant.[43]

On Tuesday, the day after the violence, Jerry Barican announced that students at UP would be staging a week-long boycott of classes to express their "vehement denunciation of police brutality and of other terroristic means being perpetrated by the Marcos administration."[44] Student leaders held a meeting at Far Eastern University (FEU), where they resolved to stage a demonstration on 30 January.[45] The next day, a Senate and House joint committee, chaired by Senator Lorenzo Tañada, was formed to investigate the "root causes of demonstrations in general."[46] Five hundred UP faculty members gathered and drafted a declaration, adopted unanimously, to "strongly denounce the use of brutal force by state authorities against student demonstrators on January 26 1970. . . . The Faculty holds the present administration accountable and responsible for the pattern of repression and the violation of rights."[47]

30 January: The Battle of Mendiola

The demonstrators regrouped on 30 January, a split emerging in their ranks. The majority, shocked by the violence of the twenty-sixth, rallied in front of Congress behind the banners of the KM and SDK denouncing the "fascism" of Marcos; the moderate student groups sent a delegation to meet with the president at Malacañang. Tensions were high. *Ang Bayan* declared that the 26 January protest "was merely the opening salvo for bigger mass actions of the near future. It is a blow against the reactionaries to be followed by more and bigger blows."[48] On the morning of the thirtieth, UP Student Catholic Action (UPSCA) circulated forged leaflets purporting to be from the UPSC, claiming that the demonstration did not have the sanction of the council and warning students, "Don't blame anyone if you get hurt!"[49]

Finding that neither camp expressed its interests, and unable to articulate an independent position, the MPKP tagged along to the KM and SDK rally. They circulated a leaflet grossly incongruous with the mood of the assembled masses, focusing on the upcoming 1971 constitutional convention. The MPKP, they wrote, "did not and does not support the slogan of 'non-partisan constitutional convention.' . . . [This slogan] is deliberately designed to create illusion [sic] about the convention and to conceal the truth that the convention, whether openly partisan or not, will reflect the bankruptcy of the present political system."[50] The leaflet continued,

> We must therefore rally the masses in a relentless struggle against neo-colonialism. The election of delegates and the convention itself may, however, be good opportunities to accomplish this principal task; but this could only be accomplished if we dispel all illusions in the minds of the masses
>
> MPKP calls for a People's Constitution that will declare illegal and obsolete the power of imperialism, feudalism and capitalism, and project the concept of people's power. The People's Constitution should be a rallying program of the struggle for national democracy.

By rejecting the call for a nonpartisan constitutional convention, the MPKP kept voting open to the two major political parties, while with its demand for a People's Constitution it promoted the idea that by voting for delegates—including representatives from the LP and Nacionalista Party—the people could secure representatives who would by legislative fiat make imperialism, feudalism, and capitalism illegal. The reformist illusions that the MPKP was attempting to promote are staggering. As Marcos's forces trained their guns on the protesters and fired, the MPKP activists had this leaflet in their hands. It made no mention—none—of the violence of 26 January, and it claimed that the central task was to elect representatives to the constitutional convention who would simply declare capitalism illegal. The events of 30 January and the public outcry that they produced compelled the MPKP to begin speaking of fascism while attempting to deflect the focus of public ire away from Marcos.

In the afternoon, Edgar Jopson, Portia Ilagan, and others from the NSL and NUSP met with Marcos. Jopson demanded that Marcos put his commitment not to run for another presidential term in writing, and Marcos, irritated by Jopson's demand, famously denounced him as the mere "son of a grocer." As they were leaving, at shortly after six in the evening, violence broke out at the entrance to the presidential palace.[51] The demonstrators had moved from Congress to Malacañang, and as Marcos emerged from his meeting with Jopson they gathered at Gate Four. Col. Fabian Ver and Major Ramos were "waiting for the President to give the order to shoot and the President did order: 'Shoot them with water and tear gas.'"[52] As security forces launched their assault, Gary Olivar issued instructions to the protesters by means of an ABS-CBN sound truck, which Lopez had apparently supplied to the protesters. Olivar used the vehicle to direct the ensuing Battle of Mendiola.[53] A fire truck arrived to blast the protesters with water, but members of the Samahan ng Demokratikong Kabataan—Mendiola commandeered the vehicle, which they crashed through the palace gates. A series of explosions followed, and the protesters retreated, constructing barricades on the Mendiola bridge as they fell back from Malacañang. They briefly held this position and then fell back again.

For several hours police and protesters waged a battle for the bridge. The police and military repeatedly fired on the student protesters, who responded with small handheld explosive devices known as pillboxes, Molotov cocktails, and rocks, setting fire to vehicles in the street to slow the passage of the military (figure 2.2). The barricades on Mendiola fell around midnight. "There was nonstop hail of bullets, deafening gunfire as we scrambled on the sidewalk on the left side of Recto Avenue [Azcarraga] towards Lepanto and Morayta."[54]

FIGURE 2.2. The smoldering remains of Azcarraga in the early morning of 1 February 1970.

As they retreated, the protesters overturned the concrete flower beds set up by Villegas along Azcarraga, and some "abandoned vehicles were cannibalized, their tires turned into bonfires that gave off the pungent smell of burning rubber and the unmistakable look of an insurrection."[55]

Preliminary radio news reports that Friday night announced that five or six protesters had been killed, but four were eventually named: Ricardo Alcantara, a student from UP; Fernando Catabay, Manuel L. Quezon University; Bernardo Tausa, Mapa High School; and Felicisimo Singh Roldan, University of the East. The dead ranged in age from sixteen to twenty-one; each had been shot by the police.[56] One hundred seven students were injured on 30 January, seventy-four of them from gunshot wounds, among them a boy from Roosevelt Academy in Cubao whose leg had to be amputated.[57] Hundreds of students were arrested. They were detained in the stockade at Camp Crame, headquarters of the PC, long past the legal maximum of six hours without charges. When protests were raised over the illegality of the mass detention, the PC charged the students with sedition, holding them for eighteen hours without food and then dismissing all charges for lack of evidence.[58]

People's Congresses of February

A wave of fear swept through the better-off layers of society; Saturday morning saw panic buying in the supermarkets and military patrols in the streets. Lacaba reported the following:

> Government troops made no effort to be inconspicuous: though supposedly no longer on red alert, they roamed the city in rumbling trucks from which carbines and armalites stuck out like sore thumbs, and occasionally made forays into the universities. Banks and stores started boarding up their glass facades with plywood or steel sheets. The stock market didn't crash, but the prices of stock took a sharp plunge that brought about an orgy of short selling. Refugees from Forbes Park nervously paced the carpeted floors of the Hotel Inter-Continental, filled to capacity for the first time since its inauguration. Classes in Greater Manila were suspended for a whole week, and for a whole week the mayors of Manila and Makati refused to grant permits to demonstrate.[59]

Everyone began to speak of martial law. E. L. Victoriano wrote in the *Philippines Herald* on 1 February, "Widespread disturbances throughout the country would give [Marcos] the excuse to declare martial law with all its unlimited executive powers." For a political pretext to be viable, there must be a social layer that ascribes it credibility. The prospect of dictatorship assuaged the so-cial fears of the upper middle class. They were the largest constituency for the politics of repression and an end to democracy, and it was to them that Marcos appealed.

Marcos delivered a nationally televised address denouncing the demonstra-tors as "Communists" and warning that he would respond to such demon-strations in the future with the force of military arms: "To the insurrectionary elements, I have a message. My message is: any attempt at the forcible over-throw of the government will be put down immediately. I will not tolerate nor allow communists to take over. . . . The Republic will defend itself with all the force at its command until your armed elements are annihilated. And I shall lead them."[60]

Marcos claimed that his political rivals were acting in cahoots with the "Maoists" to overthrow him, and on 2 February the KM published a response. Marcos was "going berserk and so fearful of popular criticism that he imag-ines at every turn that his political opponents are out to destroy him. He has even started to voice out the fear that his own vice president is interested in his assassination or his political failure."[61] Marcos's fears were not mere para-noia; there was in fact a conspiracy between Lopez and the "Maoists," and the KM knew it. The KM received financial support from Lopez to prepare and mount its demonstrations. The KM hit back, denouncing Marcos for his ties with "the Russian 'communists.'"

Immediately after the events of 30 January, the CPP published a statement in *Ang Bayan*—"On the January 30–31 Demonstration"—hailing the "four student heroes" who had been killed.[62] The CPP argued that the violence of 26 and 30 January indicated that "the entire Filipino people are increasingly awakened to the need for armed revolutionary struggle in the face of armed counter-revolution" (*FQS*, 40). The demonstrations "have served as a rich source of ac-tivists for the national democratic revolution and, therefore, of prospective members and fighters of the Communist Party of the Philippines and the New People's Army" (*FQS*, 44). *Ang Bayan* saw in the violent suppression of the students—who had gathered behind a confused array of political banners—the ideal scenario for recruitment to the armed struggle and concluded excitedly, "The revolutionary situation has never been so excellent!" (*FQS*, 45).

Determined to dispel the claim that they were insurrectionists fighting for socialism, the CPP published a statement, "Turn Grief into Revolutionary Courage," signed by both Guerrero (Sison) and Dante on 8 February.[63] To Mar-cos's claim that the demonstrations were led by "Maoists" who were "raising the issue of communism," they responded, "We communists recognize that the nature of Philippine society is semicolonial and semifeudal and that the pressing issue is national democracy. The issue now in the Philippines is neither socialism nor communism."[64] What is more, they were not fighting for an uprising of workers; rather, they insisted that "the Communist Party of the Philippines and the New People's Army are not putschists. They firmly adhere to Chairman Mao's strategic principle of encircling the cities from the countryside. All counterrevolutionaries should rest assured that the day will surely come when the people's armed forces shall have defeated the reactionary armed forces in the countryside and are ready to act in concert with general uprisings by workers and students in the final seizure of power in the city."[65]

The CPP was not fighting for socialism, and it would not act in concert with an uprising of workers until the people's war had achieved victory in the countryside. While this people's war would be of a protracted character, Sison and Dante insisted that "fascism" hastened its success, for "the use of counterrevolutionary violence, restrictive procedures and doubletalk will only result in more intensified revolutionary violence."[66] Sison and Dante gave direct political instructions to the student protesters. The party would distribute to "militant demonstrators" three works for their political education: *Guide for Cadres and Members of the CPP*, *Selected Works of Mao Zedong*, and *Quotations from Chairman Mao Zedong*.[67] Students should form "propaganda teams (of at least three members)." Such a team

> assumes the specific task of arousing and mobilizing the students and workers in a well-defined area in the city; or the students, peasants, farm workers, national minorities and fishermen in a well-defined area in the provinces.

> The mass work of student propaganda teams in urban areas and in provinces close to Manila will result in bigger and more articulate demonstrations and more powerful general strikes. The mass work of student propaganda teams in the provinces will create the best conditions for getting hold of a gun and fighting the armed counterrevolution successfully.[68]

Classes resumed across Manila on 9 February, and the MDP secured a permit to stage a rally at Plaza Miranda on the twelfth.[69] Looking to negotiate a commitment to call off the demonstration, Marcos arranged a meeting in Malacañang with the MDP leadership on 10 February.[70] The discussion lasted five hours. Marcos warned that the protests and instability would be used as a pretext for a right-wing coup, and called on the assembled leaders to cancel the 12 February protest. The delegation reassured Marcos that they "deplored the overt attempts of some sectors in the ruling oligarchy to convert student

activism into a Hate Marcos campaign."[71] The argument expressed the influence of MPKP. They presented thirteen concrete demands to the president,
including "the dissolution of the Special Forces" and "the disbandment of the
Monkees."[72] Marcos declared his intention to "grant what he could, to study
what he could not," and in return the MDP representatives agreed to call off
the Plaza Miranda rally and hold small "localized demonstrations" to discuss
issues.[73] They stated that "this move would entail minimum security risks since
smaller groups would be easier to control."[74]

The political intervention of the CPP at this moment proved decisive. Sison
immediately issued instructions to the KM to distribute a leaflet that denounced
fears that Marcos might face a military coup d'état and summoned protesters to
rally to Plaza Miranda on the twelfth. This intervention sustained the storm,
preventing it from being dissipated by the PKP, but it did so on an exclusively
anti-Marcos basis. Sison's ability to sway, in less than twenty-four hours, the
course of national events revealed the degree of control the CPP exercised over
the KM and the influence of the KM over the developing movement.[75] From this
point forward the CPP dominated the political development of the protests,
channeling mass anger behind the interests of its elite allies.

12 February: The First People's Congress

Headlines on the morning of the twelfth announced that the Miranda rally had
been called off and that separate rallies were to be held on individual campuses.
There was widespread speculation that the MDP leaders had been "bought off."
The *Collegian*, for example, ran the headline "Demonstration goes on tomorrow
in UP: Plaza Miranda plan put off due to 'risk.'"[76] The MDP held an emergency
meeting that morning and the perspective of the KM won over the majority.
The umbrella group reached a compromise: they would hold simultaneous separate rallies—largely to save face over the reversal—and then converge on Plaza
Miranda for "a People's Congress."[77] With an estimated fifty thousand participants, it was the largest rally during the FQS, as subsequent events saw fewer and
fewer people turn up.[78] The KM and the SDK were now clearly in the leadership
of the protest movement, and the conservative NUSP and NSL were not to be
seen in the plaza. The KM-SDK rivalry was rapidly disappearing, but the KM
was under direct instructions from the CPP and the SDK was not. At the first
People's Congress, the KM sought to provoke the crowd to violence, while SDK
sought to calm it. As the SDK continued its rectification process and as the CPP
recruited its leadership to its ranks, this tactical division gradually disappeared,
and by the opening of 1971 the two organizations proceeded in lockstep in

response to the instructions of party leadership. A speech delivered by the KM's Nonie Villanueva, full of irreverent profanity, established the tone that would dominate the rostrums of the storm going forward, with *putang ina* and *hindot* standing in for political analysis and program. Lacaba recounted that "each time a small group right in front of the speakers got up calling for a march to Malaca-ñang, other demonstrators surrounding the group—suspected to be one led by an LP hatchetman—persuaded or ordered them to sit down."[79] To calm the crowd, the SDK repeatedly led them in the singing of the national anthem as a means of defusing tension. As the rally drew to a close, they sung the national anthem one last time and then announced that the MDP would be holding a meeting on Valentine's Day at Vinzons Hall on the UP Diliman campus.

Ang Bayan hailed the 12 February demonstration and denounced the PKP for attempting to call it off.[80] Marcos, it argued, had secured the support of the PKP by promising that "trade and cultural ties will be instituted with Eastern European countries immediately with the sending of officially accredited rep-resentatives. The possibility of securing loans or aid from said countries shall be explored."[81] *Ang Bayan* observed, "This is obviously the booty being dangled before the Lava revisionist running dogs of Soviet social-imperialism for their cooperation with the Marcos fascist puppet regime. . . . Relations with Soviet social-imperialism . . . will only add to the intensification of the exploitation of the Filipino people. The Soviet Union is no longer a socialist country; it has become capitalist, social-fascist and social-imperialist. Soviet social-imperialist 'loans' and 'aid' are no different from US imperialist 'loans' and 'aid.'"[82]

The CPP insisted on its claim that dictatorship facilitated revolutionary struggle, openly expressing its hope that Marcos would suspend democratic processes: "How much nicer it would be if the US imperialists and reactionar-ies in the Philippines can no longer boast of their regular election! That would be a striking manifestation of how strong the revolutionary mass movement has become."[83] Thus, while the MPKP looked to defuse protests, the KM sought to provoke repression; both facilitated the declaration of martial law.

On 14 February, fifty representatives from various student and labor organ-izations met to plan the next steps of the protest movement. They resolved that the 18 February rally, which had already been scheduled, would be a Sec-ond People's Congress. The KM circulated a leaflet at the meeting calling for the "intensification of the struggle against the fascist puppet government of Marcos," who was "the primary political agent of the native exploiting and oppressing classes and of American imperialism in our country."[84] Targeting the MPKP, the KM leaflet concluded by expanding the tripartite "Down with Fascism! Down with Imperialism! Down with Feudalism!" to include a final slogan: "Down with Soviet Social Imperialism!"[85]

18 February: The Second People's Congress

An estimated twenty thousand students and "a sprinkling of workers and farm-ers" assembled in Plaza Miranda on 18 February for the Second People's Con-gress.[86] Reeling from the criticisms of the KM, the MPKP produced two leaflets for the demonstration, each written in a petulant and defensive tone. The first hailed the assembly as the development of their perspective of building "parlia-ment in the streets"[87] and declared that "MPKP views Marcos as an agent of American Imperialism. However, it does not equate the system as a whole with the person of Marcos. MPKP is well aware of the contradictions within the rul-ing class (and these contradictions tend to grow sharper in periods of crisis like the present). It therefore warns against a possible plan of rival factions of the same ruling class to seize power and create the illusion of change. The goal of the national democratic movement is to abolish neo-colonialism, not just to replace the man who presides over the operation of the same exploitative system."

The MPKP stated that the "only real alternative . . . is *people's power*—the collective might of the workers, peasants, students, and all other anti-imperialist forces," mobilized to build "national democracy." The language of this leaflet expressed the MPKP's dilemma during the FQS. They could not endorse Mar-cos and would not endorse his bourgeois opponents. The only alternative was an independent fight of the working class leading the students and peasantry in opposition to the entire capitalist class, but the Stalinism of the PKP and its front organizations was intrinsically hostile to this perspective. The MPKP thus warned against both Marcos and the "rival factions" of the ruling class while at the same time calling for a united front of "people's power" with all "anti-imperialist forces" for national democracy. The MPKP unwaveringly insisted that a section of the national bourgeoisie was a component part of these pro-gressive forces and a necessary element of "people's power," yet during the FQS they could not publicly identify which section of the capitalist class was in their opinion progressive. This was precisely because the allegiance of their leaders lay with Marcos, and to say as much in early 1970 was political suicide.

Later the same day the MPKP released a second leaflet defending them-selves against charges made by the KM that they were defusing anger against Marcos. They accused the KM of the "unwarranted resort to slanderous phrase-mongering" and distorting the MPKP political line.[88] Protesting overmuch, they stated,

MPKP never advocated shifting the people's revolutionary actions against Marcos to "dissipated attacks" against various forces. MPKP did not exculpate the blood debts of Marcos by branding the revolutionary actions of the youth as a purely anti-Marcos line. MPKP has not fallen for the Marcos "nationalist" line at all, and it does not becloud the issue of puppetry and fascism of the Marcos regime. MPKP is not disarmed by the rhetorics [*sic*] of Marcos. MPKP does not underestimate the role of Marcos in the neocolonial-bourgeois system. MPKP does not consider Marcos as only a "victim" of this system.

The demonstrators marched to the embassy, despite attempts by some of the organizers of the event to prevent them from doing so. Gary Olivar of the SDK told the crowd that there would be a rally at the Washington Day Ball at the embassy on Saturday the twenty-first and that they should hold their demonstration then. He led the crowd in repeated renditions of the national anthem in an attempt to defuse the mounting anger of the demonstrators.[89] While the SDK was carefully attempting to limit the protests and prevent violence, the KM was seeking to provoke it. *Ang Bayan* celebrated how the demonstrators "brilliantly" feinted to Malacañang, "completely outwitted practically all the fascist brutes" who deployed to the presidential palace, and then marched on the embassy.[90] At nine thirty at night, violence erupted at the embassy. Nelson Navarro, spokesperson for the MDP, stated that the organization peacefully finished its rally, and "the events that transpired afterwards it was unable to prevent or control," as demonstrating students broke into the embassy compound with "sticks, stones and homemade bombs."[91] *Ang Bayan* hailed the demonstrators who left the embassy and "broke up into several groups and attacked such alien establishments as Caltex, Esso, Philamlife and other imperialist enterprises. They carefully avoided doing harm to petty bourgeois and middle bourgeois establishments."[92]

26 February: Sunken Garden and the Raid on PCC

The MDP called off the promised Washington Day demonstration at the last moment without notifying the front groups of the PKP of the cancellation. Approximately fifty demonstrators, all associated with the PKP, showed up in front of the embassy, which was surrounded by nearly one thousand police officers. The attention of the MDP was turned to the staging of a Third People's Congress at Plaza Miranda on 26 February. Manila mayor Villegas announced on the twenty-third that he would not grant a permit for a rally at Plaza Miranda but would issue one for the use of the Sunken Gardens instead.[93] The Sunken Gardens were part of the old moat outside the southern walls of Intramuros and now served as a hazard in the nine-hole municipal golf course circling the ancient city bulwarks. While it was but a stroll away from Agrifina Circle and Congress, it was nonetheless isolated and, from the perspective of law enforcement, easily controlled. On 24 February, in a meeting of the MDP leadership at UP, spokesperson Nelson Navarro announced that the MDP would appeal Villegas's decision before the Supreme Court. The appeal was filed the next day by E. Voltaire Garcia, a member of the KM and former UPSC president now employed in the offices of Senator Salvador Laurel.[94] On 26 February, at four in the afternoon on the day of the rally, the court upheld Villegas's denial of a permit for a gathering in Miranda by a vote of 8–2.[95] MDP forces gathered outside Plaza Miranda, waiting for the Supreme Court ruling, where they confronted antiriot police "in full combat gear" who prevented them from entering.[96] On word of the decision, they moved to the Sunken Gardens, where the MDP staged a rally before marching to the US embassy.

Street battles broke out between the police, who hurled tear-gas canisters, and the protesters, who responded with Molotov cocktails. The MPD claimed that a number of demonstrators fled to the PCC compound. When the police attempted to follow them onto the campus, University President Nemesio Prudente met them at the gate and denied them entry. Late that night—at two thirty in the morning on 27 February—the MPD, having secured a warrant, raided the PCC. They tore the place apart, ripping open the ceiling, rifling through and scattering papers from office filing cabinets. In the end they arrested thirty-nine students and faculty members and claimed that they confiscated several weapons in the process.[97]

People's Marches and the End of the FQS

Denied access to Plaza Miranda, the MDP adopted a new strategy—people's marches—and on 2 March produced a leaflet announcing a People's Anti-Fascist March to be held the next day.[98] The leaflet cited the raid on the PCC as evidence of the fascism of the state and insisted that despite this fascism the movement would continue. It called on everyone to join the march, which was to begin at one in the afternoon at the Welcome Rotonda.[99]

The MDP promoted the march on national television. At the beginning of the month, Eugenio Lopez provided the MDP with a weekly television program that broadcast nationwide from nine thirty to ten thirty on Thursday nights on ABS-CBN.[100] The SDK, KM, and MDP were given extensive access to radio as well; the Lopez family and others in the media industry supplied them with regular free airtime. The MDP ran a daily two-hour program, *Impressions of the Nation*, hosted by SDK member and future New People's Army

(NPA) leader Rafael Baylosis, with the explicit intent of broadcasting material regarding imperialism, feudalism, and fascism and the program of national democracy.[101]

3 March: People's Antifascist March

A crowd of one thousand gathered for the start of the march, but the numbers "swelled ten-fold as it descended on Manila's major arteries. . . . With the students chanting, singing, banner swinging, the march heaved with energetic ideology under the bare afternoon sun." The placards that swayed over the crowd conveyed the sway of the CPP: "People's War is the Answer (KM)," "Mabuhay ang Bagong Hukbong Bayan!!" (Long live the New People's Army!!), and "Down with Soviet Social Imperialism!"[102] The MPKP, feeling isolated and exposed, circulated a leaflet among the marchers that responded to public charges that the protests were violent. The root of violence, it declared, was the "fascist repression and brutality" of the "neocolonial bourgeois state," and "an oppressed and exploited people have a right to meet force with force."[103] Certain political elements, however, bore a significant share of guilt. A majority of the MPKP leaflet targeted the KM, thinly veiled as "provocateurs": "Provocateurs must be identified and exposed as mercenary tools of the imperialist-fascist puppet factions now intensely engaged in their own fierce competition for neocolonial power and authority. Extremist and anarchistic elements must be led into the correct revolutionary line, or consciously isolated should they prove to be intractable. . . . Expose Mercenary Provocateurs! Struggle Against Anarchists!"

The KM distributed a leaflet declaring that fascism was the last weapon of US imperialism, deployed to hide the weakness of their puppet Marcos. Marcos had lost the trust of the masses, something a government needed in order to succeed, as a result of the unceasing struggle of the forces of national democracy.[104] The theme of the FQS remained unaltered—resistance produced repression, repression bred resistance.

The march followed a circuitous route through the streets of working-class Tondo, turning along the northern bank of the Pasig to pass through Binondo's ancient Chinatown. "Along the way the marchers chanced upon Chinese folk peering from windows of tall buildings." The street-level business stalls were closed, the windows boarded over, and the residents nervously hid in their second-story homes. "The marchers scream[ed] at them," the *Collegian* reported. They chanted for the "intsik" to "go home, go home!"[105] The Chinese families of Binondo had resided there for centuries and had survived multiple pogroms. Most ran small mercantile businesses. Over the next year and a half the organizations affiliated with the CPP attempted to win working-class support by means of a reactionary appeal to age-old anti-Chinese prejudices. The racial slurs and screamed threats of 3 March were the first recorded example of what would become a concerted strategy.

Ten abreast, the marchers crossed the Sta. Cruz bridge at dusk and gathered in Plaza Lawton in the neoclassical shadow of the Central Post Office. The KM raised a Philippine flag on the Liwasang Bonifacio flagpole, sang the national anthem, and in the stark illumination of television camera floodlights delivered speeches.[106] The march resumed and was quickly set upon by the police, who dispersed the demonstrators with truncheons and tear gas at Luneta.[107] The streets in the triangle between Taft, Agrifina Circle, and Isaac Peral became a war zone. Rock-throwing students darted into narrow alleyways, escaping the gunfire of roving army trucks and the ubiquitous burning fog of tear gas. Fleeing to Intramuros, Enrique Sta. Brigida, a freshman in commerce at Lyceum and a member of the Lyceum Student Reform Movement, was killed by the blow of a police officer's truncheon to his skull.[108]

The CPP drew no political conclusions from the experience; it simply repeated its stock claim—repression breeds resistance—and *Ang Bayan* declared that "the bloody suppression of the March 3 People's March failed to intimidate the masses of workers, students and youth who joined the historic mass action. It only goaded them more to wage a resolute struggle for national democracy."[109]

17 March: Antipoverty March

In keeping with this overall conception, the orientation of the CPP and the forces it led was simple: heighten and heighten yet again the confrontation between the demonstrators and the state. The violence of the state was educative and should be induced.

Prices had been rising drastically for over half a year, and painful choices confronted working-class families: which basic commodities—rice, fish, soap—would they purchase, and which would they do without? The MDP leadership met on Saturday, 14 March, and planned "an anti-poverty march" to be staged three days later (figure 2.3).[110] At nine in the morning on Tuesday the seventeenth, demonstrators assembled at three locations and marched from the north, south, and east to converge on Plaza Moriones in Tondo. The narrow rectangle of Moriones, distended along a westward line drawn from the crowded arcades of Tutuban railway station to the busy piers of North Harbor, had been a center of working-class life since the end of Spanish colonial rule. It was here that, on 7 November 1930, the PKP staged its first public rally. The marchers assembled between the overhanging wooden homes, with their

Figure 2.3. Antipoverty march, 17 March 1970. The sign in the foreground reads "Long live Dante!"—a reference to Commander Dante, head of the NPA.

sliding capiz and louvred jalousie windows, and staged what they termed a People's Court (Hukuman ng Bayan). The speakers at the rally accused Marcos and his cohort of a list of crimes "against the Filipino people," pronounced a death sentence, and hanged their effigies.[111]

The KM distributed a leaflet that declared, "Our society at present is semifeudal and semi-colonial. This is the root of the poverty and oppression of the Filipino masses." The solution to the problem of poverty and the threat of dictatorship in the Philippines, it asserted, was national industrialization and agrarian revolution under a national democratic government.[112] The MDP produced a statement that repeated, almost word for word, the KM's argument about the semifeudal and semicolonial origins of poverty. The rally "desired above all [higit sa lahat] to censure, and fight against, the current administration . . . which was none other than Marcos [na dili iba't si Marcos]," on whose profligate election spending—and not global capitalism—the MDP blamed the sharp increase in prices and the drop in dollar reserves.[113] The MPKP similarly rooted the solution to poverty in nationalism, arguing that the key was the nationalist development of the "basic industries," in particular, the creation of complex machinery using metal extracted from Philippine mines.[114]

Despite their sharp political differences, the KM and MPKP spoke with one voice. Neither mentioned capitalism or the capitalist class, nor did they breathe a word of socialism. They spoke of nationalism, of industries owned by Filipinos and not by foreigners, of the glowing capitalist future of national democracy. The MDP articulated the shared conception of every organization gathered at Plaza Moriones when it stated that the goal of the movement was to achieve "a true national democracy in which the rights and wellbeing of the masses will be the highest goal of the national democratic government."[115]

The speeches delivered from the rostrum of Moriones did not aim to educate or patiently explain; they were harangues. The KM brought out Nonie Villanueva to rouse rabble, and he revealed that for all his colorful profanity, he was deaf to the realities of working-class life. He yelled to the crowd of thousands who had trooped into the center of this neighborhood and were now seated on the plaza cement, "Even the women here in Tondo are forced to prostitute themselves [napilitang mag-puta], to sell themselves due to poverty. Even they have tattoos as well on their thighs."[116] One can imagine the reaction to these claims from the residents of Tondo, especially women, many of whom were factory workers, labandera, or domestic workers and bore the brunt of household labor as well.[117] The KM was not appealing to the working class. It was not familiar with the rhythm of workers' lives or with the nature of capitalist exploitation. Its speeches depicted workers as simply those who are abjectly degraded.[118] The orientation of the KM was to lumpen elements, and in particular to violent gangs. Villanueva called out, "My comrades in Sigue-Sigue, OXO, Bahala Na, Commando, proletariats, let us join together."[119] This was a litany of notorious rival gangs. They controlled prison economies, ran drugs, collected protection money from small businesses, and broke up picket lines. Less than a year earlier, in July 1969, Sigue-Sigue Sputnik had mercilessly attacked striking Pantranco bus drivers.[120]

The CPP had little interest in organizing the working class, but it did seek to increase political instability and provoke state repression. On multiple occasions it directed the KM to appeal to violent gangs and armed thugs in service to the interests of the party's ruling-class allies. Ramon Sanchez of SDK was the final speaker, and he built on Villanueva's appeal to the rabble, telling the crowd, "We are going to march to the American embassy, whatever you do there is up to you."[121] The KM and SDK were attempting to throw Sigue-Sigue up against the police. The protesters sang as they marched through the streets, to the tune of a Tide detergent commercial, "gamitin ninyo molotov [use a Molotov], molotooov, BOOM!"[122] The cops set upon the demonstrators that evening. Street battles raged up and down the length of Azcarraga. "Danilo Paguio, a working FEATI student was shot on the temple" and died.[123]

Eduardo Lachica reported that "the march peaked at about 5,000 strong."[124] *Ang Bayan*, however, reported that "hundreds of thousands of people" participated in the antipoverty march. The CPP's numerical estimates of revolutionary strength were jarringly unrealistic. In the same issue of *Ang Bayan*, the CPP asserted that "more than 90 per cent of the masses . . . are on the side of the revolution."[125] These figures were not merely dishonest; they were absurd. If 90 percent of the masses were on the side of the revolution in any meaningful sense of the word, the party would have already taken power.[126]

The Storm Subsides

On 5 April, the MDP and an organization calling itself Crusaders for Democracy held a rally of five thousand people at Plaza Miranda. Nonie Villanueva told the assembled demonstrators that people's war was the answer to the "threat of martial law."[127] The crowd moved from Miranda to the US embassy, but the MPD attempted to divert the demonstration with tear gas as it neared Manila City Hall. The protesters responded with Molotov cocktails and pillboxes, and the Metrocom fired their guns to disperse the crowd. It was the last gasp of the FQS.

The FQS was a student protest movement, and while the majority of these students were personally connected to the working class and peasantry, the FQS never moved beyond its social base in the student population. At no point did the leadership of this movement, which rested largely with the CPP, fight for its independence from the bourgeoisie and the traditional political elite. On the contrary, it consciously and secretly pursued the interests of a faction of the ruling class and profited from the relationship. At the same time, the CPP did not orient the protesting students to broader layers of the working class.

For an eruption of protests to survive and grow, it needs to become a political movement. This requires strategic conception and programmatic orientation. The movement must develop in a way that both keeps pace with and gives shape to the rapid development of mass consciousness. Repetition of practice is deadly as it quickly imparts a sense of stagnation and impotence. The initial stages of the FQS were a spontaneous explosion of social anger. The intervention of the CPP on 12 February allowed the mass movement to continue to grow. The leadership of the CPP, however, gave the subsequent development of protests the political shape of nationalism coupled with a strategic orientation to physical confrontations with the state as a means of provoking repression that would, they claimed, heighten resistance. The protest movement took fugal form, never growing beyond its initial theme of repression and resistance. Late February marked the height of its polyphony, but all of the various voices—MDP, KM, SDK—were counterpoint repetitions of the same notes.

This was by no means inevitable. Unresolved labor struggles simmered throughout the FQS. Workers at Northern Motors, the largest General Motors plant outside the United States, had been on strike since October 1969 and remained on strike until the middle of March.[128] Workers at US Tobacco walked off the job in early 1970 and were on strike for the duration of the storm. The strop drawn taut between skyrocketing prices and stagnant wages honed class tensions to a razor edge. One would not know it from the literature of the student demonstrations, which were entirely silent on the matter, but the FQS was marked by a series of sharp but confused class explosions. On 3 March, as students marched to Plaza Lawton, over five thousand jeepney drivers throughout Manila went on strike, shutting down most public transit throughout the city. They blocked major intersections, overturned scab jeepneys, and set several taxis on fire.[129] On 19 March, two days after the People's Court in Moriones Plaza, over three thousand taxicab drivers went on strike. They waged fierce battles against both the police and other forms of public transit, which they saw as strikebreakers. "Two buses were torn to pieces and three jeepneys were set to the torch."[130] Rising oil prices fueled the drivers' strikes, and the government responded by authorizing increases in bus, jeepney, and taxi fares. The unrest only heightened. Commuters took to the streets, hurling stones at taxis and buses when the fare hikes were announced. "The government itself had to dispatch troops to guard oil depots after receiving reports that an enraged public might blow them up."[131]

The class struggle strained forward, submerged and only partially conscious, its vast collective outrage diffused in squabbling over scraps. The ferocity of these pitched battles expressed the desperation of the working population, but their intensity contained as well an attempt to articulate a political vision that was larger and far grander than the meager ends to which they were constrained. A cabdriver's hand-drawn placard, a minor detail in a photograph in *Graphic Weekly*, gives a sense of these subterranean aspirations: "Tsuper na nagugutom sa rebolusyon. Hindi uurong." (A driver hungry for revolution. I will not move.)[132]

The FQS was a rare political opportunity—a mass radicalization of youth, under the ideological leadership of a Communist party, aligned with a tremendous upsurge of working-class struggle. The paramount task was to give the emerging movement a strategic orientation to the social force capable of sustaining a fight against dictatorship, the working class. Here the difference between the national democratic and the socialist programs was sharpest. The orientation of national democracy—of Stalinism—was ultimately to securing an alliance with a section of the capitalist class. A turn to the working class amounted to a limited, tactical maneuver to bring greater mass weight behind this alliance. A socialist perspective, in contrast, orients itself to the working class, to developing its unity and independence as the revolutionary force capable of overthrowing capitalism. The CPP made no effort to unite the storm of the student protests with the growth of the class struggle. The party's Stalinist program diffused the storm. The chanted slogans and newsprint manifestos of the FQS all directed the students to nothing but the escalation of their denunciations of Marcos and fascism, and ultimately appealed to them to join the armed struggle in the countryside. For all its fiery rhetoric and pitched battles in the street—and no matter how truly courageous and self-sacrificing many of the young people were who joined its ranks—the FQS was, in the end, merely a violent venting of steam. The political turbines through which this steam coursed were those of Lopez and Osmeña, with their scheming plots, and Marcos, who steadily readied the architecture of martial law.

As a movement composed almost exclusively of students, the storm's life was necessarily a short one. Graduation rites succeeded final examinations, and the second week of April saw the majority of students returning home to the province or taking up full-time summer work. As the semester ended and Lopez temporarily reconciled with Marcos, the storm subsided as rapidly as it had started. On 22 March, Marcos addressed the graduation rites at the Philippine Military Academy, vowing to impose martial law "in case the communist threat becomes a positive danger that would imperil the security of the country."[133] On 11 April, UP staged its graduation rites, and the MDP produced and distributed a leaflet to the class of 1970. It expressed its "firmest fraternal support for the planned protest actions at this year's UP commencement exercises by graduating national democratic activists" and denounced US imperialism and its Filipino and Chinese accomplices in the Philippines.[134] The denunciation of the local Chinese accomplices of US imperialism was a striking addition to the rhetoric of the national democratic movement, and it would develop rapidly into explicitly racist attacks on the *kumintang intsik* (Guomindang Chinese), playing an increasingly prominent role in the propaganda of the KM, SDK, and their allies over the next year. The First Quarter Storm was over.

Reaction

The danger of dictatorship grew while the social force capable of resisting it remained unorganized. Everyone spoke of martial law. *Graphic Weekly* warned, "There are talks all around of the possibility, and even probability, of the imposition of martial law and the suspension of the writ of *habeas corpus*."[135] The *Examiner*, a newsweekly known for its anti-Communist views, asked, "Are we moving towards military dictatorship?" and answered, "Yes. If we read the signs of the times correctly, we are. A military dictatorship might be a welcome change, commented some businessmen."[136]

Marcos proceeded deliberately. The mainstream English-language press had provided largely favorable coverage to the protesters, but so too had the widely circulated Chinese-language Chinese Commercial News (CCN). Unable yet to directly crack down on his bourgeois rivals, Marcos singled out the vulnerable Yuyitung brothers, Rizal and Quintin, publishers of the CCN. He had them arrested on 24 March and launched deportation proceedings against them.[137]

Rizal and Quintin's father, Yu Yi Tung, had arrived in the Philippines in the 1900s "to teach at the only Chinese school in Manila during the early years of the American administration."[138] By 1922 he had founded a newspaper, the CCN, which in the 1930s was consistently critical of Chiang Kai-shek and the Guomindang (GMD), in contrast to the leading rival Chinese-language newspaper in Manila, the *Fookien Times*, published by Go Puan Seng, which enthusiastically backed both.[139] Yu's two sons were born in Tondo—Quintin in 1917 and Rizal in 1923—and both were named after famous Filipino historical figures. Yu was executed by Japanese forces in 1942 for refusing to comply with the occupation, but his sons survived the war and resumed publishing the CCN, which became the leading Chinese-language daily in the country.[140] In 1962, President Macapagal had the Yuyitung brothers arrested for publishing material "favorable to the Communist cause in general." While Rizal was released after two weeks, and Quintin after six months, deportation orders were issued against them despite the fact that they had lived their entire lives in the Philippines. They were ordered to report to the immigration office every week for as long as their deportation case was pending. This state of affairs continued until 1965.[141]

Marcos resurrected Macapagal's charges and, on 4 May, deported Rizal and Quintin Yuyitung from the country of their birth and sent them to Taiwan, where they were tried before a military court in August. Their lawyer was not allowed to speak to them before the trial, nor were they informed of the charge they faced—"spreading Communist propaganda." The trial lasted four hours and the brothers were sentenced to several years in prison.[142] By the time of their release, martial law had been declared. Both took up life in exile from the homeland whose government had deported them as aliens; Quintin moved to San Francisco and Rizal to Canada.[143]

The *Philippines Free Press* aptly denounced the persecution of the Yuyitungs as a "Philippine Dreyfus Case."[144] The gears began to turn in the apparatus of state repression, spreading noxious fumes of reaction throughout the country—"trampling the nation under their boots, ramming back down their throats the people's cries for truth and justice, with the travesty of state security as a pretext."[145] A month later, now in fluid motion, it bore down on the KM.

On 11 June, the military arrested Nilo Tayag, head of the KM and general secretary of the CPP, in San Pablo City, Laguna, and took him north to Tarlac, where they charged him under Republic Act (RA) 1700 with being a Communist and with inciting the population to armed insurrection.[146] Preparations for the arrest of Tayag had been made over the course of several months. A subpoena had been filed against him for a preliminary hearing, and when he did not appear in court, charges of violating RA1700 were filed on 9 June, two days before his arrest.[147] The targeting of Tayag served a basic purpose for the Marcos administration: to legally establish that the KM was a front organization of the CPP.

Tayag's arrest warrant included the names of four others, among them Renato Casipe and Manuel Alabado—the president and vice president of the US Tobacco Corporation Labor Union.[148] Francisco Portem, who had been a member of the KM at Lyceum and was working as Tayag's assistant in building the CPP in the Southern Tagalog region, was arrested with Tayag although he was not named on the warrant.[149] The military denied Portem access to legal counsel and beat him repeatedly before releasing him on bail.[150] Four days later, another five "militant activists" were arrested, including Ramon Sanchez and Benjamin Gapud of the SDK, charged with supplying guns to the remote San Pablo barrio of Bautista, nestled in the eastern foothills of Mount Manabu.[151]

The news of Tayag's arrest broke on the morning of 12 June—Independence Day. The MDP had planned a rally, the "March and Congress for True Independence and True Democracy," but then rapidly reorganized the event behind the slogan "Free Nilo Tayag!" The material circulated by the KM, SDK, and MDP in response to the deportation of the Yuyitung brothers and the arrest of Tayag continued the political theme of the storm. The SDK wrote, "Should Nilo Tayag and others like him suffer the full force of the reactionary State's vindictiveness, others shall take their place, wiser and more resolute by their experience. The masses are an inexhaustible wellspring of revolutionary men and women."[152] They elaborated this argument in a Diliman campus election statement in July:

> The President has repeatedly dangled the threat of Martial Law like a hanging sword poised over the heads of the citizens. But it is apparent that even without the formal declaration, Martial Law *does* exist today.
>
> But the growing strength of the masses cannot be stifled. It has been clear that for every act of suppression committed by the Marcos reactionary and fascist forces, the opposition from the people has become louder, bolder, and stronger.[153]

The logic was clear. De facto martial law already existed, but it could not thwart the masses. The people's resistance would only grow in response to mounting repression.

The arrest of Tayag revealed that the state had massively infiltrated the organizations of the storm, particularly the KM. On 20 July, Army Sgt. Elnora "Babette" Estrada took the stand in the Tarlac court and testified to the ties between the Communist Party and the KM. Estrada was a KM National Council member and served on its finance committee; she was also a military spy.[154] On orders of the Intelligence Service of the Armed Forces of the Philippines, Estrada joined the KM while a student at Lyceum in 1967. She came to the attention of the national leadership of the organization in 1968, was asked to fill out a second application form, and became a member of the National Council. The KM knew that her family background was in the military and that her father was a colonel, that she lived in military headquarters of Camp Aguinaldo, and that she routinely had coffee with a high-ranking figure in the military who had participated in the 1965 crackdown on the Partai Komunis Indonesia (PKI). The KM did nothing. KM leader Lualhati Abreu stated that "this aroused no concern; many KM members have military brass for parents."[155]

Estrada was in a long-term romantic relationship with Antonio Tayco, the chair of the Lyceum branch of the KM. On 4 July 1970, after the arrest of Nilo Tayag, Estrada was ordered by her military superiors to leave the KM and prepare to testify against the KM's national chair. She disappeared. Uncertain how to locate his girlfriend, Tayco posted a love note to Babette on the bulletin board of the KM Lyceum office on 17 July. Three days later, she emerged in the courtroom in Tarlac.[156] When Tayco testified in defense of Tayag in early September, he claimed under oath that he had known since April that Estrada was a military spy but that he chose not to inform the KM immediately, desiring first to conduct a personal investigation to determine whether it was true.[157] In subsequent interviews with the press he claimed that he informed the KM leadership at the beginning of May.[158] No investigation was conducted, and the KM went about its business. Tayco traveled to Marinduque to work on a civic project, and when he returned he continued to work within the ranks of the KM alongside Estrada in late May and early June. Throughout this period Estrada turned over the internal documents of the KM to the military, including its membership lists, the names of new recruits, and the discussion occurring in National Council meetings. The KM knowingly tolerated a military spy in its ranks for several months and did nothing. It did not expel the agent or publicly expose the machinations of the state. Its only response was silence and denial. Estrada, they later stated, was a good activist—full of "nerve and guts during the demos." While she might have had "a low level of political consciousness," she was very diligent in carrying out the practical activity of the KM.[159]

The CPP finally responded to military infiltration in late June after Nilo Tayag had been arrested—not with political exposures but with murder. On 19 June, Benilda Macalde, a KM member who was working as an agent for military intelligence, and her boyfriend Eddie Dasmariñas, a member of the KM National Council, were murdered in Tondo. In August, Alfonso Sabilano, the eighteen-year-old vice chair of the Makabayang Tagapag-ugnay ng Tondo (Nationalist Coordinator of Tondo, MTT) was arrested on charges of murdering Macalde and Dasmariñas.[160] Sabilano confessed to the crime under torture but then attempted to retract his confession.[161] Ma. Lorena Barros wrote a lightly fictionalized account of a visit she made to Precinct Five to speak with Sabilano, revealing that he claimed that Ruben Guevarra, a Central Committee member of the CPP, was the gunman responsible for their deaths.[162] On 12 September, Judge Manuel Pamaran, basing his judgment on the coerced confession and ignoring both the retraction and the subsequent accusation against Guevarra, sentenced Sabilano to death in the electric chair. Sabilano appealed his sentence and was kept in prison until 1984, when he was acquitted of all charges by the Philippine Supreme Court on the grounds that his confession had been extracted under torture. Sabilano maintained that on the night of the murder he had been present when Ruben Guevarra executed both Dasmariñas and Macalde. Guevarra shot Dasmariñas in the head with a Colt .45, he claimed, and when Macalde attempted to flee, Guevarra held her as she struggled and shot her in the head, shooting her a second time as her body lay on the grass.[163]

Philippine Society and Revolution

The storm filled the sails of the CPP, and Sison held the tiller. The serialized publication of his *Philippine Society and Revolution* in mid-1970 strengthened his position of ideological leadership and gave programmatic direction to the mass movement. In the first week of July, Sison wrote an open letter that he signed with his real name and sent to Vicente Clemente, secretary general of the MDP. Clemente published the letter in a number of newspapers, including the *Collegian*. Sison wrote,

> The more the Marcos fascist clique resorts to the use of the army, police, courts and prisons to oppress the people the more shall it bring infamy unto itself and spell clearer the utter bankruptcy of the present reactionary state. . . .
> But fascism will only cast more fuel to the flames of the revolutionary mass movement.
> I call upon the people of every patriotic class and group to close ranks and oppose the campaign of fascist terror being waged by the Marcos puppet clique. I believe the people will never waver in fighting for and depending [sic] their own sovereignty and democratic rights.[164]

Sison repeated his rhetorical staple that fascism aided the growth of revolution, which had now become the political line of the mass movement that had emerged from the FQS. He concluded his letter, "I shall soon issue another book which I have been researching on and writing since last year." This was a remarkable slip on Sison's part, for the book he was about to publish was *Philippine Society and Revolution*, which appeared under the name Amado Guerrero. Sison, at the time, vehemently denied that he was Guerrero, and the CPP denounced anyone who made the identification.

PSR, as it came to be known, was first published in installments in college newspapers beginning in late July 1970.[165] At the time of its serialized publication, the work was titled *The Philippine Crisis*. The first chapter was published as "Review of Philippine History" in the *Collegian*; the second chapter was published as "Basic Problems of the Filipino People" in *Ang Malaya*, the student paper of the PCC; and the third was published as "The People's Democratic Revolution" in *Guidon* at Ateneo.[166] Each chapter was serialized in installments across multiple issues of the student paper, and thus each week a new chunk of Sison's work appeared on campus. In the 23 July issue, in which the first installment of *The Philippine Crisis* was published, Popoy Valencia, member of the SDK and editor of the *Collegian*, included an editorial statement: "This week we print the first part of an intriguing document mailed to the *Collegian* and purports [sic] to be a chapter of a book by one Amado Guerrero. We have no way of verifying whether the author is the same Amado Guerrero labeled by the AFP as central committee chairman of the Communist Party of the Philippines."[167] The second chapter appeared in the 21 September and subsequent issues of *Ang Malaya*.[168] The editor included a note: "This article was sent to *Ang Malaya* by mail by we-don't-know-who. We cannot ascertain whether or not this is a continuation of the article published in some school papers recently. Nor can we ascertain whether this was written by the same Amado Guerrero as there was no by-line in the copy sent. Nevertheless because of its social, political, and economic significance—and because of its literary merit—we are serializing this article to become a part of our readings."[169] In late 1970, *The Philippine Crisis* was published in book form under the title *Philippine Society and Revolution* and, according to Sison, was sold "mainly in the lobbies at UP Diliman."[170]

The text was written as a polemic against Jesus Lava, longtime leader of the PKP, not as an abstract summary of timeless political principles. That a polemic with a political adversary should become the central text of a movement was in keeping with the history of Marxism and Communism, many of the core writings of which originated in an argumentative grappling with a rival thinker over the significance of key historical developments and the programmatic conclusions to be derived from them. *PSR*, however, made no effort to situate itself in this Marxist tradition. At no point did it present itself as a development in the history of Marxism; there is not a single line dedicated to the political or theoretical continuity of Marxist thought. Its history and its outlook sharply circumscribed, *PSR* was, to its core, a nationalist document. This is why Sison inscribed the book to "every patriot in the land," and not to the international working class.[171]

The nationalism of *PSR* is particularly palpable in the text's silences. The longer one lingers over what is absent, the stronger one's sense of its parochialism grows, a feeling that *PSR* was unwilling to gaze beyond the archipelago. *PSR*, a text dedicated to revolution, makes no mention of the 1789 French Revolution, nor does it include a word on 1848 and the revolutions that rocked Europe. What was their class character? What lessons should be derived for future struggles? The silence grows; stunningly absent is 1917. Neither February nor October merited even a passing mention. *PSR* contains not a word on the seizure of power by the Russian working class and the role of the Bolshevik Party. The CPP, a party with Communist in its name, had nothing to say about the central event of the twentieth century, the event without which the party would not exist. The *Communist Manifesto* is absent; so too is *Capital*. Marx himself is absent, except as a header in the phrase "Marxism–Leninism–Mao Zedong Thought."

The history of Marxism was not the only glaring lacuna. The year was 1970, yet the critical problems and revolutionary struggles gripping the globe were similarly treated as irrelevant. The PKI was slaughtered in 1965–66, but this merited no mention. Suharto, now ruling as dictator in Indonesia, is absent. An analysis of his rise is critical to understanding the trajectory of Marcos, but *PSR* has nothing to say on this point. Ho Chi Minh, the Viet Minh, the Viet Cong—the Vietnam War was the foremost political crisis in the world, but *PSR* is silent. Lin Biao, Zhou Enlai, Liu Shaoqi—while the text heralds "Mao Zedong Thought," it makes no examination of the crisis gripping the Chinese Communist Party. The Cuban revolution is mentioned once, but here the parochialism of *PSR* is even more striking, for it is mentioned only for the impact it had on Philippine sugar production. Its class character, its outcome, the attitude Filipino workers should take toward it? *PSR* is silent. These silences do not express a want of space but rather a lack of interest. When it first appeared as a book, *PSR* was nearly three hundred pages long and it dedicated paragraphs to what "racial stocks" made up the "Filipino people," but none to the history or theoretical heritage of Marxism and none to the broader world.

Sison clearly conceived that *PSR* would become the programmatic text of the CPP and the wider movement that it led. He divided the work into three chapters: "Review of Philippine History," "Basic Problems of the Filipino People," and "The People's Democratic Revolution." This structure followed a pattern established by Mao. Writing in Yan'an in the winter of 1939, Mao published a work titled *The Chinese Revolution and the Chinese Communist Party*, which is divided into two chapters: "Chinese Society" and "The Chinese Revolution."[172] In the first chapter, Mao established that imperialism had made China a semifeudal, semicolonial country in which "the contradiction between imperialism and the Chinese nation and the contradiction between feudalism and the great masses of the people are the basic contradictions in modern Chinese society."[173] On this basis, Mao argued in the second chapter that "unquestionably, the main tasks are to strike at these two enemies, to carry out a national revolution to overthrow foreign imperialist oppression and a democratic revolution to overthrow feudal landlord oppression."[174] Mao then analyzed each of the classes in Chinese society—landlords, bourgeoisie, petty bourgeoisie, peasantry, and proletariat—drawing a sharp distinction between the "comprador big bourgeoisie" and the "national bourgeoisie," for the latter "can become a revolutionary force."[175] Mao concluded that the Chinese revolution was a "two-fold task": "to complete China's bourgeois-democratic revolution (the new-democratic revolution) and to transform it into a socialist revolution when all the necessary conditions are ripe."[176]

Modeling himself on Mao, D. N. Aidit in 1958 published a similar work, *Indonesian Society and the Indonesian Revolution*.[177] The work is divided into two chapters. The first chapter, on Indonesian Society, established that because of imperialism, Indonesia was a semifeudal, semicolonial country. Aidit expanded on Mao's opening chapter, incorporating historical material to justify the party's relationship with Sukarno and to blame Vice President Hatta for the country's political ills, including the violent suppression of the PKI at Madiun in 1948. Like Mao, Aidit concluded that the tasks of the Indonesian revolution were national and democratic in character and not yet socialist, and like Mao, he examined each of the classes in Indonesian society and drew a distinction between the comprador and national bourgeoisie. Sison followed Aidit's innovation of including polemical historical material in the first chapter and reached the same conclusions as his predecessors: the Philippines was semicolonial and semifeudal and, as a result, the tasks of the revolution were not socialist and the national bourgeoisie should be treated as an ally.

Philippine Society and Revolution gave historical and theoretical weight to Sison's core political conception: that a modified form of Rectonian nationalism could only be achieved through armed struggle in the countryside. *PSR* argued that the PKP betrayed the Philippine revolution; the Philippines was a semifeudal, semicolonial country; its feudal relations were the "social base of imperialism"; armed struggle in the remote countryside thus attacked the foundations of US rule; and the victorious revolution would establish a joint government of workers and capitalists that would carry out national democratic measures, specifically land reform and national industrialization. Recto's ends remained unchanged, but the means were decidedly more drastic.

Chapter 1: "Review of Philippine History"

The first chapter of *PSR* presents a history of the Philippines from precolonial times to the founding of the CPP, in which Sison established two basic points. He claimed that the policies pursued by the PKP were the result of the treachery of the Lava leadership, rather than the implementation of the decisions and program of global Stalinism. Sison also argued that Spanish colonialism and US imperialism had perpetuated the feudal economic structures of the Philippines, making the country's economy a "semi-feudal, semi-colonial" one.

Sison's account relies on the cultivated historical ignorance of the party's recruits to palm off his deceit as political analysis. An examination of the section "Macapagal Puppet Regime" will suffice to reveal the fluency of dishonesty in *PSR*.[178] Sison described Macapagal's land reform as follows: "To further make itself appear progressive and to swindle the peasantry, the Macapagal puppet regime enacted the Agricultural Land Reform Code. . . . The code amounts to nothing when shorn of its glittering generalities and when the provisions favorable to landlords are exposed" (*PSR*, 90).

Later in *PSR* he described Macapagal's code as "a bombastic collection of words to cover the oft-repeated lies of the landlord class" (179). Sison condemned Jesus Lava for his support for Macapagal's land reform, as well as for his "arbitrary appointments" to positions of leadership in the party, eliding the fact that he was one of the people thus arbitrarily appointed. Sison described the founding of the peasant organization, Malayang Samahan ng Magsasaka (Free Federation of Peasants, MASAKA): "The independent kingdom of the Lava's based in Manila took to using a reformist peasant organization, the MA-SAKA, to assert its fake authority in the revolutionary mass movement and also to comply with Jesus Lava's commitment to supporting the sham land reform programme for the reactionary government" (PSR, 95).

The audacity of Sison's lies is breathtaking. Sison had been the primary member of the leadership of the PKP responsible for the founding of MA-SAKA six years earlier. He, not Jesus Lava, was the leading proponent of the land reform code. He wrote the government documents promoting it, backed these up in his editorials in the Progressive Review, and gave speeches to the peasantry to mobilize their support behind Macapagal's code. The other sections of Sison's history are equally dishonest. As he blamed Jesus Lava for the policies of the party of which Sison himself was the primary mover, so too throughout his potted history of the PKP does he blame the treachery of the Lavas for what were in truth the policies of Moscow and global Stalinism, in particular the party's support for US colonial rule under the Popular Front policy, and its welcome of the return of US imperialism at the end of the Second World War.

The other task that Sison set for himself in his historical chapter was to establish that Spanish colonialism and US imperialism had perpetuated the feudal economic base of Philippine society. Sison never defined capitalism. For Marx, capitalism was a social relationship defined by the private ownership of the means of production and the manufacture of commodities. For Sison, however, capitalism simply meant industrialization. Sison conceived of capital as a thing, in the manner of a bourgeois economist, and not as a social relationship. Feudalism, for Sison, was thus agricultural production and the absence of industrialization more generally. Sison attempted to demonstrate that the development of a cash economy predominantly engaged in the production of commodities was not the development of capitalism but the perpetuation of feudalism, because the Philippines did not adequately industrialize. Examining Sison's account in this light, the evidence he presents fully invalidates his thesis. He traces the incorporation of the Philippines into the global capitalist economy and the rise of commodity production in the country. Fixated on industrialization, Sison would not see that his evidence revealed the capitalist character of the Philippine economy.

He described economic development under Spanish colonial rule. A surplus in agricultural crops was being produced for commodity exchange and "an ever increasing amount of raw material crops for export to various capitalist countries." He wrote that "the large-scale cultivation of sugar, hemp, tobacco, coconut and the like in some areas in turn required the production of a bigger surplus in staple food crops in other areas in order to sustain the large number of people concentrated in the production of export crops" (PSR, 20). Specialization in commodity production and cash crop, export-oriented agriculture—these are capitalist developments, not feudal ones.

These developments, he wrote, "necessitated the improvement of transportation and communications." The development of improved communications "aggravated the feudal exploitation of the people" (PSR, 21). How did it aggravate feudal exploitation? He continued, "The Spaniards ordered the people in increasing numbers to build roads, bridges and ports and paid them extremely low nominal wages." Sison depicted mass wage labor engaged in the development of infrastructure, including "the introduction of steamship and railroad," as part of feudal exploitation. At this point, Sison claimed that "the embryo of the Filipino proletariat became distinct. . . . They emerged in the transition from a feudal to a semi-feudal economy" (PSR, 22).

The arrival of US imperialism only perpetuated this semifeudal economy, Sison claimed. He wrote that "feudalism was assimilated and retained for the imperialist purposes of the United States" (PSR, 37). US imperialism sought the Philippines as a "source of raw materials, a market for its surplus products and field of investment for its surplus capital." US imperialism increased the production of commercial crops for export, "sugar, coconut, and hemp, aside from such other raw materials as logs and mineral ores. Sugar centrals, coconut oil refineries, rope factories and the like were built." One is almost embarrassed to point out that this is not feudalism. Sison wrote that "free trade" between the United States and the Philippines was characterized by raw materials from the Philippines and finished goods from the United States. "The free trade between these two types of commodities perpetuated the colonial and agrarian economy" (PSR, 38). This last statement of Sison's is correct with the proviso that it was a colonial and largely agrarian *capitalist* economy.

Sison goes on to say that "US surplus capital was invested in the Philippines both in the form of direct investments and loan capital. Direct investments went mainly into the production of raw materials and into trade in US finished products and local raw materials. . . . Mineral ores were extracted for the first time on a commercial basis. . . . Every year, raw material production, and therefore, the exploitation of the people had to be intensified by the colonial regime in order to increase its rate of profit" (PSR, 39). The proletariat grew, Sison admitted. "During the US colonial rule, the proletariat increased in number to the extent that the semi-feudal society became reinforced with the quantitative increase in raw material production, trade, transport and communication facilities and minor manufacturing" (*PSR*, 41).

Thus, Sison goes to great lengths to establish that the Philippine economy was not yet capitalist but semifeudal. All the evidence that he presents to this effect contradicts his own thesis. Sison either did not know what capitalism is or misrepresented it to serve his preconceived political ends.

Beams accurately summed this up:

The lack of industrialisation is continually reproduced not through feudal but capitalist social relations—the production of raw material commodities for the US market. After taking hold of the "material base of Philippines society," US imperialism turned it into a supplier of raw materials for the US market, according to the laws of capitalist production. The backwardness of the Philippine economy is spontaneously reproduced by the operation of the laws of the capitalist world market. In other words, it is the existence of capitalist relations which prevents the development of industry, not feudalism.[179]

Several weeks after the *Collegian* published what became the first chapter of *Philippine Society and Revolution*, Jesus Lava wrote a twelve-page response to Sison's accusations, titled *Paglilinaw sa "Philippine Crisis"* (Clarifying "Philippine crisis"). The text somehow found its way out of the prison where Lava was held and was disseminated in mimeographed form.[180] Lava's basic contention was that US imperialism was actively working to liquidate feudalism and replace it with capitalism in its neocolonies around the globe. He argued that US imperialism recognized that the national democratic revolution had two fundamental components: the liberation struggle of the anti-imperialist movement and the agrarian revolution. During the period that Lava termed "old colonialism," the imperialist-feudal alliance had predominated. This period was marked by exploitation carried out through the mining industry and large plantations and was based on the production of raw materials and the importation of finished products from the United States. As US imperialism was increasingly imperiled by agrarian uprisings around the world, however, this arrangement was jeopardized and Washington responded with what Lava called "bagong kolonyalismo" ("new colonialism," although perhaps better translated as "neocolonialism"). We all know, Lava wrote, that an ordinary peasant does not understand imperialism, and it is difficult to explain it to him. He does not protest against imperialism but rather against his exploitation by the hacenderos. As long as feudalism persists, the peasant will fight for agrarian revolution, and this uprising will be the strongest and most reliable force in the national democratic movement. US imperialism recognized this, Lava argued, and, threatened by peasant uprisings and national democratic revolutions throughout the world, Washington began to carry out land reform in nations around the globe. Lava argued that the imperialists, far from perpetuating feudalism, were working to eliminate it.

Sison and Lava shared a common understanding of feudalism and capitalism. For both, capitalism meant industrialization. Like Sison, Lava characterized vast mining operations and cash-crop, export-driven plantation agriculture owned by large corporations as feudalism. They agreed that the preeminent problem was the feudal character of the Philippine economy and that the tasks of the revolution were thus capitalist, not socialist. They shared the program of a two-stage revolution. They differed, however, over how feudalism was to be eliminated. Sison argued that this required an armed struggle in the countryside, while Lava favored the "Non-capitalist road to socialism"—a line that was now being articulated by Moscow. In this conception, imperialism itself was "liquidating feudalism." The task for the PKP was thus to support the government in its liquidation of feudalism, to orient it toward Moscow, and, through Moscow's assistance, facilitate the transition toward socialism. Lava did not entirely develop these ideas in *Paglilinaw*. They were, however, its ideological basis and were fully articulated by the PKP in the first months of 1973 during its Sixth Congress.[181]

Chapter 2: "Basic Problems of the Filipino People"

In the second chapter of *PSR*, Sison wrote what served as a response to *Paglilinaw*'s claim that imperialism was liquidating feudalism, focusing on what he argued were the mechanisms that reproduced and maintained the semifeudal condition of the Philippines. He opened with the statement, "Philippine society today is semi-colonial and semi-feudal. This status is determined by US imperialism, feudalism and bureaucrat capitalism which now ruthlessly exploit the broad masses of the Filipino people. These three historical evils are the basic problems that afflict Philippine society" (*PSR*, 113). Sison described what he regarded as the relationship between US imperialism and feudalism: "Feudalism has been encouraged and retained by US imperialism to perpetuate the poverty of the broad masses of the people, subjugate the most numerous class which is the peasantry and manipulate local backwardness for the purpose of having cheap labor and cheap raw materials from the country. It is in this sense that *domestic feudalism is the social base of US imperialism*" (*PSR*, 115, emphasis added).

Sison argued that US imperialism exported capital to the Philippines to secure raw material production. This was done through capitalist farming. The workers employed on capitalist farms, however, relied on other farms to produce the food that they consumed. The farms producing the food for these workers were themselves worked by peasants and tenants. This peasant agriculture was in fact directly tied to global capitalism and was itself engaged in the production of cash crops for the domestic market; this was capitalist production. Sison, however, claimed that the profits of US imperialism, extracted through capitalist agriculture, were dependent on the "feudal" production of basic staples. Feudalism was thus the "social base of imperialism." Sison argued that the entire immense weight of imperialism, described by Lenin as the highest stage of capitalism, stood upon the narrow base of peasant agriculture. This claim was the core conception of PSR, the justification for the protracted people's war of the NPA. By attacking the most backward forms of agriculture in the remotest parts of the Philippines, Sison claimed, the CPP was attacking the foundation of US empire.

Sison doubled down on this point, insisting that US imperialism "effected semi-feudalism more effectively in the countryside *by further encouraging capitalist farming and corporate ownership of land.* It put up sugar mills, abaca mills and coconut mills under corporate ownership and around which the landlords were organized. . . . Capitalist methods of exploitation are strikingly evident in lands where export crops are cultivated and feudal methods of exploitation prevail in lands where food crops are cultivated, *except in some few areas where mechanization has been introduced* by the landlords" (PSR, 169–170, emphasis added). Sison argued that the encouraging of capitalist farming and corporate ownership "effected semi-feudalism." He admitted that the only portion of Philippine agriculture that was predominantly "feudal" was food production, and he further admitted that portions had been mechanized. Sison's conception that capitalism was industrialization is here evident, for without changing the class relations in food production, mechanization somehow transformed the nature of the production from "feudal" to capitalist.

Sison was compelled to admit that industrialization to a certain extent was occurring in the Philippines, but he dismissed this development:

> It is bandied about that during the last two years, the Philippine reactionary government made heavy dollar expenditures because it imported mainly machinery, transport equipment, fuel and raw materials for domestic processing. What is falsely implied is that the Philippines is rapidly industrializing. This is a big lie because these imports have been mainly for public works projects, construction of office buildings and sugar mills, mineral extraction, spare parts, motor vehicle and home appliance reassembly and other such so-called intermediate industries as textile, flour and iron mills that rely on imported yarn, wheat and iron sheets. (PSR, 141)

Sison's refusal to understand the global nature of capitalism is here most striking. For Sison, industrialization was genuine only if it was an autonomous development, independent of the global market. Intermediate production bound up with the import and export of goods, even if it was heavily mechanized, was not industrialization according to Sison. Sison envisioned nationalist autonomous capitalism developing in the Philippines in which Philippine raw materials were processed in Philippine industries for Philippine consumption. His political correlate to "socialism in one country" was the idea of building "capitalism in one country." Capitalism is a global system and does not permit an isolated and autonomous development artificially secured within the confines of the nation-state, but this was precisely the scheme that Sison was promoting. The class interests behind such a scheme are obvious. They expressed the interests of a section of the Filipino bourgeoisie who were looking for the government to implement limited protectionist measures and provide subsidies in support of their developing industrial concerns. Sison openly articulated their interests. He bemoaned the fact that because of US imperialism, "not even the national bourgeoisie can hope to increase its share in the exploitation of the Filipino people. This social stratum is daily facing bankruptcy" (PSR, 147).

Having dealt with imperialism and feudalism—two of the "historical evils"—Sison turned to the third: bureaucrat capitalism. The bureaucrat capitalists were corrupt government officials, who were "capitalists by converting the entire government into a private enterprise from which they draw enormous private profits. They act like the local managers of the US monopolies. They serve the comprador big bourgeoisie and the landlord class which are their internal material basis" (PSR, 207). The mess of confusion in this paragraph is extraordinary. Just as Sison's "semi-feudalism" was in fact capitalism, his "bureaucrat capitalism" was not capitalist at all. Government corruption is as old as the state itself. Extracting wealth from its coffers is not a form of capitalism. Bureaucrat capitalism, according to Sison, "is nothing but an instrument for facilitating the exploitation of the broad masses of the people by foreign and feudal interests" (PSR, 210).

Sison used the category "bureaucrat capitalism" to depict this activity—class exploitation and corruption—as an aberration rather than the intrinsic function of the state. The CPP's political line called for the formation of a coalition government of the working class and capitalist class to carry out the national democratic revolution. It was therefore necessary for a state to function within a class-divided society without serving as an instrument of exploitation, foreign domination, or corruption, an idea that was fundamentally antithetical to Marxism. Sison attempted to disguise this by condemning the existing government not as the necessary expression of the state, which embodied the interests of the ruling class, but rather as an aberration based on semifeudalism—bureaucrat capitalism.

He continued this line of thought: "Bureaucrat capitalism is the basis of local fascism. The bureaucrat capitalists are too well compensated by US imperialism and the local exploiting classes to change their oppressive character in favor of the people" (PSR, 217). It followed logically that were government officials less well compensated, freer from US imperialism, they could cease to be oppressive and would govern in favor of the people. The state had the capacity to be a neutral arbiter and respond to the needs of the masses. Behind Sison's rhetoric of a people's war was the most reformist and anti-Marxist of ideas: the state could serve the interests of the people—the working class, the peasantry and the national capitalists—all of whom shared a common national interest.

Chapter 3: "The People's Democratic Revolution"

On the basis of the conceptions established in the two prior chapters—particularly that the Philippine economy was semifeudal—Sison laid out the tasks of the revolution. These tasks flowed, he argued, from "the basic contradictions of Philippine society," which were "those between the Filipino nation and imperialism, and those between the great masses of the people and feudalism" (PSR, 230). Because the Philippines was not yet capitalist, according to Sison, the class struggle between capitalists and workers was not the fundamental contradiction, for the "Filipino nation" had a shared interest in opposing US imperialism. The national democratic revolution was of a "new type," however, as it was to be led by the proletariat, Sison claimed, rather than the bourgeoisie (PSR, 231). Even though he argued that the working class was to lead this revolution, he repeatedly insisted that "it is not yet a proletarian socialist revolution. Only the muddle-headed will confuse the national democratic stage and the socialist stage of the Philippine revolution. Only after the people's democratic revolution has been completely won can the proletarian revolutionary leadership carry out the socialist revolution as the transitional stage towards communism" (PSR, 234).

Sison claimed that while the working class was the "leading force" in the revolution, it was not the "main force"; this was the peasantry, the "most numerous section of the population." He argued from the predominance of agricultural production in the country that "the people's democratic revolution is essentially a peasant war because its main political force is the peasantry, its main problem is the land problem and its main source of Red fighters is the peasantry" (PSR, 256). The working class was thus to serve as the leadership, Sison argued, of a peasant war in the countryside.

For all Sison's talk about the leadership of the proletariat, what he called for was a revolution for capitalism, not socialism; a revolution waged in the countryside, which workers could lead only if they left their jobs and the city and ceased to be workers; and which would lead to a government that sought to harmonize the interests of workers with capitalists, whose fundamental class interest is the increased exploitation of the proletariat. This was not the leadership of the working class. It was the betrayal and suppression of the interests of workers.

The goal of the revolution was to build a "people's democratic state system, which is the united front dictatorship of the proletariat, peasantry, petty bourgeoisie, national bourgeoisie and all other patriots." This government would be one that "harmonizes the interests of all revolutionary classes and strata. . . . It shall neither be a bourgeois dictatorship nor a dictatorship of the proletariat but a joint dictatorship of all revolutionary classes and strata under the leadership of the proletariat" (PSR, 288). The final phrase "under the leadership of the proletariat" was a meaningless rhetorical flourish. If this government was neither a dictatorship of the capitalists nor one of the workers, then it would not be under the leadership of the proletariat.

What Sison argued fundamentally opposed the ABC's of Marxism, most clearly articulated by Lenin in his work State and Revolution. Summarizing the perspective of Marx and Engels, Lenin wrote that the state was "the product and manifestation of the irreconcilability of class antagonisms" and "an instrument for the exploitation of the oppressed class." He continued,

> The essence of Marx's theory of the state has been mastered only by those who realize that the dictatorship of a single class is necessary not only for every class society in general, not only for the proletariat which has overthrown the bourgeoisie, but also for the entire historical period which separates capitalism from "classless society," from communism. Bourgeois states are most varied in form, but their essence is the same: all these states, whatever their form, in the final analysis are inevitably the dictatorship of the bourgeoisie. The transition from capitalism to communism is certainly bound to yield a tremendous abundance and variety of political forms, but the essence will inevitably be the same: the dictatorship of the proletariat.[182]

According to Lenin, every state is necessarily the dictatorship of a single class. Sison's joint dictatorship of the bourgeoisie, proletariat, and peasantry was an anti-Marxist conception. What would Sison's state do in the event of a massive labor struggle? Workers go on strike, and the capitalist owners bring in scabs and look to the police to break up the picket lines. There is no possible harmonious response from a joint proletarian and capitalist dictatorship. Such a government would inevitably be the dictatorship of the capitalist class, in which representatives of the CPP cooperated in the suppression and exploitation of workers.

Neither Sison nor Lava, neither the CPP nor the PKP, admitted that the Philippine economy was fundamentally capitalist. They claimed that its belated and uneven development was not a necessary expression of capitalism but rather a manifestation of feudalism. They were convinced that the tasks of the revolution were national and democratic in character, not socialist. On this basis, both worked to form an alliance with a section of the bourgeoisie. Lava and the PKP, however, argued on the basis of Moscow's line of a "non-Capitalist road" that imperialism was liquidating feudalism, that Marcos would carry out the tasks of the national democratic revolution, and that the party, by allying with him, could win him over to the autocratic construction of socialism. Sison and the CPP, meanwhile, claimed that only a protracted people's war, carried out in alliance with sections of the bourgeoisie opposed to Marcos, could effectively end the semifeudal character of the Philippine economy.

In his political report to the Second Plenum of the Central Committee, Sison described *PSR* as "a basic textbook for mass political education as well as for basic ideological training in the party." It "strives from the standpoint of Marxism-Leninism-Mao Zedong Thought to present the history, basic problems, character, motive forces, targets, strategy and tactics and perspective of the Philippine revolution."[183] *PSR* formed the core of the educational program of the party cadre as well as the party's mass educational program.[184] In August, with the party's ideological centerpiece—*PSR*—now being published in Manila papers, the CPP politburo met and issued instructions to accelerate the recruitment of new members to the party.[185]

Consolidation and Regrouping

In its 15 July edition the *Collegian* began publishing a front-page feature titled "The Movement," which summarized weekly developments in the protests, strikes, and other work in which the KM, SDK, and their sibling organizations were involved. The ability to combine these organizations and their activities into a single category—the movement—was an expression of the ongoing process of consolidation that was taking place in the ranks of the national democratic organizations under the leadership of the CPP in the second half of 1970.

The campaign of political consolidation and organizational expansion began with campus elections. What is most striking about the 1970 student council campaigns at UP Diliman is the manner in which every candidate, including the conservative Firdausi Abbas and Manuel Ortega, adopted the slogans of the national democratic movement. All four candidates denounced "imperialism, feudalism and fascism"; all four called for a "broad national united front"—the rhetoric of national democracy had become a necessary shibboleth.[186] Having opposed each other in the elections of 1968 and 1969, the campus organizations of the KM and SDK, the Katipunan-Makabansa and the Partisans for National Democracy, formed a united front campus group, the Sandigang Makabansa (Patriotic Pillars, SM), running a slate headed by KM member Ericson Baculinao and SDK member Rey Vea. Their election statement declared, "In a newly polarized society . . . all who fight for change must muster the broadest possible alliance in response. . . . Sandigang Makabansa has emerged as the broadest possible representation of nationalist groups, campus organizations, and fraternities-sororities interested simply in continuing a job well begun in the past two years."[187]

The alliance of the SM was not broad enough, however, to include the MPKP, whose election leaflet attacked the "adventurism" of the KM: "What democratic rights the people now enjoy are the product of decades of working-class struggle. Irresponsible provocation of fascist repression before the masses have attained sufficient political consciousness is counter-revolutionary and should be fought."[188] The KM responded, "In this period when the masses of the Filipino people are waking up to the reality of class dictatorship of landlords, compradors and their imperialist masters, the MPKP-BRPF group maintains that there exist 'democratic rights' within the framework created by the classes."[189] From the perspective of the KM there were no democratic rights. There would be no difference between the suspension of the writ of habeas corpus and its presence, for the writ was just the legal window dressing of already existing fascism. The KM's political line prepared people to welcome the declaration of martial law as a stripping away of what were but the pretenses of democracy.

Campus elections in 1970 saw "a landslide of victories for nationalist candidates. . . . The first victory occurred in UP Los Baños, Vic Ladlad of Samahang Demokratiko ng Kabataan and Ric Umali of Kabataang Makabayan won the council chairmanships of the College of Agriculture and of Forestry. Next in line was UP Diliman's Eric Baculinao. Victory after victory followed for the activist groups."[190] The KM consolidated its political gains by creating the Student Alliance for National Democracy (STAND) during the second national conference of the Nationalist Student Movement held on 3–6 November in Abelardo Hall on the Diliman campus.[191] STAND coordinated the decisions and activities of the various student councils over which the CPP exercised a good deal of control in the wake of the 1970–71 campus elections.[192] The CPP's control over the organization was ill disguised at best. Each delegate to the conference was provided with a book prepared for the gathering, which opened with 132 pages of quotations from Mao Zedong, continued with an article by Joma Sison, and concluded with the statement from *Ang Bayan* on the FQS, "Turn Grief into Revolutionary Courage."[193] David Ryan Quimpo, who was a member of STAND, wrote, "The CPP actually had a secret Party group inside the leadership of STAND, which was determining the conduct and direction of the alliance."[194] Just how secret its leadership was is disputable; what is certain is that the CPP controlled STAND and through it swayed the student councils.

Control of the councils was closely tied to editorial control of university newspapers. The growing radicalization of students in 1970 found expression in both the content and design of campus weeklies. PCC's *Ang Malaya*, like the *Collegian*, dedicated nearly all of its pages to reports on struggles, strikes, and protests, alongside polemics and manifestos. The editors of the radicalized campus papers formed a new organization, League of Editors for a Democratic Society (LEADS), which pooled editorial and article writing each week through an Inter-Campus News Service in keeping with the political line of the CPP.[195] LEADS's twenty-five member publications had an estimated combined circulation of two hundred thousand copies.[196] LEADS also established an independent publication, *Dare to Struggle, Dare to Win*, in early 1971. The first edition carried greetings to the newly founded organization from Sison, who wrote, "Revolutionary students should firmly hold the campus newspapers. . . . If all campus editors join up and fight for a revolutionary orientation, their newspapers can certainly become a formidable force in the making of public opinion for revolution. . . . The practice of the League of Editors for a Democratic Society in publishing pooled editorials and articles in campus newspapers is excellent."[197] Crispin Aranda, head of STAND, wrote in the same issue, "If we control the campus publications—by which we mean that they are following the national democratic line—we should use every issue to publish revolutionary publications, literature, art, etc."[198] All of the major campus papers in the country now had a common content, generated centrally by LEADS in conformity with the political line of the CPP. A regimentation of thought and vocabulary settled upon the movement.

While consolidating their political gains through the formation of STAND and LEADS, the KM and SDK formed new groups to expand their reach, focusing their efforts on the creation of several women's organizations. The crippling economic conditions encountered by the majority of the population, and the weight of the reactionary teachings of the Catholic Church, made

working-class and peasant women a doubly exploited and oppressed population. Birth control was not available, and divorce was illegal. The newly formed
women's groups, however, neither fought for the democratic rights of working-
class women nor opposed the sexist culture prevalent within the party and its
front groups. Rather, they sought to rouse and mobilize upper-class women
whom they criticized as "pampered" and "passive," seeking to win their support for the national democratic revolution. The *Asia Philippines Leader* correctly summed up the perspective of these new organizations when it wrote,

> Women's Lib in the Philippines seeks to transform the traditionally apa-
> thetic and apolitical Filipina into an active participant in the struggle for
> national liberation. It is not really a struggle against male dominance. . . .
>
> The Filipina is a virtual prisoner in her own home. She is passive,
> conservative and supports the status quo. . . . The Filipina is merely re-
> quired to look pretty and act demurely.
>
> Society has made her into a lapdog, pampered by her master, but at
> the same time fettered and immobile.[199]

No working-class or peasant woman would recognize herself in this description, but it aptly characterized the social layers to which the new women's
organizations were oriented. The Malayang Kilusan ng Bagong Kababaihan
(Free Movement of New Women, MAKIBAKA) was founded by Ma. Lorena
Barros, along with a group of women in the SDK at UP, as a means of politiciz-
ing wealthy young women attending Catholic girls' colleges.[200] The fledgling
organization staged its first protest on the coronation night of Miss Philippines,
where they denounced women for being more concerned with their appearance
than with the semifeudal condition of the country, and called on them to wake
up. The ranks of MAKIBAKA grew as women were recruited from St. There-
sa's, St. Paul, Maryknoll, and Assumption, and by 1971 the organization had four
hundred members and eight chapters.[201] Bagong Pilipina (New Filipina), a second UP-based women's organization tied to the SDK, was formed in September
under the leadership of Aimee Laurel. Where MAKIBAKA sought to reach elite
young women in religious schools, Bagong Pilipina sought to organize sorority
members on the UP campus. It put forward a perspective similar to that of
MAKIBAKA, and both organizations, along with the KM Women's Bureau,
formed an umbrella group, Katipunan ng Kababaihan para sa Kalayaan (Federation of Women for Freedom) in March 1971.

All of these organizations denounced "mainstream" feminism as "Western
and bourgeois." In December 1971, Pat Dimagiba of MAKIBAKA wrote a letter
to the *Asia Philippines Leader* in which she described Western feminism as "anti-
male, anti-bra, anti-babies."[202] In opposition to Western feminism, MAKIBAKA

and its allied organizations did not articulate the interests of working-class and peasant women. They opposed the distribution of contraceptives; they did not fight for the right to abortion or divorce. These organizations were not founded to mobilize women against their treatment within the movement—which was routinely parochial, patriarchal, and downright misogynist—or to lead a struggle against the class roots of women's exploitation. Rather, MAKIBAKA and its allied organizations primarily addressed themselves to upper-class and petty bourgeois young women, effectively attempting to shame them for their "passivity" as a means of motivating them to join the national democratic movement. They projected this passivity of upper-class women onto the Filipina (i.e., Filipino women) without regard to class. Judy Taguiwalo captured the conception of these organizations when she wrote that "within the anti-colonial and anti-feudal classes, it is the women sector which generally lags behind and is slowest to grasp the counter-consciousness that the national democratic cultural revolution is popularizing."[203] MAKIBAKA and Bagong Pilipina rooted this slow development of "counter-consciousness" in the "pampered" nature of women's lives.

Far from fighting the subordinate and traditional role of women within the front organizations of the CPP, MAKIBAKA and Bagong Pilipina reinforced it. Within months of its founding, MAKIBAKA established itself as responsible for the child care of the national democratic movement. The organization set up a "national democratic nursery," which opened on Leveriza in November 1970, and its members cared for the children of activists and taught them "revolutionary songs and stories."[204] The orientation of MAKIBAKA and Bagong Pilipina was to upper-class women with the intent of shaming them into joining the national democratic movement and then relegating them to traditional gender roles within it.

The newly formed groups were bound together with their sibling organizations in a single coordinating body, the MDP. Now made up of forty-five member organizations, the MDP met on 8 August to rearrange its leadership.[205] The secretariat, a body that had been set up in March, was overhauled, ten members were appointed, and Julius Fortuna was made general secretary.[206] A majority of the secretariat were members of the KM and SDK; Fortuna was a member of the CPP. The reorganization of the secretariat completed the removal of the MPKP and BRPF from the MDP and direct political leadership of the social unrest, which showed no signs of abating. From this point onward the leaflets and manifestos of the organizations of the PKP addressed the mass movement from the sidelines.

As the CPP secured its organizational grip on nearly the entire youth protest movement over the course of 1970, the PKP became increasingly integrated with the Marcos administration, which was continuing to deepen ties with Moscow and the Soviet bloc. At the end of July, the *Collegian* quietly announced that Lumumba University in Moscow was offering three scholarships for Filipinos to study there.[207] Celia Pomeroy, a member of the international leadership of the PKP, wrote enthusiastically to Isabelle Auerbach of the Communist Party of the USA that a great many Filipinos were applying and one had in fact begun attending.[208] Pomeroy did not mention that the attendee was Josefina Barbero, the daughter of Congressman Carmelo Barbero, a leading anti-Communist and key ally of Marcos.[209]

The CPP and its front organizations aggressively accosted the PKP in their publications, denouncing them as tools of the Soviet Union. Its back pressed to the wall, the PKP responded, decrying the KM and its allies for "splittism," "left-extremism," and "anarchism"; Moscow had nothing to do with the matter, they claimed. The initial salvos in the increasingly vicious war of words were fired by the CPP. In May 1970, the NPA released a leaflet denouncing the "Monkees—Armeng Bayan—MASAKA (Lava) Gang."[210] The NPA claimed that Lava's group had "degenerated into a handful of out-and-out agents of the reactionary government," and then proceeded to name the lot of them.[211] From the perspective of the PKP, the CPP had just publicly named almost the entire membership of its Central Committee.[212] In July the Diliman election statement of the KM attacked the PKP as "relics of the Old Left" now defending Marcos.

Unable to keep silent in the face of this onslaught, the MPKP responded in September with a statement titled "The National Democratic Struggle and the Traitor Kabataang Makabayan."[213] It charged the KM and its sister organizations with "left adventurism," their "anarchism" apparent in their "actions provoking [*napagpagalit*] the fascist state into chasing the demonstrators with clubs and guns." On 9 October the Diliman chapter of KM responded with a special issue of *Kalayaan* dedicated to attacking the MPKP, titled "Bombard the Headquarters of the Proven Renegades, Traitors and Scabs."[214] Where the MPKP accused them of "left adventurism," the KM responded that the MPKP was guilty of "right opportunism." The MPKP charged that the KM had a shadow leadership, by which they meant Sison and the CPP; the KM responded that "behind the MPKP-BRPF reactionary outfit hovers the ubiquitous shadow of the Lava renegades."[215] The MPKP accused the KM of closely collaborating with a Central Luzon senator (Aquino) and congressman (Yap) and a millionaire publisher (Lopez), and the KM responded that the "Lava renegade clique soft-pedals its attacks or makes only token attacks on Marcos, while at the same time it gloats that 'Marcos is veering towards our cause,' it has in effect closed ranks with the reactionaries."[216]

Where the MPKP accused the KM of being allied with Aquino, the KM accused the MPKP of being allied with Marcos. Both were telling the truth. The KM, however, repeatedly and directly stated that the root of the hostilities was the split between Moscow and Beijing, while the MPKP consistently attempted to cover this up. Public rancor between the two groups mounted, but the PKP still labored to sweep the entire affair under the rug. Nixon's ping-pong diplomacy in 1971 would produce a qualitative escalation of tensions; for it was then that the dam of the PKP's fury broke, the public debate turned to histrionics, and both sides turned to assassination and bloodshed to resolve their differences.

The MDP, originally an ad hoc UPSC investigative committee, had become the most significant political body of organized dissent in the country. An ingenuous agnosticism had marked its inception, and it entered the storm an ideological cipher. It proved capacious and, as the storm blew hard, inflated. There was an indeterminate, almost stochastic, character to the initial influx, the gusts of an age in brownian motion. State repression aligned the diffuse placards and conflicting visions in common cause. The trend was radicalization and the beneficiary the CPP. The forces of the PKP marched at every rally and shouted themselves hoarse, but their slogans had a halfhearted character, their cadence ill matched to the timbre of the times. Torn between Marcos and the movement, they bridged the widening gulf with noncommittal phrases and broad generalities. The storm blew past them. In August 1970 the CPP scraped the leadership apparatus of the MDP clean of any residue of its rival and filled the secretariat with its own forces. The diverse layers housed within the MDP were not yet convinced of the program of the party, and the party made little effort to win them over. While the KM and SDK were educated along the lines of *PSR*, the party led the MDP with strident slogans, not programmatic analysis. They sought an organization of breadth, not depth; clarification would entail a winnowing of the ranks and this was to be avoided. Through the MDP, the CPP exercised organizational control but not political leadership over a broad movement. It was a constituency that could be mobilized in bourgeois politics, but one that would scatter to the winds the moment the apparatus ceased to exist. It was ideally suited for the election of 1971 but utterly unprepared for martial law a year later.

CHAPTER 3

Barricades

Prices continued to soar. The rising cost of crude oil imports sharply exacerbated the rapid inflation that had emerged with the currency crisis and devalued peso. The closure of the Suez Canal in 1967, the shift of "the center of gravity of world oil production" to the Middle East, the formation of the Organization of Petroleum Exporting Countries, Gaddafi's rise to power in Libya, and the renegotiation of the barrel rate in Tehran and Tripoli drove production and transportation expenses up substantially.[1] Existing profit margins in the Philippines, where a staggering 90 percent of all power requirements depended on oil, came under extreme pressure.[2] Crude importation and the refining and marketing of petroleum were entirely controlled by the international oil cartel through local subsidiaries.[3] "In March 1970, the subsidiaries unilaterally raised their prices by about four centavos per liter, allegedly due to 'adverse effects' of the floating rate instituted a few days earlier. In January 1971, the Price Control Council granted, on signal, another round of increases to the oil companies . . . this time by about two centavos per liter."[4] When his vice president brother was unable to secure any amelioration from Marcos, Eugenio Lopez, owner of the largest power distribution facility in the country—Meralco—saw the business interests of his family imperiled. It seemed all that stood between them and ruin was the elusive powers of the state with its subsidies and rate regulations.

An almost frantic agitation gripped the bourgeois opposition. Intrigues and rumors of intrigues rattled the old year's end; a pall of fear and confusion cloaked the dawn of the new. Shadowy reports, mongered about in editorial asides and leaflet agitation, took ever sharper outline: a military coup, occasioned by strikes and protests and staged in coordination with the Communist Party of the Philippines (CPP), would oust Marcos from office and install his vice president in Malacañang. Should this fail, Marcos would retain power through the imposition of martial law. These subterranean machinations operated on a timetable, scheduled in popular conception to arrive at their denouement on the twenty-fifth of January. The glossy biweekly newsmagazine *NOW* sifted through the debris of the rumor mill a month after it had ceased to churn.

A survey of all the speculations and predictions, taken at face value, as to what would have happened on the last Monday of January, when Congress traditionally opened its regular session, might lead to the conclusion that January 25, 1971, was to be as historically significant as, say, the storming of the Bastille, the bombing of Pearl Harbor, or the Liberation of Manila. . . .

As early as December of last year, different versions of what January 25 would be in the country's history were sprouting in the idle conversations in barber shops and coffee shops. January 25 was to be the day when Marcos would declare martial law. Commander Dante would supposedly show up when the students confronted the state's forces. There were rumors that Marcos would bring armed men from Northern Luzon provinces into the city to protect him during his state of the nation address. . . . [5]

The scuttlebutt of political columnists became the stuff of headlines on 13 January when the Metrocom opened fire on protesters and Marcos took to television threatening martial law and vowing to "crush the Lopez oligarchy."[6] The next day, Fernando Lopez journeyed to the presidential palace and resigned as secretary of agriculture and natural resources. Marcos had an acceptance letter already prepared and handed it to his vice president. "While you were a member of my Cabinet, the Lopez interests . . . were engaged in fomenting unrest and inciting the already militant and impassioned groups who advocate anarchy and assassination. The media controlled by the Lopez interests are still engaged in this, have in fact intensified their campaign against me."[7]

On the fifteenth, the *Chronicle* published Marcos's letter with an accompanying point-by-point rebuttal; and the day after, the famed political cartoonist

Gat launched a series of front-page cartoons in the paper that ran for three straight months, lampooning Marcos's wealth and corruption. The newly established League of Editors for a Democratic Society wrote that "the isolation of President Marcos was now complete. His rift with the Lopezes exposed his fading image even among his erstwhile colleagues."[8] Everyone breathlessly awaited the twenty-fifth.

An Anticipated Military Coup

The available evidence reveals that the opposition anticipated that rumblings of social unrest would build to an eruption at the State of the Nation address, a repeat of the events of the previous year, and they intended to use this as a pretext for a military seizure of power from Marcos. At the center of these efforts stood Lt. Victor Corpus, an instructor at the Philippine Military Academy (PMA), who for several years had been a "member of a secret CPP cell within the government military."[9]

The son of a colonel, Corpus graduated from the PMA in 1967, where he studied under Dante Simbulan. Simbulan maintained direct contact with Sison and the Kabataang Makabayan (Nationalist Youth, KM), and as Corpus and Simbulan "developed a close relationship,"[10] Corpus was brought into Sison's ambit. He was a student at the PMA in 1966 when Sison lectured there. In his speech, "The Correct Concept of National Security," Sison appealed to the officer corps to "serve the national interest."[11] Corpus was drawn to Sison's idea of a nationalist military force and began meeting with Sison regularly. "Later, as a constabulary officer, Corpus stayed in touch with Sison, sometimes dropping by in uniform to visit the communist leader at his apartment in the Manila suburb of Quezon City."[12] Corpus was frequently in the company of KM and Samahan ng Demokratikong Kabataan (Federation of Democratic Youth, SDK) activists, and he met and married an SDK member, Germelinda Tanglao.[13] Upon his graduation from the PMA, Corpus joined the KM.[14]

Corpus spent the next three years in the Philippine Constabulary (PC), the section of the military apparatus responsible for the physical suppression of dissent. By the middle of 1970, he returned to the PMA to work as an instructor in political science, teaching the course Government 411. McCoy writes that Corpus "junked the curriculum and substituted . . . questions on how to stage a coup d'état,"[15] and organized among the cadets. "In a clear breach of regulations, Corpus began meeting outside of class with the leaders of Class '71, including their first captain, Gringo Honasan."[16]

The future trajectory of this batch reveals how far the coup plotting instruction and organization of Corpus advanced. Honasan and the class of 1971, in alliance with Defense Minister Juan Ponce Enrile, played a leading role in the attempted military coup against Marcos in 1986, which led to his ouster under "People Power." Honasan went on to become the country's leading coup plotter and, subsequently, a senator. Honasan later recalled that "most of the radical thinking of our class was his [Corpus] influence."[17] McCoy notes that "Class '71 became leaders of a military revolt against civil authority. Not only did these coups define them, but the class itself defined the role of the coup d'état in Philippine politics. Apart from providing the leadership for five major coups, these eight-five graduates supplied fifteen of the seventy-seven officers involved in two or more coups—by far the highest of any single class."[18] This history bore the indelible mark of the elite conspiracies of 1970–71, orchestrated by Sison and the CPP through Victor Corpus.

In October 1970, Corpus traveled to the town of Cauayan, Isabela, where Sison was living in the home of the mayor, Faustino Dy, to whom he had been introduced by Aquino.[19] The province of Isabela climbed eastward from the fertile loam of the Cagayan valley to the impenetrable rainforest of the Sierra Madre mountains skirting the Pacific. Sison had drawn up plans in August 1969 to make Isabela the center of all New People's Army (NPA) activity, a liberated zone from which they could stage operations and to which they could fall back.[20] Dy, who was a leading figure in the Liberal Party (LP), was "instrumental in enabling the NPA to develop a base in the province." The NPA, in return, assisted Dy in getting elected governor in 1971.[21] On Dy's instructions the NPA received assistance from the police in the region, and through his introduction, they established collaborative relations with logging interests.[22] Sison and Corpus spent hours plotting a raid on the PMA armory to be staged at the end of the year and the defection of Corpus to the NPA. Corpus's defection would be immediately followed by a mass walkout of PMA cadets, led by Honasan and orchestrated by Corpus, signaling a withdrawal of military support from Marcos. In a manner suggestive of the far larger conspiracy of which this was a component, Dy—the LP politico—was an integral part of their planning, arranging for the Cauayan police to escort Corpus and his forces through the province after the raid.[23]

A team of NPA cadre, led by Juanito Rivera, traveled to Baguio City in late December, and on the evening of the twenty-ninth they met Corpus and slipped south to the grassy plateau and whitewashed halls of the PMA.[24] The journalist Gregg Jones recounts,

> While much of the PMA security force was guarding President Marcos as he vacationed in Baguio, where the academy was located, Corpus drove

to the city's downtown Burnham Park. There he was met by 9 guerrillas. They returned to the academy, Corpus in his military jeep, the rebels in two cars, and they were waved through the gate. Inside, the rebels quickly tied up the armory guards and loaded 21 automatic rifles, 14 carbines, 6 machine guns, 1 bazooka, grenade launchers, and more than 5,000 rounds of ammunition into the cars. They drove all night to reach Cauayan, the entry point for the NPA base camp in the nearby Sierra Madre foothills. Corpus and the raiding team were escorted by Mayor Dy's police to a rendezvous point at the base of the mountains, where they were met by Dante and 10 guerrillas. After walking all day and all night, they reached the camp.[25]

Sison moved to Manila, staying in the home of Ricardo Malay, a reporter for Lopez's *Manila Chronicle* and a member of the CPP. Sison drafted the party statement on Corpus's defection and gave it to Malay to take to the *Chronicle*, which published it on the second of January.[26] The successful raid dominated the front page of every major paper.

Sison and Corpus planned the raid and defection to dramatize disaffection in the ranks of the junior officer corps with widespread corruption in the upper echelons of the Armed Forces of the Philippines (AFP). They calculated that the action would stimulate a withdrawal of significant military support from the Marcos administration. That corruption was the core grievance they targeted was brought into sharp relief by a second defection three months after Corpus's raid, that of Lt. Crispin Tagamolila.

Tagamolila graduated with a degree in business administration and marketing from University of the Philippines (UP) Diliman in 1966 and enrolled at the PMA. He was sympathetic to the cause of protesting youths as early as 1966, and his younger brother, Antonio, became a leading member of the SDK and was editor of the *Collegian* from 1970 to 1971. Crispin Tagamolila was made a finance officer, responsible for "delivering huge sums of payroll money to the different camps in central Luzon."[27] By 1970, Tagamolila, like Corpus, had become a faculty member. He was responsible for teaching "nationalism" to the PC at Camp Panopio, a notorious detention center in Cubao.[28] He participated in "discussion groups" with Corpus and "other progressive young officers," before Corpus joined the NPA, a fact that reveals the extent of Corpus's organizing, reaching far beyond the PMA in the northern city of Baguio.[29] On 29 March 1971, Tagamolila defected, an act he coordinated with the CPP to carry out on the second anniversary of the NPA's founding. Tagamolila left behind a four-page letter in which he declared that corruption and theft at the highest levels of the military were his primary motive for defection.[30] He wrote of huge kickbacks in construction projects that resulted in substandard military facilities, of officers who did not receive adequate supplies, of disbursing officers who deposited army funds into their personal accounts, of provincial commanders pilfering arms and selling them to local warlords, and of generals running protection rackets.

Neither Corpus nor Tagamolila denounced the Armed Forces as the repressive instruments of bourgeois rule. Rather, they targeted the corruption of the Armed Forces and expressed a frustrated desire for a thorough-going reform of the military. It was a carefully chosen cause. There is an ideological polyvalence to outrage over corruption; forces across the political spectrum carry its banners. Figures like Honasan saw corruption eroding the capacity of the military to function as an effective apparatus of repression, and the fight against it was thus made the watchword of the right-wing coup plots of his Reform the Armed Forces Movement cabal in the 1980s. Honasan and a number of Corpus's other students organized a mass walkout of the entire cadet corps to protest against PMA corruption, but the heightened security in the wake of the December raid prevented the student strike.[31]

The CPP was instrumental in the coup plots of the bourgeois opposition of 1970–72 and in the process created the future coup leaders that plagued the country's politics from the 1980s onward. The party, however, did not wish for the opposition to take power through a military putsch without the support of a mass movement. If a withdrawal of military support for Marcos removed him from office in conjunction with a broad social upheaval under the leadership of the CPP, then the party would be guaranteed a seat at the table. A palace coup, on the other hand, would see the CPP excluded from the spoils. On 3 January *Taliba* published a Tagalog statement from Corpus explaining his actions: "As an officer I could have joined a group of fellow officers to stage a coup d'état. I know that many officers are always saying that seizing the [presidential] palace will solve our national problems. But I believe that a coup d'état, because it is carried out from above and does not have the support of the masses, especially the workers and peasants, could be seized by the enemies of the people."[32] The machinations of the officer corps, solicited and, to an extent, organized by the CPP, had to be coupled with a mass movement. This would secure power for their bourgeois allies in a manner that left them beholden to the party's constituency. The party would secure seats in the overhauled state, which it would term a coalition government of new democracy.

Sison launched an adventurist policy calculated to destabilize the Marcos administration and align with a military coup, bringing the energy of mass protests and strikes behind the plots of the party's elite allies. He wrote the Political Report to the Second Plenum of the Central Committee in September 1970, and the report was published in *Ang Bayan* on 15 October.[33] Sison did not instigate unrest; he politically disarmed it. The thrust of his report solicited audacity reckless of strategy. He directed protests with an eye to securing an intervention from on high, in the form of either a coup or dictatorship. Rather than warning workers and students of the imminent dangers they confronted and orienting their efforts toward a struggle for power, he downplayed—even welcomed— these perilous possibilities. The repression being carried out by the Marcos regime, he argued, was beneficial to revolution. "The Marcos fascist puppet clique imagines that the brutality of its minions will terrify the people. The truth is that it is only hastening the advance of the revolutionary masses."[34] Should Marcos declare martial law, it would have similar consequences. "The Marcos fascist puppet clique shamelessly boasts that it will use all the forces at its command to suppress the democratic rights of the people. It can only fan the flames of revolutionary war in the country."[35] The upsurge could not be interrupted; it confronted no grave dangers. Repression would only hasten revolution. Sison showed no concern to safeguard the mass movement or marshal its forces. He urged the restive youths and workers into confrontation with the state but gave them no strategy for battle. *Makibaka, huwag matakot* (Struggle, don't be afraid). Salt spray dashed against the rubble breakwaters of dictatorship.[36]

"The Revolution that Never Was"

Administrators from a number of private universities met and formulated a joint policy to quell student radicalism by expelling "undesirables" and refusing to accept transfers, thus ensuring that those who were expelled were removed from higher education entirely. In late November, the schools of the university belt required students enrolling for the second semester to sign statements that "they are satisfied with the facilities and personnel of the school, that they are not members of any progressive organization, and that their enrollment is good only for the current semester." Students deemed undesirable at the end of a semester would be given non-readmission notices.[37] Universities expelled an initial three hundred students, and the number grew to nearly eight hundred by early December.[38] The elected leaders of student councils and the editors of several campus papers were denied readmission, deemed "undesirable" for having "led riots."[39] The university belt institutions were known as diploma mills for a reason; they would not allow a flimsy thing like freedom of thought to interfere with the production of interchangeable cogs for the apparatus of profit.

The KM and SDK denounced "campus fascism" and called for "campus revolution." On the first of December, the KM wrote, "They [militant students] should no longer rely on the old methods of struggle which highly depend on negotiations with the dispensers of economic and political power in society. New tactics should be developed and creatively applied."[40] There was not a word on the character of these new tactics, but the leaflet concluded with the slogans "Make Revolution in the Colonial Universities and Colleges!!! . . . Long Live the University Rebel Committees!!!" The next day, the SDK put out a leaflet denouncing the "sinister plot to cripple student activism" and singled out the "fascist school administration of FEATI" as primarily responsible.[41]

Students demonstrated in Manila on 4 December demanding the Marcos administration Department of Education compel the reenrollment of the expelled.[42] As they marched in front of FEATI, a thrown pillbox hit the head of Francis Sontillano, a fifteen-year-old Philippine Science High School student, and exploded. His skull blew open and he died instantly.[43] Brownshirted and wicker-shielded, the Metrocom dispersed the angry crowd with tear gas and left Sontillano's corpse in the street.[44]

The UP Student Council (UPSC) called on students to "answer fascism with campus revolution! Avenge Comrade Francis!"[45] Sontillano's funeral became a mass demonstration on Monday, 7 December, and students at UP boycotted their classes until Wednesday, when fifteen thousand protesters marched to Plaza Lawton.[46] Metrocom and the Manila Police Department violently dispersed the crowd, shooting three of the demonstrators and beating seven with truncheons.[47]

The KM circulated a remarkable leaflet. The death of Sontillano "proved once again that the united front of revolutionary workers, peasants, nationalist bourgeoisie and militant students are prepared to give their lives [*nakahandang magbuwis ng buhay*] for the progress and victory of the movement whose aim is to attain national democracy." The KM continued, "Death surely comes to the life of every creature, but death can have many different levels of importance. To die for the nation [*mamatay para sa bayan*] and the first steps toward a just society is a death that can never be equaled [*hindi kailanman mapapantayan*]." Sontillano's death was an "inspiration for our protracted struggle." The leaflet concluded, "It is time for us to develop our methods of struggle, methods that will show that we too are prepared to kill if necessary for the success of our goal [*handang pumatay kung kinakailangan sa ikapapagtagumpay ng ating adhikain*]!!!"[48]

There was a certain involution to the fiery student rhetoric of December: campus revolution waged against campus fascism, university rebel committees.

To an extent this was a response to the repressive policies of university administrations, but it expressed as well a narrowing of vision. As the intensity of student agitation heightened, outstripping the broader mass movement, its political scope contracted in inverse proportion. The charged mood of pinpoint desperation, palpable in leaflets that spoke of armed struggle and campus revolution, flashed out in February in the sheet lightning of the Diliman Commune.

January intervened and the students were wrenched into the wider world by a mass transit strike. Strained by the soaring price of oil, jeepney drivers shut down the majority of public transportation in Metro Manila, and the strike spilled over into the neighboring provinces of Bulacan, Rizal, and Cavite and reached as far as Batangas, Laguna, Cebu, and Davao.[49] Students raised barricades in support of the strike in downtown Manila and around a number of college campuses, shutting down several critical thoroughfares.

On Wednesday, 13 January, as the strike entered its fourth day, over ten thousand drivers, students, and workers marched on Plaza Miranda to protest the oil price hike.[50] Both the radicals and the moderates, the National Democratic (NatDems) and the Social Democratic (SocDems) groups, were involved in the jeepney drivers struggle—as well as the plots of 25 January—and the protest brought them together in common cause. Tensions between the two groups were sharp. The radical slogan "Long live the New People's Army!" and chants cursing the police left the well-to-do moderates ill at ease.[51] Manila mayor Antonio Villegas refused to issue a permit for a rally at Plaza Miranda, and the police cordoned off the square. The protesters filled Quezon Boulevard from the foot of the bridge to the front of the church and speakers addressed the crowd.[52] The police attempted to arrest a marshal of the march and struggle broke out. Accompanied by vigilantes, the police attacked the protesters with truncheons; when they did not disperse, the police opened fire on the crowd. Over one hundred were injured and four were killed in the ensuing violence: a pillbox blew up in the face of Arcangel Sioson, age twenty, of Sampaloc; Edgardo Bolano, fifteen, of Quiapo, was shot in the head; Winifredo Enriquez, eighteen, of Quezon City, was shot in the chest; and Roman Flora was likewise killed, although there are no details on his death.[53] A leader of the SDK, Sixto Carlos Jr., fled the police onslaught with members of the SocDem organization Kapulungan ng mga Sandigan ng Pilipinas (Gathering of the Pillars of the Philippines, KASAPI) to the nearby Padre Faura campus of Ateneo de Manila University. Undeterred in their pursuit, the Metrocom raided the Ateneo campus and opened fire on several buildings.[54]

The connections between Fernando Lopez and the protesting workers and students were apparent. From favorable press coverage to funding, it was obvious that the family and business interests of the vice president were tied to the unrest. The Lopezes had used vehicles from their nationwide radio news network, Radyo Patrol, to ferry demonstrators to Quezon Boulevard.[55] Marcos delivered a nationwide address on the evening of 13 January, denouncing his vice president by name and openly threatening to impose martial law. "If violence continues, if there should be massive sabotage, if there should be terrorism, if there is assassination, I will have no other alternative but to utilize the extraordinary powers granted me by our Constitution. These powers are the power to suspend the writ of habeas corpus under which [suspension] any man can be arrested and detained any length of time; and the power to declare any part or the whole of the Philippines under martial law. These powers I do not wish to utilize and it is for this reason I appeal to our people tonight."[56]

Lopez resigned his cabinet position the next morning. Marcos announced a moratorium on oil price hikes while his Price Control Council reviewed the proposed new rates. He secured a temporary end to the strike, defusing some of the social tensions that were building toward 25 January. The barricades were lifted.

The CPP, Partido Komunista ng Pilipinas (PKP), and SocDem groups each regathered their forces. The *Collegian*, under the full editorial control of the front organizations of the CPP, put forward the party's perspective in its 21 January issue.[57]

> First, it must be borne in mind that the Marcos regime could impose martial law *only at the risk of isolating itself completely from the masses.* Crisis after crisis have intensified the anti-Marcos feeling to its boiling point. The growing rift between the President and the Lopez bloc has magnified beyond controllable proportions the former's fading image among his erstwhile supporters. . . .
>
> Any move that the President does at this stage will inevitably lead to his own downfall. . . .
>
> Fascist power is concentrated in the city, and "encircling the city from the countryside" is the only logical maneuver of the people's revolution. . . .
>
> The immediate task in the city is the prolongation of the legal struggle for as long as the political situation allows it. Now that there is a tangible split in the power elite, it is politically desirable to broaden the United Front by creating conditional alliances against the common fascist enemy.[58]

Marcos could not impose martial law without being isolated completely. The immediate task was to facilitate the armed struggle in the countryside by mobilizing the masses in an alliance with the ruling-class opponents of the president. This would provoke fascist repression, which would increase mass resistance, and when Marcos was finally compelled to declare martial law, he would topple from power. The CPP's national democratic forces redoubled their preparations for the twenty-fifth.

The SocDem organizations issued a public appeal to the military to stage a coup against Marcos. On 19 January, KASAPI, Lakas ng Diwang Kayumanggi (Strength of the Brown Spirit, LAKASDIWA), and UP Student Catholic Action (UPSCA) marched from the Loyola Heights campus of Ateneo de Manila through the army headquarters of Camp Aguinaldo to Camp Crame, home of the PC, where they met with Undersecretary of Home Defense Jose Crisol and Brig. Gen. Eduardo Garcia, head of the Constabulary.[59] They distributed an open letter appealing to the military to oust Marcos. The letter was addressed to the formal honorific Ginoong Kawal (Gentleman Soldier). They appealed to "everyone serving in the military" to oppose the "rotten administration of President Marcos which is conspiring with heartless foreigners [*mga walang pusong dayuhan*]." The letter concluded with the injunction "Oust President Marcos!"[60]

Two days later the SocDem organizations abruptly reversed course. Raul Manglapus, a central figure in the coup plotting of the bourgeois opposition from 1970 to 1972, hastily arranged the formation of a new umbrella organization, Prente para sa Demokrasyang Sosyal (Front for Social Democracy, PDS), headed by Edgar Jopson and claiming the allegiance of LAKASDIWA, Christian Social Movement, Federation of Free Workers, KASAPI, and National Union of Students of the Philippines.[61] Through the PDS, Manglapus instructed the SocDem groups not to participate in the 25 January demonstration, which threatened immense bloodshed and would be the final pretext for martial law. He declared that everyone should "defend civil rights . . . by staying at home" and called on the SocDem groups to stage a separate rally on Saturday, 23 January, rather than participate in the Monday demonstration during Marcos's State of the Nation address.[62] It is clear from the ad hoc organization and abrupt reversal that this was a sudden decision arrived at in the final week before the intended denouement. It seems likely that having appealed to wider layers of the military for the ouster of Marcos, Manglapus and company sensed that their gambit would not succeed. A temporary retreat was necessary to prevent Marcos from consolidating dictatorial rule. The SocDem organizations gathered at Agrifina Circle on Saturday as instructed, marched to Malacañang, and quietly dispersed.[63]

The alliance between the SocDem and NatDem forces was fleeting and strained, commencing with the Plaza Miranda massacre and Ateneo raid and falling apart on 23 January. On Saturday morning, as their erstwhile companions rallied in Agrifina Circle, the Movement for a Democratic Philippines (MDP) held a meeting on the Diliman campus of all its affiliated organizations to which they invited representatives from the military and police.[64] A professionally printed four-page leaflet published in both English and Tagalog called on everyone to follow the leadership of the MDP and rally on the twenty-fifth, and decried the SocDems.

> The clerico-fascists have once again exposed their political and ideological bankruptcy by refusing to join in the historic January 25 State of the Nation Rally and advocating instead a cowardly "keep-off-the-streets" campaign. They have openly made a break with the national democratic movement whose vocabulary, methods, and goals they have been all the while passing as their own. They are the special detachments of the reactionary segment of the Church to preserve her vested economic and political power by all devious means, as well as frequent tools for intrigues spread by the Central Intelligence Agency (CIA).[65]

The front organizations of the PKP issued a joint statement. This was not a hastily prepared and mimeographed leaflet, but a neatly laid out and carefully polished statement of the party.[66] It opened by announcing that "our country is in the grip of a political and economic crisis qualitatively different from those that have been brought to bear upon the Filipino masses since the reimposition of US imperialism in 1946. Class contradictions, complexed with the rabid power struggle among the power blocs of the ruling classes, have developed to a degree approximating a revolutionary situation, as an increasingly larger number of people are drawn into the center of the political storm."

The effect of the deteriorating conditions of life for the Filipino masses, the statement argued, was that Marcos could no longer serve as an effective puppet for US imperialism. US imperialism had begun "to take a hard look at Marcos and saw that another puppet had lost its usefulness in the service of imperialist interests. One contradiction after another drove a wedge between the US policy-makers and the Marcos gang. As the CIA mounted its campaign to discredit the puppet Marcos regime, it looked askance in search for new puppets, new forces to be developed to manage the imperialist hegemony." The PKP identified the CIA's preferred new puppet, writing that the agency sought the "possibility of accelerating the succession of Vice President Fernando Lopez to the presidency." The next section of the leaflet was headlined "The CIA vs. Marcos" and stated that

> in the process of discrediting Marcos, the CIA has employed various tactics. It has manipulated the contradictions among the political and

economic groupings in the ruling classes, channeling these conflicts to a concerted anti-Marcos movement. But perhaps the height of CIA cunning expresses itself in redirecting the anti-Establishment, or even revolutionary, sentiments of the youth pointedly at Marcos, complete with anti-imperialist phrase-mongering. The pseudo-revolutionary groups which have thus been developed have served another purpose for imperialism, namely, as a vehicle for the divisive tactic employed to break up the unity of the anti-imperialist forces.

The leaflet continued, "As the CIA's anti-Marcos forces gather strength, Marcos does not stand in passivity. . . . He has announced his readiness to use the extraordinary presidential prerogative of declaring martial law and suspending the writ of habeas corpus. Can President Marcos afford to fight US imperialism openly or will the CIA succeed in assassinating him before he could deliver the first blow?" While the leaflet still referred to Marcos as a "puppet," he was now a discredited puppet who was being pushed by the CIA into fighting US imperialism and was preparing to use martial law as a weapon in this battle. It would take but one additional logical step for the PKP to call for support for military dictatorship as a necessary measure in the fight against imperialism. The PKP did not yet openly articulate this conclusion but declared that two tasks confronted the Filipino masses. The first task was the struggle for "unity, unity, and greater unity of all anti-imperialist forces." If Marcos was taking up the anti-imperialist struggle, regardless of his reasons, this logic would necessitate unity with him. Second, the PKP stated that "we must continuously expose the role of the pseudo-revolutionaries in the imperialist-directed anti-Marcos campaign and progressively isolate them." As the nation approached the knife's edge of 25 January, the PKP stepped forward in defense of Ferdinand Marcos.

The tension of the final weekend hung thick over Manila. Antonio Tagamolila wrote, "Never has an impending mass action brought such anxiety, rumor and tension as the projected rally on Monday. . . . Talks abound to the effect that martial law will be imposed."[67] Another column read, "Everyone—from the sidewalk hawker to the white collar workers—seems to be in suspended animation. No one, it appears, is in a position to gauge what comes next. Understandably, the threat of martial law coming as it does from the Marcos regime, hangs uncomfortably like Damocles' sword over the broad masses of people. . . . Political uncertainty is fever-pitched in Greater Manila."[68]

The Manila Chronicle, Manila Times, and Daily Mirror ran a pooled editorial, an exceptionally rare action. "The Philippine Republic is faced with a crisis threatening its very stability," it declared. The editorial assessed this crisis, and with each line the voice of the propertied classes became increasingly audible.

Peace and order, an infrastructure as fundamentally necessary as road and bridges, are non-existent. Organized hold-ups have become common. Armed robbers break into homes, and do not hesitate to kill. The streets are no longer safe. . . .

What we hear is talk of revolt or revolution, of assassination as a solution, of large-scale arson as a warning of things to come, of violent mass action and organized acts of civil disobedience. . . .

Now, what will the President do? How long will the people's sufferance be? Does he believe the broad masses of the people can stand the siege of his Administration for three more long years?[69]

These were the opposition papers—the *Chronicle* belonged to Lopez—but they did not oppose martial law or defend democracy. The elite opposition, angling for a military coup, sought law and order.

The nation held its breath.

Marcos readied a pretext for martial law. On 23 January, Soliman and the urban guerrillas of the PKP, almost certainly with the assistance of Marcos's military forces, bombed the offices of the Esso and Caltex oil companies, killing one worker and injuring three others in the blast. They left behind leaflets at the bombing signed by the People's Revolutionary Front, but Marcos blamed the NPA.[70] The justification for military rule was now in place.

Looking to stem the possibility of a coup by strengthening the loyalty of his military brass, Marcos sent "helicopters to fetch certain officers and they came to him in Malacañang and he promoted them at three o'clock in the morning! [25 January] . . . For the first time, in the Commission on Appointments, we confirmed 191 full colonels. Walang natira. [No one was left.] They were called in the morning and Imelda shook hands with all of them on the eve of the so-called-revolution-that-never-was."[71] Having quelled any rumblings in the military, Marcos sought to secure the support of the streets as well, and he arranged for sixty busloads of paid demonstrators to cheer his speech outside of Congress.[72]

Marcos's forces, both the military and the paid demonstrators, surrounded the congressional building. He arrived and departed under massive armed escort; soldiers stood at attention, ten ranks deep, to guard his pathway.[73] There would be no errant papier-mâché crocodiles this year. Twelve thousand protesters arrived, only to find themselves displaced from the western entrance and compelled to assemble at the northern fringe on the lip of the Lagusnilad vehicular underpass. A navy helicopter circled ominously overhead.[74] The MDP—now composed of sixty-eight member organizations—staged a Kongreso ng Bayan (People's Congress) and presented two demands: that Marcos resign on the grounds that he was a "fascist" and that "speedy justice" be granted to the four victims of the 13 January violence.[75] It was a light-minded slogan, calling on a "fascist" to "resign."

In the legislative chamber, over the space of two hours, Marcos delivered what would become one of the more famous speeches of his political career: "The Democratic Revolution." Marcos's ghostwriters included Adrian Cristobal, a man closely connected to the PKP, and the speech drew on the party's conceptions to present Marcos's policies and threats of dictatorship as "revolutionary." All was not well in the Philippines. He told the assembled legislators, "I come to speak of a society that is sick, so sick that it must either be cured and cured now or buried in a deluge of reforms."[76]

Marcos singled out the two great ills plaguing society: oligarchs and demagogues. The oligarchs were the *ancien*, those members of the elite who "use the combination of media and economic power to coerce and intimidate the duly elected leaders of the people and to advance their privileges and financial gains, there is no course left but to eradicate them." The oligarchs blocked all meaningful social reform and preyed on economic inequality. In their wake sailed the demagogues. "The illness of our society is aggravated by agitators who would make us so enamored of equality that we would prefer to be equal in slavery rather than unequal in freedom." While he proposed to eradicate his elite enemies—the oligarchs—he did not propose to target the wealthy universally. Social harmony, not equality, was the goal. "We shall move, ladies and gentlemen, to harmonize—and not to alienate—the classes of our society; but this can only be achieved by ending privilege and the exercise of irresponsible power."

Marcos proposed to right the crisis-tossed ship of state by eradicating his elite opponents and crushing demagogues and agitators. Marcos pointed to the "decreasing American presence in Asia"—a reference to the Nixon Doctrine—and called for a "review of our relations with the United States of America to make them serve more fully the mutual interests of the two countries." While recalibrating ties with the United States, he declared that "for the purpose of widening the opportunities of diversified trade, we must now open our doors to other countries, to the Soviet Union and Socialist countries in Eastern Europe which comprise huge untapped markets for Philippine products."

The reorientation of Philippine foreign policy and the suppression of the oligarchs and demagogues would likely require authoritarian measures. Marcos fired a shot across the bow of his coup-plotting rivals. "As for the loyalty of the Army, I have never doubted the fidelity of the Armed Forces to their nation and to constituted authority." He concluded with words whose full and chilling import would be made clear in less than two years: "I ask that our people brace themselves for a democratic revolution that will reach to the roots of our institutions. And if it is the nation's wish that the President himself lead this revolution, then I accept the challenge."

No violence erupted outside. Marcos departed the legislature and the MDP vacated Lagusnilad. Well-to-do residents of Metro Manila turned off their radios and eyed their stockpiled goods with a sense of mingled relief and chagrin. All was not well, but the voice of the president—that calculated and measured Mephistopheles—extended an offer of stability.

January 1971 was a dress rehearsal for September 1972. The bourgeois opposition agitated for a coup d'état, and the CPP brought the energy of social unrest behind their plots. The PKP shored up Marcos's rule, and the president retained the loyalty of the military brass. At the critical moment the elite conspiracy collapsed, leaving the mass unrest without direction and the CPP isolated. Marcos spoke the last word on 25 January.

The Diliman Commune

The KM and SDK greeted the outcome with consternation. Where was the anticipated storm? In an editorial published in the *Collegian* amid the quiet remains of January, Antonio Tagamolila voiced this frustration. "Peace has a way of beclouding the issues the way violence has. . . . The issue to clarify it once more, is that the people are still at war, a war declared and imposed by the ruling classes led by their fascist puppet chieftain."[77]

The thwarted sense of upsurge intensified the earlier involution of radical rhetoric. Since 1967 the ideas of cultural revolution had shaped campus politics: university youth would serve as a vanguard to instigate and inspire a broad shift in popular consciousness that would propel the working masses to armed struggle in the countryside. It was an anarchistic outlook, seeking not to educate but to rouse. Even in periods of upheaval such as that which gripped the Philippines from 1969 to 1972, the class struggle has an uneven and lurching character. The national democratic youth, impetuous and impatient, filled out the temporary lulls and retreats as surrogates for the working class. They erected barricades that workers did not man; they swelled the ranks of unions in workplaces where they were not employed. The attendant excesses of cultural revolution placed a philistine imprint on their politics. When the visiting Bolshoi Ballet staged a free public performance of *Swan Lake* in Luneta Park in May 1969, the KM and SDK turned out to hoot and jeer the event, which they deemed an "unabashed celebration of bourgeois sensuality" and "elitist fantasy."[78] In December 1970, a week after the killing of Francis Sontillano, the radical group Ligang Demokratiko ng

Ateneo (Democratic League of Ateneo, LDA)—a member of the MDP—piled "anti-nationalist" books in the Ateneo quad and burned them.[79] These ideas deepened when the SDK staged its First National Congress on 30–31 January on the UP Diliman campus with the theme "Unfurl the Great Red Banner of the National Democratic Cultural Revolution!"[80]

At the beginning of the year, Dioscoro Umali, the dean of UPLB, announced that he had information that the SDK was intending to take over the Diliman and Los Baños campuses and occupy the administration buildings. The SDK denounced this as a "fairy-tale" and a "fantasy" from his "ever-recurring night-mares."[81] Umali's claim was not at all far-fetched. On 5 October 1970, students at Diliman occupied Quezon Hall, the main administrative campus building, presented a set of fifty-seven demands for campus reforms to University President Salvador Lopez, flew the Philippine flag upside down, and placed an Uncle Sam top hat on the famed campus statue, Oblation.[82] Ericson Baculinao, chair of the UPSC, told President Lopez that if their demands were not granted by the beginning of the next semester, they would stage a "permanent occupation" (*walang tigil na pagsakop*) of campus facilities.[83]

The plans for campus occupation refracted through the recently adopted tactic of barricades. On the morning of 11 January, the KM barricaded the streets in support of the striking drivers. Over three hundred students formed a human barricade on University Avenue, the main entrance to the Diliman campus, to prevent vehicles from entering. Metrocom, working with UP security forces, broke up the barricade.[84] The conflict was more substantial at UPLB, where students set up barricades on the provincial highway blocking all traffic.[85] The PC called out a fire truck to break down the barricades, but the next morning the students rebuilt them. The PC returned and violence broke out; there were explosions, and the police began beating the barricaded students and workers. Forty-seven protesters were arrested and taken to Camp Vicente Lim, six of the wounded were taken to the UPLB infirmary, and many more were taken to various private medical facilities.[86] That night the protesters again rebuilt the barricades, and there was the expectation of greater violence on the morning of the fifteenth, but a further assault did not occur. Marcos declared a one-week moratorium on the oil price hike and the students tore down the barricades.[87]

"Amid the hubbub over the violence at the January 13 rally and the threats of violence at the First Quarter Storm (FQS) anniversary rally, the issue of the oil price hike got somewhat sidelined. Gasoline prices were not rolled back."[88] On the first of February, the jeepney drivers launched a renewed strike and the KM and SDK launched a coordinated campaign of obstructing thoroughfares throughout the country, resurrecting the barricades at UP Diliman and Los Baños and raising new ones in the university belt.[89] The solidarity of the students on the barricades for the striking drivers was genuine, but their coordination was negligible. The barricades arose around campuses, not over the central routes of public transit; the students acted on behalf of the strikers, not with them. The barricades provided the state with a pretext to break up the strike and arrest its leaders. On 2 February, Lupiño Lazaro, general secretary of Pasang Masda, the primary jeepney driver union involved in the strike, was arrested without warrant near the University of Santo Tomas (UST) on the orders of Mayor Villegas on "suspicion of creating disorder in the city."[90] Within three days the strike had largely fizzled, but the students at the barricades continued their protests and campus occupations. It was the political energy of the twenty-fifth of January—temporarily thwarted and now concentrated on the campuses—that fueled what became known as the Diliman Commune.

On 1 February the strike resumed and the barricades went up. According to the account in the *Mirror*, "About 60 per cent of public vehicles, including jeepneys, buses and taxicabs continued operating that Monday in Manila and the rest of the Metropolitan area."[91] The students "barricaded streets, solicited strike funds from drivers of passing vehicles, stoned buses and cars that did not stop when they directed them to turn back." They built a bonfire at the junction of Azcarraga and Lepanto; traffic through the vicinity was shut down and all Divisoria-bound vehicles were routed through Quiapo. "Passengers in the few buses operating pulled up the window shades to avoid stones." The next day bloodied the barricades. Students threw rocks, pillboxes, and Molotov cocktails, and the police fired on the protesters, killing three: Danilo Rabaja, nineteen, of PCC; Renato Abrenica, twenty-four, UST; and Roberto Tolosa, a twelve-year-old sweepstakes vendor, who died of a bullet in the back. Twenty-nine others were injured. The barricades stood in the university belt throughout the first week of February, and by Friday two more students had been killed. Fernando Duque, a nineteen-year-old UST student who was "fleeing from police and drivers battling the students," was hit on the head by a pillbox explosion. A "battle took place on Dapitan street when students resorted to stoning the vehicles, hurting passengers and drivers. The drivers fought back with stones." To the south, barricades sealed the main entrance of the Los Baños campus by 4 February, and additional barricades shut off all traffic to the university on the eighth.[92] The strike largely ended by 6 February. The students maintained and expanded the barricades, but they "permitted [*pinayagan*] the drivers to operate up to the barricades."[93] At least one jeepney driver, after the majority ended the strike, attempted to drive his vehicle through the barricades and the students assaulted him, throwing pillboxes at his vehicle.[94]

Monday, 1 February

While street battles raged on Azcarraga and provincial traffic was shut down in Los Baños, the KM and SDK erected barricades on the UP Diliman campus. The Physical Plant Office had installed loudspeakers in the Arts & Sciences (AS) building on the request of the UPSC, and the council used these speakers to instruct students to boycott their classes and man the barricades, while "groups of activists made rounds of classes being held, interrupting proceedings in the classrooms."[95] The campus at the time was still a public thoroughfare; its wide, acacia-lined streets from Commonwealth to Katipunan were open, and a good deal of traffic passed through on a daily basis. The barricades were initially erected to "stop public utility vehicles from entering campus,"[96] but *Bandilang Pula*, the paper that the students manning the barricades began publishing on 5 February, wrote that all vehicles, public and private, were being stopped and asked to take another route, and anyone who wished to enter campus was instructed to get out and walk.[97] The students manning the barricades were armed with pillboxes and Molotov cocktails and waved a red banner. Young men prevented vehicles from entering the campus, and young women solicited funds from those who had been turned away.[98]

Hearing of the disruption to traffic on campus, President Lopez instructed Col. Oscar Alvarez, chief of campus security forces, to request that faculty vehicles be allowed to pass. Alvarez inspected the barricades and returned to report to Lopez that "everything was in order."[99] By midday, many of the students wished to go to lunch, but there were not sufficient numbers to maintain the obstruction. So, they knocked over a tree and placed it in the road. The security forces returned and attempted to remove the tree that was blocking traffic. "A skirmish developed, during which pillbox bombs and gasoline bombs were thrown at the UP security guards. One guard drew his side-arm and fired warning shots. The students retaliated with bombs resulting in the injury to [*sic*] five security guards. More students arrived and reinforced the barricades. Their number was variously estimated at two to three hundred."[100]

At twelve thirty in the afternoon, UP mathematics professor Inocente Campos arrived in his car. Campos was a known figure on campus, having on several occasions threatened students with failing grades if they participated in demonstrations. Students complained that he had pulled out a gun in the classroom and menaced them with it—on one occasion going so far as to fire three "warning shots."[101] Campos's abusive and violent behavior had been reported by students to the campus administration for over a year, but no measures were taken against him.[102] At the barricade, Campos accelerated and attempted to drive through the barrier. "Upon recognizing the professor, students on University avenue began throwing pillboxes at his car. The left rear tire exploded, forcing the car to a stop."[103] An account written by the barricaders themselves reported that when the students saw Campos, they shouted, "It's Campos . . . throw pb [pillboxes] at him . . . he's a fascist!"[104] Campos emerged from his damaged vehicle wearing a bulletproof vest and a helmet and opened fire on the students with a shotgun. Dean of Students Armando Malay later described the "grim smile" on Campos's face as he shot into the crowd of young people. Campos reloaded his shotgun and fired again, shooting one of the students, Pastor "Sonny" Mesina, in the forehead.

Members of the UP security forces, who had been standing nearby since their attempt to remove the tree barricade, arrested Campos and took him to the Quezon City Police Department (QCPD). The students burned his vehicle.[105] Mesina was taken to the UP infirmary and then transferred to Veterans Memorial Hospital, where he was unconscious for several days and died Thursday evening.[106] Mesina was seventeen years old, a first-year student at the university who had joined the SDK a week earlier, and on the day of his death had opted to march with some of his friends rather than go to a movie with others. While Mesina was in the hospital, Tagamolila wrote an editorial stating, "The hero of the day is undoubtedly Pastor Mesina, a freshman activist, who was seriously wounded by an insane man we had allowed to roam in our midst." Mario Taguiwalo, chair of SDK Diliman, wrote that "Sonny was not an activist nor a revolutionary, but he tried."[107] The Bantayog ng mga Bayani monument would later inscribe that Mesina "earned the honor of being considered UP Diliman's 'first martyr' . . . he gave his life for academic freedom."

Salvador Lopez had been watching the events through binoculars. About fifty students angrily left the barricades and marched to the university administrative building of Quezon Hall, storming Lopez's offices, tearing plaques off the wall, shattering windows, and throwing rocks. One student threw a piece of wood at Lopez, hitting him in the chest.[108] Baculinao confronted Lopez and demanded to know why he sent security forces to the barricade without first informing him. Baculinao blamed Lopez for the actions of Campos, claiming that if the security forces were not present he would not have been emboldened to shoot.[109] Tension mounted, and it seemed increasingly likely that a student might physically assault the university president. Baculinao led the group in a loud rendition of the national anthem and they departed the office.

Lopez later recounted that he was summoned that afternoon to the military headquarters of Camp Aguinaldo for a meeting of a shady cabal known as the Peace and Order Council.[110] Justice Secretary Vicente Abad Santos, the chair of the council; Executive Secretary Alejandro Melchor; Defense Secretary Juan Ponce Enrile; Col. Tomas Karingal, head of the QCPD; and Gen.

Eduardo Garcia, head of the PC, discussed how best to suppress the students at the flagship state university. The council called for the forced entry of the police onto the campus, but Lopez protested, citing a prior agreement with Quezon City mayor Norberto Amoranto to keep the city police off the campus and leave policing to campus security forces.[111] The council stated that the agreement was not legally binding. A decision was reached, over Lopez's dissent, that the police would enter the university and clear out the barricades; it was further decided that if the police could not successfully carry out this action, the constabulary would be deployed. Enrile warned that if the mayor refused to allow the deployment of Karingal's forces on campus, the PC would take over city hall. The council went to Quezon City Hall to inform Amoranto of the measures they were taking. Lopez's account of his meeting with this junta provides a rare insight into just how advanced were the preparations for military rule. If elected leaders or democratic norms interfered even slightly in the suppression of unrest and dissent, the military leadership was poised to strip their powers away.

With the police deployed at every approach to the university, students set up new barricades on the west entrance guarding Commonwealth Avenue. Lopez continued to protest against police on the campus, but Karingal disregarded him; at three in the afternoon, the QCPD broke down the barricades and arrested more than eighteen students.[112]

Tuesday, 2 February

Early Tuesday morning, the students rebuilt their defenses, incorporating the burned-out remains of Campos's car into the barricades.[113] Hastily prepared leaflets circulated, vying for leadership over the growing student rebellion. A group calling itself the "decent elements of the UP Student Council" denounced "student fascism." With a crudity of prose matched to the crudity of its ideas, their leaflet read "UP vilent [sic] activist Sonny Mesina was shot in the head yesterday, when in self-defense Prof. Inocente Campos fired at fascistic students who want to reign supreme in UP."[114] The Samahan ng Makabayan Siyentipiko (Federation of Nationalist Scientists, SMS) appealed to the student body to continue their support for the jeepney strike and opposition to fascism on campus. The final line summoned students "to the barricades!" This was the last mention of the strike during the Diliman Commune; after the morning of 2 February, it was forgotten entirely.[115]

Police and students eyed one another tensely over the barricades. The MPKP broke the standoff, driving a jeep through the makeshift defenses, a sickle-blazoned flag flying from the vehicle.[116] They carried a leaflet that argued that "the massing of hundreds of PC troopers and Quezon City policemen armed with high-powered firearms in the University is a naked act of fascist repression. . . . However, we also see the necessity of criticizing certain elements within the student ranks who committed acts of unwarranted violence against UP personnel and property."[117] They called on students to "sustain the struggle against American oil monopolies" but also to "expose and oppose petty-bourgeois pseudo-revolutionary elements." Behind their jeep came the police, firing tear gas. The students at the barricades retreated before the onslaught. The front organizations of the PKP had played no part in the barricades until now. They stood on the opposite side in this battle, and as they entered Diliman they were accompanied by the military.

At midday Salvador Lopez demanded that QCPD chief Tomas Karingal remove his forces from the university campus. After several skirmishes with the students, the police appeared to withdraw, and at two in the afternoon the students declared that UP was a "liberated area."[118] A group calling itself the AS Rooftop Junta seized the upper floors of Palma Hall—the AS building—and flew a red flag from the roof. They stocked the rooftops of Palma and its symmetrical counterpart across the campus oval, Melchor Hall, with Molotov cocktails and pillboxes to hurl down on the police.[119] A barricade guarded the elegant rectangular facade of Palma Hall.

> But police took the road behind the building, cutting off the students' retreat and many of them were caught.
>
> Students battled the militarists at Vinzons hall where activists held their meetings. Fourteen students were injured when Metrocom soldiers captured the area. . . .
>
> QC Major Elpidio Clemente ordered the attack on two girl dormitories where ten male students fighting the police with bombs sought refuge. In ten minutes the Sampaguita and Camia halls reeked of gas fumes and the cries of 200 occupants resounded. Girls trapped inside broke glass windows and squirmed through broken glass, lacerating or bruising themselves. They were in tears.[120]

The students poured water on the road to dampen the effect of the tear gas, and shouted out to the Metrocom that it was gasoline. The Metrocom began to attack from the grass, where pillbox bombs would not explode on impact.[121] Low-flying helicopters circled over the campus dropping canisters of tear gas.[122] The students began streamlining the production of Molotov cocktails, using Coke bottles taken from the cafeteria, two drums of crude oil, and the curtains from the AS building. The exchanges between the Metrocom and the students continued late into the night. The students set fire to the barricades, and their embers still smoldered at morning light.[123]

Wednesday, 3 February

DZMM, a radio station owned by Eugenio Lopez, sent its Radyo Patrol truck to the campus on Wednesday morning. The truck broadcast an appeal by Dean Malay to the nation to provide food and supplies to the barricaded students.[124] Salvador Lopez called on the entire university community to gather on the wide front steps of Palma Hall, where KM leader Boni Ilagan opened the assembly, recounting to the students the events of the past two days. Lopez addressed the students and told them that the militarization of the campus was at stake in the struggle over the barricades.[125] Mila Aguilar, journalist and instructor in the UP English department, reported that at the end of Lopez's speech "a band of white-helmeted fascists were sighted at the corner of the Engineering building 100 meters away from the Arts and Sciences steps, where the gathering was being held." The students grabbed "chairs, tables, blackboards" and brought them down into the street.[126] The barricade rapidly extended down the length of Palma Hall, and Molotov cocktails and pillboxes were distributed up and down the line. The students occupying the rooftops were given *kwitis* (fireworks) to launch at helicopters flying overhead.

A negotiating team, including the dean of the College of Arts and Sciences, some faculty members, and student representatives, went to meet with the police—the "white-helmeted fascists"—under the command of QCPD Major Clemente, who had been told by Defense Minister Enrile that if he did not remove the barricades the Constabulary would take over the campus.[127] The negotiations stalled and conflict raged throughout the afternoon. The police repeatedly opened fire on the students at Vinzons Hall at the far end of the campus oval. During one of the police assaults, a student, Danilo Delfin, was critically wounded by a gunshot to the lung.[128]

At five in the evening, Aquino, along with Senators Salvador Laurel and Eva Estrada Kalaw, came to the barricades with food for the students.[129] They proclaimed "their concern over the military force under control of President Marcos. They called upon the military units on the edges of campus to withdraw."[130] The senators met with Salvador Lopez in his office to discuss the affair. While they were in conference, Marcos called Lopez and stated that he was ordering the withdrawal of all troops and that students would not be issued a deadline for the removal of the barricades.[131] Marcos, it seems, astutely decided to allow the students to tire of the barricades, which lasted for five more days. Marcos ordered Clemente to have his men stand down as long as Lopez and the university administration took responsibility for the situation. Buses were rerouted down Commonwealth Avenue, skirting the north side of the campus.[132] The barricades stood.

All police and military incursions on the Diliman campus ended on Wednesday night, according to the students' own publications.[133] Lopez issued a press statement that evening calling for the resumption of classes, stating that he was "unalterably opposed" to police entering the campus, but called on students to tear down the barricades so that classes could resume.[134] This was the turning point in the self-isolation of Diliman. Until this moment the students had been defending themselves against the police; now they occupied the university. Defying Lopez, the students tore down the stage lights from the AS theater and installed them on the top of Palma Hall as a searchlight. The campus newspaper, which the students prepared that night, spoke for the first time of the "Diliman Commune."[135] As the campus was renamed, so too were its facilities. The accounts of the renaming are contradictory. According to various sources, Abelardo Hall became Dante Hall, the Faculty Center became Jose Ma. Sison Hall, Palma Hall also became Dante Hall, and Gonzales Hall became Amado Guerrero Hall.[136] The only renaming that I can independently verify is Jose Ma. Sison Hall, because the students scrawled Sison's name in large red letters on the walls.

Thursday, 4 February

Like the slogan "makibaka, huwag matakot," the activity on the barricades expressed an intensity of momentum without conscious orientation. The inertia of political enthusiasm carried the barricades beyond their initial justification. Support for the striking jeepney drivers became the defense of the campus against military incursion, which became the Diliman Commune. The barricades became the end in themselves, disconnected from the social reality they had expressed; content was dissolved in form. Isolated on the rural eastern fringe of Quezon City, the students were left to role-play revolution until they lost interest. Their numbers petered out. By Thursday morning, a majority of the student body had left and the university streets were deserted. Those who remained at Diliman were the members of the UP chapters of KM and SDK who had been joined by members from other universities.[137] They elected a provisional directorate with Baculinao at its head.[138]

The occupying students, now styling themselves as "communards," broke into and seized the DZUP radio station, renaming it Malayang Tinig ng Demokratikong Komunidad ng Diliman (Free Voice of the Democratic Community of Diliman).[139] *Bagong Pilipina* described the "liberation" of the station: "The university radio station which used to play and cater to well-educated bourgeoisie [sic] listeners (who else could afford to appreciate Beethoven's symphony, who else could find time to relax at night and listen to bourgeois' [sic] music?) was liberated and occupied by the progressive sector."[140] The KM and SDK began broadcasting, receiving extraordinary assistance from the Lopez family. DZUP had a broadcast radius of five kilometers, and according to Armando Malay, "nobody (but nobody) had been listening to it before."[141] ABS-CBN, the national broadcast network owned by Lopez, announced that the station had been captured and that it was being broadcast at 1410 AM. The student operators managed to burn out the transmission tubes of the radio station, but these were promptly replaced by an anonymous donor. Lopez arranged the nationwide rebroadcast of the students' programming. The little campus radio station now reached the entire archipelago.[142]

Eugenio Lopez did not merely supply the means of broadcast to the students; he also supplied the content. As part of Marcos's presidential campaign in 1969, he had commissioned the production of a film depicting what were supposed to be his years as a guerrilla during the Second World War. The film, *Ang Mga Maharlika*, starred Hollywood actors Paul Burke as Marcos, and Farley Granger. Dovie Beams, a B movie actress, played Marcos's love interest.[143] Throughout the course of 1969 and most of 1970, Beams and Marcos carried on a love affair and, without Marcos's knowledge, Beams recorded the audio of each of their encounters. Imelda Marcos, stung by the scandal, arranged to have Beams deported as an undesirable alien in November 1970. Beams responded by threatening to release the recordings. Ferdinand Marcos made an offer of $100,000 to Beams for the audiotapes, and the US consul carried out the negotiations on his behalf. Beams refused and called a press conference during which she played a portion of her recording, featuring Marcos singing "Pamulinawen"—an Ilocano folk song—as well as the sounds of their lovemaking. A pair of reporters broke into Beams's hotel room and stole the audiotapes, and the tapes wound up in the possession of the Lopez media conglomerate.[144] Much as they desired to humiliate Marcos, they could not broadcast the hours of recorded bedroom conversation and noises over their radio network. The Diliman Commune provided an ideal opportunity to do so, and they supplied the students with the material. The KM and SDK cheerfully played Beams's audiotapes, punctuated by performances of "The Internationale," and the Lopez radio network carried the broadcast nationwide to the immense humiliation of Marcos. The KM and SDK had the means of addressing the entire nation, yet they made no attempt to present a political perspective. They occupied their time broadcasting explicit sexual recordings in an attempt to embarrass Marcos on behalf of a rival section of the bourgeoisie.

By midafternoon on Thursday, the students had broken the lock off the door of the university press, intending to use it to print a newspaper for the

Commune. Expressing concern that the students might break the press, Dean Malay offered to provide them with several regular press employees—"one or two linotypists, a makeup man, and others you might need."[145] By the next morning the students had published a newspaper for the barricades, which they titled *Bandilang Pula*, a name taken from the Tagalog performance of Brecht's *Mother*, which had been staged by the SDK on the eve of the barricades.[146] In addition to the press and radio, the students took over the chemistry lab and used it for the production of Molotov cocktails and other explosives. On the fourth, Tagamolila, at the head of the *Collegian*, published an editorial on the commune, writing, "The scholar turned street fighter becomes a truly wiser man. The political science professor hurling molotovs gets to know more about revolution than a lifetime of pedagogy. The engineering and science majors, preparing fuseless molotovs and operating radio stations, the medical student braving gunfire to aid his fellow-activist, the coed preparing battle-rations of food, pillboxes, and gasoline bombs, by their social practice realize that their skills are in themselves not enough—that the political education they get by using those skills against fascism is the correct summing up of all previous learning."[147]

Friday, 5 February–Tuesday, 9 February

As the threat of police invasion receded, life on the Diliman campus settled into a routine. Before departing the campus, the police arrested the cafeteria workers, for unspecified reasons, leaving the students responsible for their own food. "The President of the UP Women's Club undertook this task. Foodstuffs came in as donations; they were cooked up at the Kamia Residence Hall and brought in as ration to the various barricades."[148] A resident of Kamia, Babes Almario, wrote a sympathetic account of the Commune in which she claimed that an "agent . . . was caught in the act of sabotaging the molotov cocktails we had neatly laid out as if in preparation for a buffet, and he was dealt the revolutionary punishment of the communards."[149] Almario did not specify what this punishment was. The number of students continued to dwindle. Kamia, which customarily housed two hundred students, housed only twenty by Friday.[150] The production of literature likewise began to taper off. On Friday morning, UPSCA issued a statement that hailed the student victory over the "fascist" invasion of campus but stated that the threat had passed and called for the removal of the barricades.[151] On Sunday, the AS Rooftop Junta issued a manifesto of little substance, announcing, "So long as these MONKEYS keep pestering us, we will never cease to fight."[152] There had been no sign of the police since Wednesday.

Nine days after they erected them, the few students remaining on campus voluntarily tore down the barricades, and life at the university returned to normal. In his history of the campus, Sison wrote that the Diliman Commune ended "only after the administration accepted several significant demands of the students and the Marcos regime accepted the recommendation of the UP president to end the military and police siege, and declare assurances that state security forces should not be deployed against the university."[153] Sison's account is entirely false. The military siege had been lifted days before the commune ended; assurances that state forces would not be used against the campus existed before the commune and the events of early February marked a significant step toward their rescinding; and while the commune did publish a set of eight demands, only two were eventually partially granted and none were granted prior to the lifting of the barricades.[154] According to Jerry Araos, whose SDKM played a key role in the arming of the barricades, "the barricades ended only when a decision from the underground [that is, the CPP] ordered their abandonment."[155] The barricades in the university belt and at UPLB were lifted on the same day in a coordinated manner; they had all received instructions from the CPP leadership.[156]

Major explosions and fires broke out on both the Los Baños and the Diliman campuses as the barricades were being taken down. Whether this was carried out by provocateurs, students opposing the lifting of the barricades, or the "communards" as a final action before their removal is unclear. At three in the morning, thirteen drums of gasoline on the Diliman campus, "set aside by students at the Sampaguita residence hall[,] suddenly caught fire [*biglang lumiyab*]," while several hours earlier, a large explosion took place at the UPLB armory.[157] *Ang Tinig ng Mamamayan*, the publication of the Los Baños barricades, speculated that it might have been set off by the NPA, but a week later SDK UPLB chair Cesar Hicaro said that the idea that "activists" were responsible was "laughable [*katawa-tawa*]." He alleged that Dean Umali, in cahoots with the constabulary, carried out the bombing to frame the activists.[158]

On 12 February, three days after the removal of the barricades, the Malayang Komunidad ng Diliman published its second and final issue of *Bandilang Pula* and explained the fate of the short-lived commune. "The conditions of the barricades which were those of an emergency and of actual resistance, cannot be maintained as a permanent condition. The fascist military—of course for its own purpose—has [*sic*] by and large withdrawn its own force by Thursday. . . . The constant exactions, limited resources, both human and material, and the necessity for consolidation were circumstances that also had to be considered."[159]

Aftermath

The police filed nine charges against Ericson Baculinao: attempted murder, illegal detention, arson, malicious mischief, and five counts of theft. Two taxi drivers filed charges against several students; one claimed that they had detained his vehicle for ten hours, the other that they had set his taxi on fire.[160] Malay, whose account is highly sympathetic to the students, wrote that the students had "commandeered" a motorcycle with a sidecar from a local driver, detached the sidecar, and incorporated it into the barricades, while the motorcycle was used by the student leaders on campus. The owner requested from Malay that the motorcycle and sidecar—his source of livelihood—be returned to him, and Malay instructed him to speak to Baculinao.[161] On 8 February, UP student councilor Ronaldo Reyes wrote a memo enumerating acts of violence and theft that he alleged unnamed outsiders had committed behind the barricades, including the death by stabbing of an Esso security guard who lived on the UP campus.[162]

Returning students found the walls of campus buildings festooned with graffiti. "Revolutionary slogans" covered the facades of Palma and Melchor Halls, red paint caked the Oblation, and the name "Jose Ma. Sison" was scrawled across the walls of the Faculty Center.[163] The AS cooperative store had been looted and classrooms ransacked. Chairs, tables, blackboards, wall clocks, and bulletin boards had all been smashed and burned. It dawned on the leaders of the barricades that the commune had proved unpopular with the majority of the student body. They undertook a two-part response: officially defending the barricades while denouncing "outsiders" for "excesses." The UPSC under Ericson Baculinao passed a resolution declaring that "barricades are fine. . . . The UP Student Council endorse barricades as a form of protest." A second resolution was passed on the same day, commending the "revolutionary heroism" of Mesina, Delfin, and others.[164] The official endorsement of the barricades did little to improve their image. Seizing the opportunity, the MPKP began putting up posters on campus attacking the KM and SDK, some of which read, "Wage revolution against American Imperialism, not against UP."[165] The KM and SDK leadership, in the second and final issue of *Bandilang Pula*, admitted that "because of a lack of organization, many suspicious infiltrators [*maraming mga kahina-hinalang impiltrador*] were able to enter and safely sabotage the property of UP breaking into and robbing many places [*iba't ibang lugal*] on campus during periods of confusion."[166] We know, however, from the students' own accounts that the "communards" themselves broke into many of the buildings on campus and took university property. The literature of 1–9 February is replete with accounts of breaking windows and crawling into labs to get acid and other chemicals for explosives, for example. Rather than defend these actions as necessary for the defense of the barricades, the leadership disavowed them, claiming that they were carried out by infiltrators.[167]

On examination, the barricades, and particularly the affair known as the Diliman Commune, proved to be an unmitigated defeat for the KM and SDK. They lost almost all connection with the striking jeepney drivers and a great deal of support from the student body. And, as a direct result of the barricades, the SM lost the 1971–72 campus elections. The barricades were taken down without a single demand being granted. They provided yet another pretext for Marcos's declaration of martial law. At the end of nine days, at least one student was dead, another was paralyzed, and many were wounded; if we include the university belt barricades, the death toll grows to seven. The barricades were, in the final analysis, neither a spontaneous expression of student anger nor a response to police encroachments. They were a calculated policy, planned in advance and implemented by the leadership of the KM and SDK, with the motive of service to a section of the bourgeoisie that in early 1971 was looking to topple Marcos.[168]

In September 1971, less than a month after Marcos's suspension of the writ of habeas corpus, Gintong Silahis staged a drama, *Barikada*, at UP Theater. *Barikada* described itself as a play freely based on the events of 1–9 February. The program for the event informs us that the makeup for the performers was done by Beautifont, high-fashion cosmetics, "distinctively formulated for the Filipina"; the next page of the program was headlined "Destroy the state machinery of the ruling classes."[169] There was an anarchistic tone throughout the performance, calling for the destruction of the old culture and the smashing of the state, but never for the seizing of state power. Behn Cervantes staged the production, which was modeled on the style of Peking Opera, with choreography and songs titled "Paper Tiger" and "The People Are What Matter." It concluded with fifty red flags waved throughout the auditorium and the singing of "The Internationale." The event was sponsored by La Pacita Biscuits, and repeat performances were held 8–9 October.[170] Fernando Lopez, vice president of the Philippines, arranged for the play to be staged at his family's prestigious Meralco Theater.[171]

Inocente Campos was acquitted on all charges. In September 1972, a judge ruled that Campos "acted upon an impulse of an uncontrollable fear of an equal or greater injury."[172] Campos shot Mesina, the judge argued, because he feared "a greater injury" than the death that he dealt to an unarmed seventeen-year-old. A week later, Marcos declared martial law.

Fragmentation of Labor

The plots of 25 January, the barricades, and the commune were not the only ultraleft measures taken by the CPP at the beginning of 1971. The party attempted, by organizational maneuver without any political preparation, to launch a general strike. This culminated in a reckless attempt to wrest control of two large union umbrella organizations from their existing leadership by means of subterfuge.

One of the difficulties in writing this book was the sparsity of detail available on the labor struggles in which the CPP and PKP were involved in the early 1970s. While they produced copious printed material for protests and rallies, there is practically no residue of their involvement in strikes or in the working class more generally. The dearth of material on the role of the CPP and PKP and their front organizations in these labor struggles is more than an accident of the archive. It reflects a fundamental fact about the class orientation of both Stalinist parties: these were not parties of the working class. Their membership was not drawn from its ranks and their orientation was elsewhere. This is not to say that the CPP and PKP did not intervene in labor struggles; they did, although not consistently. When they did, it was to orient the workers' struggles to interests alien, and often antithetical, to those of the workers themselves. The CPP and PKP produced very little documentation of these betrayals. They did not produce material explaining capitalism to the working class on the basis of the workers' concrete experiences; they did not document the record of workers strikes or explore the lessons to be gained from these struggles.

Using the thin layer of material available, it is possible nonetheless to reconstruct, at least in outline form, the role of the CPP and its front organizations in the labor struggles of the period. The interventions of the CPP with the working class had a particular character. Young people in the KM and SDK would be sent to existing picket lines, where they would stage "revolutionary dramas"—street theater productions of a moralistic and motivational character. The youths would sing "revolutionary songs" and conduct "criticism-self criticism" sessions among the workers. These interventions felt like a church outreach, inviting the workers to Sunday School. The other aspect of the KM and SDK interventions with the workers' picket lines was their deliberate escalation of tensions with the police, as they came armed with pillboxes and Molotov cocktails and, at times, actively sought to provoke violence. State repression was educative, the CPP claimed, and would propel the workers to armed struggle, for this was the goal of the CPP's interventions with the working class: directing workers to leave the city and take up arms in the countryside.

In early 1971, the Central Committee wrote the CPP's *Guide to Building Organs of Political Power*. In this document the CPP stated that the task of the party in carrying out work among the working class was threefold: first, to secretly control the actions of the union (*pamunuan ng lihim ang kilos ng unyon*); second, to send to the countryside those workers who were ready to or needed to join the NPA (*papuntahin sa kanayunan ang mga manggagawang handa or kinakailangan sumama sa Bagong Hukbong Bayan*); and third, to spread the overall mass movement of workers in alliance with the movement of other democratic classes.[173] This was a codification of the work in which the party was already engaged, and the threefold orientation of the party outlined in the 1971 *Guide* had been the basis of the CPP's activities in the working class from the founding of the party. Sison, in October 1970, described this work "of building organs of political power" as already underway.[174]

The impact of this policy was an immense boon to the bourgeoisie. The most politically advanced and militant workers were taken out of the workforce and sent to the hills. The CPP functioned as a social safety valve, overseeing a constant venting of steam from the system of capitalist exploitation that it diffused across the countryside. Those workers who remained in the factories were often directed to ally with their exploiters, the capitalists, who were, after all, one of the "other democratic classes." Strikes that came under the leadership of the CPP were thus treated as means of ensuring crackdowns by the state to hasten the deployment of advanced workers to the countryside. By the rationale of the Maoists, a defeat on the picket line would be far more politically effective in propelling the workers toward armed struggle than a victory, and the CPP thus exercised no care or caution for the well-being of the striking workers. Of all the strikes in which the KM and SDK were involved and that I have been able to document, not a single one ended with the striking workers returning to work, let alone securing even a minor victory. The workers were uniformly arrested, thrown out of work, or killed. The only time the workers managed to retain their jobs was when they voted the KM-SDK union out of their workplace.

The patient political education of the working class, which Lenin detailed in his work *What Is to Be Done?*, involves the systematic and persistent explanation to workers of their objective conditions and of the tasks that history has posed before them. No police truncheon beating can fill the need for careful education in the political program of the party. Revolutionary leadership does not consist of provoking violence and relying on the state to "educate" workers with its blows.

The CPP was thus, explicitly and programmatically, not engaged in a struggle against the capitalist class. When workers organized themselves and courageously mounted the picket lines, they were acting in direct opposition to the capitalist owners. The role of the CPP was to dispel this confrontation, and it fulfilled this role quite effectively. The most articulate workers and the fiercest fighters were sent to the countryside; those who remained were eventually beaten back into submission or removed from the job.

The CPP's interventions among the working class served the interests of a section of the bourgeoisie in another way as well. The CPP would not call strikes at companies belonging to its bourgeois allies, as these national capitalists were part of the progressive national united front and were, the CPP told the workers, their allies. The CPP would instruct workers in these companies not to strike but to focus their energy on the larger political struggle against imperialism, feudalism, and bureaucrat capitalism. The CPP promoted strikes at companies owned by Chinese businessmen or, occasionally, Americans—the business rivals of their capitalist allies. Every strike during this period that I have been able to trace, and in which the CPP intervened, occurred in a business the CPP deemed to have foreign ownership. The overwhelming majority were owned by Chinese Filipinos.

The CPP's chief point of contact with the labor movement was Central Committee member Carlos del Rosario.[175] Known as Charlie, del Rosario was born in 1945 to a comfortably well-off merchant family. His parents owned a dry goods store on Blumentritt Street, and his father, Feliciano del Rosario, was the vice president of the Vendors Association.[176] Carlos del Rosario was a founding member of the KM, and as early as March 1965 he was speaking at rallies.[177] He became head of the KM at Lyceum and then general secretary of the entire organization, replacing Prospero Palma.[178] In 1970, del Rosario became a member of the MDP secretariat.[179] He met Frances de Lima, the sister of Juliet de Lima, in Joma and Juliet's home. Carlos and Frances married in October 1970, and del Rosario became Joma's brother-in-law. Del Rosario taught in the political science department at PCC.[180]

Del Rosario was on the board of the Socialist Party of the Philippines (SPP) and was closely connected to the National Association of Trade Unions (NATU), the union federation run by labor lawyer Ignacio Lacsina. Lacsina, along with Sison, had been a member of the Executive Committee of the PKP in the early 1960s and had been instrumental in the party's support for then president Diosdado Macapagal.[181] When the party split in 1967, Lacsina found himself somewhere in between the PKP leadership and the forces who would go on to found the CPP, a labor union operator who was no longer a member of the leadership of a Communist party. He was far closer, however, to Sison than to the PKP. Working closely with Lacsina was Rodolfo del Rosario, his right-hand man since at least the early 1960s.[182] The relationship between the

CPP and Lacsina became increasingly tense between 1969 and 1971. Lacsina and NATU backed Marcos in the 1969 election, a fact the CPP chose to ignore. Relations with Lacsina collapsed in the beginning of 1971 around the 25 January machinations of the bourgeois opposition when Lacsina thwarted the party's attempt to launch a general strike through NATU.

Sison issued a statement in *Ang Bayan* whose headline, "Cast Away the Labor Aristocrats," was the slogan of the intrigues of February. He called for the formation of "revolutionary trade unions."[183] This appeal was not in itself misguided. The union heads were functioning as the agents of capitalism, stifling and selling out the struggles of the working class. Sison, however, did not mobilize the working class to fight for their political and organizational independence. He orchestrated an attempt to secure by subterfuge the party's slipping bureaucratic hold over layers of workers that it sought to mobilize in service to the political interests of a faction of the capitalist class. The party treated the workers not as the members composing the union, to whom an appeal should be issued, but as the resources that the union contained, to be wrested from the hands of rivals.

The impact of the CPP's policy on the working class was most clearly demonstrated at the US Tobacco Corporation (USTC), which was in the midst of a long-standing labor dispute. For half a decade, workers at the USTC had been struggling to break free of the Philippine Transportation and General Workers Organization (PTGWO) union, headed by Roberto Oca, which was functioning as a labor contractor on behalf of USTC management. They organized an independent union, the US Tobacco Corporation Labor Union (USTCLU), and affiliated with the PKP-aligned Federacion Obrera de la Industria Tabaquera de Filipinas (FOITAF). The legal process to certify the new union was protracted, and USTC management did everything possible to obstruct it in court. The PKP saw the USTCLU as valuable political capital, and FOITAF attempted to cut a secret deal with USTC management to secure the union's certification. When the USTCLU workers caught wind of the betrayal, they broke with FOITAF and affiliated with Lacsina's NATU.[184] In early 1970, the USTCLU went on strike to contest the endless certification process and demand that workers be allowed to vote for their union representation.

An earlier election, contested by management before the Court of Industrial Relations, had secured six hundred votes for the PTGWO and over two thousand for the USTCLU.[185] The striking workers demanded that either these results be upheld or a new vote be staged. With the assistance of management and the police, the PTGWO engaged in "bloody and repeated picket-busting."[186] Peter Mutuc, a vice president of the USTCLU and a member of the CPP, described the strike: "It has been characterized by the most brutal and undiscriminating violence against our workers and student activists by scabs and hired goons, protected and often actively aided by the Manila police, Metrocom, and even the PC. Management has always turned down our basic demands, and instead has systematically sought to maul, arrest, or kill our union leaders."[187] The striking workers scheduled a union certification vote in the first week of July, but management secured an injunction from the Court of Industrial Relations canceling the election. The workers voted, in defiance of the court, but the police seized their ballot boxes.[188] The delayed certification election would not be held until February 1971, when its outcome would be decided by the machinations of the CPP.

There is no evidence that the CPP issued any political appeal to the working class to stage a general strike in the final weeks of January. They did, however, attempt to orchestrate such a strike through the apparatus of the various union umbrella groups over which they had influence—in particular, NATU, SPP, and the jeepney driver unions. The barricades, the protests, and the machinations toward a military coup were meant to coincide with an explosive general strike on 25 January. But this failed, because none of the organizations that the party sought to sway followed its lead.[189] The CPP redoubled its efforts, attempting to launch a general strike in conjunction with the barricades of 2–9 February and the Diliman Commune.[190] Lacsina, determined to prevent this, kicked out "two KM members from the SPP executive board" in the final week of January.[191]

Desperate at losing its means of launching the intended strike, the KM attempted to seize control of NATU's unions by subterfuge. They put up posters throughout Manila that read "Ibagsak si [Down with] Lacsina—PC informer" and "Lacsina—huwad na labor leader [phony labor leader]."[192] With the support of twenty-one people in the upper ranks of the USTCLU, the KM broke the union's ties with NATU without informing or involving the three thousand members of the union.[193] In the same fashion, with a breathtaking simultaneity, the KM and SDK gained control of other NATU unions by bureaucratic intrigue. They succeeded in securing a hold over the Northern Motors Free Workers Union, a significant force with 775 members, but the majority of the unions they wrested from Lacsina represented handfuls of workers in small, Chinese Filipino–owned factories and stores in Caloocan and Malabon.[194]

The outcome was catastrophic. The membership of the USTCLU was deeply confused by the machinations of the KM, and many called for a general meeting in order to learn the reason for the break, which the union leadership, now held by the KM-SDK, refused to convene.[195] Less than two weeks later, on 15 February, the long delayed certification vote was held. The KM-SDK called on workers to vote for the USTCLU, now broken from NATU. Voltaire Garcia, attorney for the KM-SDK, signed the minutes of the election, certifying that there had been no cheating. Oca's PTGWO won by a large majority, roundly defeating the USTCLU. The confused and disillusioned workers, straining to find independence, were thrust back into the clutches of management by the conspiratorial plots of the CPP. The CPP hailed the results as confirmation of its analysis. The victory of the PTGWO clearly revealed, SDK leader Benito Tiamzon claimed, "the hopelessness of legal struggle. Even though one life had already been lost [*isang buhay na ang binuwis*] in ten months of strike here, the union of the conscious workers at USTC did not win."[196]

Jess Rivera, vice president of NATU, denounced the KM, stating,

What is the benefit for workers of being made "sacrificial lambs" and after [the KM] makes a brief flare (throwing pill boxes while shouting "Revolution" and "Long live Mao Zedong") and disappears, the striking workers are abruptly left to be picked up by the police and PC? Has KM secured any union victory? Why is the result always defeat for the workers while these youths are "heroes?" Why do all strikes to which they give "help" end in injunctions and are made illegal? . . .

Who now emerges as the destroyer of the union? Why are these purveyors of black propaganda themselves the servants of capital? Is it because they are scabs?[197]

The plot to seize control of the labor movement extended beyond the attempt to wrest organizations from NATU.[198] In a synchronized, conspiratorial fashion the KM-SDK moved to take over the jeepney driver unions as well, but this attempt also failed. At the beginning of February, Lupiño Lazaro, head of the leading jeepney driver union, Pasang Masda, had been arrested without warrant as a result of the barricades erected by the KM and SDK, and his arrest had contributed to the failure of the jeepney driver strike. When they tore down the barricades of the university belt, Los Baños, and Diliman on the tenth, the KM and SDK issued a call for a "third general strike" on the twenty-fifth. Lazaro claimed that the KM was attempting to instigate a "violent revolution. Because of that, Lazaro said, he would advise against the resumption of the jeepney strike on February 25."[199] The KM responded, denouncing Lazaro's stand on the strike as "bakla" ("homosexual"; the KM used the word here as a vulgar synonym for "weak").[200]

Rather than issue an appeal to the drivers, the CPP, as it had done with NATU, attempted to take over their union by organizational maneuver. The *Philippines Free Press* reported that the KM tried to seize power in Pasang Masda, "but Lazaro, a lawyer, was not to be caught napping."[201] Lazaro and Glicerio Gervero, head of Malayang Pagkakaisa ng mga Samahan ng Tsuper (Free Unity of Driver Federations, MAPAGSAT), expelled the KM and SDK from the alliance of jeepney driver unions.[202] The KM announced that it would hold a People's Congress on 18 February to launch a jeepney drivers strike on 25 February, but as a result of the expulsion, the KM was compelled to call off the strike and delay the congress until the twenty-sixth.[203]

The CPP was left holding scraps of the labor movement. The party's machinations lost it both the trust of significant layers of the working class and access to their organizations. In the final week of February, the CPP staged two workers gatherings to consolidate its supposed gains. On 26 February, the KM led the founding of a labor federation, Katipunan ng mga Samahan ng mga Manggagawa (Federation of Workers Associations, KASAMA), bringing together seven unions under its umbrella.[204] Two days later, a group of jeepney drivers founded a new umbrella organization, Pambasang Samahan ng Makabayang Tsuper (National Federation of Nationalist Drivers, PSMT), and Leto Villar, former spokesperson of Pasang Masda, was made spokesperson.[205] PSMT was not an independent organization, and it had few drivers in its ranks. The headquarters of the newly founded union of jeepney drivers was in Vinzons Hall on the Diliman campus, where it shared office space with the KM, SDK, and other UP student organizations.[206]

Carlos del Rosario, who acted as the connection between the CPP and Lacsina, was murdered less than a month later. While Lacsina had removed several KM members from the SPP executive board, he had been unable to remove del Rosario.[207] Lacsina staged a press conference on 29 January in which he attacked the "fanatical fringe" of the national democratic mass movement and "the cult of Mao."[208] He disclosed to the press that del Rosario was "representing Jose Maria Sison," thus publicly associating him with the underground Communist Party.[209] Carlos del Rosario was last seen at ten at night on 19 March. On the evening he disappeared, del Rosario was tacking up posters for the National Congress of the MDP in the heart of the university belt when a fraternity rumble broke out, injuring a number of PCC students. Del Rosario was expected in Cubao for a preparatory meeting of the National Congress of the MDP at eleven, but he never arrived.[210] The KM and SDK published statements claiming that the military had murdered del Rosario after his association with the CPP had been exposed by Lacsina.[211] Sison added that Lacsina had instructed his right-hand man, Rodolfo del Rosario, to threaten Carlos del Rosario with murder.[212] Little more was said. Within a year of Carlos del Rosario's disappearance, Rodolfo del Rosario reunited with the CPP and KM. They had denounced him as corrupt, blamed him for sabotaging the workers' movement, and staged protests against him in 1971. In 1972, the KM wrote that "Kasamang [Comrade] Rody, a member of the KM consultative council who was active in the nationalist labor movement, is noted for his devotion to the organization and politicization of the working class in the mass movement."[213] This man who a year earlier had been denounced as a traitor and implicated in the murder of Carlos del Rosario was again embraced as a comrade. No explanation was given to the working class, nor was any accounting made for who had been at fault or what political line had been altered, whether that of the party or that of Rodolfo del Rosario. The CPP buried the past and with it Carlos del Rosario.

Within three months of its founding, over twenty unions had joined KASAMA. Most represented workers in small retail and manufacturing businesses run by Filipinos of Chinese descent in Caloocan, Navotas, and Malabon on the crowded northwestern fringes of Greater Manila.[214] The CPP sought to consolidate its hold over these workers by supplanting class struggle with a racist nationalism, identifying the workers' enemies not as capitalists but as "intsik," a common slur for Chinese.[215] The literature associated with the party from 1971 and 1972 repeatedly singled out "the Intsik" as responsible for the economic plight of workers.

The attacks began immediately. In March, *The Partisan* published an article titled "The Chinese Kumintang in the Philippines and US Imperialism," denouncing "big-time Chinese middle-men, the comprador bureaucrats who lie behind the curtain of anonymity, who are ultimately responsible for the vise-like grip of aliens over our national economy. . . . The Chinese control of our internal economy extends beyond mere middlemanship into banking, insurance, industry and export. . . . The time has come for the middleman to be evaluated and judged by the people."[216]

These ideas were extensively developed in July by the SDK. In a historical analysis of the category "comprador bourgeoisie," the SDK clearly established that it was referring to Chinese businessmen and claimed that the cause of rising prices was the Chinese monopoly on trade, which allowed them to dictate prices.[217] The SDK dredged up every imaginable anti-Chinese stereotype. "So that their profit can flow and so that their big bellies can continue to swell [*tuluyang mabundat ang kanilang malalaking tiyan*], the comprador bourgeoisie employ tactics that are beyond cruel. Their only desire is to raise the price of all commodities so most of the time they keep them hidden in their warehouses."[218] The Guomindang Chinese, the SDK argued, do not merely strangle the Filipino people with rising prices; they also push "evil vices" (*masasamang bisyo*), "examples include opium, their running of brothels, and peddling of pornography [*nataguriang* bedtime stories] in the streets, not only to poison the Filipino masses but also to grow their profits even more."[219] The article noted that Filipinos should distinguish between Chinese workers in the Philippines and Chinese businessmen, but the tenor of the piece was a filthy racist diatribe, a salvo in an ongoing campaign of national chauvinism.

The anti-Chinese campaign served the interests of a section of the Filipino bourgeoisie that was looking to get its hands on businesses owned by Chinese Filipinos. In November 1971 one of the eleven demands put forward by the MDP was a call to "Filipinize the wholesale trade dominated by the Guomindang Chinese"—that is to say, to transfer ownership to another section of capitalists on the basis of their race.[220]

A year later, at the end of February 1972, KASAMA held its First National Congress. A forty-page document distributed at the congress gave instructions for building unions, getting workers to break from "yellow" unions, and leading strikes. KASAMA stressed to its members that it was important for actual *workers* to be involved in the strikes. It wrote that there were many occasions when "the only people picketing are youths and students. Often *we* are the only ones producing manifestos, placards, slogans, letters, etc. Workers should play this role in accordance with *our* leadership of their movement. [Ang mga manggagawa ang dapat kumatawan dito ayon sa pamamanutbay natin sa kanilang kilusan.]"[221] The pronouns are noteworthy. The CPP's labor union federation, KASAMA, did not identify itself with workers but rather with the students and youth who were "leading" the workers and picketing on their behalf, and it stressed to the students that at least some workers needed to be part of the strike. The document inadvertently but aptly encapsulated the class basis of the CPP's involvement in the working class. Their union federation, the product of a series of provocations and secretive machinations, was not composed of workers at all but of activists.

In February 1971, the party attempted to seize control of the labor movement through conspiracies and backroom plots. As the ruling class's preparations for dictatorship reached a fever pitch, the CPP fragmented the working-class movement without any explanation. They were not interested in educating the working class but in controlling it. On a programmatic and fundamental basis, the party opposed the political independence of the working class and sought either to subordinate workers to a section of the capitalists or, failing that, to send them to the hills to take up the armed struggle for national democracy.

May Day Massacre

Workers and youths, led by the KM, SDK, MDP, and the newly founded KASAMA, marched on 1 May from the España rotunda down the length of España, across the Quezon Bridge, and gathered on P. Burgos in front of the congressional building, waving their flags and banners. Military helicopters ominously followed them as they marched. Food and drink vendors passed through the crowd peddling their wares to the thirsty demonstrators. Behind them stretched the grassy expanse of the Muni Golf Links skirting the rough southern bulwarks of Intramuros.

At five in the afternoon, Jimmy Lacsamana, president of a union currently on strike, addressed the crowd. A KM contingent from Tondo arrived, and someone attempted to lower the Philippine flag and reverse it, so that the red field was uppermost. A member of the armed forces in civilian clothing struck the person touching the flag and threatened to kill him if he took the flag down. USTCLU vice president Peter Mutuc, who was the emcee of the event, took the microphone and attempted to calm the crowd. According to the journalist and screenwriter Ricky Lee, who was present at the event, some of the demonstrators began throwing pillboxes at the troops in front of the congressional building.[222]

It was at this point that the protest became a massacre. Members of the Fifty-Fifth Company of the PC, fresh from an "anti-Huk" campaign of counterinsurgency warfare in the countryside, had been incorporated into the Metrocom the day before. They were deployed as snipers with machine guns on the roof of the legislature and trained their sights on the crowd. Snipers were positioned on roofs in Intramuros as well, prepared for those who would flee. Uniformed and plainclothes police officers, armed with guns and truncheons, surrounded the demonstrators.[223]

The rooftop snipers began to spray the crowd with machine-gun fire. Panic gripped four thousand demonstrators and they scattered in all directions. They screamed, frantically and ineffectually attempting to hide behind lampposts or within a scrawny thicket of *gumamela*. They fell over each other in their panic. Ricky Lee recounts toppling over a *kariton* (cart) laden with steaming corn. The military helicopter circling overhead began to drop tear gas canisters on the scattering protesters.[224] *Tsinelas* (rubber slippers) and books were cast about on the pavement. The machine-gun fire continued unabated.

Ninotchka Rosca wrote, "A deadly rain drops from the impassive facade of Congress, from above the granite heads of the late nationalist leaders Sergio Osmeña and Manuel L. Quezon."[225] Lee captured the horror of this moment: "The wails and pleas and crying mingle with the whizz of bullets and the ratatat of armalites." A *palamig* (iced desserts) vendor reported that the bullets skipped off the pavement and the grass like a swarm of "tipaklong" or grasshoppers.[226]

Three demonstrators were killed in the rally. Richard Escarta, known to his friends as Dick, was a secretarial student at Rodriguez Vocational School in Sta. Mesa Heights. Dick had recently married, and he and his wife, Amerita, had a four-month-old child. The day before the May Day rally, she had asked Dick if they could get a photograph taken of their child so they would have something to send home to the province. He told her that they could not afford it. Dick ran from the machine-gun fire and hid, only to find that he had lost his tsinelas. Since he could not afford to lose them, he bent over and raced back to P. Burgos, where he managed to recover his footwear. When he ran back to the golf course, however, he was shot in the thigh. "I'm hit," he called out. Then a second bullet hit him, this time in the head, shattering his skull. He fell forward, his face buried in the grass, and was still.[227]

Liza Balando had moved to Manila from Samar three years earlier when she was nineteen years old. She had initially found work as a domestic helper but eventually landed a job in Caloocan at Rossini's Knitwear, where she worked as a cap seamer making three pesos a day. She was a proud member of the union in her workplace and by everyone's account was of a vibrantly cheerful disposition. She made it as far as the grass before she was shot dead. It would be more than a week before her family in Samar learned what had happened to her.[228]

Ferdinand Oaing was only sixteen years old. He was a sidewalk vendor and had been radicalized while selling snacks and cigarettes at the fringes of rallies. He became an active member of the Quiapo branch of the KM. Ferdie ran beside his fifteen-year-old friend, Dante Cocquia, and they managed to make it to a dip in the grass where they took shelter. Seeing the bodies of the wounded writhing on the pavement, Ferdie ran back to attempt to pull one to safety. A bullet caught him in the forehead. Dante ran to his side, and with his last breath Ferdie asked his friend to take the few items in his pockets so that the Metrocom would not get their hands on his only possessions. Dante dragged Ferdie's body across the pavement toward safety, but as they got out of the range of gunfire and approached an ambulance, a Metrocom officer stepped up and cursed Dante, chasing him away. Ferdie's corpse was left on the pavement.[229]

Still the machine guns fired. A quarter of an hour had passed, and bullets continued to chip away at the pavement. Red Cross workers and emergency rescue personnel arrived in ambulances and attempted to crawl to the bodies of the wounded, but the snipers' guns spit fire and they retreated.[230]

Plainclothes officers waited in Luneta and swung their truncheons, beating those who ran south for safety. Guns fired from rooftops in Intramuros. Rosca reported, "Roberto Valenzuela is shot in the face—gun emplacements seem to be elsewhere, in the surrounding buildings, other than Congress itself—and falls writhing to the ground."[231]

Twenty minutes after the massacre started, the guns fell silent. In addition to the three demonstrators killed, eighteen were wounded and hospitalized.

The number of wounded is always far higher than that reported in the papers, as only those hospitalized are mentioned. The injured and the bleeding workers could ill afford a trip to the hospital and many bandaged themselves. Only the severely injured went to the hospital. The police arrested over a score of demonstrators, and many of those arrested reported that they were beaten in the precinct and in their cells.[232]

The MDP staged a press conference on 2 May and denounced the massacre. Spokesperson Chito Sta. Romana, standing beside Ericson Baculinao, announced that they would stage an indignation rally on 8 May. Dick Escarta's father told the press that he had no idea how he would pay for his son's funeral. Then, admitting that he had never been a political person, he announced, "I'm going to join the SDK, I will continue the work left behind by my son, even if I need to lead."[233]

Mudslinging and Obloquy

From the stifling days of early April to the sodden remains of late July, the CPP and PKP waged a pitched battle in the glossy pages of mainstream magazines and the manila newsprint of their own broadsheets and leaflets. Prior political struggles were but pale foreshadowings of this immense explosion of anger. Denunciations and imprecations commingled; character assassination was followed by assassination of a more literal sort. The PKP's orientation to Marcos painfully constrained its response to social tensions. The stifled political energy of its cadre massed as fury behind a dam of self-restraint until geopolitics unleashed it. Mao sought rapprochement with Nixon, and on 10 April the US table tennis team traveled to Beijing; Henry Kissinger's secret visit followed in July. The opening of ping-pong diplomacy in April pried away the last stones of political temperance, and the party's ill-concealed rage flooded the pages of the press.

The Jacinto family's launching of a national news weekly, the *Asia Philippines Leader*, with the intent of defending their interests in the steel industry against Marcos, provided a timely outlet for the public dispute between the CPP and the PKP. Looking to strengthen its anti-Marcos position, the *Leader* opened its pages to articles by the various front organizations of the rival parties. Although it published the statements of both sides, the Jacintos' opposition to Marcos meant that the paper's editorial predilection strongly inclined to the CPP. By remarkable coincidence, the news weekly published its first issue on 9 April, the day before the US table tennis team arrived in Beijing. It was thus in this very public forum that the accumulated vitriol of the rival Communist parties finally exploded into the open, and by the second issue, on 16 April, they were hysterically denouncing each other in the pages of the *Leader*.

Ninotchka Rosca, a staff writer for the *Leader*, fired the opening shot with an article titled "View from the Left: Word War I."[234] In a flagrant conflict of interest, Rosca failed to mention that she was a founding member of the SDK. Unsurprisingly, the MPKP and Bertrand Russell Peace Foundation (BRPF) came out quite poorly in her version of events, while the SDK was given the final word on the matter. Rosca followed this piece with an article in the next week's issue titled "Word War II: Lava versus Guerrero," which rooted the acrimony between the various organizations in the dispute between rival Communist parties, and this dispute in turn in the Sino-Soviet split.[235] Every subsequent issue carried a denunciation from the rival political groups. A sampling will suffice. On 30 April, Lacsina announced that the KM worked for the CIA; the KM retorted that Lacsina was allied with the "Soviet social-imperialists."[236] Teodosio Lansang, long tied to the PKP, denounced Sison as a "Trotskyite" on 14 May; a week later, the radical organization Samahang Molabe announced that it had expelled Lansang for his "counter-revolutionary attitude."[237]

The dispute turned to murder. On 11 June, Trinidad Calma, former secretary of Samahang Molabe, wrote an article for the *Leader* that quoted an MDP memo, authored by Liwayway Reyes, that had been circulating on college campuses. The memo identified every member of the Central Committee of the PKP—many of whom were closely tied to the Marcos administration, some in salaried government positions—and Calma named each of them.[238] The memo claimed that UP professor and PKP Central Committee member Francisco Nemenzo Jr. told Reyes that the PKP expected that "a few killings would silence the 'Sison group' and would teach Lacsina and the others to toe the line."[239]

Violent suppression was intrinsic to the DNA of the PKP and the CPP. The political program of Stalinism was predicated on securing hold over a constituency, the working class, whose objective interests it did not articulate, in order to subordinate it to a hostile class, capitalists, and by these means extract concessions on behalf of a privileged bureaucratic caste. This control over the working class could not be achieved by honest discussion; the political ends of Stalinism required deception and subterfuge. When the manhandling of the truth would not suffice, the well-worn alternative was suppression—not reason but an icepick. As the histrionics continued, and with their machinations increasingly exposed, both sides began to reach for their guns. In late May—when Liwayway Reyes published her memo identifying the entire Central Committee of the PKP and declaring that they were plotting "a few killings" to "silence" the CPP—Francisco Sison, the brother of Joma, was murdered.

The BRPF had published a special issue of *Struggle* in January 1971 in which it announced that Sison's older brother, Francisco, worked for the Marcos administration as the assistant deputy director of the Presidential Economic Staff.[240] Having been warned that his life might be in danger, Francisco Sison applied for and was granted a fellowship to study in Germany for two years.[241] In the early morning of 24 May, he was en route to Goethe-Haus "to take a proficiency examination in German" when both he and his driver, Elpidio Morales, "properly armed . . . with weapons issued by virtue of [his government] position," disappeared.[242] Their bodies were never found.[243] The disappearance was not immediately reported. Aware of the danger facing his brother, whom he affectionately knew as Paquito, Joma Sison wrote a letter to the *Leader* that was published on 11 June. Sison denounced the BRPF as "cheap informers of the enemy" and attempted to shield his brother from its charges.[244] The next day, the *Manila Times* announced the disappearance of Francisco Sison. Joma Sison wrote a letter to the *Collegian*, which was published on 9 July. He had learned, he said, of the disappearance of Paquito "through newspaper reports." He concluded his brief note, "I hope that the disappearance of Paquito will arouse all my kinsmen for the revolution. Let the loss of one man multiply the revolutionaries among you."[245]

The murderous intrigue and bitter exchanges of April, May, and June were but a foretaste of the frenzied month of July. On 9 July, Henry Kissinger traveled to Beijing and met with Zhou Enlai, and on the sixteenth his travels were disclosed and Nixon's intention to visit Beijing in the coming year announced. On 21 July, less than a week after the announcement of the growing rapprochement between Nixon and Mao, the PKP published an issue of *Ang Komunista* headlined "Pingpong Diplomacy." It was the PKP leadership's declaration of war on the CPP. "We have been silent," the front-page editorial declared. "It's time for counter-attack."[246]

Ang Komunista concluded that "it would be interesting now to watch how these local-bred parrots of Beijing will twist their avowed position to accommodate the latest turn in their master's foreign policy." It did not have to wait long to find out. Within a week of the PKP's publication, the CPP and its front organizations hailed Nixon's statement that he intended to travel to China as a victory for Beijing. *Ang Masa*, for example, headlined the Sino-US talks "Nixon, Surrenders to Mao!"[247] On 30 July the CPP Central Committee published a statement in *Ang Bayan*, titled "On the Lavaite Misrepresentation of the Proletarian Foreign Policy of China," responding to the 21 July issue of *Ang Komunista*.[248] The CPP argued that pursuing diplomatic and economic ties with Washington was not incompatible with China's established policy of "providing assistance to the revolutionary struggles of all the oppressed people and nations." In truth, it drastically altered China's geopolitical stance. When Nixon ordered the mining of Haiphong harbor and launched the Linebacker I and II bombing campaigns in North Vietnam in 1972, Beijing tolerated Washington's aggression and refused a request from Hanoi to use southern Chinese ports to circumvent Haiphong. A fundamental shift in Beijing's foreign policy was underway. China began to initiate ties with dictatorships around the globe, including the shah, Pinochet, and Marcos. The Yan'an of world revolution was closing its borders, and Mao opened the economic and diplomatic ties that led to the restoration of capitalism in China.

These two statements from the leadership of the PKP and the CPP attacking and defending the foreign policy of Beijing established the political terrain on which the rapid-fire attacks staged by the two parties' various front organizations were launched. The rhetoric of the organizations of the PKP closely resembled that of the Maoists: inflammatory but politically vague. Each new publication carried acid prose without content; the rivals lobbed caustic bubbles at each other. The BRPF published a new edition of *Struggle*, titled "Facts which ought to be known about a proven warrior of counter-revolution."[249] The organization denounced "the black leaders of these yellow groups" and launched an extended personal attack at Sison, that "Judas," "congenital liar," "stubborn," "infantile," "obsessive," "hypocritical" "boot-licker," whose followers, the "long-haired extortionists" in the KM and SDK, had been "brainwashed to fanatically regard him as a demi-god whose word is their gospel truth."[250] The SDK hit back in an article titled "Ibunyag at Tuluyang Itakwil ang Kontra Rebolusyonaryong MPKP—Ahente ng Reaksyon sa Hanay ng Kabataan" (Expose and continue to renounce the counter-revolutionary MPKP—agent of reaction in the youth front), which declared, "Truly anything that imperialism desires, such as having an opportunist line, the MPKP and the whole Lava gang desires as well."[251] The KM published an issue of *Kalayaan* titled "Palisin Lahat ng Pesteng Maka-Lava!" (Brush away the Lavaite pests!) attacking the MPKP and the other front organizations of the PKP. "Sison's detractors," they wrote, "only expose their utter bankruptcy with every ridiculous attack they make on him in their puny attempt to deny his role in the present upsurge in the revolutionary mass movement."[252]

On 20 July Sison submitted a report titled *On Lavaite Propaganda for Revisionism and Fascism* to the Central Committee of the CPP, which was then printed and distributed by the CPP later in the year.[253] The final document was 193 pages and yet said very little that was new, as Sison simply summarized and repeated the positions articulated in previous publications and documents. This compilation of the arguments of the party was presented because "the Executive Committee of the Central Committee has deemed it necessary and appropriate in the interest of truth and in compliance with the demand of the masses to show comprehensively the degeneration of the Lava revisionist renegades into fascist criminals and special agents of the US-Marcos clique against the Communist Party of the Philippines, the New People's Army and the revolutionary movement in general."[254]

The report did not explain this degeneration or give a political definition of a "fascist criminal" or clarify how a Communist party had become such a political entity. It compiled a list of the alleged crimes and intrigues of the PKP, most of which the PKP was actually guilty of. It did not account for them politically, however, beyond the usual imprecations and denunciations. Sison accused the PKP of carrying out "cheap Trotskyite tricks" and denounced the leadership of the PKP as "little Trotskys."[255] At another point Sison accused the PKP of "fascist trickery." He used the words "fascist" and "Trotskyite" interchangeably, like an angry child attempting to curse. Despite its length, Sison's report added nothing of substance to the political discussion in 1971.

In late July the CPP produced an unsigned leaflet titled *Deception and Murder Is the Meaning of the Lavaite "Theory of Physical Affinity" and "Armed Struggle as a Secondary Form."*[256] The leaflet claimed, without any substantiation, that the "Lavaites" held to a "theory of physical affinity." This theory was not explained, but the pamphlet implied that the PKP held family members of revolutionaries to be fair targets for harassment and assassination. According to the pamphlet, "Lavaites are old experts in unprincipled assassinations, which they call 'liquidation' in their Mafia parlance." The CPP's response to the campaign of political murder being waged by the PKP was not the defense of principled politics but an escalation of the violence. The CPP threatened the PKP Central Committee members with assassination, identifying each of the members named in Liwayway Reyes's memo, listing their places of employment and their relation to the party.

The exchanges died down at the end of July. The mudslinging in the pages of the *Leader* went on until 6 August, when the editor announced, "With this issue the *Leader* declares the debate on the Left officially closed."[257] The attention of the rival organizations was for a time focused elsewhere. In late July the KM and SDK were unexpectedly and roundly defeated in the Diliman campus elections; August followed with the bombing of Plaza Miranda and the suspension of the writ of habeas corpus; the November election loomed after and the front organizations of the CPP strained every nerve and sinew to secure victory for the Liberal Party. It was not until late November that the diatribes and assassinations resumed. For the historian, and one has to imagine for the contemporary reading public, the truncation of the summer salvos of

1971 was a welcome respite. Reading through the material of April to July is a wearying affair; one strains through page after page of inarticulate anger and murderous threats to sift out the stray lines of political coherence. The CPP and the PKP were given open access to the pages of the mainstream press and they had nothing to say, but they said it very loudly.

Defeat at Diliman

When the *Collegian* resumed publication at the end of the summer break, it was under the editorship of leading SDK member Rey Vea. He began printing weekly press releases from the CPP, and by the middle of July, the articles of the Communist Party were running in the campus paper under the prominent masthead of *Ang Bayan*, featuring the hammer, sickle, and armalite. A similar radicalization of *Ang Malaya* at the PCC had taken place, but in its case the adoption of the imagery of the Communist Party was in the masthead of the student paper itself. The front organizations of the CPP controlled campus politics in 1971 in an unprecedented fashion, their influence spreading across the country from the center of student political life on the flagship Diliman campus. They received university funding to provide mandatory nationalist orientation to every enrolling freshman; published the statements of the Communist Party in the campus paper; broadcast its statements on campus radio, which Lopez then rebroadcast throughout the nation; and their unions, youth groups, and sectoral organizations controlled the entire sprawling fourth floor of Vinzons Hall, with office space to spare. Their influence was poised to expand further. On 23 July, Kaunlaran, the Los Baños student party of the KM and SDK, won the campus election by a landslide, securing twenty-eight of thirty seats on the student council.[258]

Then came the election debacle of August 1971. The SM was roundly defeated in the Diliman campus election, losing not only the chairmanship of the student council but a majority of seats as well. The CPP seized on the election outcome to reorient its front organizations in the week before the Plaza Miranda bombing, initiating a sharply rightward political lurch. It instructed the membership of the KM and SDK to join traditional, conservative organizations, particularly religious sodalities and community groups, and "broaden the united front," by which they would form an alliance with layers they had previously denounced as reactionary. This policy served the interests of the LP and the elite anti-Marcos opposition, whose paramount concern in the wake of the bombing was no longer the destabilization of Marcos—who having suspended the writ of habeas corpus was perilously close to implementing military dictatorship—but the consolidation of public sympathy and support behind their election campaign.

The 1971 Diliman campus election was a dirty affair. Campaigning opened on 26 July, and elections were staged on 6 August. Sandigang Makabansa (Patriotic Pillars, SM) held a convention on 17 July to select its candidates, choosing Rey Vea to run for chair of the UPSC, against Manny Ortega, of the Katipunan ng Malayang Pagkakaisa (Federation of Free Unity, KMP).[259] Seventy students competed for forty-four seats, and both sides engaged in mudslinging, malicious propaganda, and physical violence.[260] Over the past year the KM and SDK had worked to win the support of a number of campus fraternities. Willie Nepomuceno, a spokesman for SM, wrote that the majority of campus fraternities had now "adopted the mass line" and become "national democratic organizations" in the "forefront of the people's democratic struggle."[261] The move effectively politicized the traditional fraternity rivalries on campus and turned the election into a bloody frat rumble.[262] On 2 August, violence broke out during the campus election convocation and several students were injured. Both sides immediately accused the other. The SDK issued a leaflet within hours of the altercation, claiming that members of the KMP came to the debate carrying sticks, rocks, guns, and smoke bombs that they "mercilessly threw at the students who were quietly watching."[263] The KMP rebutted that SM members came to the convocation wearing "conspicuous red armbands" as "very convenient identifying marks," and the fight broke out when the KM-SDK threw a pillbox at the Ladies Auxiliary Corps of the KMP, injuring two young women.[264] Neither the KMP nor the SM presented a coherent or consistent version of events. Who started the violence is a point that cannot be resolved. It is clear, however, that both groups entered the university theater armed and engaged in the equivalent of a street battle.[265]

Armando Malay, dean of student affairs and chair of the University Election Board, issued a call for students to submit evidence regarding the violence during the convocation with a deadline of 19 August.[266] Both sides had engaged in violence and were alarmed that Malay would rule against them; thus, the SM and the KMP united in denouncing the dean. On 4 August another debate was staged, held on the AS steps under the sponsorship of UPSCA, and both the SM and the KMP used the forum to take turns denouncing Armando Malay for serving the interests of the rival party.[267] The KMP crudely derided Malay as "Dean of Homosexuals," while the SM attacked him as an ally of Marcos.[268] On 3 September the *Collegian* declared that Malay's investigation had yielded no results, as those who testified were deemed biased in favor of either the SM or the KMP. Malay claimed that neither the University Security division nor the Health Division had given any information, and students who had taken pictures of the event did not come forward to turn in photographs. The incident went unresolved.[269]

Sandigang Makabansa lost the election. Ortega received 5,358 votes; Vea 4,978. KMP took a majority of the council seats.[270] KM and SDK members, who had gathered from as far as Tondo to support the campus election, were stunned by the defeat. An SDK member later recounted, "That was when I learned how significant the campus election was to national politics."[271] The initial response published by the KM was short on details, stating simply that "reactionary diehards resorted to underhanded tactics such as sowing intrigues and dissension in the ranks of the national democratic movement and fear in the hearts of the masses of the students."[272] By 9 August, the SM was attempting to spin the outcome, claiming that while it lost, it won an "actual majority of politically conscious students."[273] The logic of the statement seems to be that those who voted for KMP were not politically conscious, and those who voted for SM were. This was nothing but rhetorical sleight of hand. At the same time, the SM depicted its defeat as the result of various machinations carried out by the KMP, which succeeded in deceiving the student body. The SM gave no accounting for why the student body, after over a year of political control by the SM in the student council, was deceived. What is more, the SM fared particularly poorly in what should have been its stronghold: the College of Arts and Sciences. They wrote, "Ironically [!] it was at the College of Arts and Sciences where Sandigang Makabansa fell victim to the unprincipled, albeit programmed and voluminous, black propaganda assaults of the ideologically bankrupt KAMP."[274]

The SM published a public accounting for its defeat in the *Collegian* on the thirteenth. The KMP, the SM claimed, had won by means of "deceit" and "black propaganda," above all the painting of graffiti in campus buildings, presented as the handiwork of the SM, on the morning of the election.[275] The SM noted that "the walls of the Arts and Sciences second, third and fourth floors were un-KM-SDK'lly [!] painted with such meaningless scribblings as 'Mao' and such wrongly-worded phrases as 'Fight Liberalism' and 'Destroy Book Worship.'" Everyone knows, the SM insisted, the correct slogan is "Oppose Book Worship."[276] Situated in the historical context of 1971, this explanation makes no sense. The Diliman Commune had left the campus covered in graffiti and the Oblation doused in red paint; Joma Sison's name was scrawled on the walls. A regular assignment for KM members was Operation Pinta work (that is, scrawling slogans in paint on the walls of buildings both on and off campus). What is more, despite the SM's claims that the slogans on the walls were "incorrectly"—"un-KM-SDK'lly"—written, the slogans left behind by the

Diliman Commune show no such scholastic care in their formulation. "Destroy Liberalism," for example, was painted on the walls of Palma Hall. If the student body chose to vote against vandalism, then it was not because of any "black propaganda" work carried out by the KMP.

What conclusion did the leaders of the SM draw from these pieces of evidence? They wrote that the "Malacañang think-tank must have admitted (if grudgingly) the strength of the national democrats' political line when they resorted to blatant chicanery and distortions as were manifested during the elections." SM released a second statement on the defeat, writing that "wine must have flowed freely from the ruling classes' tables," and concluded, "Put daring above everything else and boldly arouse the masses! All reactionaries are paper tigers!"[277] The initial response of the SM was thus to see the defeat as confirmation of its political line—a perspective it would drastically revise within days.

The truth was that, more than anything else, the UP students in 1971 were *voting against the Diliman Commune* and the conduct of the KM-SDK leadership of the student council. The members of the SM recognized this fact when they attempted to defend themselves by arguing that even "the KMP standard bearer himself at one time, before Molave Hall residents, admitted to his approval of the barricades." Rather than defend the barricades as the policy of the SM, they sought to spread the responsibility for the barricades onto both parties. Over the preceding year, the UPSC, under the leadership of Ericson Baculinao, had been repeatedly accused of forcing the views of the KM and SDK on UP students and on their fellow council members. Disagreement with KM policy was not tolerated. On 7 December 1970, the UPSC had called for a boycott of classes in response to the killing of Francis Sontillano, and the Engineering Student Council responded, expressing a growing sentiment among the students,

> We, members of the Engineering Student Council of the Philippines, are in wholehearted agreement and support of the move to boycott classes in protest of the bomb-slaying of student demonstrator Francis Sontillano.
>
> However, we decry the actions of the activist movement in the forced manner in which the engineering students were made to stay away from their classes. In the morning of December 7, 1970, the doors of classrooms and offices at Melchor Hall could not be opened on account of bits of paper and wood plugged into the keyholes.
>
> We consider this kind of action an infringement on the freedom of the individual student. As it was, the individual had been deprived of his right of choice between going for or against the boycott.[278]

The election defeat entailed the immediate loss of political sway on the campus. Having won the student council, the KMP, under Ortega, announced that the offices in Vinzons Hall belonging to the Student Cultural Association of the University of the Philippines, Malayang Kilusan ng Bagong Kababaihan (Free Movement of New Women, MAKIBAKA), SDK, and other organizations affiliated with the KM were being reallocated to other student organizations. The KM burned Ortega's effigy in a campus bonfire, and SDK member Butch Dalisay denounced Ortega and the KMP as "fascist lice."[279] Far worse setbacks loomed for the SM, including the loss of the Nationalist Corps—the campus organization responsible for the nationalist orientation of incoming freshmen—and editorial control of the *Collegian*.

Lurch to the Right

Within days, the KM and SDK held meetings reexamining their tactics and reaching the conclusion that "it was necessary to enter moderate groups and transform them into nationalist groups."[280] They would carry this out through community service work, a tactic that would allow them to integrate more closely with the SocDems and to whip up support for the LP in the election. The task was no longer primarily to destabilize Marcos but to integrate with "moderate" forces. Every statement produced by the front organizations of the CPP from mid-August to mid-September carried a similar theme. Anticipating an electoral victory for the LP in the wake of the 21 August bombing of Plaza Miranda, the front organizations of the CPP prepared to ride on its coattails.

On 15 August, the Executive Committee of the SDK, under the leadership of Antonio Hilario, wrote a lengthy reassessment of the policies, strategies, and tactics of the SDK in light of the defeat on the UP campus, which was published in September in the SDK's internal paper, *Talang Ginto*.[281] The document reoriented the movement from barricades to community service drives. Activism needed to begin, it argued, with the everyday needs of the masses— for example, concerns over trash disposal. By focusing on these things, the SDK would win the confidence of the masses and gain the opportunity to raise their subjective consciousness to the level of strategic needs. The "clerico-fascists," SDK claimed, by taking precisely this approach, have been able to win the masses and mislead them. Opposition to this new line, Hilario argued, was "left opportunism," and the leadership needed to "gradually pull out the roots of excess democracy that are deeply buried in the history of the SDK," correcting what "might be called a 'UG' [underground] style" in its chapters.[282]

"A large portion of our membership and even of our leading members were captured by the temptation of 'leftism.' For example, some have a mindset that we could call 'gunpowder brain' [*utak pulbura*]. These are the ones with the mindset that it is only with combat and barricades that we will be able to arouse and bring together the masses."[283] These were dogmatic errors, the document asserted, rooted in an incorrect assessment of the Philippine situation.

A key component of the rightward reorientation of the SDK was the transformation of its interventions among the working class. The document dealt with the Labor Committee of the SDK, which it admitted had seen very little success over the past year—"for all our work we have earned but a crumb of success" (*kakarampot ang aning tagumpay*).[284] It attributed this to the difficulty of factory-level union work and called for the campaign among workers to be carried out at the level of the community and not the factory, declaring that the Labor Committee was to be made a part of the new Sectoral Organization Bureau. This turn from the factory to the community was part of the overall turn of the SDK toward basic community service work as the new center of political strategy. The SDK, in other words, would no longer focus on building within the working class in their workplaces, but rather on campaigns built around issues like trash disposal in poor communities.

Hilario thus reoriented the entire work of the SDK to reform-driven community organizing, and this served as the center of its political activity from the bombing of Plaza Miranda until the declaration of martial law. It subordinated all work in the working class to this struggle, and it sought to eliminate any dissent or alternate patterns of action within the organization as "excess democracy." The turn away from workers as a class in factories and workplaces to a sector within a neighborhood was in part an attempt to win over forces in shantytowns who were otherwise organized under KASAPI and the SocDems. Through this campaign the KM and SDK secured control of the organization of squatters, Zone One Tondo, from the SocDem forces and invested itself heavily in community outreach programs such as Operation Tulong in the wake of the August 1972 flood. SDK National Executive Committee member Jaime Regalario recounted that, as a result of this policy, by the beginning of 1972, "because we had focused too much on the basic sectors, the number of lumpen members grew, so our expansion contracted [*dumami ang mga lumpen members kaya nagcontract ang expansion*]. The quality of activists retrogressed such that they could not even draw the correct political line any more."[285] Smaller community outreach projects included Operation Tambak Lubak—filling potholes in the roads with stones—and Operation Linis, cleaning the canals.

The elite character of community service projects flying banners denouncing imperialism, feudalism, and bureaucrat capitalism while tidying up the neighborhood was made particularly clear in San Juan. Some women in the community reportedly complained that their husbands were engaged in cock-fighting, so the SDK staged a "lie-in" "to prevent it from operating and demanded from then Mayor Joseph Estrada that he shut down the cockpit."[286] These efforts seemed to have been more along the lines of Carrie Nation and the temperance movement than of Mao.

The first *public* reassessment of the Diliman election debacle was written by Sonny Coloma in the pages of the *Collegian*, and he put forward the same political line as Hilario. Coloma wrote that the defeat meant that it was necessary to "rectify errors and resolutely struggle to raise the cultural revolution to new heights."[287] What was needed, he argued, was "intensive political work in order to win over the middle and backwards elements who are most susceptible to counter-revolutionary enticement." Winning over these elements by engaging in conservative community organizing was the new political imperative. Carrying out this line, the SM declared its "tactical unity with all groups, which *through their deeds* manifest genuine anti-fascist sentiments. . . . We may give benefit of the doubt to other hitherto opposing groups for the support they may manifest."[288] Romeo Candazo, of the SDK, recounted that "the next day [after the SDK reassessment] I applied to UP Aletheia," a moderate religious organization.[289]

From October 1970, when Sison's Political Report to the Second Plenum was published, until August 1971, the political orientation of the KM and SDK, in keeping with the instructions of the CPP, had been to seize control—of student groups, of unions, even of the university itself. Now they were instructed to join conservative organizations and gradually win them over. Those they had decried as clerico-fascists in January were now their allies.[290] The party lurched to the right. The bulk of the new united front was formed of conservative religious students, bound to the front organizations of the party by the thin threads of anti-Marcos nationalism. The reorientation of the front groups of the CPP in August 1971 was a question of organizational practice and strategy, but not of rhetoric. Despite their merger with sodalities and catechists, the KM and SDK did not drop the language of armed struggle in their internal documents; rather, they doubled down on it. Their rightward trajectory required radical posturing, and drawings of M-14s adorned leaflets calling for unity with UPSCA.

The party could not remain unaffected by this alliance. The social ends of Marxism were alien to the Catholic Church; violence, however, was not. "Political power flows from the barrel of a gun" was a formulation that suited Ignatius de Loyola as well as Mao Zedong, while materialism suited neither. The limited but nonetheless sincere secular humanism of the founders of the

CPP was buried beneath the church militant. A range of religious groups, many tied to the bourgeois opposition, had already begun mouthing the phrases of the Communist Party. On 4 July 1971 the Student Christian Movement of the Philippines (SCMP) called on worshippers to

> let our wrath bring us out of the cover of our religious buildings and join the "People's Anti-Imperialist Congress to Oppose the Oil Price Hike and the Transport Fare Increase." In just anger. This red afternoon. In a United Front against US imperialism.
>
> We call on our fellow Christians to turn the churches from whited sepulchres into red barricades against US imperialism, domestic feudalism and bureaucrat capitalism. In God's glory and honor.[291]

The party hastened to adapt to these layers. SDK leader Gary Olivar wrote a letter from prison in early 1972 for the Sunday bulletin of the Church of the Risen Lord, and his quotations from Mao Zedong's tribute to Norman Bethune ran next to an announcement that a new mezzanine had just been christened.[292] By 1972, the party had formed its own religious front organization, Christians for National Liberation (CNL). Less than a month before martial law was declared, the CNL staged a mass that culminated in a candle-lit religious procession to the church of the Black Nazarene in Quiapo. The CNL termed this a Prusisyon ng Bayan laban sa Militarisasyon (People's Procession against Militarization) and called on "all Christians" to join this "religio-political act."[293] The party would continue to speak of the "unfinished revolution" of Bonifacio, but they had stripped it of its anticlerical content. Damaso was a useful ally and the crucifix a facile tool for recruitment.[294]

The party's lurch to the right was presented as a response to the defeat on the Diliman campus, but this was only partly true. The movement had been stunned by the defeat and a reassessment was required. The careful national coordination of the shift reveals, however, that more was at stake. The reorientation was launched with just enough of a window—six days—to allow the party's various front groups to alter their practice before the 21 August bombing of Plaza Miranda. In the wake of the terrorist bombing, the CPP and all of its organizations strained to muster every manifestation of social opposition and sympathy from the voting public and bring it to the November ballot box on behalf of the LP. That this policy was launched six days before the bombing strongly suggests that the party leadership knew what was about to take place.

CHAPTER 4

The Writ Suspended

Plaza Miranda was the nation's public space, "the center not only of the city but of the country itself—the hub, the forum, the crossroads of the nation."[1] The plaza stretched between the off-white earthquake baroque facade of the Quiapo Church and the crowded arcades of the market, situated beside the rise of Quezon Bridge over a bend in the Pasig. It was in Plaza Miranda that the critical political disputes of postwar democracy were aired. Here the major parties held their rallies, here radicals gathered to protest. The demonstrations of the Kabataang Makabayan (Nationalist Youth, KM) and Samahan ng Demokratikong Kabataan (Federation of Democratic Youth, SDK) in the early 1970s spilled out of the plaza, beyond the towering curved exterior of the Mercury Drug building, and clogged the entirety of Quezon Boulevard. A popular anecdote of Ramon Magsaysay recounted how he asked of a proposed law, "Can we defend this in Plaza Miranda?" It was in this tradition that on a Saturday night, 21 August 1971, the Liberal Party (LP) mounted the plaza dais to stage its *miting de avance*—officially announcing its slate to the public and launching its midterm election campaign. Ten thousand assembled to witness the event, which was live broadcast across the nation on television and radio. Shortly after nine that evening, three fragmentation grenades were thrown from the audience onto the stage, two of which exploded (figure 4.1). "The crowd stampeded and dispersed." Nine

FIGURE 4.1. The crowd flees from the grenade explosions at Plaza Miranda, 21 August 1971.

people in the audience, among them a five-year-old boy, were killed, and over one hundred were wounded, including eight of the LP candidates who were on stage at the time.[2]

Within two and a half hours, Marcos secretly issued presidential order 889, suspending the writ of habeas corpus. The proclamation blamed the bombing on "lawless elements" who were guided by "Marxist-Leninist-Maoist teachings" and received "the moral and material support of a foreign power."[3] Defense Secretary Enrile, who had stepped down to run for Senate on the Nacionalista slate, issued a press statement that he would "bag the culprits" within forty-eight hours.[4] Police and military forces carried out raids without warrant and arrested widely, targeting the activists of the front organizations of the Communist Party of the Philippines (CPP). Two hundred Metrocom troopers raided the Philippine College of Commerce (PCC) less than twenty-four hours after the bombing, seizing alleged subversive materials and arresting several professors.

Benigno Aquino was notably absent from the Plaza Miranda rally, and as the most important event of the LP's entire election campaign was bombed, the leading representative of the LP was nowhere to be seen. Writing on 3 September, Ninotchka Rosca recounted, "After the headcount, through the numbness, the question that immediately pops up is where in god's name is Benigno Aquino Jr., the so-called Wonder Boy? Ninoy appears later, unscathed, by virtue of what, he recounts later, is an amazing series of coincidences and the closest of calls. He was not there, he says, but was on the way when Plaza Miranda cracked up in that violent explosion."[5] Late that night, Aquino was photographed by the press carrying a submachine gun in his hand as he raced to visit the hospital rooms of the injured representatives of his party.[6]

The bombing of Plaza Miranda remains one of the most contentious events in the history of the Philippines. Marcos blamed the CPP, and the CPP blamed Marcos, but no one has ever been prosecuted for the crime. In the months leading up to the Plaza Miranda massacre, a string of bombings and terror attacks had taken place throughout the city, and they continued in the wake of 21 August, targeting government facilities such as the National Water and Sanitation Authority (NAWASA), City Hall, and Commission on Elections (COMELEC). This sequence of attacks from June through September was quite different in character from the Miranda bombing, however. They took place in the dead of night, targeted key infrastructure, and produced very few casualties. We know from the publications of the Partido Komunista ng Pilipinas (PKP) that it was responsible for at least some of these bombings.[7] There is also strong evidence that Marcos had military forces stage bombings in both 1971 and 1972 to provide a pretext for the declaration of martial law.[8] We know, based on Enrile's own testimony in 1986, that Marcos and Enrile staged an ambush on Enrile's motorcade in September 1972 as the final pretext for the declaration.[9] The PKP members directly responsible for the bombing campaign, particularly Commander Soliman and Ruben Torres, had intimate ties to the Marcos government. Their travel, as we have seen, was facilitated by Marcos, and Torres was employed in Enrile's office at the time of the 1971 terror campaign. It seems likely that the PKP and the military worked together to carry out this campaign from June to September 1971. Miranda, however, did not fit their modus operandi at all. Who was responsible for the bombing of Plaza Miranda?

Accusations

As he suspended the writ of habeas corpus, Marcos blamed Communist "subversives" for the bombing, and the student activists blamed Marcos. The majority of the population seems to have sided with the student activists. It was widely known that the KM and its allies were in a close alliance with the LP, and it was also common knowledge that the KM was closely tied to the Communist

Party. Why would the CPP bomb its allies? Within a few months, the official target of investigation was not the CPP but Antonio Villegas. The LP had selected Ramon Bagatsing as its Manila mayoral candidate, replacing Villegas. In an act of revenge, the story went, Villegas hired men he released from prison to carry out the bombing. This became the central focus of the government investigation by 1972. With the declaration of martial law in September 1972, the question of Plaza Miranda largely disappeared, reemerging briefly at the trial of Ninoy Aquino in the form of the accusation that his Communist allies had told him of the bombing in advance.

The CPP's possible involvement in the bombing came up in government and military circles on a number of occasions before exploding into public view in 1989. As we will see, in 1972, the government captured the minutes of a CPP military tribunal that documented a party member's claim that he had carried out the bombing on instructions from Joma Sison. Rolando Abadilla, head of Marcos's military intelligence, would later claim that Central Committee member Noli Collantes, upon surrender to the government in late 1972, had testified that the party was responsible for the bombing and that Aquino was complicit.[10] Jones recounts that when Central Committee member Ruben Guevarra was captured, or surrendered, in 1981, he made "a voluminous statement" detailing how Sison gave orders for the bombing.[11]

In August 1986, Victor Corpus wrote a letter to Jose Lacaba claiming that he had been present when Sison and a few other members of the Central Committee were plotting the Plaza Miranda bombing. Lacaba was in the process of writing the screenplay for a film titled *Operation: Get Victor Corpus*.[12] Lacaba had depicted Corpus as being captured in 1976, which was the official story, but Corpus wrote to Lacaba that he had in fact surrendered to the military on 13 January of that year. Corpus claimed that he had been troubled by criticisms that he had failed to voice during the plenum of the Central Committee held in Bataan in December 1975 and had contacted a former Philippine Military Academy classmate to arrange his surrender.[13] In his letter, Corpus claimed that he was present "when some leaders of the Party headed by Joma plotted the bombing of the Liberal Party (LP) rally at Plaza Miranda."[14] In November 1986, during the "God Save the Queen" coup, which was part of a string of military coups during the Corazon Aquino presidency, Defense Minister Juan Ponce Enrile leaked Corpus's letter to the press, with the calculated political intention of driving a wedge between Aquino and the CPP and ex-CPP members around her administration. Corpus held a press conference on 8 November confirming the authenticity of his letter.[15] The allegations received very little press coverage and were largely written off as either part of a promotion campaign for the new movie or part of the machinations of Enrile, or both. Aquino herself had little desire to see this matter investigated. Her husband, the myth of whose political sainthood was the bedrock of her administration, was possibly implicated in the affair.

It was in the middle of 1989 that the possibility of the CPP having orchestrated the bombing came to public prominence. Gregg Jones, an American journalist, had just completed a book on the history of the party based on interviews with the leadership and former leadership of the CPP. In a chapter titled "The Ghosts of Plaza Miranda," he claimed, on the basis of anonymous interviews with four former Central Committee members of the party and several other leading members, that Sison had ordered the bombing and the party had carried it out. He developed his argument in considerable detail on the basis of these interviews.[16] From 3 August to 6 August 1989, Amando Doronila serialized in his column in the *Chronicle* Jones's chapter on Plaza Miranda based on the galley proofs of the book, which had not yet been published. On 23 August 1989, the New People's Army (NPA) northern command published a letter in Tagalog in the *Inquirer* that denounced Ariel Almendral, Victor Corpus, Pablo Araneta, and Ruben Guevarra "and other traitors who are being vaunted as witnesses to the role of the CPP/NPA in the Plaza Miranda bombing." It claimed they were all on the payroll of the "US-Aquino regime."[17] It was striking that while Almendral's, Araneta's, and Guevarra's names had not yet been mentioned as sources in the press, the NPA was aware that they were privy to information regarding the bombing. On 24 August 1989, the *Chronicle* published a letter from someone identifying himself as Emilio Ricarte, the spokesman of an unknown organization he called the "CPP Reformist Underground Cell." Ricarte claimed that Ninoy Aquino had known of the bombing in advance because Ruben Tuazon had informed him. Fluellen Ortigas, who in 1971 had been both national spokesperson for the KM and paid employee of Ninoy Aquino, responded in an interview with the *Chronicle* on the same day that Tuazon had informed him that "NPA members did not tell Aquino there was going to be an attack but purposely kept him away from the rally by insisting on meeting with him that night."[18] Tuazon had been a member of the Central Committee of the party and, at the same time, an employee of Ninoy Aquino.

Sison responded to the charges in an article titled "Communist Party and Plaza Miranda," which was serialized in the *Chronicle* from 9 September to 11 September 1989 and then published in full in the *Inquirer* on 25 September.[19] Sison accused Jones of being a CIA agent and identified Jones's sources as Corpus, Almendral, Guevarra, Ricardo Malay, and Ibarra Tubianosa. He dismissed all these as renegades from the party, several of whom he accused correctly of now being either military or intelligence operatives.

Evidence

What evidence was presented that the party had carried out the Plaza Miranda bombing?[20]

While Jones's account of the Plaza Miranda bombing is based on anonymous sources, a careful examination of his footnotes—cross-referencing when the interviews were conducted and how Jones identified the party rank of the interviewee—makes it possible to identify his sources.[21] Jones's account relies on interviews with Victor Corpus, Ruben Guevarra, Ariel Almendral, Ricardo Malay, Ibarra Tubianosa, and Julius Fortuna. The motives of many of these sources were deeply problematic. Corpus had been restored to the military and given the rank of lieutenant colonel, "three ranks above the one he held before defecting to the rebels."[22] His account of the party's involvement in the Miranda bombing was published in the introduction to his book, *Silent War*, which is a detailed military handbook proposing strategies and tactics for suppressing the Communist insurgency.[23] Ruben Guevarra had become a ranking military intelligence officer. The rest of those giving evidence were, at the very least, disgruntled with the party. Like those of Jones and Corpus, Guevarra's account was initially published in 1989, in the book *The Story behind the Plaza Miranda Bombing*.[24] Corpus and Guevarra certainly brought forward their evidence with ulterior political motives, as their testimonies were a coordinated part of the endless coup plotting of the late 1980s.

This fact does not, however, invalidate their claims or those of the other CPP members who all stated that Sison had ordered the bombing. An examination of the evidence is necessary. What follows is a reconstruction based on all the available sources of the narrative of CPP responsibility for the bombing. I document the evidence given for each claim and then assess the credibility of the account after its reconstruction.

Plotting

In early February 1971, Sison, Tubianosa, Jose Luneta, and the party's chief finance officer met in Manila and "laid out a plan for Party operatives to attack an opposition Liberal party rally."[25] Sison traveled to Isabela, where he met with Dante and Corpus, who had defected to the party but months prior, and where they were joined by Luneta. "The Party had a dilemma, Sison told his comrades. Hundreds of rifles and other weapons would be arriving from China in the months ahead, yet the NPA had only about 90 fighters in Isabela at the time."[26] The source for Sison's meetings in Isabela was Corpus. The idea of weapons arriving in "the months ahead" is a bit of an overstatement, as the arms shipment from China on the *Karagatan* did not arrive until July 1972. Jones claims that Sison never explicitly spelled out the Miranda plan in Isabela, but Corpus in his book claimed that "it was in a jungle camp of Commander Dante, then the Commander in Chief of the New People's Army, in the Isabela portion of Sierra Madre Mountains that the plan to bomb the Liberal Party rally at Plaza Miranda was first hatched."[27]

Sison returned to Manila in June 1971, and Danny Cordero was selected to lead the bombing team. Jones cites three "former party veterans" as the source for this claim.[28] We know that Cordero was at this time the chair of KM Caloocan and was a relative of Caloocan mayor Macario Asistio, whom the KM would denounce as a fascist in October 1971.[29] Cordero would have been a credible choice to carry out a terrorist act, as he had in the past been assigned to raise money for the KM and CPP by robbing gambling joints at gunpoint.[30]

In mid-August, Ruben Guevarra arrived in Manila from Isabela, and on the evening of 21 August, Magtanggol Roque and Noli Collantes drove Guevarra to a safe house in Parañaque, where Sison, Hermenigildo Garcia, and Monico Atienza were present. Sison was meeting with Danny Cordero, Cecilio Apostol, and Danilo Valero when Guevarra entered the room. Cordero and his two companions left to carry out their mission, and Sison instructed Atienza to inform Guevarra of the plan. Ruben Guevarra himself is the source for this meeting in Parañaque, while both Garcia and Atienza later denied that such a meeting ever took place. Cordero, as we will see, would later publicly claim that it had.[31]

Cecilio Apostol died in an encounter with the military in late 1971. Danilo Valero, who joined the NPA in 1971, had been an activist from Sta. Ana, Pandacan, Manila, and was a student at the Philippine College of Criminology. He was present at Cordero's trial and execution and died in an encounter with the military in 1977. All three men who are claimed to have thrown grenades at Plaza Miranda were leading members of the KM in the months before they received orders from Sison. Senator Jovito Salonga, who was permanently injured in the blast, would claim in 2001 that the man (whom Salonga did not name) who drove Cordero and his companions to Miranda had confessed to Salonga his part in the bombing.[32]

The next day, Ruben Guevarra returned to Isabela. Cordero, Apostol, and Valero also traveled to Isabela on 22 August but traveled separately from Guevarra.[33] Rolando Abadilla, head of Marcos's military intelligence, claimed that Noli Collantes informed him that Aquino had Cordero and his companions transported to Isabela in his helicopter.[34]

The Execution of Danny Cordero

Between September 1971 and June 1972, Cordero and Guevarra had a disagreement that culminated in the execution of Cordero. This fact is not disputed.

The Isabela forces of the NPA began preparing for a shipment of arms
from China, which would arrive in early July off Digoyo Point on the party's boat, the MV *Karagatan*. In preparation for the delivery of arms, the
NPA, under the leadership of Corpus and Guevarra, began to minimize its
encounters with the military, with the goal of securing as small a military
presence in Isabela as possible. The majority of the NPA members, including the leadership, were not informed of the reason for the sudden quies-
cence, and Cordero and a number of forces around him were angered by it,
seeing it as a political retreat. Cordero began to discuss secretly and then to
plot actively to depose Guevarra from leadership, and to this end he obstructed Guevarra's orders and issued counterorders in an attempt to gener-
ate armed encounters between the NPA and the military. Among Cordero's
companions in this were Pablo Araneta and Herminio Espiritu.[35] Guevarra
claimed that Cordero issued orders to Crispin Tagamolila to attack a military squadron in April, and Tagamolila died in the firefight. Whether or not
Cordero was responsible for this, Tagamolila's attack was not in line with
the NPA's policy in Isabela at the time, and it resulted in his death.[36] In an
effort to strengthen his position against Guevarra, Cordero began to brag
about how important he was to the party. In this context, it seems, he began
to mention his role in the Miranda bombing and that he had been ordered
by Sison to carry it out.

In late June, as the *Karagatan* arms were already en route from China, Guevarra convened a meeting of the Isabela forces. When Cordero and his companions arrived, Guevarra announced that the meeting was a military tribunal.
He charged Cordero, Araneta, and Espiritu with "inciting [their] command to
rebel against the CPP leadership" and attempting to sabotage NPA operations.[37] Cordero was also charged with slandering the party, by claiming it
had been responsible for Miranda. Pablo Araneta, who stood accused alongside Cordero, had graduated from seminary in Iloilo intending to be a priest,
but had thought better of it and took up engineering and then political science at the University of the Philippines (UP) Iloilo. He joined the SDK there
and then the CPP. Araneta had participated in the Diliman Commune after
attending the SDK congress on the Diliman campus, and in late 1971 the party
sent Araneta to Isabela.[38] Araneta later claimed that among the roots of the
disgruntlement that he, Cordero, and Espiritu felt were the privileges of Guevarra and others in the leadership. Even such trivialities as the leaders getting

Marlboros while the rank and file made do with local tobacco stung Cordero and Araneta and contributed to their rancor.[39]

The tribunal hearing the case against Cordero, Araneta, and Espiritu was composed of nine members. Guevarra identifies them: Magtanggol Abreu, Elizabeth Principe, Marcelino Cadiz, Hermogenes Pagsulingan, Mario de la Cruz, Daniel Gallardo, Rene Espinas, Fortunato Camus, and Guevarra. Guevarra chaired the tribunal, and thirty members of the NPA observed the affair.[40] Ariel Almendral was assigned by Guevarra to serve as the defense for the three accused. Almendral had been a student at UP who had joined KM. He had relocated to Baguio in late 1970, where he headed the Baguio chapter of KM. After Plaza Miranda he joined the NPA in Isabela, and he had thus been in the NPA for less than a year when he was assigned to defend Cordero and the others.[41] The trial began on 2 July and ended in the evening of the same day.[42]

Danny Cordero, charged with slandering the party, insisted that he had in fact been ordered to carry out the Plaza Miranda bombing, and he called on Danilo Valero, who was present at the trial, to confirm this. Guevarra states that he had warned Valero of the consequences if he divulged the Miranda mission. Thus, at the trial, only two others knew that Cordero was telling the truth: Valero, who kept silent, and Guevarra, who chaired the tribunal.[43] At the end of the presentation of evidence, the tribunal met separately. They voted to demote Araneta and compel him to engage in "self-criticism in front of comrades"; they voted to expel Espiritu for one year, also compelling him to public self-criticism; and they voted to execute Danny Cordero.[44] The final verdict was a split vote, with four voting to execute, and four voting for a more lenient punishment. Ruben Guevarra cast the deciding vote to execute Danny Cordero, and on the morning of 3 July 1972, after the tribunal sang "The Internationale," Elizabeth Principe shot Cordero in the back of the head.[45]

The *Karagatan* arrived later that day. Upon nearing the shore, it experienced some problems, leading to conflict between CPP and military forces. In the debacle that ensued, the military entered the camp where Cordero had been executed, and seized the notes of the trial, which had been held two days prior.[46] Pablo Araneta surrendered to Romy Eugenio, the mayor of Isabela, in April 1973, and would in the 1980s provide corroborating evidence regarding the trial of Danny Cordero.[47]

China Delegation

A second body of evidence pertaining to the Miranda bombing comes from the large delegation of CPP leaders sent to Beijing in July 1971, just before the bombing.

This delegation may have been in part responsible for negotiating an arms shipment from China to the Philippines, but this does not seem to have been its primary task, as the principal negotiator of the shipment was Fidel Agcaoili, who arrived in Beijing in September. Jose Luneta had been the party's representative to Beijing since 1968, but he had returned to the Philippines in mid-1970 to report to Sison. With the capture of Nilo Tayag, Luneta was made general secretary of the CPP and Carlos del Rosario was sent to China in Luneta's stead, arriving in December 1970 to finalize arrangements for the CPP delegation to travel to China.[48] It was on del Rosario's return to the Philippines that Sison and others are alleged to have begun plotting the Miranda bombing. Del Rosario was intended to lead the delegation to China in July, but he was killed in April and Ibarra Tubianosa was made the new head of the delegation.

By late July 1971, Ricardo and Charito Malay, Ibarra and Calay Tubianosa, Mario and Alma Miclat, and Roger Arcilla had all journeyed to China.[49] It is striking that they traveled as couples, almost as if they expected not to return for some time. On 20 August, the day before the bombing, Sison sent his children to China with a delegation led by Ericson Baculinao, which included Chito Sta Romana, Jaime Florcruz, and Rey Tiquia.[50] Ricardo Malay reported to Jones that Tubianosa told several members of the group "about the plan to bomb Plaza Miranda—*a few weeks before the attack took place.*"[51] Mario Miclat, who was part of this delegation, wrote a book in 2010, in which he too claimed that Tubianosa had told them of the bombing in advance.[52]

The delegation did not depart China until the mid-1980s.[53] That it was a coincidence that Sison sent his children to China a day before the bombing, where they stayed safe throughout the duration of martial law, strains credulity.

Assessment

Certain facts are irrefutable: four former Central Committee members of the CPP accused Sison of plotting the bombing of Miranda, Danny Cordero raised the same charge and was executed for it, and at least two members of the delegation to China claimed they were told in advance of the bombing.

The narrative of the bombing plot and its aftermath that emerges out of these accounts is surprisingly coherent. If the CPP did not in fact carry out the bombing, then we have to assume that Cordero was lying during his trial and that Guevarra, Corpus, Malay, Fortuna, and Miclat were lying in a coordinated fashion.[54]

Sison, Hermenigildo Garcia, and Monico Atienza all denied the charges. Sison argued that the majority of the evidence being presented against him was hearsay and therefore inadmissible. Were the task of the historian that of the prosecutor I would be compelled to agree, as there is certainly insufficient evidence to convict Sison of the bombing in a court of law. The task of the historian, however, is not to establish guilt beyond reasonable doubt; it is to demonstrate what the preponderance of evidence suggests and to establish on this basis what likely happened. Additional evidence may further substantiate this conclusion or compel its revision.

Sison argued that the party did not carry out the bombing on the grounds that it did not engage in putschist or anarchistic acts. This is demonstrably false. The CPP regularly instigated violence during protests in an attempt to provoke state repression, claiming that this would hasten the revolution. Mauro Samonte, who was a leading CPP member in Katipunan ng mga Samahan ng mga Manggagawa (Federation of Workers Associations), the CPP labor umbrella organization, wrote in 2014 that he had been given a fragmentation grenade and instructed to throw it during a protest rally in front of the US embassy in July 1972.[55]

Sison repeatedly claimed that on 22 February 1986 among Enrile's confessions was that Marcos was responsible for the 1971 bombing.[56] This is not true. Enrile announced that he and Marcos had staged the ambush on his motorcade in September 1972 as a pretext for martial law, but he made no mention of Miranda.[57]

Sison also claimed that US intelligence knew that the party was not responsible for the bombing and cited as evidence Raymond Bonner's 1987 book on the Marcos dictatorship, in which Bonner claimed that US intelligence was convinced that the Communists were not responsible. Bonner's evidence for this claim is a single unnamed CIA officer who stated that the CPP was a "fledgling organization with fewer than 100 members, and they were very disorganized. Moreover, their efforts were concentrated in rural areas, building for a peasant revolution along the lines of Mao's in China. They had no urban capacity."[58] These claims are absurdly off base. The figure of one hundred members is off by an order of magnitude, as by the end of 1971 the party had approximately one thousand members, many of whom were operating in urban areas. It had the leadership of nearly all the radical protest organizations of the day and directly gave them instructions. Its members and loyal supporters controlled the majority of university student councils and determined editorial policy in every major campus paper. It was intimately allied with one of the two major bourgeois political parties, and it was receiving regular funding and support from some of the wealthiest and most influential sections of the elite.

What motive would the CPP have had in carrying out the bombing?

According to Jones, Sison's underlying motives were twofold: first, the LP would blame Marcos and ally more closely with the CPP; and second, Marcos would crack down on the population, and the CPP anticipated that the increased repression would breed increased resistance. Both of these points correspond closely to the outlook of Sison and the CPP. The CPP was forever striving to use "contradictions" within the ruling class in order to win over the "middle forces"—in other words, to ally with a section of the bourgeoisie. On 15 August, six days before the bombing, the CPP, through the KM and SDK, issued instructions reorienting its front organizations to a policy of heightened integration with these middle forces. I have documented in detail how the CPP repeatedly argued that repression was good for revolution, that it spontaneously bred resistance.

The preponderance of available evidence strongly indicates that Sison and leading members of the CPP carried out the Plaza Miranda bombing. I suspect that smoking gun evidence of this exists in the archives of the Chinese Communist Party (CCP). Just as it has now emerged that Mao and the CCP leadership knew of the September 30 Movement in Indonesia in advance, the balance of probability suggests that Carlos del Rosario in December 1970 and members of the CPP delegation in July 1971 discussed the plot with the CCP as part of their negotiations over the shipment of arms.[59]

In the end, this book's argument that the CPP made possible the declaration of martial law is not tied to whether the CPP executed the Miranda bombing. Marcos was preparing to declare martial law without the Miranda bombing, and his military operatives and leading members of the PKP were engaged in a joint bombing campaign to provide a pretext for military dictatorship. Miranda accelerated the process but did not determine its outcome. The CPP facilitated the declaration of martial law not through the Miranda bombing but by subordinating the opposition to military dictatorship in the working class and youth to a rival section of the ruling class who were conspiring to become dictator themselves.

The Writ Suspended and the 1971 Election

On 21 August, within three hours of the bombing, Ferdinand Marcos issued proclamation 889 suspending the writ of habeas corpus. He waited thirty-six hours before announcing that the writ had been suspended, however, using this window of opportunity to carry out a series of quiet arrests.[60] His purposes achieved, Marcos held a press conference at noon on 23 August, announcing the suspension, and again in the evening of the twenty-fourth, outlining the "legality, desirability and acceptability of his decision."[61] The proclamation, only half a page long, was predicated entirely on the claim that "lawless elements," "whose political, social and economic precepts are based on the Marxist-Leninist-Maoist teachings and beliefs," "acting in concert through front organizations that are seemingly innocent and harmless . . . have succeeded in infiltrating almost every segment of our society."[62]

The KM had moved into a new headquarters building on Kamias Road, and the day after the bombing the leadership met to discuss naming it after Charlie del Rosario.[63] At two in the afternoon a group of men claiming to be reporters from the *Herald* arrived and requested to interview Secretary General Luzvimindo David. When he emerged from the meeting to speak with them, they revealed that they were armed, forced him into their jeep, and drove off.[64] The police and military, no longer bound by the niceties of evidence and procedure, conducted similar "arrests" throughout Manila. A wanted list of 63 students and activists was published in newspapers, and in late August the *Manila Times* reported that 120 people had been arrested under proclamation 889.[65] The majority of those seized were members of the front organizations of the CPP, but the police, turned loose by the suspension of the writ, arrested indiscriminately, rounding up grassroots members of the Malayang Pagkakaisa ng Kabataang Pilipino (Free Unity of Filipino Youth, MPKP) in the provinces.[66]

While the president doubtless aspired to arrest his bourgeois rivals, who were, he knew, plotting either his assassination or his ouster in a military coup, he was not yet prepared to do so. The suspension of the writ of habeas corpus was a dry run for military dictatorship; Marcos was testing out its implementation. While he would not yet arrest Aquino, he readied the pretexts for 1972. Marcos accused the CPP of a July-August plan to seize power by destabilizing the government through a bombing spree of which Miranda was but a component part. Marcos himself had orchestrated the majority of these bombings, which were carried out by military operatives in conjunction with the armed wing of the PKP. Marcos went further and attempted to associate Aquino with this plot, publicly accusing his rival of ties to the Maoist CPP and claiming that Aquino had introduced Joma Sison to Commander Dante and had thus facilitated the creation of the NPA. Aquino denounced these claims as political slander. The mutual hypocrisy of Marcos and Aquino is extraordinary. Marcos was funding and aiding the PKP as they carried out a bombing campaign on his behalf; Aquino was intimately tied to the CPP and was facilitating their armed struggle, and it is likely that he had been aware of the Miranda bombing plot.

Needing to defend his leading bourgeois ally, Joma Sison wrote a letter to the Manila press denying that he had any ties to Benigno Aquino or the Miranda bombing. On 30 August, the *Collegian* published his statement, which was signed on the twenty-fifth and had been published in Tagalog translation in *Taliba* on the twenty-eighth.[67] Sison wrote,

> I deny the allegation made publicly by Mr. Marcos in his Tuesday radio-TV hook-up interview that I met Sen. Benigno Aquino together with Commander Dante in 1968 and again in 1969. I can only describe his allegation as a brazen lie. . . .
>
> I state categorically that Commander Dante, Senator Aquino and I have never met together in all our lives. . . .
>
> It is true, however, that I have warm regards for a number of LP leaders who were victims of the Plaza Miranda carnage and it is simply malicious, incoherent and mad for anyone to make groundless insinuations contrary to the fact. . . . Marxism-Leninism-Mao Zedong Thought condemns terrorism and anarchist bombing. . . .
>
> I agree with the Liberal Party that the Marcos clique itself has been responsible for the "climate of violence" now prevailing in the country.

Aquino did arrange the meeting of Sison and Dante; Sison lied categorically on this point. Sison spoke the truth, however, when he declared his "warm regards" for the LP leadership. The CPP and its front organizations, meanwhile, denounced Marcos for the bombing of Miranda. They hailed the suspension of the writ as hastening the advent of revolution and threw themselves into the LP election campaign. An article in *Eastern Horizon* accurately described the public understanding of the attitude of the KM and SDK to the suspension of the writ and the threat of martial law: "Both the KM and the SDK, however, refused to be cowed; they instead advanced the thesis that martial law would merely hasten the politicization of the masses and the waging of an all-out people's war."[68] On 22 August, the day after the bombing, the Manila-Rizal Regional Committee of the CPP issued a statement, which declared, "We call on the broad masses of the people, including the Liberal Party and the democratic elements or sections of the Nacionalista Party, to build a broad united front to defend national and democratic rights against the criminal plots of the enemy. In struggling against the enemy, we will not use grenades, or the throwing of bombs or molotov bombs [*hindi tayo gagamit ng mga granada, o paghahagis ng bomba o molotov bomb*], methods which are used by the Marcos terrorists with the intention of falsely accusing their own victims."[69]

This was a remarkably direct, open articulation of the political ties of the party. The CPP painted the Stalinist line-drawing of the progressive section of the national bourgeoisie by the numbers of the LP. On 30 August, the

League of Editors for a Democratic Society and the College Editors Guild of the Philippines (CEGP) published a joint editorial statement on the suspension of the writ, which built upon this orientation. "The best laid of plots often fail. In the face of widespread opposition from the people: progressive senators, congressmen, and con-con delegates, from the press people, from civil-liberties groups and from the broad masses whom he cannot effectively silence much less fool. The naked truth of Marcos fascist puppetry to imperialist interests will only lead to wider and more massive mobilization of the people behind the national democratic banner."[70]

Repression, they claimed, roused the people and united them—capitalists and workers, senators and peasants alike—behind the banner of national democracy, which the CPP waved for the election campaign of the LP. A new organization was founded to house this expanded unity: the Movement of Concerned Citizens for Civil Liberties (MCCCL).

MCCCL

The MCCCL formed over the course of the politically fraught week that stretched from the announcement of the suspension of the writ of habeas corpus to the end of August. The group was the broadest alliance the CPP ever built; its ranks consolidated barrio catechists, Jaycees, and Communist Party cadre behind a common platform of opposition to the president.[71] The party strained to bring every conceivable organization, other than those directly loyal to Marcos and the PKP, into its fold.[72] It instructed its members to enter each of these groups and influence and win them over, adapting as necessary to their conceptions in order to secure their support for the MCCCL, an organization whose program was so limited it could be scribbled on a napkin. While its awkward acronym implied the defense of constitutional rights, its leadership was composed of retired military intelligence men, coup plotters, and CIA agents; these were not democratic forces.

The class character of the organization found expression in the moniker "Concerned Citizens," a name that historically has smacked far more of right-wing populism than opposition to the danger of fascism. This assessment is borne out by developments. In the first week of October, armed gangs of lumpen elements in Caloocan, adopting the name "concerned citizens," assaulted demonstrators, killing several, including children. Rather than denounce the usurpation of the name, the CPP publicly appealed to these "concerned citizens" to join the broader movement. The MCCCL called for the formation of "vigilante groups" and "neighborhood watch" organizations, clearly revealing that it was not drawing its language from the historical phrasebook of democracy.[73] For all its talk of civil liberties, the MCCCL proved to be an organ for opposition to Ferdinand Marcos and not to martial law.

The party replaced classes with neighborhoods as the base of its organizational work in its rightward lurch initiated on 15 August with the resolution of the SDK executive committee. A week before the Miranda bombing supplied the CPP with the public pretext, the party had covertly launched organizational measures in preparation for full integration with the bourgeois opposition. Under the oversight of the Sectoral Organization Bureau, the SDK rapidly worked to form community organizations, and the KM did likewise. Out of this effort was founded Malayang Kapulungan ng Makabayang Samahan (Free Assembly of Nationalist Federations, MAKAMASA), which was the "Quezon City alliance of progressive groups"; the Ugnayan ng Kilusang Progresibo (Progressive Movement Association, UKP) was formed to play a similar role in Caloocan.[74] In each city and region, the CPP worked to establish a comparable organization and to throw it into support for the MCCCL and the election of the LP.

The MCCCL cohered out of protests against the suspension of the writ, which were staged from the twenty-fourth to the thirty-first. On 24 August, five thousand students rallied at Liwasang Bustillos to protest the suspension of the writ, and the KM and SDK issued a leaflet accusing Marcos of bombing Plaza Miranda, City Hall, Congress, and COMELEC.[75] The next day the KM and SDK staged a rally at one in the afternoon at Liwasang Bonifacio, where Senator Jose Diokno addressed the crowd.[76] On 26 August, a group calling itself the Citizens Movement for the Protection of Our Democratic Rights (CMPDR) issued a statement declaring its strong beliefs that the Plaza Miranda bombing was "part of an organized plot to annihilate the growing opposition to the Marcos regime" and directly accusing Marcos of ordering the bombing.[77] Marcos carried out the bombing, they claimed, with the goal of cracking down on "the most formidable critics of his corrupt and violent administration"—that is, "the Liberal Party, the progressive mass media men, the youth, the militant workers, rural dissenters, and the intellectuals." On the same day, a group of KM-affiliated organizations issued a statement calling for the formation of the broadest possible alliance in "your respective neighborhoods."[78] On Monday, 30 August, the Movement for a Democratic Philippines (MDP) staged a rally at Malacañang; on Tuesday there was a rally on the UP campus; Wednesday saw a CMPDR rally; MAKAMASA staged a "mass action" in Quezon City on Thursday; and on Friday, the Student Alliance for National Democracy held a rally.[79]

On 31 August, Senator Jose Diokno resigned from the Nacionalista Party (NP) in protest over the suspension of the writ. He immediately moved to found a new umbrella organization, the MCCCL, and was made its chair.[80] The MCCCL deepened and expanded the alliance of the front organizations of the CPP with the LP, bringing them into close contact with thoroughly reactionary figures such as Bonifacio Gillego, a man known to have worked for the CIA as a leading agent of Philippine military intelligence. Along with others in the Workshop Group, Gillego spent 1971 plotting to assassinate Marcos, and he thus became an intimate ally of the CPP. The SM invited him to speak to a rally on the UP campus, where he told the assembled students that "without revolutionary theory, there is no revolutionary party. And without a revolutionary party, there is no revolution."[81] Gillego declared that it was necessary to "destroy the present oppressive and exploitative system in the Philippines in order to truly free the Filipino masses, and such destruction requires violence."

The protests continued to grow.[82] On 7 September, six thousand protesters rallied in front of Malacañang, and the *Collegian* wrote that "the march and rally held Tuesday [7 September] far exceeds previous participations of UP in all past mass actions."[83] On Monday, 13 September, the newly formed MCCCL staged its first demonstration against the suspension of the writ, marching from Welcome Rotonda to Plaza Miranda. In October, the publication *Welga!* estimated over fifty thousand people attended the rally, whose speakers included Diokno and Bal Pinguel.[84] The MCCCL made three demands: "immediate restoration of the writ," "freedom to all genuine political prisoners," and "expose and oppose militarization."[85] It is unclear how the last item was a demand. The insertion of "genuine" before "political prisoners" was a weasel word designed to exclude the imprisoned members of the PKP. These became known as the Three People's Demands, and they constituted the entire platform of the MCCCL. The KM, SDK, and MDP repeated these demands at every rally they staged for the rest of 1971.

The dizzying rightward lurch of the CPP, its sordid new allies, and its conciliatory vocabulary were disorienting to the members of its front organizations.[86] Oyie Javate, MDP representative in the leadership of the MCCCL, recounted that she faced the challenge of reassuring members that "we were not giving unnecessary concessions to the more conservative forces."[87] At the same time, the front organizations of the CPP worked mightily to restrain their members to the conservative boundaries established by the new alliance. The SM published a leaflet for the 13 September rally of the MCCCL, *Avoid Slogans That Tend to Alienate Others*, telling protesters "that this is a united front. Cries of 'Rebolusyon!' [revolution!], 'Sigaw ng Bayan—Himagsikan!' [The

people's cry—revolution!], 'Sagot sa "martial law"—Digmaang bayan!' [The
answer to "martial law"—people's war!], 'Amado Guerrero' and the like should
be temporarily avoided."[88] To allay concerns among students and youth about
the new conservative politics of the KM and its allies, they wrote, "We are not
in the united front to compromise, much less to yield our correct political line."
The remedy was to

> grasp the two essential points in our work in the current situation:
> 1—GIVE FULL PLAY TO CREATIVITY AND INITIATIVE.
> 2—PUT DARING ABOVE EVERYTHING ELSE!![89]

The screaming capital letters could not mask the vapid rhetoric. Revolution was gone, leaving in its stead one word: daring. The CPP would direct
workers and youths to *dare* to cast their ballots for the LP slate.

The Election

The LP met the KM halfway. While the front organizations of the CPP adopted
a more conservative approach, the candidates of the LP took up the rhetoric of
revolution and its politicians became adept at mouthing the slogans of the front
organizations of the CPP. Particularly skilled at this was LP congressman John
Osmeña, who was in his mid-thirties but looked eighteen, the scion of an elite
political dynasty, nephew of Sergio Osmeña Jr. In 1971, John Osmeña was
running for Senate. The LP adopted the style of youth activists before the
bombing. On 22 May, the KM, SDK, and MDP staged a rally at Plaza Miranda
to denounce Marcos. John Osmeña addressed the crowd, waving a book before
the audience, a copy of the penal code. He cursed the "fascism" of Marcos and
then set the book on fire, burning it onstage while the crowd cheered.[90] In Cebu
City, Osmeña's home turf, the political ties of the KM and the LP took on an
even more grotesque form. On 12 June, the KM and SDK staged a rally for Osmeña, and he took the stage as the Cebu City Band played "The Internationale." The Philippine Constabulary and local Boy Scout troop stood at
attention. Future historian Resil Mojares, then working as a journalist, wrote
of the event, "Rep. Osmeña struck a responsive chord in the crowds as he repeatedly rapped the *fascist* administration of President Marcos, the *imperialist*
control of the economy, the excesses of the *feudal landlords* and *big compradors*,
leading one to wonder, as he went on with his speech, whether we have here
the beginnings of a Liberal Party design to ride back into power by representing itself as *progressive* through a *co-optation* of the vocabulary of the radicals."[91]
This is precisely what was occurring, and it was a co-optation gladly facilitated
by the front organizations of the CPP. Even the more conservative members of

the LP adopted this strategy. Jovito Salonga told a crowd in July, "If the Marcos Administration repeats its conduct during the 1969 elections in 1971, then we know what we will do: 'Ibagsak si Marcos; itanghal ang baril.' [Down with Marcos; take up the gun.]"[92] The statement was an indication of the desperation of the opposition: they could not be excluded from power again.

The bombing and the suspension of the writ brought immense public sympathy behind the LP's campaign. *Graphic Weekly* interviewed Aquino in October, asking, "How do you perceive the impact of the suspension of the writ of habeas corpus on the attitudes of people in the provinces [to the LP campaign]?" Aquino answered with obvious enthusiasm, "Tremendous, pare! [dude] . . . The reception is fantastic."[93]

On 1 October, the UKP and a range of allied organizations, including KM, staged a rally in Caloocan in support of MCCCL and in protest against the suspension of the writ.[94] Hundreds of armed men organized in gangs, acting on instructions from Mayor Macario Asistio, a retired military colonel and key ally of Marcos, attacked the marchers (figure 4.2).[95] The police assisted in the attack, beating protesters with their truncheons, and four marchers were seriously injured.[96] On 4 October, the KM and its allies called for a rally to be staged the next day in Caloocan, this time to protest the "fascism" of Asistio, whom they began calling "Pasistio"; five thousand protesters gathered on the fifth.[97] Asistio's

FIGURE 4.2. The confrontation moments before violence broke out in Caloocan, 5 October 1971.

armed thugs, styling themselves as "concerned citizens" organized in the Pederasyon ng mga Organisasyon sa Kalookan (Federation of Organizations in Caloocan, POKA), gathered to again attack the marchers. As the UKP marchers approached La Loma Cemetery, POKA assaulted them. The police joined in, opening fire on the marchers. At least four people were killed in the ensuing violence: Ernesto de Lara, age ten; Romeo Antonio, age twelve; Ricardo Barrientos, twenty-one, a member of KM-Santa Ana; and Onofre Tibar, twenty-eight, president of Rossini's Knitwear Worker's Union.[98] A nineteen-year-old KM member had part of his face blown off by a pillbox explosion.[99] The *Collegian* reported that in the first five days of October, specifically on the first and the fifth, 10 people were confirmed killed, including young children (figure 4.3), 51 critically injured (*agaw buhay at malubhang nasugatan*), and 155 arrested.[100] Asistio's political rule in Caloocan was associated with his close ties to Chinese busi-

FIGURE 4.3. The lifeless body of a child murdered by police and hired goons in the confrontation in Caloocan.

nessmen, and the KM and its allies furiously denounced not capitalists but the "kumintang intsik" for the deaths of October 5.[101]

The slogan for the rallies on both the first and the fifth of October was the Three People's Demands of the MCCCL.[102] The MCCCL, under Diokno and Joaquin Roces, led a rally of about eight thousand in Caloocan against Asistio and the violence of 5 October, which was staged at Caloocan City College on 12 October.[103] Diokno told the press that the 12 October march "showed Asistio . . . that the Filipino race [lahing Pilipino] is not afraid of the threats and suppression of the state." Diokno's reference to the Filipino race was part of the campaign to blame the "intsik" for the violence in Caloocan.[104] During the 12 October rally, Bal Pinguel, the national spokesperson of KM, issued a direct appeal to the "ruffians [maton] and goons" of Asistio to "join the national democratic movement."[105] Pinguel was publicly soliciting the support of the forces who but a week prior had murdered the protesters, including young children. The rotten, rightward elasticity of the label "concerned citizens" was here manifest; the only prerequisite for membership in the MCCCL was opposition to Marcos and his allies. In Caloocan, the UKP, KM, and company were backing the LP candidate for mayor against Asistio's reelection and thus sought to secure every vote in the city, bringing them under the umbrella of the MCCCL; it was this interest that Pinguel was articulating in his appeal. This was not an unfortunate stray phrase in a speech, but the central thrust of the organization. It was repeated on 19 October, when the UKP staged another rally in Caloocan in which they again called on the "concerned citizens" of Caloocan to "purge themselves" of the Marcos puppet, Asistio, and back his LP rival, Marcial Samson, for mayor.[106]

The economic crisis continued to worsen, a majority of the population could not afford basic necessities, and the writ of habeas corpus had been suspended. In this charged atmosphere, Marcos recognized that the principal political danger he faced in the 1971 election was not the LP itself but the mass outrage being mobilized behind it by the front organizations of the CPP. It was necessary to attack the youth, who were, after all, at the center of the LP campaign. In early October, a series of television advertisements were broadcast claiming that Communism was behind the current unrest and calling on viewers to "rally against Mao."[107] They depicted young people as adherents of Mao, drug addicts, and disrespectful. One spot had a young person refusing to kiss his elderly parent's hand in respect; another had a young person throwing a Molotov cocktail at the statues of Mary and Jesus in the Quiapo Church.[108] It was widely known that Marcos was behind the advertisements.

Looking to build on anti-Chinese animosities, subordinate social unrest to the LP, and deny allegations that they were promoting Communism, the MDP staged the People's Long March against Poverty and Fascism from 20 October to 24 October. The planning group of the MDP met on the UP campus on 10 October and chose the slogan for the march: "Strengthen the United Front against the Fascist Puppet Dictatorship of Marcos" (Patatagin ang Nagkakaisang Hanay Laban sa Papet Pasistang Diktadura ni Marcos).[109] The MDP staged a kickoff rally on the twentieth at Plaza Miranda, then commenced the march from two starting points: Los Baños, Laguna, in the south and Angeles City, Pampanga, in the north. Two jeeps drove in front of each group of marchers—one carried the baggage and sound system of the marchers, and the other carried the marchers' food and medical supplies. The marchers would leaflet and perform in each of the towns they passed through on their way to Manila, appealing to each community to support the united front against Marcos by voting for the LP.

The leaflet distributed by the MDP throughout the four-day march denounced the Marcos government as the chief puppet of the enemies of the people, identified as US imperialists, hacenderos, Kumintang Chinese middlemen (kumintang na intsik middelmen (sic)), and "our rotten politicians" allied with Marcos.[110] The leaflet insisted that what was needed was a national democratic revolution to build a new society (bagong lipunan), but reassured its readers, "This new society will not be communist, because instead of killing capitalism, it will strengthen and spread it in order to put an end to foreign imperialism and to develop our economy toward the growth of industry and the broadening of trade." Imperialism would be ended, the front organizations of the CPP proclaimed, by strengthening capitalism. The Chinese middlemen and Marcos's corrupt cronies were thwarting progress, but a vote for the LP would ensure the healthy development of capitalism, freeing the country from imperialism and the clutches of the intsik, and setting it on the path to prosperity.

The Nationalist Businessmen's Association, an affiliate of the SDK, also released a leaflet for the march denouncing the "kumintang intsik" business owner—"that devil! [lintik!] he won't even pay enough money to buy rice [pambigas lang]."[111] The NBA stated that the "progressive youth" will "in every town explain the need for National Democracy and National Industrialization. This has not been dictated by the supreme chairman Mao Zedong. [Hindi ito idinikta ng kataas-taasang tagapangulong Mao Zedong.] This is only based on a scientific investigation of the development of any society."[112] On 24 October, the two marches, now numbering thirty thousand, converged on Plaza Miranda, where the front organizations of the CPP turned over the microphone to LP stalwart and Aquino relative Alejandro Lichauco to deliver the final political appeal to the assembled People's Congress.[113]

While the front organizations of the CPP organized and marched, the members of the PKP generally kept silent in the election of 1971. The period of the suspension of the writ of habeas corpus was for them an unpleasant

and politically perilous time. They could endorse neither Marcos nor the opposition, and they would not call for the political independence of the working class. When pressed they declared that they were calling for a boycott, but
they did not actively campaign for one; it was a rhetorical cover for the fact
that they were biding their time through a pained political interlude. Everyone seemed to be aware of this and targeted the party's weakness. On 13 September, as fifty thousand rallied behind the MCCCL in Plaza Miranda, the
Bertrand Russell Peace Foundation (BRPF) denounced the Vanguard Fraternity for distributing a phony BRPF leaflet titled "Parliamentary Struggle Is the
Answer" three days earlier.[114] The disputed leaflet hailed Marcos for suspending the writ in order to suppress the Maoists. The strength of the forgery lay
in its open articulation of what everyone suspected the PKP was privately longing to declare. In opposition to the stance of the fake leaflet, the BRPF sought
to distance itself from Marcos, stating, "In fact, the BRPF is now actively campaigning for the *total boycott* of the 1971 elections."[115] It concluded, "The only
recourse is to forge a broad, united front. . . . At no other time in our history
is the word UNITY most sacred, and treachery most vile." The largest "united
front" in decades had in fact been formed and the PKP was not a member,
precisely because the MCCCL was opposed to Marcos. Class independence
was alien to the Stalinist PKP and unity with Marcos unspeakable; it was thus
compelled to call out the verb "unite" while choking on the predicate.[116]

Gary Olivar, spokesman for the MDP, spent the day of the election, 8 November, at the Lopez-owned ABS-CBN studios where he appeared alongside
Ninoy Aquino on the nationwide election day broadcast "Bilang ng Bayan"
(Count of the Nation) calling on viewers to vote for the LP.[117] As he was departing the studio, he and two companions were arrested by five men. His two
companions were subsequently freed, but Olivar remained imprisoned.[118]

The 1971 senatorial elections were a great victory for the LP. Six of the eight
candidates endorsed by Marcos lost, including Enrile and Blas Ople, who were
quickly reappointed as defense and labor ministers. It was the bloodiest election
the country had ever seen, with the official tally at 206 killed and 217 wounded.[119]
Marcos delivered a televised address to the nation two days after the polls closed,
in which he called for "unity." He offered to consult closely with the LP and requested the cooperation of the media to end the feud with his administration;
"let us start anew," he appealed, "and be as humble as we can be."[120] Gerry
Roxas, president of the LP, "welcomed" the appeal and declared that the opposition would now be consulted "before actual decisions are made." Marcos
stopped making charges against Aquino and his ties to the Communist Party.
Both sides regrouped. The writ was still suspended, the scramble for martial law
continued, but now was the time to quietly maneuver.

The MDP hailed the election victories of the LP as a "victory of the people," writing that "the Filipino masses intelligently saw thru the transparent democratic mask of the fascist administration and fully repudiated the fascist regime of Marcos."[121] One is inclined to wonder what intelligence is required to see through a mask that is already transparent, but what is clear is that the front organizations of the Communist Party depicted the outcome of the election as the full repudiation of fascism. Not content to depict this shift in the tides of elite power as the repudiation of fascism, the MDP characterized the election of the LP as a "preference for Communist leadership." They wrote that Marcos's "tirades against Senator Aquino, supported by affidavits from dead persons and 'revelations' by gangster Commander Melody, had but charged the Liberal Party as a Communist Front. . . . By his own logic, the people then have expressed preference for Communist leadership and have resoundingly rejected the Marcos type of misleadership."[122] On 3 December, the MCCCL hailed the 8 November election victory of the LP, stating that "an aroused people spoke on November 8 and repudiated the undemocratic policies of the Marcos regime."[123]

In the analysis of the CPP, the issue was not the danger of dictatorship, for which both parties were secretly positioning, but that hazy yet unpleasant abstraction—fascism, a policy choice that the electorate had seen fit to repudiate, rejecting it with a wave of the hand from the proffered political bill of fare. The writ of habeas corpus was still suspended, but six LP senators had been elected; the front organizations of the CPP hailed the "victory" of the "aroused masses." For all its rhetoric that people's war was the answer to martial law, during the closest approach to military rule before its full implementation, the CPP mobilized every bit of its strength behind a rival section of the ruling class. The people's war but added heft to the endorsement it weighed on the scales of bourgeois politics.

The election of 1971, staged under the lengthening shadow of dictatorship, publicly exposed the strategy of the CPP. The party would provoke repression, anticipating resistance, and then channel the entire force of this resistance behind its ruling-class allies, looking to them to lead the struggle against Marcos. What conclusions did the working class draw from the experience of 1971? The bankruptcy of the program of the CPP was palpable. While the Stalinist roots of this bankruptcy were far from apparent, all could see that these "communards," these Molotov-throwing criers of revolution, first hailed the suspension of the writ of habeas corpus as good for revolution and then served as the local campaign managers for the political representatives of the sugar barons.

CHAPTER 5

Martial Law

The year 1972 opened with a whimper. Marcos calmly accepted his electoral defeat; on 11 January, he fully restored the writ of habeas corpus but continued to pursue plans for dictatorship, which were nearly complete.[1] The pretexts were numerous and growing, the precedent now established, and all that remained was to outmaneuver and split the opposition. The alignment of the ruling-class opponents of Marcos was a conjunctural grouping at best. They loosely shared a common grievance: Marcos had been in office for too long and needed to be removed. The tide of dynastic power had not turned in 1969 but continued to ebb; alarmed, they gathered in common cause, a political syzygy, and ebb turned to flow in the election that ended 1971. In its wake, their conflict and confusion of interests broke to the surface. They began jostling, eyeing each other uncertainly. The more electorally minded elements saw redemption imminent in the presidential election of 1973 and planned an off year of consolidation and jockeying for position. For others, who felt their interests better measured in balance sheets than ballot boxes, the turning of the tide meant that they could now negotiate to recoup their losses.

The contentions began immediately, and by March they were being publicly remarked upon. The *Asia Philippines Leader* wrote in April, "The current intramurals within the Opposition have been fanned by speculation on who will be the lucky Liberal Party (LP) standard bearer in 1973." There were two contenders—"Senators Gerardo Roxas and Benigno Aquino Jr., LP president and secretary-general respectively. The keen infighting for the coveted nomination next year is anchored on the belief that whoever wins the LP convention will win the presidential election hands down."[2] It was fully expected that mass social opposition would sweep whomever secured the LP nomination into office. Gerry Roxas was a rather dull political figure; his power expressed itself in the backroom, not on the rostrum, but his weight within the leadership of the LP was unrivaled. He sought an immediate nomination of the party's presidential candidate by closed convention, knowing that he could, given the current balance of forces, secure the nomination by these means. Aquino recognized that he could not win on these terms, but he also saw that Roxas would in this way split the opposition. Laurel, Lopez, Diokno—these forces had left Marcos's camp and largely broken with the Nacionalista Party (NP). Where would they now go? Aquino thus called for an open convention—which would include the participation and nomination of independent candidates—to be staged six months before the election, declaring that this strategy would "dangle a carrot" before Lopez, Laurel, and company.[3] He anticipated that the loose and straining opposition would hold given these terms, each angling for a slot on the ticket, but expected, given the weight he would carry in an open convention, that he would secure the nomination, while Laurel would likely stand as his running mate. The opposition was reaching a breaking point, "the whole problem boiled down to the rivalry between Roxas and Aquino," and Aquino played an uncharacteristically cautious game, looking to delay the battle; "he kept his loquacious self out of the picture."[4]

The opposition broke unexpectedly, as its strongest link proved also to be its weakest. In May, Lopez made peace with Marcos. Business interests and not political advantage were paramount to the Lopez brothers. Fernando Lopez was three times a vice president, never a president, yet this did not perturb him. Malacañang concerned them only as a means to an end, and that end was Meralco. Marcos astutely recognized that the Lopezes, fearing that Aquino was losing out to Roxas and that the opposition would fragment, were inclined to strike a deal with the president while they still carried the political clout of the united opposition. Marcos ensured their profits and they called off their attack. For the Lopez brothers this was victory, but for Marcos it was a gambit in a larger game. The neutralization of the Lopez family was the moment he had been waiting for: the opposition had lost its strongest backer; the time to strike was now, before the opposition recovered its forces. He launched all his plans for military rule—bombing campaigns, preparatory propaganda, foreign delegations to secure international support. Within four months he had successfully declared martial law.

The program of the Communist Party of the Philippines (CPP) sought to articulate the interests of a section of the capitalist class in order to secure their allegiance. Its allies on the platform of old money eyed one another with suspicion from January until May, and the CPP perforce hesitated, waiting for a clear signal. The party sought to secure gains in the wake of the successful election by uniting with the conservative and right-wing forces around the Liberal Party (LP) with whom it had campaigned—"the middle forces." But the specter of a common enemy was in early 1972 a diffuse motivation; the slogan calling for unity against Marcos led to what exactly? They had just voted against him and won. What was the political imperative now? The first half of the year was thus a time of consolidation without any particular goal; binding together disparate forces without a specific cause was a difficult task. The protests staged by the front organizations of the CPP thus bore the imprint of their allies' standoff; they were desultory, disjointed affairs, halfhearted and largely pro forma. Flabby campaign followed flabby campaign, each increasingly enervated and ephemeral.

Thus, in the wake of its successful maneuvering in 1971, the CPP entered 1972 in a position of surprising weakness. Having worked for the election victory of its bourgeois allies, the spoils were not forthcoming. Financial support continued, but at a languorous pace as the opposition was preoccupied with jockeying among themselves. What is more, the CPP had lost some of the more significant and radical elements on its periphery. The experience of the latter half of 1971 had been disheartening for those convinced by the earlier rhetoric of pillbox and storm. Community service projects had replaced barricades, and protest marches were nothing but election rallies; this was not what they had signed up for. The CPP sought to shore up its ranks by recruiting new forces, drawn in their majority from conservative religious groups, bound to the party only by a thin nationalist opposition to Ferdinand Marcos.

The danger of martial law had not gone away. Both Marcos and Aquino spoke of it regularly, and it was widely understood that it was being readied. The opposition's frenzied jostling over 1973 was in part an expression of the fact that a great many suspected it would be the last election held for a long time. This was the common concern of the ruling class, simultaneously uniting and dividing them: a social explosion was imminent and military rule was needed. The *Asia Philippines Leader* concluded its article on the infighting within the opposition with this line: "Overshadowing all these is the most important question of all: Will the next President of the Republic . . . ward off that impending revolution?"[5] The disjuncture between this imminent peril and the tepid and disoriented actions of the CPP and its front organizations is perhaps the most striking feature of the year of martial law.

Seeking to ally with the middle forces, the front organizations of the CPP cobbled together a number of broad but shallow organizations in the first months of 1972. Each proved short-lived. In January they formed the Alyansa ng Bayan Laban sa Pagtaas ng Presyo ng Langis (People's Alliance against Oil Price Hikes, ABLPPL), which hosted an alphabet soup of organizations of such politically disparate character that there was not a single programmatic line on which they could agree or that could hold them together. The Jaycees and the Samahan ng Demokratikong Kabataan (Federation of Democratic Youth, SDK), the Lion's Club, the Democratic Car Owner's Association, and gasoline dealers—all were progressive sectors according to the CPP.[6] January's alliance quickly dissipated and was followed in February by the formation of the Movement for Democratic Reforms, an umbrella organization opposing the threatened closure of the University of the Philippines (UP) Tarlac.[7] It disappeared from the historical record in the month of its founding. March saw the formation of the Anti-Imperialism Movement (AIM), an alliance founded on racist nationalism in support of "FILIPINO capitalism." It targeted "aliens in our midst," above all the Chinese, as "ENEMIES. They must be DESTROYED."[8] AIM sought to consolidate relations between influential radio personality Roger Arienda's political apparatus, Ang Magigiting (The Brave), and the front organizations of the CPP. Nothing came of it. The party turned its attention to yet another issue-based coalition in May, overseeing the formation of the Kilusan ng Bayan Laban sa Batas Medicare (People's Movement against the Medicare Law, KBLBM), dedicated to protesting Marcos's proposed Medicare Act. The act provided limited state-run medical coverage for workers funded by contributions from the workers themselves. Articulating the interests of the middle forces, KBLBM denounced the act as "socialized medicine," declaring that the country remained "semi-feudal, semi-colonial" and was not ready for "socialism."[9]

The demonstrations of early 1972 bore the imprint of this orientation. They were markedly different from those of the preceding two years, and there was an air of general unseriousness to their proceedings. During the State of the Nation address, the KM and its allies staged their annual rally, holding a People's March led jointly by the MDP and various Social Democratic (SocDem) groups. Ten thousand students, youths, and workers attended.[10] Where previous years had seen fiery political tirades, 1972 witnessed Willie Nepomuceno—launching his career as a stand-up comedian—perform comic impersonations of Marcos and Villegas, interspersed with his renditions of Popeye.[11] The KM and SDK organized campus sporting events at Diliman in which various national democratic teams with names like the Keglerettes competed.[12] Volleyball nets were strung up where barricades had stood a year before.

Each organization and demonstration was an isolated event, only tenuously connected with a larger political struggle. Yet even as it allied with conservative forces and launched weak demonstrations, the KM continued to declare that military suppression and dictatorship only served to hasten the revolution. On 16 March, the KM wrote of the death of Arsenio Rienda, who had been shot in the back, they claimed, by security guards at Arellano University while he was marching in a protest. According to the leaflet, the "forces of the revolutionary people are reaping victories," and "the ruling class more than before [*higit sa rati*] must use violence." The leaflet concluded, "This will only further inflame the eruption [*mag-aalab ang silakbo*] of the national democratic struggle."[13]

While it hailed repression for building revolution, its rightward orientation led the CPP to embrace sections of the repressive apparatus of the state. On May Day, the KM, SDK, and MDP staged their annual labor day rally, and among those in attendance were the striking workers of LK Guarin in Malabon.[14] On 23 April they had been attacked on the picket line by the Philippine Constabulary (PC) and Metrocom, as the PC drove a weapons carrier through the workers' barricade and opened fire with armalites and machine guns, killing an unknown number of workers and arresting sixty workers and activists.[15] The MDP led the demonstrators during the May Day rally to chant "Mabuhay ang Makabayang Pulis!" (Long live the nationalist police!), followed by "Ibagsak ang Pasistang Pulis!" (Down with the fascist police!). While law enforcement murdered workers on the picket lines, the MDP praised what it claimed were its nationalist, progressive sections. They did not want the middle forces to think that they were opposed to the entire state security apparatus, only to its "fascistic" elements. The nationalist police were the good guys and should be embraced. In recognition of this, the MDP invited a member of the Malabon police to serve as a featured speaker at its May Day rally.[16] Two days later the Malabon police again attacked the picket line of striking workers at LK Guarin.

The CPP worked to scoop up the aimless middle elements who served as a bulwark of detritus around the squabbling bourgeois opposition. The result was inert purposelessness in a context of imminent repression, and the ranks of the KM and SDK bore the twin pressures of social tension and political ennui. As its ruling-class allies lost their common orientation, the front organizations of the CPP, uncertain where to channel the energy of the streets, fell to squabbling as well. Aquino and Roxas turned from haggling to backstabbing, Lopez eyed the exits, and in March and April 1972 the old disputes between the KM and SDK, long buried under shared political purpose, reemerged.[17] The tensions between the SDK and the KM never reached a breaking point, not because they resolved their dispute but largely because martial law rendered it moot. By the end of 1972, both organizations had effectively vanished from political life, and by 1975 they were formally dissolved.

Diplomacy and Dispute

The machinations in Manila took geopolitical form. Nixon continued to pursue a policy of détente with Mao. In October, Kissinger again visited Beijing, making the final arrangements for the US president's visit in the coming year. On the twenty-fifth the People's Republic of China (PRC) was admitted to the United Nations as "the only legitimate representative of China."[18] In late February 1972, Nixon traveled to Beijing and met with Zhou Enlai. The week before his arrival, US forces in Vietnam launched the heaviest bombing campaign in the war to date, but Beijing said nothing. Nixon and Zhou issued a joint communiqué at the end of Nixon's visit, declaring their agreement "to facilitate the progressive development of trade between their two countries."[19] While the Soviet bloc had felt compelled to vote for the admission of China to the United Nations, the various pro-Moscow parties around the globe howled in protest at the tightening bonds between Washington and Beijing.

Marcos, meanwhile, sought closer relations with Moscow. In March 1972 Imelda Marcos traveled to Romania, Yugoslavia, and the USSR, where she visited Moscow and Leningrad, a trip that marked a significant step to the opening of full diplomatic ties between the Soviet bloc and Manila.[20] On 10 March, in the midst of her visit, Ferdinand Marcos announced the opening of formal diplomatic relations with Yugoslavia and Romania. In Moscow, Imelda Marcos met with Soviet premier Alexei Kosygin for extended discussions over the course of three days, as well as with the deputy premier, foreign affairs minister, and foreign trade minister, issuing a statement that she hoped the talks would lead to "the normalization of relations between our two countries."[21]

The ruling-class opposition, in contrast, was traveling to China. From 17 to 22 March, as Imelda Marcos was returning from Moscow, Salvador Laurel journeyed to the PRC, where he met with the vice premier to discuss Manila's possible future foreign relations with Beijing, declaring his support for a One China policy. The *Asia Philippines Leader* aptly described his visit as "an opening salvo in the coming battle for Malacañang."[22] Laurel, a disgruntled NP member, was weighing running for vice president on the Aquino ticket.[23] Laurel's visit to Beijing in March was an anticipatory quid pro quo, seeking popular support through the front organizations of the CPP. The foreign policy maneuvers of the bourgeois opposition were carried out with both eyes fixed on 1973.

At the beginning of the new year, as Nixon prepared to visit Beijing, the Partido Komunista ng Pilipinas (PKP) launched a furious new series of attacks on the CPP. Each was increasingly unhinged in its rhetoric and rooted in the conflict between the rival Communist parties in the Sino-Soviet split. The PKP published a special issue of *Ang Komunista*, "Issues in the Ideological Dispute between Maoism and the International Communist Movement."[24] The MPKP denounced Sison and his "political juvenile delinquents" for "parroting the Beijing line."[25] In March the PKP declared that China was "no less counter-revolutionary than the Nixon government" and in April that it was "on the road to capitalist integration."[26] The CPP was silent throughout these attacks. Having published at the end of July 1971 a single, brief defense of the "proletarian foreign policy" of Beijing, they held their tongue. The Nixon-Zhou communiqué, with its promises of increasing ties and burgeoning economic trade, issued while more and more bombs rained down on the people of Vietnam, was an embarrassment. The less that was said about it, the better. Scenting blood, the PKP pressed on the geopolitical weakness of its rival, but in late May, Nixon traveled to Moscow. After repeatedly denouncing Mao's dealings with Washington, the PKP immediately hailed Brezhnev's deal with the American president as "a victory for peace and socialist foreign policy."[27] The hypocrisy was mutual; the PKP stopped publishing attacks on the pro-imperialist policies of Beijing and its local lackeys in the CPP.

The published broadsides, which had become repetitive and dull, ceased entirely; but while the ink was left to dry, blood continued to flow. Street battles—waged between these two Communist parties, now the armed gangs of a cutthroat bourgeois rivalry—commenced in earnest. Early rumbles, staged in the wake of the election, produced individual victims, but by the middle of 1972 rallies left a body count in scores.

The language of the rival organizations was of wartime propaganda. A leaflet from the Bertrand Russell Peace Foundation (BRPF) and the MPKP, for example, reported that at dawn on 23 November the "fascist provocateurs and anarchists of the KM-SDK-Sison traitor gang made a treacherous assault against Paterno Castillo, an MPKP labor organizer and member of the National Council." Castillo was killed by a pillbox thrown at this head.[28] The BRPF called on its members to "crush the Kabataang Mamamatay-tao [murderers] and their front organizations!!" and demanded "retribution" against the "murdering Maoist henchmen of the ruling classes that now run amuck under the disguise of being 'national democrats.'" Several weeks later the MPKP and BRPF accused the New People's Army (NPA) of being "bandits who rob, rape and kill the rural population of Tarlac, Isabela and neighboring provinces."[29] They described the First Quarter Storm and Diliman Commune in viscerally hostile language. "These crackbrained schoolboys raised hell in the cities to force the masses to revolt with them. Toward this end, the pillbox loving fanatics of Sison staged senseless violent demonstrations in which they caused the sadistic sacrifice of the lives of their 'comrades' and the untimely deaths of innocent bystanders."[30]

There was more than a note of desperation in the chorus of odium sung by the PKP from late 1971 to the middle of 1972. While the CPP kept silent, intimately allied with political forces on the make, the PKP flailed, looking to remain relevant. The PKP was tied to the hated Marcos; its youth wing was a staid, straitlaced outfit, ill suited to the era of the Molotov cocktail. The party's published attacks bore the imprint of geopolitics and the ire of Moscow is present in every line, but its concern that it was becoming a spent force lent their formulations a double share of vitriol. The PKP was doing quite well at present, its leadership comfortably ensconced in salaried government positions from which to negotiate the interests of the Soviet bureaucracy, but shadows limned the future. The PKP's influence with Marcos would persist only so far as it remained politically useful; Marcos would discard the party should it prove otherwise, and it knew it.

For Marcos, the party had two significant functions. First, its bombing campaign allowed him to manufacture a pretext for martial law. In the final analysis, however, this function could be played by the military alone, and the role of the party, while useful, was expendable. The party's second and far more important function for Marcos was to provide his administration with sway over the masses, a political influence and prestige to counter the clout of the Communist Party wielded by his rivals. Retaining utility for Marcos thus required that the PKP have a robust hold over a section of youth. Herein lay the crux of the party's dilemma: retaining ties with Marcos required securing the support of youth; securing the support of youth required opposition to Marcos.

Francisco Nemenzo sought the resolution to this dilemma in the creation of the Young Communist League (YCL), a new organization of PKP youth that recruited almost exclusively on the basis of the romanticized image of the guerrilla. The new group spoke of neither Marcos nor Aquino but of .45 caliber ammunition, gun battles, and fiery-eyed warriors. The YCL was thus tailored to secure a grip over the imagination of a broader layer of youth while providing a cover to expand the bombing campaign whose explosions were tallied one by one in the whereas clauses of Marcos's declaration of military rule.

In July 1969, *Ang Bayan* wrote of the PKP, "At the moment, the two 'independent kingdoms' of the local revisionist renegades are already separately set to support the 'New Revolution' of Marcos."[31] The article noted that while "a majority within [the PKP] determines the character of the clique as a puppet of Soviet revisionist social imperialism," the party was "wracked by internal contradictions." The contradictions of which *Ang Bayan* wrote were almost certainly a reference to Nemenzo and his group within the party, whose allegiance was to a set of political ideas derived from Havana. This group was attached above all to the image of the petty bourgeois guerrilla as the archetype of the future, and far less to the political line dictated by Moscow. Before September 1972, the rival orientations of the Nemenzo group and the majority of the party leadership did not take the form of opposition, for they shared a common enemy—the Maoists—and worked closely together. The guerrilla orientation of the Nemenzo group provided the basis of the YCL. As the curtain of martial law rung down, however, tensions within the party fragmented Nemenzo and a portion of the YCL from the majority of the PKP, with bloody consequences.

To understand these developments, it is necessary to examine the theoretical conceptions of Nemenzo as they had been articulated by Régis Debray and Carlos Marighella. Nemenzo was drawn to the Cuban Revolution and saw in the tactics of Castroism the means of waging revolution in the Philippines. Castroism was a guerrilla movement that sought to secure the ends of Cuban nationalism in opposition to the Fulgencio Batista dictatorship. Fidel Castro, who as a student had been politically influenced by the ideas of Falangism, had no orientation to Communism or Marxism. He sought to seize political power through armed guerrilla bands, organized in centers or *focos*, and the promise of limited agrarian reform measures. He was opposed in this by the Stalinist Communist Party of Cuba, which had in the 1940s entered into the Batista government. In the end, the Batista regime fell not because of the armed might of the few thousand men organized under Castro but because it lost the support of the Cuban bourgeoisie and of Washington, which imposed an arms embargo on his government. Castro initially sought friendly relations with Washington, but when the United States sought to dictate economic terms to the new regime by cutting Havana's sugar quota, he turned to Moscow for aid. The Cuban Stalinist Party was instructed to support the Castro government and to supply it with an ideology.[32]

The clearest articulation of the ideology of Castroism written for the foreign press was Régis Debray's *Revolution in the Revolution?*, which took the pragmatism of Castro's foco guerrilla tactics and dressed them up in the theoretical language of Stalinism.[33] The present, Debray claimed, needed to be "freed from the past" (*RR*, 19), as the principles of Marxism, the lessons of the revolutions of 1917 and 1949, and the struggles in Vietnam were not only irrelevant but their implementation would in fact be deleterious. Debray wrote that by "a stroke of good luck" Castro had not read Mao, and "he could thus invent, on the spot and out of his own experience, principles of a military doctrine in conformity with the terrain" (*RR*, 20). Castro's ignorance facilitated the correct development of his tactics, and these pragmatically derived tactics were the basis of all else. Debray argued that "the right road, the only feasible one, sets out from tactical data, rising gradually toward the definition of strategy" (*RR*, 60). The historically derived lessons of past struggles, the scientific understanding of revolution, society, and class forces—these were detrimental to the development of revolution. Marxism should be reduced to the tactical campaign for power by guerrillas; the rest should be scrapped.

The foco, the center of guerrilla operations, was not a base but a mobile unit, an independent band freed from any ties to the civilian population (*RR*, 32, 41). It did not emerge out of the masses but was separate from them. Debray wrote, "Whereas in Vietnam the military pyramid of the liberation forces is built from the base up, in Latin America on the other hand, it tends to be built from the apex down—the permanent forces first (the *foco*)" (*RR*, 52). Winning the population over to the *ideas* of revolution was irrelevant, for the revolution was not based on ideas at all. What mattered were military victories. "The destruction of a troop transport truck or the public execution of a police torturer is more effective propaganda for the local population than a hundred speeches" (*RR*, 53). Debray boasted, "During two years of warfare, Fidel did not hold a single political rally in his zone of operations" (*RR*, 54). Military successes needed to be heralded, however, and thus leaflets would be left behind proclaiming the victories of the foco.

Most importantly, Debray argued, in the second section of his work, titled "The Principal Lesson for the Present," these roving armed focos, free from both the broad population and any semblance of political thought, could not be subject to the leadership of a vanguard party, for the focos themselves were in fact the embryos of a future revolutionary party. They drew into their armed ranks individuals from all parties, bourgeois and working class, and made them into a new unit. "Gradually, this small army creates rank-and-file unity among all parties, as it grows and wins its first victories. Eventually, the future People's Army will beget the party of which it is to be, theoretically, the instrument: essentially the party is the army" (*RR*, 105). He expanded, "The vanguard party can exist in the form of the guerrilla *foco* itself. The guerrilla force is the party in embryo" (*RR*, 106). No external political authority to the focos could exist, and "the guerrillas must assume all the functions of political and military authority . . . must become the unchallenged political vanguard, with the essential elements of its leadership being incorporated in the military command" (*RR*, 109). Debray concluded on this point,

For the moment there is a historically based *order of tasks. The people's army will be the nucleus of the party, not vice versa.* The guerrilla force is the political vanguard *in nuce* and from its development a real party can arise.

That is why the guerrilla force must be developed if the political vanguard is to be developed.

That is why at the present juncture, *the principal stress must be laid on the development of guerrilla warfare and not on the strengthening of existing parties or the creation of new parties.*

That is why *insurrectional activity is today the number one political activity.* (RR, 116)

For Debray, the solution to the Sino-Soviet dispute lay in a "shortcut" (RR, 123)—the abandonment of politics entirely. *"Revolutionary politics, if they are not to be blocked* [by the Sino-Soviet dispute], *must be diverted from politics as such.* Political resources must be thrown into an organization which is *simultaneously* political and military, transcending all existing polemics"[34] (RR, 124). These conceptions served as the basis for the political activity of Nemenzo and the YCL: insurrectional activity was the primary political task, and, although Nemenzo did not yet openly articulate this, it would be carried out by units independent of the PKP. Through the YCL, Nemenzo began organizing a foco in opposition to the party of which he remained a leading member.

Debray's ideas, however, were refracted for Nemenzo through the writings of the Brazilian Stalinist Carlos Marighella. Marighella, a member of the Central Committee of the Partido Comunista Brasileiro (PCB), rebelled against the leadership of the party when it refused to adopt methods of armed struggle against the military dictatorship that had been imposed by coup in 1964, ousting the João Goulart administration with which the PCB had been allied. Marighella traveled to Havana in 1967, where he adopted the perspective of Castroism articulated by Debray, and in response was ousted from the PCB. Marighella adapted the principles of the foco to an urban setting, transforming the rural guerrilla units of Castroism into urban hit squads engaged in acts of "terrorism." In 1969, Marighella published his conceptions in a manual dedicated entirely to the practical details of urban terrorism, *Minimanual of the Urban Guerrilla.*[35] In keeping with the conceptions of Castroism, Marighella was entirely concerned with tactical matters. He detailed how to carry out kidnappings, executions, sabotage, terrorist bombings, and bank robberies but gave no political program to which these actions were subordinate. The fundamental political task, however, was clear: small urban focos, of approximately five members, would carry out terrorist acts to destabilize the military dictatorship. These urban guerrillas would bomb government facilities and foreign-owned firms and would leave behind leaflets as a means of distinguishing themselves from bandits and counterrevolutionaries.[36] Nemenzo circulated a mimeographed version of Marighella's *Minimanual* within the ranks of the YCL.[37]

The YCL was organized at the beginning of 1971, recruiting from the MPKP and other PKP front organizations and training them as members of the party.[38] The impact of the YCL, however, was far broader than its membership, for it cultivated the image of the PKP as an organization of rebellious youth taking up arms against an oppressive system. In December 1971 the YCL published the first issue of a new journal, *Ang Mandirigma* (The Warrior).[39] The founding editorial stated that the "primary function" of *Ang Mandirigma* "will be that of a collective agitator and organizer of the youth. It will serve to inspire all the revolutionary youth to deliver hard and mortal blows against the neo-colonial state machine. It will prepare them to pass on to higher forms of struggle, at the same time making them realize the inevitability of armed struggle as the final path to take as the ruling classes will not step down on their own accord."[40] Armed struggle was inevitable, but where *Ang Bayan* would have spoken of the US-Marcos regime, *Ang Mandirigma* hid the identity of its enemies behind the formulation "neo-colonial state machine." This was not because it was opposed to the entire bourgeoisie, but rather because it could not name the section to which it was loyal.[41]

The armed struggle was, for *Ang Mandirigma*, less of a means to an end and more of an end in itself. To become a guerrilla was an ideal to which one aspired, not a recourse to which one was driven. It was a romantic archetype, not a political strategy. When a member of the Hukbo Mapagpalaya ng Bayan (People's Liberation Army, HMB) was killed, the paper honored him for having been "a fast draw with his .45" but made no mention of his ideas.[42] The February-March issue of *Ang Mandirigma*, which opened with a quote from Che Guevara, dedicated a significant portion of its pages to romantic biographies of the party's guerrillas.[43] An article by Vangie de Castro, for example, was dedicated to Soliman, the head of the People's Revolutionary Front (PRF). De Castro wrote that Soliman was an "urban guerrilla" and "very manly [*lalaking-lalaki*]. His movements are smooth, confident and discreet. . . . While carefully entering his strictly guarded 'hideout', one notices that he is wearing a long-sleeved 'paisley' shirt, appropriately cut black pants, and suede shoes [*sapatos na gamusang*] that are clearly well-cared for, all of which help to create a 'suave' effect ['*suwabeng*' *epekto*]." The biography of Commander Angela reads in a similar manner: "In front of the burning wood that only intensifies the fire in her eyes, her male comrades armed with carbines, armalites and .45s, breathlessly wait to hear her words. . . . Like her revolutionary namesake,

Angela Davis in the United States, Commander Angela has reached the high level of revolutionary struggle."[44] Angela was twenty-two years old, we are told, had married a fellow guerrilla, and was "now recognized as a Commander." "For her, it is of great value to be skillful with a .45."

While these guerrillas were glorified, they did not live in the countryside, not with their paisley shirts and their suede shoes. Angela rejected the Maoist perspective on guerrilla struggles in the countryside, stating, "You can't organize anything in the mountains except wood." The interview with Soliman stated that the PRF was created as a rejection of the Maoist line of encircling the city from the countryside, arguing that the true Marxist military strategy was to balance forces in the city and the countryside. Soliman stressed that the first task to be carried out by the armed wing of the party was urban sabotage and "armed propaganda" through bombings. He claimed to have bombed Caltex and Esso in January 1970[45] and further claimed that his group had bombed the Joint US Military Advisory Group, the Jefferson Library, the Constitutional Convention at the Manila Hotel, and other buildings.[46] With these repeated open declarations of responsibility for the bombings plaguing Manila, it is unsurprising that there was a growing public awareness that the explosions, which Marcos was citing as a possible pretext for martial law, were being staged by the PKP. The KM issued a leaflet denouncing the "Lava-MPKP-BRPF revisionists" for working with the Marcos regime in carrying out "terrorism," "arson," "bombings," and "theft."[47]

On 15 March, PKP bombed the Arca building on Taft Avenue, which *Ang Mandirigma* proudly headlined as a "victory for armed propaganda" and claimed that Soliman had "carefully" chosen to use only seven kilos of explosives so as not to damage adjacent buildings.[48] Soliman announced that "there will be many more attacks of this kind in the coming months."[49] On 22 September, Marcos would place the Arca bombing at the head of his list of reasons for declaring martial law and would lay the blame at the feet of the Maoists.

Street Battles

In the first weeks of May, Ferdinand Marcos and the Lopez brothers made peace. Marcos revealed the acuity of his political insight in his recognition that the giant of the opposition was its weakest link. The dispute within the LP deeply concerned Fernando and Eugenio Lopez, as they saw their clout weaken at a time when their business interests were deeply imperiled. "By early 1972, Meralco was in a deep hole because of a combination of its high costs, interest rates rising out of control and outdated power rates. In March 1972, it filed an application with the Public Service Commission (PSC) for a rate increase of 36.5%. The next presidential elections were not until November 1973. Under the most optimistic scenario, even a change to a sympathetic administration meant that Meralco would not get rate relief until nearly two years later—an eternity given the scale of the financial shortfall. So a ceasefire—if not necessarily a lasting peace—was vital to Meralco."[50]

To carry out his ends, split the opposition, and launch the final preparations for martial law, Marcos had to make the reconciliation with the Lopez brothers look like a defeat. He humbly petitioned them to resolve the dispute in April, offering generous terms. The Lopez brothers would not come to Malacañang, so on 10 May, Benjamin Romualdez, brother of Imelda Marcos, personally drove Marcos to Eugenio Lopez's house, where they concluded the negotiations. Marcos granted Meralco its rate increase.[51] The Lopez brothers immediately altered the oppositional stance of the *Chronicle* and ABS-CBN, and thus, in the final months before dictatorship, the nation's largest television and radio broadcast network adopted an editorial policy conciliatory to Marcos.

As the Lopez brothers broke from the opposition, Aquino found a renewed sense of purpose. He was no longer biding his time for 1973, seeking through patience and silence to outlast Roxas; now was the time for action. There were rumblings from sections of the military loyal to Aquino and Osmeña that Marcos would attempt to implement martial law by the end of the rainy season.[52] The imperative was no longer long-range electoral jostling but immediate maneuvers against the possible seizure of power by the president. The music reached a frenetic tempo and only two men were left competing for the throne: Aquino and Marcos. Roxas, the man of the political machine, was as ill suited to these heady final months as his rival had been to the torpor of January to May. The reckless and headstrong Aquino came to the fore, self-assured and relentless. The CPP and its front groups drew renewed energy from their revived ally and sought to mobilize the entirety of the middle forces in the final battle for Malacañang. The conservative groups among whom the CPP had been working since the bombing of Plaza Miranda met the Communist Party halfway in this endeavor. The Jaycees and Catholic Student groups began chanting the slogans of the KM and marched alongside their allies into street battles marked by pillbox explosions and gunfire, while the Sandigan Makabansa (Patriotic Pillars, SM) ran a campus election slate dominated by its conservative partners. The community service projects continued, but now they distributed both relief goods and the literature of the Communist Party. This common purpose did not express an ideological meeting of the minds, but the renewed focus of the bourgeois opposition that summoned both its Right and Left flanks behind it in disciplined lockstep.

Rallies immediately reverted to their earlier incendiary tactics and strident language, and within ten days they had again turned bloody, with gunshots fired and pillboxes thrown. The occasion for the unleashing of this renewed militancy was the war in Vietnam. In late April, as the United States launched a massive bombing campaign against Hanoi and Haiphong and Nixon announced that US forces had mined Haiphong harbor, protests broke out around the world. A mass demonstration staged on 20 May 1972 marched toward the US embassy but found that the police had erected barricades in their path. At the head of the joint SocDem and National Democratic (NatDem) forces marched Bonifacio Gillego, a former military intelligence officer and now a leading coup plotter against Marcos.[53] The rally of ten thousand people was inching forward, pressing up against the blockade while singing the national anthem, when explosives were thrown. Lacaba wrote that "no one can say where the first pillbox came from. . . . The demonstrators do not deny that before the first blast died away some of them had reached for their pockets like fast-draw gunslingers, pulled out their own pillboxes, and hurled these into the ranks of the Metrocom." Some of the explosives thrown at the demonstrators came from the upper floors of the nearby Shellborne Hotel.[54] The Metrocom opened fire on the protesters, wounding fifty of them, eight critically. Ninety were arrested, seventy-five of whom were subsequently released. The remaining fifteen, the government claimed, had been "abducted by a rightist terrorist group." They were not heard from again.[55]

As the KM and its conservative allies united in the streets, Marcos deployed the front organizations of the PKP, which were directly funded by Malacañang, to confront them. From 7 to 12 June, the KM and its allies staged the March against American Imperialism for National Democracy, marching from San Fernando, Pampanga, to Manila and concluding with a demonstration in front of the US embassy on 12 June, Independence Day. The CPP medical front group, Makabayang Samahan ng mga Nars (Nationalist Federation of Nurses), claimed that the marchers were attacked by members of the MPKP while they were marching through Bulacan.[56] The MPKP responded that it was they who had been attacked by the KM and called for the violent crushing of their rival: "The oppressed mass of our country will march to victory and freedom . . . over the debris of the Maoist apparatus!"[57]

By early July the ambushes and assaults turned into open street battles, in which scores were wounded and kidnapped and murdered. On 4 July, the MDP staged a rally at Plaza Lawton, where a battle broke out between its diverse array of forces and those of the MPKP. Both sides threw pillboxes, and thirty-five people were wounded in the conflict. Several elderly peasant demonstrators were beaten with sticks.[58] In the wake of the bloodletting, the rival

Communist parties denounced each other. Both sides were in fact violently assaulting each other. They had turned sections of their demonstrations into roving armed groups, the street-fighting proxies of Marcos and Aquino as they vied for military dictatorship. While the KM and SDK were renowned for their street battles and Molotov cocktails, it was the forces of the MPKP that were largely responsible for instigating the bloody conflicts of mid-1972. Soliman later recounted to Nick Joaquin, "Ruben [Torres] and I were among the marchers. . . . As everyone knows the KM was very fond of pillboxes and it greeted us with a shower of pillboxes. Many among us were wounded. In the ensuing rumble we succeeded in catching the pillbox-throwers; in fact that was the reason for the rumble, in which, of course, Ruben and I participated. We turned over the KM pillbox-throwers to our provincial forces, who could be ruthless with troublemakers. I don't think those KMs got home that day."[59] Soliman's laconic "in fact that was the reason for the rumble" clearly suggests that the PKP deliberately provoked the fight, with the intention, it seems, of capturing and killing a number of KM members. Ruben Torres, Central Committee member of the PKP, was overseeing its street battles against the KM while working as a salaried Marcos administration official.

On 30 September 1971, Fidel Agcaoili traveled to Beijing on behalf of the CPP to negotiate an arms shipment from China, bearing Sison's request that the Chinese Communist Party (CCP) supply the CPP with M-16 assault rifles and deliver the weapons by submarine. The Chinese party leadership responded that they would supply M-14s but that the CPP would be responsible for delivering the arms to the Philippines themselves.[60] Agcaoili traveled to Japan and purchased a fishing trawler in rather poor shape that the CPP christened *Karagatan*.[61] A crew of nine Filipinos trained in China for three months before the ship embarked for the northeastern coast of Luzon in June 1972 at the onset of typhoon season.[62] *Karagatan* arrived at the mouth of the Digoyo River on 3 July. Danny Cordero had been shot in the back of the head earlier that morning. The crew attempted to ferry the arms in a small boat, but *Karagatan* ran aground on a sandbar barely a hundred yards offshore, driven by the winds of Typhoon Edeng.[63] The CPP forces on the beach were spotted by a plane operated by a logging company executive who promptly reported the suspicious activity to the military, which sent a boat to investigate.[64] A firefight broke out between Corpus's forces onshore and the military in the boat. The NPA had managed to off-load the weaponry and supplies onto the beach but had not yet moved much of it into the shelter of the jungle. The next day the military deployed F-5 jets and helicopter gunships that strafed and bombed the beach. Corpus and the NPA were forced to retreat, and the government forces captured 738 M-14 rifles, 150,000 rounds of ammunition, and 500 rocket shells.[65]

The story of the *Karagatan* arms shipment broke in the Philippine press on 7 and 8 July. Both Ramon Mitra and Aquino told the press that they had evidence that the *Karagatan* affair was a hoax staged by Marcos to justify martial law.[66] The opposition press ridiculed the idea that arms were being smuggled from China. The *Asia Philippines Leader* depicted the government's account as drawn from an Ian Fleming novel in which the NPA operated a "labyrinth of air-conditioned tunnels packed with electronic gear, the nerve center of international conspiracy."[67] Four soldiers had been killed in the encounter, so the CPP and its allies could not dismiss the affair as entirely fabricated but claimed instead that an ordinary fishing vessel had run aground at a location where the government had engaged in a minor firefight with the NPA. Seizing the opportunity, Marcos had arms planted on the beach to depict this as a major incident involving an international arms shipment.[68]

Typhoon Gloring followed Edeng, flooding much of Luzon.[69] "Entire towns and villages remained under water for weeks when the Laguna Lake rose by two meters and overflowed its shores, inundating hundreds of villages and laying waste the vast rice fields of Laguna, Bulacan and Pampanga province. The importation of more than 400,000 tons of rice from Thailand, Taiwan and Japan became a matter of national survival as the prices of commodities soared by 25%."[70] The MDP reported that over 260 people died in the floods.[71] The front organizations of the CPP launched Operation Flood Relief, a massive community service program that distributed relief goods and an eight-page anti-Marcos comic book, *Ang Bayan at ang Baha* (The nation and the flood), which advocated armed struggle under the leadership of the party.[72] The PC attempted to seize the relief goods and carried out a raid on the headquarters of a local union, arresting forty-two doctors, interns, and volunteers.[73] Over the next month, the military would stage a series of similar raids and mass arrests as the final preparations for martial law were set in motion.

Imposition of Martial Law

President Marcos announced the declaration of martial law (figure 5.1) and Minister of Public Information Francisco Tatad read the entire text of Proclamation 1081 in a nationwide broadcast in the late afternoon of the twenty-third of September, but the public had become aware of the imposition of military rule earlier in the day when their radios greeted them with nothing

FIGURE 5.1.   Ferdinand Marcos announces the declaration of martial law on national television, 23 September 1972.

but static and no morning papers could be purchased. The steady flood of publications, daily papers, and news weeklies, with their revelations, allegations, and counterallegations, all abruptly stopped. The curtailing of journalism thins the archival record to a trickle, not only for the period after the imposition of dictatorship but also for the weeks leading up to it. Each publication was tied to a rival ruling family and served it as a political weapon; thus with a predictable regularity the backroom deals of contending sections of the elite would emerge within months to public consciousness in the form of interviews and exposés popularly referred to as *bomba*. The censorship of martial law not only ended daily coverage of developments; it truncated the exposure of the final political maneuvers on both sides from July to September.

The last months are poorly documented, but the tenor and thrust of the final machinations can nonetheless be adequately traced. The tide of dictatorship was rising, it had to be taken at the flood. Both Marcos and Aquino sought to use their own Communist parties to secure military rule; the NPA attempted, and spectacularly failed, to smuggle arms from China; the PKP, working with the military, launched a frenzied bombing campaign throughout Manila; and the KM and SDK latched onto the August inundation to distribute both relief goods and the anti-Marcos literature of the CPP. Washington readied to accept either side as victor; it had numerous assets in both camps and would endorse whichever man finally sat secure on the "throne of bayonets."

The denouement proved stunningly lopsided. Aquino's reckless self-assurance and will to power were no match for the remorseless calculation of Marcos as he moved through the final stages of the plot he had carefully calibrated over the course of two years. Aquino's failed bid for dictatorship in 1972 was one of the grossest miscalculations in Philippine political history; it proved so slight, so insubstantial, that most are unaware that it was even attempted. Throughout his entire political career he had never lost, and it went to his head. He seems to have genuinely believed that Marcos's final steps toward martial law would occasion a spontaneous upsurge of the masses led by his allies in the CPP in coordination with coup-plotting elements in the military and thrust him into power. In retrospect, he resembles a vainglorious prizefighter posturing in the ring before being knocked out in the opening seconds of the first round. The subjective psychology of the man, with his ill-fated sense of invincibility, was not the determining factor in the defeat of the opposition, but it did lend the entire affair a biting irony.

In the final analysis, the weakness of Aquino's gambit expressed the irresolution of the entire opposition and was intrinsic to its class. They sought martial law; they did not oppose it. The danger of a social explosion mounted, they could all sense the rumbling, imminent threat to their class position and privileges and agreed that an apparatus of repression was required. Until it was in place, they were, in the words of Rizal, "dancing on a volcano." They fought tooth and nail for the throne, but when the music stopped, so too did their scramble. They would tolerate the Bonapartism of the occupant of the palace and endure his occasional predations, as long as the great unwashed were kept in their place. The bourgeois opposition maneuvered desperately to be in power until the morning of 23 September. When military dictatorship was fully implemented, in their vast majority they acquiesced, resigning the political field with an apparent sense of relief. They had accepted every step toward dictatorship; their objection had never been to military rule but to Marcos, not the apparatus but the occupant.

Aquino intended to seize power through an uprising led by the CPP in conjunction with a military coup and then immediately implement martial law. For this to succeed it was imperative that he have the support of Washington, and on 12 September, Aquino held a private meeting with two political officers of the US embassy. Aquino first made clear that he supported military dictatorship regardless of who implemented it. The embassy officers summarized Aquino's position: "Marcos must take strong actions in the near future and these will include martial law. If the President follows this course, Aquino said that, 'for the good of the country,' he will support Marcos."[74] The embassy reported that "the growing threat from the dissidents, the worsening law and order problem, the serious economic setback that has resulted from the floods in central Luzon . . . were cited by Aquino as reasons why stronger central government action is needed. Such action means martial law. Were he President, Aquino indicated that he would not hesitate to take such strong action and would, for example, execute several corrupt officials at the Luneta Park in Manila as a lesson to other officials that he meant business."

Having established that he would either back martial law or impose it himself, Aquino then informed the embassy political officers that he might in the near future attempt to seize power. "Aquino believes that the possibilities of his becoming head of government by legitimate means are quickly diminishing, and he is accordingly keeping open an option to lead an anti-Marcos revolution in alliance with the Communists."[75] During the same meeting, Aquino informed the embassy officers that

> he had recently held a secret meeting with Jose Maria Sison, Chairman of the Central Committee of the Communist Party of the Philippines/ Marxists-Leninist (CPP/ML).[76] Aquino and Sison discussed the possibility of forming a broad united front in opposition to the Marcos Administration. Aquino said that he had been offered, and had declined as being premature and unwarranted by the present situation, the position of leading a revolutionary government "in the hills" in alliance with the CPP/ML. Aquino also subsequently provided Sison with a statement of his principles and program for review by the CPP/ML. In Aquino's view, however, the internal security and socio-economic situations in the Philippines are rapidly deteriorating. He believes that President Marcos intends to stay in power indefinitely and that his own chances of becoming head of the government by legitimate means are slight. He thus may be willing at some point in the future to ally himself with the Communists as the leader of a revolution, if he is convinced that this is the best way for him to realize his ultimate political ambition.[77]

Aquino was dissembling as much as he was revealing. Many of the formulations recorded by the embassy political officers in this summary statement are decidedly false. The idea that Sison and Aquino discussed the "possibility" of a "broad united front" is absurd, for the CPP had been at the core of such a united front with Aquino for the past four years, mobilizing its forces on his behalf while funded and salaried by him. Several of its leading members worked on his staff. The phrase "government 'in the hills'" is similarly ridiculous. Aquino did not aspire to be president of the Sierra Madre and Sison knew this; he sought full control of Malacañang and would go to any length to seize it. Between the lies, Aquino was informing the embassy that he was about to attempt to seize power with the assistance of the Communist Party. The outlines of the plot are clear, although its details are hazy. The CPP was engaged in a coup plot involving sections of the military brass with ties to Manglapus, which was being orchestrated through Danilo Vizmanos. Both the CPP and its bourgeois allies saw their plan to put Aquino into power as effecting something akin to Salvador Allende's relationship to the Communist Party and the military in Chile. The CPP would characterize this as a "revolutionary coalition government" with combined representation of the CPP and the military, a formulation in close accord with the founding document of the party, the *Programme for a People's Democratic Revolution*.[78]

Aquino was not naive, and he knew that Washington would look askance on a Communist seizure of power. He sought to allay these concerns by declaring his support for martial law and informing the embassy that if he succeeded in taking power he would implement military dictatorship and publicly execute dissidents.

While Aquino readied his plot to seize the presidential palace, Marcos took the final steps to gain permanent hold of it. A string of bombings rocked Manila. A bomb was set off at Joe's Department Store on Carriedo Street on 6 September, leaving one dead and scores wounded.[79] On 18 September, Samahan ng mga Guro sa Pamantasan (Federation of University Teachers, SAGUPA) published a statement claiming that among those "arrested in connection with the Carriedo bombing and the aborted Good Earth Emporium bombing was a PC Sergeant, a top-notcher in a PC special course on explosives handling."[80] More bombings followed: Manila City Hall, two Meralco power stations, the water main in San Juan, the telephone system in Quezon City, and Quezon City Hall.[81]

On 13 September, Aquino delivered a privilege speech in the Senate accusing Marcos and the military of orchestrating the bombings in a plot to justify martial law. He claimed the plot had the code name "Operation Sagittarius," and cited "confidential sources in the Armed Forces."[82] Aquino had intimate ties to sections of the military leadership, and his information was correct, but only partially so. Sagittarius was a military plan, drawn up by Armed Forces of the Philippines (AFP) chief of staff Gen. Romeo Espino in early August. It was not a bombing plot, however; it was the military blueprint for responding to riots and "massive civil disturbance" during the early stages of dictatorship. Sagittarius was not the pretext for martial law but a component of its implementation.[83] Aquino's allies in the front organizations of the CPP published and circulated his speech, adding to his accusations that the PKP was working closely with the military to carry out the bombings. On 11 September the KM staged a protest rally at Plaza Miranda, where it circulated a leaflet accusing the "junior fascist Lavaite gang HMB-MPKP" of carrying out the terrorist bombings that were being used as a pretext for the possible declaration of martial law, and claimed that the MPKP had "braggingly admitted" that it was responsible.[84] The September issue of *Kalayaan*, the publication of the KM, featured a caricature of Marcos and Lava jointly holding a gigantic grenade labeled "terrorist bombings" at the behest of Richard Nixon, wearing a tall Uncle Sam hat.[85] On 19 September, the SDK issued a statement citing the April-May issue of *Ang Mandirigma* as proof that the PKP HMB was behind the bombing spree, listing eighteen bombings or attempted bombings that had taken place since 3 July. The SDK claimed that these had been carried out "by the puppet military with the help of their Lavaite cohorts," and called on readers to join a rally of the Movement of Concerned Citizens for Civil Liberties (MCCCL) on 21 September against the danger of martial law.[86]

On 14 September, Marcos gathered a council of twelve men to implement the declaration of martial law; ten were members of the top military brass, and two, Juan Ponce Enrile and Danding Cojuangco, were civilians. This group would later become known as the Rolex Twelve, as Marcos, after his successful imposition of dictatorship, gave each a commemorative watch. Marcos informed the group that he intended to impose martial law, and they discussed the logistics of the declaration and the targets for arrest, holding daily meetings from the fourteenth to the twenty-second of September to hammer out the details. Their plotting carefully drew on Suharto's experience in Indonesia in 1965–66, and at least two of the Rolex Twelve had been in Jakarta at the time.[87] Two days later, an article in the *Far Eastern Economic Review* stated that Marcos "hinted this week that, for the second time in two years, he may resort to emergency measures such as the suspension of the writ of habeas corpus in the face of growing threat from subversives and anarchists," and added that "a so-called militarization bill was pending in the lower house of Congress seeking to make all civil officials and government employees technically members of the military service."[88]

Marcos blamed the CPP for the bombings and continued to point to its ties to Aquino. The *Far Eastern Economic Review* reported that Enrile claimed that "a fifteen-man liquidation team—led by two ranking NPA commanders, Noli Villanueva (alias Ka Temyong, a former leader of the militant youth organization Kabataang Makabayan) and Benjamin Sanguyo (alias Commander Pusa)—is at large in Manila."[89] Sanguyo was closely tied to Aquino, and his name would be used to add weight to Marcos's charges against his rival. Repeating the line of Marcos's administration, the article declared that "the NPA itself has made no attempt to contradict reports blaming it for the bombing incidents." This was an outrageous falsehood. The CPP and its front organizations had repeatedly denied culpability and had pointed to copious evidence that the PKP itself had claimed responsibility for the bombings. Despite the PKP's multiple publications proudly claiming responsibility for the bombings, at no point did Marcos accuse the organization. He intended to use the bombings as a pretext not only for imposing military rule but also for rounding up the leaders of the front organizations of the CPP prior to the official declaration, breaking key links between the bourgeois opposition and the mass movement. At dawn on the seventeenth, the PC launched a wave of arrests, capturing approximately fifty leading members of the CPP and its front groups and shutting down thirteen of their organizational headquarters.[90] In response to the mass arrests, the MDP called on its members to join the protest rally of the MCCCL on 21 September.

The Rolex Twelve continued to convene each day. Aquino, meanwhile, began to gather with his coterie in a suite of rented rooms at the Hilton Hotel. The MCCCL prepared for a massive rally against Marcos to be staged on 21 September. The SM issued a leaflet on 19 September with the heady yet correct title *The Situation Is Critical—What Is to Be Done?* It laid out the steps Marcos had taken toward the imminent declaration of martial law, then answered its crucial political question in one sentence, calling on readers to "act as we did during the period of the writ suspension." During this period, the front organizations of the CPP had channeled all opposition behind the LP, and they were doing so again now. This entailed building for the MCCCL's protest rally on the twenty-first and continuing "militant protest actions in the University."[91] These actions in the university were speaking opportunities for Marcos's elite opponents. That afternoon, Diokno led a rally on the steps of the Arts & Sciences (AS) building at UP, telling the gathered audience of one thousand students and faculty members to "do mass protests now against the Marcos administration and against Marcos manufactured situations, if we are to maintain our freedom and prevent a Marcos takeover of the government."[92] The danger was not martial law itself but Marcos; it was a Marcos takeover that needed to be prevented. Diokno downplayed the danger of martial law, telling his audience, "The implications of martial law, if implemented, are the following: firstly, the President would in effect have the highest priority in issuing orders as the commander-in-chief of the Armed Forces; secondly, the Constitution of the Philippines would not be suspended nor will the writ of habeas corpus be suspended if the situation did not warrant it. Our constitutional rights would still be intact if the imposition of martial law materialized." Two days before military dictatorship was firmly imposed, Diokno informed protesters that martial law would effectively change nothing. The president was already commander in chief, and, according to Diokno, constitutional rights would remain intact. The next day, Bonifacio Gillego, Bal Pinguel, and Roger Arienda spoke from the AS steps. Gillego and Diokno were leaders of the elite opposition. They spoke alongside CPP members such as Bal Pinguel, who would whip up the crowd with tall tales of the NPA and marshal its support for the coming storm. The leadership of the MCCCL was not opposed to martial law; they were opposed to Marcos. While the CPP rallied protesters to listen to their speeches, Aquino advanced his scheme to secure the reins of dictatorship.

On 20 September, Marcos staged a televised press conference in which he announced that Aquino had met with Sison earlier that month. He cited Enrile, who claimed that Aquino had personally revealed this to him and that he had in turn informed Marcos.[93] Aquino responded in a speech in the Senate on the twenty-first, denying that he had met with the CPP. He claimed that the Marcos administration was making this up as a pretext to assassinate him and then claim that the NPA had carried it out.[94] It is highly implausible that Aquino informed Enrile of his meeting with the CPP, and it is much more likely that Marcos learned of this from the US embassy. Enrile also claimed that Aquino spoke of a plot by "men in the AFP" backed by "big financial supporters in Manila" to bomb Malacañang with "commandeered Air Force planes."[95] This claim was not out of keeping with the schemes in which Aquino, Osmeña, Diokno, and Manglapus were engaged. If there was any truth to the claim, the CPP would have been a subordinate component of the plan and not at its center, as Enrile alleged.

What is most striking in the political flurry of the last week before dictatorship is that the majority of accusations being hurled were accurate. Aquino and the CPP charged Marcos with having the military and the PKP stage bombings throughout the city as a pretext for martial law. Marcos accused the CPP of smuggling arms from China and working with Aquino, in conjunction with elements in the military, to plot the president's ouster. The broad details articulated by both sides were true.

On the same day as Aquino's speech, fifty thousand people assembled at a rally in Plaza Miranda under the leadership of the MCCCL, of which there are few available details, as the press was silenced the next day.[96] What is noteworthy is that there was mass opposition to the danger of martial law, but it had been mobilized behind Diokno, the MCCCL, and the bourgeois opponents of Marcos by the front organizations of the CPP.

On the evening of 22 September, Marcos and Enrile concocted the final pretext for the declaration, which they had drawn up weeks before. Enrile staged an armed assault on his own motorcade and blamed the Communists. This "ambush" was the final straw, Marcos stated, and he declared martial law at midnight that night, backdating the proclamation to 21 September, in keeping with his superstitious predilection for the number seven and its multiples.[97]

A series of prepared orders were signed into law that night and put into immediate implementation. Marcos issued general orders for the government to take over all media outlets and all public utilities, including electricity, water, telephone, rail, and air travel. Schools were closed for a week and a nightly curfew imposed. Mass arrests were ordered and a military tribunal created to prosecute those charged. Anyone carrying a firearm outside their home without permission from the military would be punished with death; carrying a pillbox or Molotov cocktail would be punished with fifteen years' imprisonment. Rallies, demonstrations, and strikes were banned. Filipinos were not allowed to leave the country, nor were they allowed to send money abroad. All films, domestic or foreign, deemed subversive were to be banned by a board of censors. The wages of the military were raised.[98] Martial law was the legal architecture for social repression. The Marcos dictatorship, installed with its measures, would arrest over seventy thousand people without warrant, kill at least thirty-two hundred, and torture thirty-five thousand.[99]

Marcos immediately had his leading opponents arrested.[100] Aquino was at the Hilton with a cohort of opposition figures when military forces under Col. Gatan came to arrest him. "Aquino merely smiled, believing Marcos to have made a monumental blunder. 'Colonel,' he congratulated Gatan, 'you have just made me the President of the Philippines!'"[101] This was not mere bravado; Aquino was convinced that the declaration would spark an uprising that would lead to his seizure of power. Aquino's allies held the same conception. Manglapus was in Japan on the twenty-second and "his first instinct when he heard that martial law had been declared was to come home and join the 'resistance.' He telephoned his family and told them so. What resistance?—they cried."[102]

The character of the arrests varied greatly depending on the class of those detained. Abaya recounted that "a number of Left sympathizers in plush Makati villages had also packed overnight bags, dressed and waited for the dreaded knock on the door, but it never came—somewhat to their chagrin. They were safe, by National Intelligence Coordinating Agency (NICA) standards. It was a different story for the young activists and ideologues who bore the brunt of the inquisitors' blind fury."[103] While the activists arrested may have borne this "blind fury," the leading bourgeois political figures—Aquino and his cohort—were quite comfortable. Abaya wrote that the morning after their arrest, "breakfast, self-service style, was a pleasant surprise—eggs, boiled or scrambled, bacon, *pan del sal*, *longaniza*, fried rice, coffee, and Danish pastries no less, but not enough to go around. And lunch was fried chicken in picnic boxes."[104] Smuggling kingpin

Lino Bocalan was among those arrested, and he made arrangements so that every day they had "Native delicacies and hot coffee in the morning, full meals at lunch and supper, prepared by Bocalan's second lady from the day's catch by his Capipisa crew. We passed our rations on to our security guards, and Bocalan saw to it that they also had a share of the specials, like prawns, crabs and lobsters."[105] Thompson writes, "All traditional politicians and their close allies who had been arrested were released within weeks except for Senators Jose Diokno . . . and Aquino who were held two and seven and a half years respectively. . . . Although properties were confiscated from a few top oppositionists, most members of the Philippine elite were left alone by the Marcos regime."[106]

Sergio Osmeña Jr., Eugenio Lopez, Raul Manglapus, and Salvador Laurel—many of the key leaders of the elite opposition to Marcos—were out of the country when martial law was imposed.[107] Some took up life in exile, others returned and pledged loyalty to the dictator. Laurel returned to Manila on December 10 and personally informed Marcos, "Mr. President, martial law, which you now hold in your hands, is a double-bladed weapon. It can be used for good or for evil. Use it to cut for good, Mr. President, and you won't have to worry about me."[108] The elite opponents of Marcos stumbled over themselves in their haste to declare loyalty to the regime. Prominent political signatories to a manifesto circulated on September 21 opposing martial law sent desperate back-channel appeals for the manifesto to be buried.[109]

The Liberal Party dropped all opposition to Marcos and supported martial law. It issued a statement that "the sweeping Marcos reforms coincide with the reformist goals of the opposition." Martial law, the LP declared, was "necessary to offset the communist conspiracy, destroy the serious cancer of the sick society, bring down ill-gotten power and privilege, and achieve new national discipline."[110] The Constitutional Convention, assembled in 1971 to make changes to the country's charter, had been dominated by forces hostile to Marcos prior to the declaration. Former president Diosdado Macapagal, president of the convention and one of the most influential figures in the Liberal Party, led the convention to vote for the dictatorship. Macapagal met with Marcos in Malacañang on the day martial law was declared and launched a campaign to bring the support of the entire opposition behind the declaration.[111] Hoping that an endorsement of martial law would secure Aquino's release, Raul Roco, who was both the head of Aquino's legal staff and a delegate to the constitutional convention, announced his support for a yes vote on the constitution. Roco told the handful of delegates still contemplating a no vote, "It is meaningless to vote 'No' anyway. The important question was what possible harm could there be in voting 'Yes'?"[112] Within eight weeks of the declaration, Macapagal secured the nearly unanimous passage of a new constitution, which ratified martial law and ceded all political power to the executive branch.

Aquino was outmaneuvered and abandoned. Imprisoned in Fort Bonifacio, where he was to spend the better part of the next decade, he asked his lawyer, Senator Jovito Salonga, "Where are the young people who said revolution would follow the declaration of martial law? Where is the Liberal Party? Ano'ng nangyari? (What happened?) Has everyone accepted martial law?"[113] It was more a cry of despair than a question. The opposition to Marcos had collapsed and Aquino's elite allies and co-conspirators had embraced the dictatorship.

In its vast majority the bourgeois opposition was not suppressed, and within weeks a mere handful remained imprisoned. Those released acquiesced to Marcos's military rule and resumed a comfortable existence. They had lost the contest for the palace, but the real threat to their interests would be effectively stamped out; no social uprising would jeopardize their class position and privileges. Intimate friends gathered in a quiet *sala* might jealously gripe—while their household servants replenished their drinks—at the gaucheness of the First Lady and her shoes, but they would not organize, nor would they imperil the dictatorship; it served a useful end. The outcome might not have been ideal, but things were quieter now and they would cultivate their gardens. It was different for the working class and peasantry. "Between September 1972 and February 1977 a total of nearly 60,000 had been arrested for political reasons by the martial law regime."[114] The great mass of those arrested were neither traditional politicians nor members of the CPP; they were workers, peasants, and students, and they bore the brunt of state repression throughout the martial law period.

Immediately after the declaration, Executive Secretary Alejandro Melchor flew to Washington, where he met with top officials and held a press conference on 25 September, while Ambassador Carlos Romulo announced the declaration before the United Nations.[115] Washington approved of the military dictatorship. The American Chamber of Commerce announced its full support for martial law. In the first week of October, the US State Department announced an additional $30 million in military aid for the Marcos administration. On 24 November, the *New York Times* published an editorial by Ambassador Leon Ma. Guerrero justifying the declaration.[116] Washington wrote Marcos's land reform bill, which attempted to provide a reformist justification for military dictatorship. In 1973, Nixon stationed his old intelligence hand, William H. Sullivan, who had been responsible for the conduct of the US secret war in Laos, to serve as the US ambassador in the Philippines under the

Marcos dictatorship.[117] On 24 September, Marcos sent House Speaker Corne-lio Villareal to Moscow to formally announce the declaration of martial law and to expand diplomatic ties with the Soviet Union.[118] Marcos had until this point been negotiating diplomatic and trade ties with Moscow under the aus-pices of the executive trade authority extended to him by Congress in 1967, but this authority had lapsed and Marcos's dealings were in violation of the anti-Red trade law. Martial law removed this hurdle and made ties with the Soviet Union possible.[119]

On the morning of 23 September, before the official announcement from Malacañang, the Civil Liberties Brigade of the UP Student Council issued a statement, "Marcos, the mad bomber, has imposed martial law!" It provided a few cursory details of arrests and then asked "what is martial law? . . . Martial law is nothing but the last card of the US-Marcos regime to prevent its total col-lapse in the face of massive opposition from the Filipino people. We have noth-ing to fear. . . . Marcos has still to learn that the Filipino cannot be cowed!" The leaflet concluded with now-familiar language: "A movement supported by the people is invincible. Try as they might to suppress it they will only miserably fail. For every patriot they arrest, two or more from the masses come forth to replace them."[120] A new group calling itself Nagkakaisang Mamayan ng Pilipinas Laban sa Taksil at Pasistang Pangkating Estados Unidos-Marcos (The United People of the Philippines against the Treacherous and Fascist US-Marcos Clique), whose rhetoric revealed its ties to the CPP,[121] wrote, "Martial Law has finally been declared. . . . Brute military force now rules our lives," and continued,

> We must unite in the face of outright suppression of our democratic rights. We must form underground anti-fascist, anti-US Marcos clique alliances. . . . We can make it difficult for the hired goons to move about by the organization of anti-fascist alliances in communities, factories, schools and offices. . . . One way of counter-acting the media black-out is by writing letters to friends. . . . Another way is by passing this paper around. . . .
>
> Let the US-Marcos clique shiver at the sight of an awakened people. We should always bear in mind that the defeat of the US-Marcos clique is the victory of the Filipino people. . . . We the Filipino people have the spirit to fight the enemy to the last drop of our blood. Thousands upon thousands of Filipino martyrs have heroically laid down their lives for the people; let us hold their banner high and march along the path crimson with their blood.[122]

The immediate response of the front organizations of the CPP and their allies was to double down on their nationalism and insist on unity with the bourgeois opposition. The defeat of Marcos was now proclaimed as *the* victory of the Filipino people—that is to say, the defeat of Marcos would be the victory of the national democratic revolution. The US-Marcos clique would "shiver" in the face of the antifascist alliances—yet to be formed—and . . . chain letters. The CPP fully expected its bourgeois allies to continue to fight against Marcos. The silence that followed was deafening.

The CPP: Utterly Unprepared

The declaration of martial law found the CPP utterly unprepared. By September 1972, the party had grown to nearly two thousand members, and its network of front organizations was vast.[123] In Proclamation 1081, Marcos accurately stated that the KM had a membership of fifteen thousand and the SDK fifteen hundred. This entire apparatus was founded on the political strategy of supporting a section of the bourgeoisie, and the CPP, at the head of the KM, SDK, and their allies, had carried out this strategy with precision. It had cultivated alliances with the sections of the bourgeoisie opposed to Marcos, carefully serving their interests and exacting concessions and support in return. It was not an error in the implementation of the political line of the party that led to its utter lack of preparation for martial law, an event it had been anticipating for years. My examination of the record of the CPP from 1969 to 1972 reveals that the leadership generally exercised tactical skill in the implementation of their program. It was precisely the program itself—Stalinism—that made possible the declaration of martial law and left the party floundering.

The CPP allied with a section of the bourgeoisie, but in the face of martial law its allies disappeared. A handful were arrested, some left the country, a few joined the apparatus of the dictatorship, but the majority acquiesced. Had history proceeded along an alternate track in which Aquino outmaneuvered Marcos, martial law was just as inevitable. The rival Stalinist parties had allied with the leading contenders for the throne, and both were positioned to ride the coattails of dictatorship. Neither scenario—victory for Marcos and the PKP or Aquino and the CPP—provided a way forward in the struggle against dictatorship and repression. In the event, Aquino was defeated and the CPP was left desperately repositioning itself. As martial law was announced, the CPP immediately sought to facilitate the continuation of opposition under its bourgeois allies. Rigoberto Tiglao, head of the party's Manila-Rizal Regional Committee, instructed members of the party to mobilize a demonstration that would gather at the Sta. Cruz church in Manila, where, he stated, they would be joined by congressmen and senators who would vote against Marcos's declaration of martial law. The party was to "protect the assembly inside the church with the might of the mass movement, and with armed resistance if necessary." The oppositional gathering of senators and congressman under the protection of the Communist Party never took place, as only a handful of legislators arrived. The police arrested a few of those guarding the church, and the rest moved to another church in Binondo, where, along with a few congressmen, they staged a mass.[124] If their appeals for bourgeois intervention went unheeded, perhaps they could secure divine intervention instead.

The party continued to reach out to the coup plotters, examining in a November publication the various sectors of dissent within the military leadership and appealing to them to join the anti-Marcos struggle. Manglapus was in exile, however, and Diokno and Aquino in prison; the purse strings of dissent drew tight. The loyalty of the disgruntled brass had been to the highest bidder, and none would venture from the barracks for the scant rations on offer. Like its counterparts in uniform, the CPP lost its patrons. It issued repeated appeals to the bourgeoisie to join a united front against Marcos but was greeted with silence. It sweetened the terms and expanded the market, offering to protect the business interests of anyone—landlord or capitalist—who would fund it. Eventually there were takers: landlords and logging interests in the hinterlands that knew a deal when they saw one and rented out the affordable muscle of the NPA. The mesh of ties to the bourgeoisie, however, who kept their heads down for half a decade, would not be reestablished until 1978.

Martial law shattered the front organizations of the party. Some of the leaders were arrested, a great many of the rank and file went into hiding or exile, and the debris was swept into the countryside. Of the fifteen thousand members of the KM in September 1972, the majority took up neither arms in the countryside nor enforced residence in a Camp Crame cell. They looked to the party for leadership, and the party dug through the ashpit of its history and located the cindered remains of the single-file policy, dusted it off, and dressed it up with a new name—Student Revolutionary Committee (SRC). Whether bound together in the remnants of old organizations or absorbed into the gelatinous structures of the new, those who sought direction from the CPP were given very little to say. The party had reduced its political platform to the denunciation of martial law and claimed that dictatorship would bring about the revolution. The actual imposition of military rule thus found it at something of a loss for words. The front organizations of the party denounced restrictions on miniskirts at Santo Tomas or lights-out curfews in the UP dormitories. They sought to cobble together opposition behind the banner of the most tepid reformism, recruiting from layers within the Reserve Officers' Training Corps (ROTC) and the Lion's Club.

The party effectively emptied the cities of trained and dedicated cadre, sending everyone to the hills. The ranks of the NPA swelled slightly, not through an influx of new forces but through the redeployment of the old. The squadrons roaming the Sierra Madre and the byways of Bicol, however, no more threatened Malacañang than a comparable bunch in the Adirondacks would endanger the White House. The vanguard abandoned the working class, leaving them in the city without leadership, to bear the brunt of dictatorship. Tens of thousands were arrested, and thousands were tortured and murdered. Their mutilated corpses were tossed among the sparse tufts of *talahib* in the trash-strewn lots of Cavite, Rizal, and Bulacan. Through all this, Sison celebrated the imposition of dictatorship. Repression bred resistance, he claimed, and the more Marcos brutalized workers, the more they would rise up. In the cracking bones and bloodied faces of the Filipino working class, Sison found cause to rejoice.

SRC: Return to the Single-File Policy

On 9 October, a new group calling itself the Student Revolutionary Movement issued a three-page appeal to students to take up the struggle against the Marcos regime. Written by the CPP, the document called on students to read *Philippine Society and Revolution* and assured them that the CPP would contact them shortly. This first set of instructions issued by the CPP to its urban network in the wake of the imposition of martial law exposes with startling clarity the extent of the damage that had been inflicted on its apparatus. Printed seventeen days after the declaration, the instructions attempted to reconstitute—in an unplanned, ad hoc fashion, through chain letters and personal acquaintances—the movement that the party had painstakingly built over the course of years of struggle and consolidation. The document declared that the "US-Marcos military dictatorship is hellbent on 'dismantling' all student organizations. . . . Student leaders have been incarcerated. . . . Student publications have been banned and all forms of organizations, from Christian organizations such as the Student Christian Movement to national democratic organizations, such as the Students' Alliance for National Democracy are now the target of military suppression."[125] Despite the repression, the party claimed that the movement had never been stronger.

> In its sick thinking, the US-Marcos clique imagines it can crush the revolutionary mass movement. . . . But the imposition of martial law and the suppression of all dissent has only served to raise ever higher the level of revolutionary consciousness and strength among the students and the people for effective resistance. . . .

The cultural revolution it [the student movement] has waged can never be suppressed; it will continue to awaken the masses of the people and mobilize them against the US-Marcos military dictatorship. The US-Marcos fascist dictatorship has only inflamed the revolutionary students and youth throughout the country. (*FSY*, 1)

The document called on students to unite with "all forces and individuals" opposed to Marcos (*FSY*, 2). This drastic expansion of the bloc of four classes was in keeping with the strategy that the party had adopted since the November 1971 election and that it had implemented through the MCCCL. Its alliances were as broad as the social structure of the Philippines, yet were bound together solely by opposition to Marcos; their breadth was limitless but their depth negligible. One could wade across the expansive ocean of the MCCCL and scarcely wet one's feet. Unity with "all forces and individuals": CIA operatives and landlords, clerics and corrupt politicians—it did not matter. If they opposed Marcos, they were welcome.

The masses were inflamed and the alliance limitless, the CPP declared; but the organizational apparatus in which to house this will and expansive network had been effectively suppressed. Seeking to rebuild, the CPP called for the adoption of "the particular form of organization of the Student Revolutionary Committee (SRC)."

These SRCs can assume the general task of organizing and mobilizing the students, peasants, farm workers, the national minorities and fishermen in a well-defined area of the province. We can effectively combat the US-Marcos military dictatorship's attempt to crush our organizations by keeping the membership of such committees unexposed while still boldly organizing hundreds of committees. Every student must assume the responsibility of organizing his closest friends or schoolmates into such a committee. Every member of such a committee must then assume the task of organizing his own friends into another new committee, and each member of the new committee must then organize other new committees, and so forth. (*FSY*, 3)

This was a revolutionary pyramid scheme, a sort of Stalinist Amway. Less than three weeks after the declaration, the CPP was scrambling to rebuild its urban front organizations from the ground up by means of spontaneous networks of friends and classmates. The party instructed students to expand their networks and circulate political material by "chain-letter" campaigns, writing out by hand copies of political material and mailing them to a broader group of acquaintances (*FSY*, 2). The party depicted these steps as a security measure. "To guard against enemy suppression and infiltration, the members of one committee need not be known to other members of other committees. Thus will the revolutionary mass movement protect itself and rapidly expand the underground movement to transform the masses into a sea of flames in which to drown the US-Marcos military dictatorship. Every patriotic student must be integrated into these SRCs and we must build these committees into cohesive and self-sacrificing cores of revolutionary leadership" (FSY, 3).

The SRC policy of the CPP repeated almost verbatim the single-file policy of the PKP under the Lavas, which Sison had made the target of so much political ire. Like the single-file policy, the formation of SRCs eliminated the possibility of any democratic discussion within the movement, for when you were contacted your task was simply to pass on directives. What is more, the SRC did not provide additional security but drastically weakened the defenses of the CPP. The security of a revolutionary organization rests in its disciplined centrism, not its decentralized structure. The SRC policy made it the simplest matter for agents to form committees, join committees, and arrest individuals and groups without anyone else's knowledge. An agent who was exposed could simply join a different committee and no one would be the wiser.

Attempting to dispel concerns that this policy represented an immense setback for the party, the document continued,

> The students who take the initiative of forming their revolutionary committees should be confident that many others are doing the same in the city. They shall be approached by the proletarian revolutionary party for recruitment and cooperation on the basis of what they have already contributed to the national democratic movement. The masses of students should feel confident that the revolutionary mass movement and the revolutionary organizations have been unscathed. The revolutionary mass movement has expanded more vigorously than ever, in other forms of organizations and struggle to advance the people's democratic revolution against US imperialism, feudalism, and bureaucrat capitalism to victory!!! (FSY, 3)

What this document spells out is that the legal front organizations of the CPP, every sectoral alliance and umbrella group, were completely unprepared for the declaration of martial law. Having denounced its advent for over three years, they had not made even the most rudimentary of preparations; their mimeograph machines were seized and their leaders arrested or fled. No amount of lies stating that the "revolutionary organizations have been unscathed" could cover over the fact that the movement was attempting to reestablish itself from scratch. If they were unscathed, why were the SRCs necessary? The publications of the KM and SDK vanished, and the SRC was an attempt to reconstitute an underground student movement out of the ashes. A retrospective by the KM in 1984 stated that

> KM was not caught napping. . . . In fact, the core of KM's leadership had started to partially go underground in 1969 and to completely go under-ground in 1971 upon the suspension of the writ of habeas corpus.
>
> The full-blown fascist dictatorship could not make wholesale arrests of KM officers and members, except in areas where they did not make ample preparations. On the whole, only a few could be arrested. The KM could continue to operate from the underground, with [illegible] of lead-ership intact. Many KM members were unidentifiable to the enemy.[126]

It is accurate that the majority of the KM leadership, and of the SDK for that matter, were not arrested. They burrowed so far underground that their muffled political instructions could no longer be heard. The paramount con-cern of an underground revolutionary apparatus is that it is still able to pro-vide leadership in conditions of repression.[127] Going underground does not mean disappearing entirely, in the manner of the front organizations of the CPP, for there is no difference between this underground work and resigning oneself from political life. Safe houses had been prepared throughout Manila and its environs for the leadership of the party's front groups, and they rap-idly absconded to them. The air in the safe houses was thick with conspirato-rial plots and tobacco smoke. The party had no shortage of ideas for rekindling relations with military officers inclined to coup d'etat or for securing support from the bourgeois opposition, which, like the CPP leadership, had suddenly vanished. What it lacked entirely was a politically educated mass base and an underground organizational apparatus through which to lead it. The party scrambled to construct the latter under conditions of military dictatorship.

An immense blow to organizing this effort was the loss of the party's mim-eograph machines. A core aspect of a party's ability to exercise leadership under repressive conditions is the dissemination of ideas, but for this to be ef-fective requires print. The majority of mimeograph machines operated by the front organizations of the party were neither safeguarded nor hidden, and with the declaration of martial law they were confiscated. The writ of habeas cor-pus had been suspended, and they did not hide their machines; the headquar-ters of their organizations had been raided but a week before the dictatorship, and still they did not hide their machines. Everyone knew that martial law was imminent, and yet when it was declared, most of the party's means of printing were seized by the state with ease. This abject failure on the part of the leader-ship of the CPP was a manifestation of its confidence that its ally, Aquino, would succeed in seizing power. Two weeks later, the party was left to call on students to handwrite messages and mail them to their acquaintances.

The rank-and-file members of the front organizations of the party, along with the broad periphery that saw the CPP as the center of opposition to dictatorship, now looked to the party for leadership. They took precautionary measures, burned all party literature, visited uncles or aunts; those who could go home to the provinces did so. They nervously busied themselves with mundane tasks and waited for instructions. Some gathered in groups and independently attempted to oppose the dictatorship, employing tactics in equal measure courageous and silly. For most, however, instructions never came, and gradually, with an acrid distaste, they grew accustomed to military rule. Those who had money sought exile overseas, but the majority took up jobs at home and led lives of quiet desperation, never free of the fear that the man boarding the jeepney might be PC. The hesitation and gradual despairing acceptance did not root in a shortage of courage. These forces lingering before Proclamation 1081 had been steeled in the storm; they had in large numbers marched before truncheons and tear gas and regrouped under fire. Now, bewilderment and disorientation, a sense of political purposelessness, gripped them; and the healthiest layers of the nation were taken by malaise.

They were given no leadership nor had they been prepared. The party's instructions to form SRCs embodied the dilemma of the rank and file: on what basis should they build or recruit to these committees? There was no content, no program, not a single principle held up to guide them, just the party's vapid watchword: unite with everyone against Marcos. On this point hinges the entirety of the failure of the CPP: the party had not educated the working class in its political tasks, and as a result the social layers around the party did not know how to fight dictatorship. They had not been trained to act independently. The political and theoretical education of the most advanced layers of the working class and youth must be the paramount concern of a revolutionary party when preparing for repression. In the event that the party's organization is suppressed, the forces gathered around it will be able to continue their revolutionary struggle on the basis of this training. And when the time is right, the apparatus of the party can rapidly reconstitute itself.

What education had the CPP provided to the rank-and-file members of its front organizations and its broader periphery? Martial law will hasten revolution. A section of the bourgeoisie is our ally. It is not yet time for socialism; we must limit ourselves to national and democratic ends. It is impossible to educate a politically independent cadre on this basis. The program of Stalinism requires that the membership and periphery be dependent on the leadership of the party, for at its core is an alliance with a section of the bourgeoisie, and how could anyone independently anticipate the vicissitudes of the party's alliances? The political imperative, as Sison had repeatedly stressed, was to be prepared to zig and zag as ties with different sections of the bourgeoisie ebbed and flowed.

Accepting these alternating alliances required cultivating amnesia within the cadre, who received a systematic political miseducation that justified every abrupt turn in occluded and dishonest language. Training in the history and program of the revolutionary movement is the strongest preparation of the cadre for conditions of repression, because it allows each of them to act independently as a disciplined leader of political struggle. The shifting alliances of the party, however, were not the product of principles but of haggling opportunism, serving interests alien to the revolutionary struggle against dictatorship. Macapagal is progressive, they cried; no, wait, he is reactionary. Marcos is progressive, they declared; no, wait, he is reactionary as well. Aquino is progressive, they claimed . . . No political education could prepare the cadre to adjudicate the progressive or reactionary character of sections of the bourgeoisie on their own, for this was assessed not on the basis of program but on the pragmatic conjunctural ends mutually agreed on by the leadership of the party and the bourgeoisie. The political education of the cadre was thus not to judge for themselves but to accept thoughtlessly, to swallow whatever new alliance had been formed.

The CPP's lack of preparation for martial law, so fundamental to Marcos's successful imposition of dictatorship, was thus intrinsic to the program of Stalinism.

In response to the instructions from the CPP, students began forming SRCs, but the lack of political direction was palpable. On 6 December, the UP SRC published the first issue of a paper called *Dissent*. The paper had little substance, focusing on increased dorm fees and the mandatory putting out of lights at ten at night in the UP School of Nursing.[128] The UP SRC wrote, "The new heroes of the people's democratic struggle unhesitatingly raise high their clench [sic] fist to defy and once and for all crush the US-Marcos dictatorship."[129] How was such "crushing of dictatorship" being carried out? The paper proclaimed that "mass actions in the form of silent marches, chanting protest songs, spontaneously singing the National Anthem in the AS lobby, and the simultaneous pounding of spoons and forks on the table to the tune of 'Marcos, Hitler, Diktador, Tuta' in the cafeterias, have been successfully staged by the awakened studentry" (figure 5.2).[130] This revolutionary plate tapping was likewise cited in another leaflet that heralded the tapping as the "fearless student masses creating new forms of protest."[131]

FIGURE 5.2.   Cafeteria protest (*Dissent,* December 1972).

Norman Quimpo, an activist with the Student Christian Movement of the Philippines, recounts,

> In the urban areas, youth groups like KM had such tasks as carrying out anti-martial law propaganda and protest actions. These campaigns were meant to combat feelings of helplessness and prove that dissenters could still be active despite the overwhelming grip of the military on the city.
>
> KM was naturally among the first with novel urban propaganda activities. A week after the declaration of martial law, it organized groups to launch "lightning rallies." A handful of activists would suddenly gather at a public place, shout out anti-martial law slogans, and quickly disperse.[132]

Quimpo describes "one such rally at Farmers Market in the Cubao district": "[The KM] prepared cards with anti-Marcos slogans and hung them on chickens, which they carried in *bayong* (market bags made of woven palm fronds). At a couple of busy intersections in the labyrinthine passageways of the mall, they released the chickens, shouted slogans, and dispersed quickly."[133] This was not a one-off event, as protesters continued to attach handwritten slogan cards to animals and set them free in public locations; and on the UP campus, the protesters painted in red the letters MHDT—Marcos, Hitler, Diktador, Tuta—on the backs of cats.[134] Over fifty thousand people had flooded Plaza Miranda on 21 September denouncing the threat of martial law, but after it was declared, the remnants of the KM were posting slogans on chickens. Historian Dante Ambrosio aptly described this period as a "time of groping in all directions" (*panahon ng pangangapa sa iba't ibang lugar*).[135] On 15 November, five hundred students staged a silent protest march within the AS building, quietly walking up and down the hallways. A pillbox explosion was set off, and the SDK wrote that a "stupid policeman was running frantically like a mad bull when a pillbox exploded a meter away from him. The students clapped enthusiastically in support of the pillbox explosion."[136] The explosion, the SDK claimed, had been carried out by "a militant student." This protest—silently pacing the halls of a single building on the UP campus and then disappearing into classrooms accompanied by the throwing of a small bomb—had been organized by the UP SRC.[137]

In February 1973, the *Collegian* reported that as many as three thousand students had not reported back to school after the reopening of campuses in the wake of the declaration of martial law.[138] Many had, in an admixture of fear and political despair, simply gone home.

Recovering Publications

The majority of the publications of the front organizations of the CPP disappeared. An occasional leaflet, most often typewritten, appears in the archival record, but the newspapers, manifestos, and endless stream of revolutionary ephemera vanish. This was a result of the capture of their mimeograph machines and the loss of the leadership that had been responsible for their production, as some were now in safe houses, others in the hills, and still others in prison. In the wake of martial law, a new set of publications began to appear; the first regular underground paper to emerge was *Taliba ng Bayan* (The People's Vanguard).[139] In its first issue *Taliba ng Bayan* wrote that "Martial Law has made even clearer [*lalong nagpalinaw*] the contradictory forces in Philippine society, the force of reaction and the force of revolution. More than ever before [*Higit kailan pa man*] the national united front has grown now in all classes, groups, elements and individuals who are prepared for an armed struggle against the fascist dictatorship of Marcos and his boss, American imperialism. Martial Law did not lengthen [*hindi nagpalawig*] but shortened the remaining days of the fascist US-Marcos regime."[140]

On the same page, *Taliba ng Bayan* informed its readers that "the moment that the fascist dictator Marcos declared Martial Law, the armed struggle in the countryside grew even more. A hundred thousand peasants [*Daang libong mga magsasaka*] have truly taken up the path of armed struggle as the only cure." This was a flagrant lie; a hundred thousand peasants did not take up armed struggle on the declaration of martial law. The dishonesty of the publication was matched by its unserious tone throughout. The first issue, for example, concluded with a "Rebolusyonaryong Pinoy Medli" of songs. The following song, sung to the tune of the folk nursery rhyme "Sitsiritsit Alibangbang," was part of the collection:

Sitsiritsit, pakinggan mo
Ang sekreto ng bayan ko
Ang pangulong sira ulo
Nagdeklara ng *martial law*!
(Sitsiritsit,[141] listen to
The secret of my people
The crazy president
Has declared *martial law*!)

Having nothing to tell the working class, the publication instead insinuated dictatorship into a children's nursery rhyme in the same manner that one might write doggerel on Hiroshima to the tune of "London Bridge Is Falling Down." Not content with this insipidity, the first issue published a story about a barber who was initially excited by the declaration of martial law because short haircuts would now be mandatory. At first, no one came to his barbershop. Finally, a group of soldiers came to get their hair cut and he jumped up and down with joy. After cutting their hair he awaited his payment, but was given only a New Society lapel pin. As the soldiers turned to leave, he took his scissors and stabbed them in the neck. The story was titled "Culture for the Masses."

Taliba ng Bayan routinely referred to the military, PC, and other forces of the Marcos government as *Hapon* (Japanese), playing off resentments and memories of the Second World War. The word "Hapon" was used (essentially as the equivalent of "Jap") on every page of the first issue of the paper—for example, on page 5, "the 'Japs' are drinking the workers' money," and on page 6, "the 'Japs' invaded UP." The light-minded celebratory tone of *Taliba ng Bayan* persisted in subsequent editions. The third issue, which again trumpeted that "people's war is the answer to martial law," denounced the University of Santo Tomas for upholding its ban on miniskirts and called on students to rise up against the restrictions.[142] The paper adopted the slogan "Dare to Struggle, Dare to Win!" on its masthead.

Taliba ng Bayan was directly run by the CPP out of a safe house in Novaliches. The paper's staff was overseen by leading CPP member and *Manila Times* business editor Satur Ocampo. Jose Lacaba, a journalist with a remarkable facility for prose, edited the paper, and its correspondents included the poet

Bayani Abadilla, experienced journalists Bobbie Malay and Joann Maglipon, and gifted screenwriter Ricky Lee.[143] The asinine, semiliterate glee of the paper in the face of repression expressed not a want of talent but of content. Martial law had been declared, but this was good because now the masses would take up arms against the "Japs" and possibly against restrictions on miniskirts as well. On one of the only printing presses left to the party, this was the publication it chose to produce and disseminate.

Other publications briefly appeared in October and November 1972, pursuing a similar line. The paper *Bangon!* launched a three-page leaflet on 5 October. Like *Taliba ng Bayan*, it denounced the "Japs," adding that this time "the enemy is no bandy legged child of the Rising Sun."[144] The next issue referred to the PC as "Kempetai."[145] The repeated references to the "Japs" were intended to do more than whip up racism as a means of cultivating dissent; they sought to equate martial law with the Japanese occupation to invoke the historical precedent of creating the broadest possible united front. As Stalinism around the world had used the pretext of the antifascist struggle to justify uniting with the major imperialist powers and with every class and social layer at home, so too the CPP sought to ally with coup-plotting elements tied to the CIA, politicos favored by Washington, and brutal hacenderos. Without any sense of irony, the CPP placed Ninoy Aquino, son of a leading collaborator during the occupation, at the center of this anti-"Hapon" united front.

On 14 November, *Taliba ng Bayan* dedicated its front page to a demonstration at UP. According to the paper, at ten in the morning on 3 November, students gathered on the second floor of the AS building to sing the national anthem. "Government agents" were too "dazed" (*tulala*) by the protest to arrest anyone. A great many of the accounts of the early days of martial law record that forces around the CPP regarded the singing of the national anthem as an act of protest. Where previously the KM and SDK had led their followers in loud performances of "Lupang Hinirang" as a means of defusing tensions, now the same verses were hoarsely sung as if they were a form of dissent. A week later, *Taliba ng Bayan* reported that students at Manuel L. Quezon University protested by shouting, "If you want freedom, you need revolution!" from the roof of the building and then throwing their manifestos in the air for students on the ground floor to catch or pick up, before fleeing. Such protests involved an amount of courage, at times even a certain inventiveness, but these scattered leaflets and shouted slogans were the weapons of the exceedingly weak and unprepared. By September 1973, the headlines of *Taliba ng Bayan* had largely returned to the staid politics of the united front. "Diokno needs to see a Doctor" and "Aquino: 'It's better to die with honor'" occupied the front page. The lead on Aquino concluded with the report that the masses gathered in the rain (*nakatayo sa ulan*) outside the courthouse, shouting "Mabu-hay ka, Senador Aquino!" (Long live Senator Aquino!), while the inner pages of the paper were still dedicated to the stirring victories of the NPA, complete with illustrations of women throwing grenades and AFP soldiers cowering.[146]

In the middle of October 1972 the party began publishing *Liberation*, the official newspaper of the National Democratic Front (NDF). The founding of the paper served as an organizational means of recovering ties with sections of the bourgeoisie. Just as *Taliba ng Bayan* peddled both Aquino and grenades, so too *Liberation* immediately began printing fictitious reports of victorious campaigns waged by the NPA, running them in tandem with inspiring quotations from the bourgeois opposition. At the beginning of December, it published a report of an entire three-hundred-member battalion of the AFP being "wiped out" in Isabela, stating that over 250 soldiers were killed, while in the same issue approvingly publishing quotations from Senator Soc Rodrigo: "As long as the seed of freedom is in the hearts and minds of our people, time will come when the climate will be favorable, and that seed will germinate and flourish once again."[147] Rodrigo had delivered the keynote address to the 1956 Asian People's Anti-Communist League Conference, but now he was an ally in the struggle against Marcos. From its inception, *Liberation* was bent on dishonest cheerleading. Its second issue, published in the first month of martial law, was headlined, "The Cultural Revolution Gains New Heights as the US-Marcos Dictatorship Is Encircled from the Countrysides [*sic*]."[148] By mid-December it claimed that the AFP was on the run in Isabela, Central Luzon, and Marawi.[149]

Both Aquino and the CPP had fully expected martial law to sweep them into Malacañang. When it did not, the CPP spent several months publishing flagrant lies about how close it was to seizing power. The AFP was on the run, the CPP claimed; hundreds had been wiped out by the NPA in a single encounter; over a hundred thousand peasants were taking up arms. In early October, *Bangon* wrote that "martial law is so unpopular that Marcos is a virtual prisoner in Malacañang."[150] These repeated dishonest claims added to the disorientation of those looking to oppose the dictatorship, for they were grossly incongruous with reality and everyone knew it.

As it solicitously but ineffectually appealed to the bourgeoisie, so too the party reached out to coup-inclined elements in military leadership. In November, *Kontres*, the umbrella publication of the front organizations of the CPP in the arts, called for carrying out "revolutionary propaganda among the officials and troops of the reactionary armed forces. Very many of them [*marami-rami sa kanila*] are opposed to the US-Marcos dictatorship."[151] In the CPP's analysis, the armed forces were divided into three camps: those supporting Marcos; those opposed to him and looking to carry out a coup; and those, like

Corpus and Tagamolila, who supported the national democratic movement. It was, as always, on the middle group that the CPP focused its attention. It further divided this group of coup plotters into two subgroups: one that would await a guarantee of support from US imperialism for the coup attempt, and another that did not need this support. The latter group of independent coup plotters, from the rank and file to the top brass, should be encouraged, the CPP argued, in order to win their support for the masses of the people.

The thrust of all the publications the CPP created in the wake of the imposition of martial law was not to provide leadership to the forces that looked to it for guidance. They were left to tap on plates, sing the national anthem, tie cards with slogans to chickens, and write chain letters. The CPP used every bit of its strength, which it amplified with outrageous lies, to appeal to the bourgeoisie and its coup-plotting allies in the military for a renewed united front. The ruling-class opposition, however, no longer had any interest in the alliance; the majority welcomed martial law, even in the hands of Ferdinand Marcos. If he used it to suppress their erstwhile allies in the Communist Party, so much the better.

"Hinggil sa Legal na Pakikibaka"

Seeking to recover the alliance with a section of the ruling class, the CPP deliberately curtailed militant activity in the working class, channeling all urban political work into the mildest possible reformism. This strategy, which amounted to leading workers to appeal to the martial law regime for improved trash service, was not designed to secure the safety of the working class under repressive conditions, but to win over the middle forces, who in their majority had embraced martial law. On 4 November 1972, the Manila Rizal Regional Committee of the CPP released the document "Tasks of the Party in the Manila-Rizal Region in the New Situation," which argued that "we must advance limited demands and forms of struggle acceptable to the masses according to the specific conditions at a given time and place and the degree of political consciousness of the masses. . . . We must wage steady and sure struggles in conformity with the principle of waging struggles on just grounds, to our advantage, and with restraint and utilize every legal measure and social custom that suit our purpose."[152]

While *Ang Bayan* hailed martial law as the onset of a massive revolutionary upsurge, the party turned to piecemeal reformist politics in the city, carried out by legal means. It sought to excuse this orientation by pointing to the low level of existing consciousness among the masses, never seeking to reconcile this flagrant contradiction to their shibboleth that the masses had been inflamed by the declaration. It was not the consciousness of the working class to which the party was adapting, for any worker who transgressed the boundaries of its reformist orientation was rapidly herded into the hills to take up arms with the NPA. The party was adapting yet again to the middle forces, and under conditions of military dictatorship, the CPP demanded of the working class that it exercise "tact, more tact, still more tact!"[153]

This perspective found extended articulation and justification in a document written by Antonio Hilario in January 1974 for the SDK, *Hinggil sa Legal na Pakikibaka* (On the legal struggle).[154] Hilario vividly depicted the confusion that reigned in the party and its front organizations in Manila in the wake of the declaration of martial law. Everyone, he claimed, was trying to resolve the problem of how to carry out the legal struggle in the city; and while it had been over a year, this problem was still far from a solution, and there was considerable disunity over how to proceed. He described this confusion as follows: "If four horses pull in different directions, one north, one south, one east, and one to the west, you can be sure that the carriage will not budge [*siguradong hindi titinag ang karwahe*]" (*Hinggil*, 1). A significant reason for this disunity, he argued, was that most did not have a systematic understanding of the nature of work in the city. Because of this deficiency, they were moving with their eyes blindfolded (*nakapiring ang mata*) and running wildly without direction (*takbo nang takbo, walang tinutungo*).

Hilario laid out what he regarded as the correct understanding of urban work, which he argued would necessarily be in its majority a legal struggle. Political work in the city was limited, he claimed, for several reasons. The cities were the stronghold of reaction, the countryside that of revolution. The task of the revolution was to encircle the cities from the countryside, while the task of those in the city was to support the armed struggle in the countryside. This was not, however, exclusively a matter of sending new recruits to the armed struggle, as the city forces also needed to organize the masses in order to split the forces of reaction, compelling some of the forces of the state to concentrate on the city (*Hinggil*, 2). City work was also limited, he claimed, by the weak condition of the forces in the city at present, and by what he characterized as the low level of political consciousness among the masses (*Hinggil*, 3).

We knew that martial law was coming, wrote Hilario, and yet we were inadequately prepared (*hindi naging sapat ang ating aktuwal na paghahanda*) (*Hinggil*, 3). In the end, however, it did not matter that the party had lost the majority of its organizational apparatus, for the revolutionary could reach the masses through any organizational means and the movement simply needed to find new means of legal struggle that were adapted to the martial law epoch. Despite this claim, Hilario was compelled to admit that "we are in a new stage of repression, and yet after a year, the correct form of organization and struggle against this repression" has not yet been found (*Hinggil*, 7). Having stated the problem, Hilario pointed the way forward for urban work: the legal struggle, which he characterized as any struggle that was not suppressed by the state, carried out through existing organizations (*Hinggil*, 10). Under conditions of sharply curtailed freedom, Hilario argued that the party needed to limit its urban work to what the state deemed acceptable. It should not focus on underground, illegal activity, organizing the working class in the struggle for power; anyone inclined to such activity should be sent to the remote countryside. Further, the working class should not form its own, independent organs of political work; it should enter into existing structures, which were of a deeply conservative and reactionary character. Hilario described three types of organizations that the party's urban forces should enter: traditional religious and social organizations; existing legally recognized organizations, such as the Jaycees and the Lions; and the organizations of martial law such as the ROTC and Civilian Army Training (*Hinggil*, 11). The work in these legal organizations, he stated, was based on the mass line, and its goal was to reach the middle and more backward elements of the masses by adapting to their existing levels of consciousness and winning their trust through day-to-day interaction (*Hinggil*, 13). The support of the middle layers would be won by carrying out minor reformist struggles in their daily lives. Hilario explained that if the state granted reforms, then the masses would learn of their democratic power; but if the state denied the reforms, then this was even better, for the masses would learn that only revolution could solve their problems (*Hinggil*, 18). If the party did not carry this reformist integration into existing legal organizations, Hilario claimed, it would have practically no influence in the city (*Hinggil*, 16).

The party directed the working class to enter into right-wing social organizations—the Jaycees, religious groups, and the ROTC—to win the trust of the middle forces (that is, the bourgeoisie and petty bourgeoisie). Those workers, straining under conditions of brutal dictatorship, who might not be content requesting improved delivery of municipal services through participation in a local civic group were directed to go to the hills. Most workers joined neither the Lions Club nor the NPA, but this was all that the party offered them. They hunkered down and looked to weather the dictatorship. Open working-class struggle would not resume until October 1975, when workers courageously went on strike at the La Tondeña distillery, in defiance of not only management and the martial law regime but also the CPP, as the party repeatedly told the distillery workers not to go on strike.[155] For the first three years of martial law, the cities were quieted and emptied of opposition. Marcos could not have secured better aid in stabilizing military dictatorship if he had drafted the strategy of the Communist Party of the Philippines himself.

"Conditions . . . Have Been Tremendously Enhanced"

Joma Sison and the Communist Party had spent years arguing that martial law and repression were the triggers of massive revolutionary struggle, and that the greater the repression, the greater the resistance. Yet, when martial law was declared, they were utterly unprepared. As silence pervaded Manila, as protests and strikes were replaced with tapping forks and chickens bearing slogan cards, Sison insisted that the masses were rising up and that this was due to Marcos and military dictatorship. He wrote a lengthy piece making this argument, which was published in *Ang Bayan* on 1 October 1972, less than two weeks after the declaration.[156] Martial law was "the complete self-exposure of the US-Marcos dictatorship," and as a direct result of its imposition, "the conditions for the rapid advance of the Philippine revolution against US imperialism, feudalism, and bureaucrat capitalism have become far more excellent than ever before" (DR, 5). He repeated this refrain throughout his analysis, declaring that because of martial law, "the ranks of the revolutionary movement have greatly expanded and fighting cadres as well as allies are all over the archipelago determined to conduct people's war. These things would not have stood out as clearly as now were it not for the fascist viciousness of the US-Marcos dictatorship" (DR, 30). A page later he stated, "We consider the present situation far more favorable to the revolutionary movement than ever before" (DR, 31). One can almost hear Sison thanking Marcos in these passages.

Sison advocated two critical steps in response to the declaration: the party should liquidate the urban organizations of the working class, both legal and underground, and should appeal to the bourgeoisie for funds. He stated that anyone who could "no longer conduct legal work or underground work in cities and towns should be dispatched to the people's army as the Party's principal form of organization" (DR, 33). The party's urban organizations had been shattered; they were not being rebuilt. As martial law was imposed, Sison emptied Manila of trained cadre.

By sending them to the countryside, Sison argued that the party would benefit from Marcos's suppression of workers. "The more the fascist dictator madly goes after all kinds of workers' organizations, the more it will aggravate its already isolated position. The more the workers' rights are suppressed, the more will the workers become fearless of the US-Marcos dictatorship. . . . The violent suppression of workers' unions and strikes can only yield more determined fighters for the revolutionary cause, provided the Party does well its duty of arousing and mobilizing the workers" (*DR*, 34). The falsity of this claim was starkly exposed in December 1972 when the party's ties with the working class suffered a deadly blow as a result of state repression. Central Committee member Noli Collantes, head of the party's trade union bureau and son of Marcos's undersecretary of foreign affairs, was arrested and immediately began to inform the police and military of the location and identity of all the party organs in the labor movement. In January 1973, the "principal underground houses of the trade union bureau under the organization department of the general secretariat were raided," crippling the party's apparatus in the working class.[157]

Sison's policy for the party's ruling-class allies had a markedly different character: "The Party should win over members of the national bourgeoisie, in the cities and in the countryside, to give political and material support to the revolutionary movement. Since they themselves cannot be expected to bear arms against the enemy, they can extend to the revolutionary movement support in cash or kind or allow use of their facilities."[158] Sison did not ask the bourgeoisie to take up arms against the dictatorship; the party would lead workers and peasants to do that on their behalf. Rather, he asked that the capitalists and landlords, the entirety of the elite opposition, give the party cash. "In return," he wrote, "such legitimate interests of theirs as those which do not harm the people can be protected" (*DR*, 37). While Sison welcomed the repression of the working class, he extended to the elite a promise: support us financially and we will protect your interests.

Sison's subsequent writings repeated the refrain that martial law was good for revolution. In March 1973 he wrote, "This fascist puppet dictatorship has more than ever made the situation excellent for armed revolution. . . . The ruling system has hopelessly cracked up from top to bottom."[159] Far from cracking from top to bottom, Marcos's hold on power was more secure than that of any prior figure in Philippine history. Sison continued this line for years, repeatedly declaring that martial law was good for revolution and the people were spontaneously rising up and taking to arms. Facts at times compelled him to admit that this was not true, but he would quickly double down on his insistence on the growing revolution of the masses. In October 1975 he published "An Assessment of the Fascist Martial Rule after Three Years," which stated, "Oftentimes, the fascist dictator and his henchmen comfort themselves by claiming that the people are acquiescent to their usurpation of power."[160] Sison continued, "The broad masses of the people have never been cowed: they have only become more prudent than before the fascist rule" (*DR*, 272). Sison was here compelled to admit that far from a growing revolutionary struggle, what prevailed was "prudence" (that is, silence), but two months later he wrote, "The toiling masses of workers and peasants and the urban petty bourgeoisie and other middle forces have been so oppressed that they are convinced of the necessity of revolutionary armed struggle" (DR, 310).

Sison celebrated the declaration of martial law. From his political perspective, what was needed to lead a revolution was not the patient struggle to build leadership in the working class by explaining to them their conditions and their tasks, but rather the blunt brutality of a dictator. If Marcos simply clobbered the workers enough they would rise up. Marcos did in fact brutalize the Filipino working class. The vast majority of the victims of martial law were neither the bourgeois opponents of the regime nor members of the Communist Party, but ordinary workers. They were arrested, tortured, and murdered, and yet the masses did not rise up. What was lacking was revolutionary leadership.

The PKP: Endorsing Martial Law

The CPP welcomed martial law; the PKP needed it. If the curtain of dictatorship did not ring down on the present act, the PKP would be shunted from the political stage, spent actors who had exhausted their lines. The continued existence of the party, and the achievement of its aspirations, required an abrupt end to the drama, with the sole copy of the script left in the hands of the *dictador*.

The PKP had bound itself to the president. Unlike prior ties to Macapagal and the LP, the PKP's ties to Marcos were not easily loosed. The murderous tensions in the ruling class meant that having cast the party's lot with Marcos, there remained no other section with whom it could ally. The party would rise or fall with him; Proclamation 1081 was the Rubicon of their shared political fate. Military dictatorship was not an unfortunate evil to which the party was prepared to accommodate itself in the furtherance of its interests. It was a measure immediately necessary for the securing of its ends, and the PKP labored mightily to achieve it.

Martial law consolidated the political power of their ally. Marcos would employ its sanction to padlock the legislature and pocket the key, and he could thus build ties with Moscow without parliamentary interference. He would wield its knout against their Maoist enemies, and the leadership of the PKP, as they moved into key positions within military intelligence, would gain a firm grip on the haft.

The PKP provided the pretexts—both ideological and military—for dictatorship. It wrote statements justifying martial law in the language of Stalinism and clothing Marcos in the diaphanous *piña* fiber of the progressive national bourgeoisie. Marcos was abolishing feudalism, it claimed, and with the support of Moscow he could be led down the noncapitalist path of development. The party ghostwrote Marcos's apologia for military rule and had the occupant of Malacañang cite Lenin in support of his machinations. In conjunction with the military, the PKP staged bombings throughout Manila, each of which was neatly tabulated by Defense Minister Enrile and subsequently reported on national television by Minister of Public Information Tatad as he listed the grounds for dictatorship.

The Rubicon was crossed and September closed in silence. Marcos himself expressed amazement at the ease with which he finally assumed the throne. It fell now to the leadership of the PKP in exile to secure support for Marcos from Moscow-aligned parties and their fellow travelers around the globe. Over the course of the past decade, Moscow had become practiced in the art of peddling its dictator-allies as progressive, and in this manner had sold arms to the Indonesian military with which to slaughter the Beijing-oriented Partai Komunis Indonesia and embraced Suharto. William Pomeroy, no longer a man of the forest, put the party's bottles of snake oil liniment and tonic on display in the pages of the *Daily World*, cleared his throat, and launched his rehearsed pitch: martial law was a means of opposing imperialism and would facilitate the rapid implementation of the national democratic revolution. It was not a credible claim, but the tincture contained a quantity of laudanum sufficient to allow the Moscow bureaucracy's supporters around the world to stomach looking at their erstwhile conscience in the mirror. They had weathered Khrushchev's revelations and endorsed the crushing of the Hungarian revolution; they saw themselves represented in the cold apparatchik rule of Brezhnev; they could embrace Marcos as well.

Domestically, matters were more complicated. The PKP leadership moved with alacrity, long abeyant, to endorse the dictator, yet it took two years to complete the process. They had to exact from their followers a public oath of loyalty to the permanent occupant of the presidential palace and to his apparatus of rule. The majority of the membership had not joined the party in furtherance of this end, and a mixture of lies and violence was required to bring it about. Each of the different class constituencies of the party required an adapted set of methods to be brought to heel.

The bulk of the party's leadership was composed of academics, professionals, and government officials. Against the "lost, violent souls" of the KM stood the hollow men of the PKP—gray and faceless, their dried voices suited to their thin words, men who "crossed with direct eyes" into the kingdom of martial law.

They brought in their wake the majority of the PKP's rank and file and periphery: the peasantry organized by the party in Malayang Samahan ng Magsasaka (Free Federation of Peasants, MASAKA). Beginning in the early 1960s with the founding of MASAKA, this mass of small peasants, predominantly based in Central Luzon, had been politically educated to appeal to the executive for the implementation of land reform in opposition to the interests of the large landowners. Joma Sison had written this orientation into the founding documents of the organization, and it had been built on this groundwork. The PKP, on Sison's expulsion, had retained control of the peasant wing and continued to lead it on the meager and conservative basis he had established. The sole political labor of MASAKA for the decade leading up to martial law had been to seek the consolidation of small property holdings through a powerful and sympathetic executive branch, which would carry out measures against the massive estates of the hacenderos.[161]

Marxism had long analyzed the character of the peasantry as an undifferentiated embryonic class, with both conservative and revolutionary tendencies. A small property-owning class, it inclined toward the defense and consolidation of its holdings, an orientation that bound it to the capitalist class. An oppressed and impoverished class, it often lashed out at the conditions of its exploitation, an orientation that bound it to the proletariat. Marx lucidly analyzed the political implications of the conservative aspect of the peasantry in *The Eighteenth Brumaire of Louis Bonaparte*. As they were an economically heterogeneous and geographically disparate group,

> they are consequently incapable of enforcing their class interest in their own name, whether through a parliament or through a convention. They cannot represent themselves, they must be represented. Their representative must at the same time appear as their master, as an authority over them, as an unlimited governmental power that protects them against the other classes and sends the rain and the sunshine from above. The political influence of the small peasants, therefore, finds its final expression in the executive power subordinating society to itself.[162]

Marx stressed that in its conservative tendencies the peasantry served as the bulwark for dictatorship. The struggle against this tendency required cultivating in the peasant class a sense of its own revolutionary power, not its dependence on rain and sunshine from above, and this in turn required strengthening the bonds of the peasantry with the working class. The peasantry would be won to the side of either the capitalists or the workers. Their loyalty to the working class would be secured not by adaptation to the conservative aspects of their character but by the revolutionary struggle for socialism.

In keeping with its Stalinist program, however, the PKP sought to subordinate the peasantry in MASAKA to a section of the capitalist class, first mobilizing it behind Macapagal and then behind Marcos with promises that one of these two men would use his executive power to represent the interests of the peasantry. The PKP thus carefully cultivated within the peasantry the most conservative aspects of its nature. In the month after Marcos declared martial law, Washington drew up a new land reform plan for his government. Marcos used the scheme to seize the landholdings of some of his ruling-class rivals, including Aquino. The PKP leadership promoted the plan as a revolutionary solution to liquidate feudalism, and the peasant wing of the party was won to the dictatorship.

Unlike the CPP, which headed a firebrand union federation noticeably uncontaminated by actual workers, the PKP headed a staid apparatus of older, established unions and, with the reincorporation of Lacsina into their ranks in mid-1971, its network was extensive. The unions' political influence, however, was disproportionately small. The unions of the PKP were not political engines of the working class; they were headed by niggling negotiators who ran them as apparatuses for securing sinecures, not for the militant struggle or political education of the membership. Where the CPP sought to provoke repression on the picket lines, the PKP labored to keep workers on the assembly lines; both methods served to break the independent struggle of the working class. While the hollow men at the head of Federacion Obrera de la Industria Tabaquera de Filipinas and the Confederation of Trade Unions in the Philippines leaned together and pledged loyalty, they could not move the majority of the membership to either support or opposition. The organs they had built could not secure such political ends; they were lifeless, a "papier-mâché Mephistopheles" designed to be propped up in a corner and pointed at occasionally during backroom negotiations. The loyalty of labor pledged by the PKP to the dictator brought to him but the service of its bureaucrat barterers. Between the motion and the act fell the shadow.

The social weight of MASAKA gave political clout to the party but lent its front organizations a diffuse and conservative character. The majority of its youth wing in the MPKP were the sons and daughters of MASAKA members, and a significant number followed their parents in the embrace of Marcos.[163] Many of the youth in the MPKP and the BRPF, however, had been naively led to the shore of the tumid river and would not cross. This left them with little political recourse, for what precisely could they do? Join the KM? It had vanished. One option remained for the youth and workers around the PKP who were horrified by the seemingly abrupt leap of their leaders into the camp of dictatorship: the foco guerrilla units of Francisco Nemenzo and the YCL, which, looking to incorporate all the oppositional elements of the PKP into its ranks, transformed itself into the Marxist-Leninist Group (MLG). The leadership of the PKP could not enter Marcos's cabinet if a sizable fraction of the party took up armed struggle against the dictatorship and they turned in cold fury upon their own membership. Summoning the specter of "Trotskyism," they systematically assassinated the opposition in a rampage that drowned their insubordinate rank and file in blood.

The protracted mechanisms through which the party endorsed the dictator are not entirely clear. They were implemented in the shadows by men skulking in the dark corners of history; those who carried this out are understandably loathe now to speak of their role. They secured salaried positions and negotiated the interests of the Moscow bureaucracy. Their victory, however, was a political crime and it was not forgiven; their very success spelled the eventual demise of the party. The martial law government funded its publications, but they had no audience. The threadbare mantle of credibility slipped off their shoulders and left them utterly exposed. They staffed the Labor Bureau and became colonels of military intelligence, responsible for suppressing the Maoists and the working class generally. Their periphery ghostwrote Marcos's vanity multivolume history of the Philippines, *Tadhana*. With Marcos's downfall in the mid-1980s, some of the individual leaders of the party were able to dress themselves up again as nationalist intellectuals, and the CPP, looking to secure new allies, assisted them in affecting this. The PKP, however, was finished. The Sino-Soviet split was buried. Nationalism required but one party to subordinate the working class to the bourgeoisie, not two, and the PKP was not that party.

Today's Revolution: Democracy

Marcos had from the beginning of his presidency incorporated a number of leading fellow travelers of the PKP into the inner circle of his administration, among them Blas Ople and Adrian Cristobal, who served as secretary and undersecretary of labor, respectively, while maintaining intimate ties with the leadership of the PKP.[164] Cristobal not only served as undersecretary of labor but also functioned as a ghostwriter for Marcos, and in this capacity he wrote Marcos's book *Today's Revolution: Democracy*.[165] The book was published in late 1971, in the wake of Marcos's suspension of the writ of habeas corpus. It argued that the political task of the day was the democratic revolution, which would be implemented by the Marcos government, not from above the Philippine polity but from its center, a conception that corresponded closely to Sukarno's guided democracy. The book stated that Marcos might declare martial law; such a declaration would not be in opposition to democracy but in aid to its fuller implementation against those who threatened the democratic revolution.

Cristobal, in writing the book, attributed to Lenin Stalin's theory of a two-stage revolution, and *Today's Revolution: Democracy* put in the mouth of Ferdinand Marcos the phrase "To Lenin we owe the statement that there could not be revolution without a revolutionary theory. . . . Lenin conceived of the revolution in two steps: first the bourgeois, then the proletarian."[166] Cristobal's Marcos asserted that the democratic revolution in the Philippines was "nationalist" (*TR*, 64) and entailed above all dealing with social inequality, and stated that "the dominant characteristic of our society which demands radical change is the economic gap between the rich and poor" (78–79). This, Marcos argued, was rooted above all in the Philippines' "oligarchic society." Not all of the wealthy were oligarchs, he continued, and "when I speak, therefore, of oligarchy, I refer to the few who would promote their selfish interests through the indirect or irresponsible exercise of public and private power" (*TR*, 96).

The book laid the political foundation for depicting Marcos's seizure of his political rivals' assets through the mechanisms of dictatorship as the implementation of the "democratic revolution." In like manner it depicted the curtailing of the freedom of the press as a necessary measure. The oligarchs, Cristobal's Marcos claimed, controlled the press, and the press therefore needed to be regulated or controlled, as the oligarchic institution of journalism abused the name of "public service" and was "pandering" to the "low taste of the masses" (*TR*, 100). The issue of inequality, Marcos wrote, was "inescapable. As I have said earlier, there are two alternatives: socialization and democratization." By socialization Marcos meant the seizure of wealth and its redistribution, something he fiercely opposed, and to which he presented democratization as the alternative. Democratization meant that the center—Marcos and his administration—would seize the assets of the oligarchs and use them for "democratic" purposes, while the wealth of all those not deemed "oligarchs" would be secure. Among the assets of the oligarchs was the press, which would be controlled in the interest of "democracy." The implementation of these measures, the book openly admitted, might require martial law.

In modified Stalinist rhetoric, *Today's Revolution: Democracy* laid out Marcos's proposal to declare himself dictator, seize the assets of his rivals, and shut down the press. The PKP thus had one of its leading supporters write the document, which it then used as the pretext to show that Marcos and martial law were progressive and which Marcos himself used as the justification for dictatorship. Jesus Lava wrote a public response to the release of *Today's Revolution: Democracy*, effusively describing the book as "a brilliant analysis of the ills of Philippine society as well as a prescription for a 'revolution' from the center."[167] The party's leadership awaited the declaration that everyone knew was coming; they were poised to support it.

Pomeroy: "It Is All to the Good"

In 1971 William and Celia Pomeroy, Jose Lava, and "two others" met in Moscow to form an international committee outside the Philippines that would function as an "arm of the party's international department." Celia Pomeroy was appointed head of the committee, but Jose Lava objected to her appointment and attempted to remove her by intrigue. Looking to secure support for his leadership bid, Jose Lava attempted to send a conciliatory letter to Beijing, but the Pomeroys, being advised of Lava's machinations by Moscow, prevented its transmission.[168] William and Celia Pomeroy were thus the heads of the international leadership of the PKP in 1972 when Marcos declared martial law, and routinely traveled to Moscow to coordinate their work.[169] On 1 October, less than two weeks after the declaration, William Pomeroy wrote to James S. Allen, a leading member of the Communist Party of the USA (CPUSA) who had been instrumental in the early development of the PKP, in which he rehearsed the party's justifications for its support. "So far there is nothing in any of the press reports we have seen to indicate whether any of our people have been affected. Our movement of course is and has been for a longtime underground, and it has been expecting the Marcos move for a couple of years, so we doubt if many would be caught off-guard."[170]

This was a lie. While the party had anticipated martial law, it had prepared for it not by sending its leadership underground but by securing salaried government positions. Ruben Torres was traveling to Moscow on the payroll of Malacañang; Haydee Yorac, Romeo Dizon, Merlin Magallona, Ernesto Macahiya, and Domingo Castro, all Central Committee members, held salaried government offices from which to conduct the work of the party; Felicisimo Macapagal, head of MASAKA and secretary general of the PKP, was a paid official of the Land Authority, responsible for Marcos's agrarian reform program.[171] Pomeroy continued,

> There are certain reasons why the steps taken by Marcos would even be beneficial to us at present. Those who have been arrested from the Liberal Party and the Catholic groups and from the press are those who have had links (an alliance, actually) with the Maoists and have been publicizing and encouraging Maoist propaganda and action against the PKP as well as Marcos. The CIA and other American agencies have had connections with precisely these elements. If the vicious Maoist propaganda can be stifled, it is all to the good. . . .
>
> Although the politics of Marcos have been benefiting the Americans, he is apparently not wholly their boy. He has business links with Japanese

corporations in rivalry with US interests, and he has said in interviews with European newsmen that he wanted to force more equalized and balanced international relations. Do you know, he has also been the first president to take serious steps toward relations with socialist countries, a process slammed by the political opposition that used it to make anti-communist propaganda against him.

In general, we reserve complete judgment on the developments until we have more detailed information. We don't have any illusion about any sector of the Philippine ruling classes, but there are differences and antagonisms that we need to recognize and to work with.

Love from Celia and me.

Pomeroy's logic was clear and well thought out. Martial law, he argued, could "even be beneficial to us"; if Marcos suppressed the Maoists, this was "all to the good." Marcos was suppressing the pro-Beijing party and opening ties with Moscow; the PKP should support this. James Allen wrote back on 6 October to express concern.

I was rather surprised by the positive note in your first DW [*Daily World*] article, and again in your letter. While there may be certain side effects which in passing may be of benefit (say, breaking up the Maoist-type alliances in the PI [Philippine Islands]), these seem to me far overshadowed by the entrenchment of the most reactionary forces by the imposition of martial law. . . .

That the bona fide CP forces are already well underground and had anticipated such a move, while the open allies of the Maoists had been caught by surprise, is hardly ground for optimism . . .

True, Marcos has taken steps of reconciliation toward the socialist countries (so did Franco) and the Maoists have been discomforted. (Remember when the CPUSA did not lift a finger when the Smith Act was first used against the Trotskyites, only to get it in the neck very soon?)

True, as you say, it is complex—but the above is the way I see it initially. Perhaps you have other information—and second thoughts. Let's hear.

Best to you and Celia, Jim.[172]

The historical analogy of the Smith Act, invoked by Allen, is worth examining. The 1941 Minneapolis trial of twenty-eight leading members of the Socialist Workers Party (SWP), which was at the time the US section of the Fourth International, was carried out under the Smith Act as "the first peacetime federal prosecution for sedition in American history" and was an important aspect of the Roosevelt government's preparations to enter the Second

World War.[173] The Smith Act made advocating the *idea* of the overthrow of the government a crime. The Roosevelt government used the law to go after the Trotskyist SWP, without touching the Stalinist Communist Party, as the CPUSA was giving its full-throated support to US entry into the Second World War, while the Fourth International opposed the war as imperialist. James Cannon, head of the SWP, issued a warning to the Stalinist Communist Party that the Smith Act would eventually be used against them as well, but the Stalinists enthusiastically supported the prosecution of the Trotskyist party. After the war, as Cannon had warned, the Smith Act was used against the Stalinist party in 1948. The SWP immediately offered to form a united front with the CPUSA against the Smith Act. Farrell Dobbs wrote to the CPUSA Central Committee on behalf of the Political Committee of the SWP. His letter stands in such stark contrast to the behavior of the CPP and PKP that it is worth quoting at length.

> The indictment of 12 leaders of your party under the Smith Act is another sharp reminder that in this gag law the rulers in Washington have a diabolical weapon whose barb is aimed at the working class political and trade union movement. . . .
>
> Now that you are under attack, we, the first victims of the Smith Act offer you our aid. We are convinced that only a united struggle by the whole labor movement—by all the tendencies within it—can defeat this conspiracy to deprive you of your democratic rights. . . .
>
> We ask you not to permit the profound political differences between your party and ours to stand in the way of a broad united front of the working class in defense of Civil Rights. While you did not come to the defense of the Trotskyists when we were persecuted under the Smith Act, we have already made public our opposition to your indictment and are fully prepared to further assist in your defense.[174]

The SWP called for a united front, despite "profound political differences," in order to defend the interests of the working class against the danger posed by the state's crackdown under the Smith Act. The CPUSA ignored the SWP's letter, refusing to acknowledge the call for a united front. The concerns that Allen voiced in his October letter to Pomeroy went unheeded. The PKP, which Allen had helped to found, had long mapped out what it intended to do, and it moved rapidly to endorse martial law. A month later, Allen was removed from the Central Committee of the CPUSA, a position he had held for twenty years, and he dedicated himself to heading the editing of International Publisher's forthcoming editions of Marx and Engels *Collected Works* in English.[175]

Toward Endorsement

While the political motive for supporting the dictatorship of Marcos originated in the alignment of the geopolitical interests of Moscow with a section of the Philippine bourgeoisie, the nationalist politics of the PKP required a domestic pretext to sell its support convincingly, and it found this in Marcos's land reform.

Marcos's land reform program, like Macapagal's 1963 code, had been drawn up in Washington. "Only two weeks after martial law was declared, Dr. Roy Prostermann, of the University of Washington, author of the 1970 land reform in Vietnam (and the subsequent program in El Salvador) arrived in the Philippines with a draft decree in his pocket."[176] For Prostermann and Washington, the impetus for land reform was the fight against Communism, and according to development studies scholar James Putzel, Prostermann pursued land reform with "anti-communist vigour."[177] Where the 1963 code reflected the liberal anti-Communism of an earlier generation of State Department officials, that of 1972 expressed the post–Bretton Woods predilection for authoritarianism as the bulwark of US interests. For Marcos, the land reform code was part of his move to consolidate power from his political rivals, as political scientist David Wurfel notes: "For the President himself, land reform's most important political function was to strike a blow at the 'oligarchy,' those wealthy elite who had formed the core of his political opposition. Not surprisingly the Aquino estates were among the first to be expropriated. The subsequent pattern of implementation helped to confirm this interpretation."[178] Marcos adopted Prostermann's document as his own and announced on 21 October that he would be carrying out land reform through what he termed the Farmers' Emancipation Act.

The 1972 land reform code, drafted in Washington and deployed by Marcos against his political rivals, provided the PKP the pretext it needed to initiate open relations with, and give public support to, a martial law regime. Jennifer Franco writes, "Shortly after Marcos signed a new agrarian reform law on October 21, 1972, . . . negotiations between [Felicisimo] Macapagal's group and the government began that led to a political settlement. . . . After reaching a 'national unity agreement' with Marcos in 1974, MASAKA established a government relations committee and changed its name to *Aniban ng mga Manggagawa sa Agrikultura* (AMA), or 'Federation of Agricultural Workers,' and continued to exist quietly under the new martial law regime."[179]

The party readied to endorse the dictatorship in its own name, to place the Stalinist imprimatur upon Marcos's martial law regime. While it viewed Prostermann's decree as tolerable pap for its peasant wing, official public support from the Central Committee required a more elaborate justification. In December 1972, the British Communist Party, of which William Pomeroy was a leading member, published portions of a PKP statement in *Comment*, with the note that "the following are extracts from a statement issued by the Communist Party of the Philippines."[180] This was its sales pitch.

The PKP argued that pressure, brought to bear on Malacañang by both foreign monopoly capital and the militant struggle of the Filipino working class, was compelling the "fascist" Marcos government to implement the necessary steps toward national industrialization, which the party identified as a progressive measure in the furtherance of national democracy. Marcos's growing alliance with Moscow meant that his administration could grow beyond these compulsory national democratic steps to move in the direction of socialism in approximately five years. The PKP thus needed to support him in this endeavor in order to assist his "fascist" regime in carrying out its progressive tasks. War was peace; fascism was progressive, or could be made so provided the Communist Party gave it full support. The PKP opened its argument by pointing to the weakening of US imperialism by economic crisis and losses in Vietnam, writing, "In the light of this, US imperialism formulated the Nixon Doctrine. Abandoning trade embargo and boycott against the socialist countries, the Nixon Doctrine broadened trade relations with them. . . . This development—a decisive victory for the forces of progress and socialism—opened an era of détente between the two social systems."[181]

This was the geopolitical terrain of martial law. In the face of the global crisis of capitalism in the early 1970s, and confronting defeat in Vietnam, the hegemony of US imperialism was weakening and it sought to restabilize its dominance through dictatorial forms of rule around the world. Neither Moscow nor Beijing responded with the international struggle of the working class to bury capitalism at long last, but instead pursued rapprochement with Nixon, each against the other, and in so doing shored up the tottering position of US imperialism, embracing its new doctrine and dictators. The document turned to the implications of the Nixon Doctrine for the Philippines. US imperialism was weak; this was why it was carrying out the industrialization of the Philippines and why Marcos was susceptible to pressure. "The Nixon Doctrine underscores the major policy changes in the Philippines, including the imposition of martial law. In foreign affairs, overtures for diplomatic relations with socialist countries and the subsequent opening of trade relations with them were initiated—a progressive shift which has been misleadingly announced by government propagandists as an indication of Marcos' independence from US imperialism."[182]

A progressive shift was underway in Philippine foreign policy, implemented by the Marcos administration—the opening of diplomatic relations with

Moscow. This was not being carried out in opposition to the dictates of Washington but in keeping with the reorientation of US imperialism itself. Nixon was compelled to accept the "decisive victory" of socialism; Marcos had to follow suit. The crisis of global capitalism not only compelled Washington and its puppets to accept diplomatic relations with Moscow but also forced them to end "feudal" relations in countries of belated capitalist development and to develop a national capitalist infrastructure, albeit by dictatorial means.

> On the part of US imperialism, there are two complementary reasons for the imposition of fascist rule. The first is to suppress the national liberation movement, and the second is to pave the way for a more accelerated development of the capitalist system in the Philippines. . . .
>
> The Marcos military-technocratic dictatorship is reforming the government by weeding out official corruption in response to the demand of foreign capital for an efficient administrative machinery.

The Marcos government, the PKP declared, had imposed "fascist rule" at the behest of US imperialism. By these means, however, Marcos would accelerate the development of capitalism, something that both Stalinist parties had long proclaimed as their goal. He was achieving a progressive end by fascist means. These measures, they claimed, benefited the peasantry and the working class and were a response to their militant struggles.

> The "New Society" is doubling efforts to implement a land reform programme. . . . The people do not owe the Marcos administration any favour in speeding up the land distribution. Marcos has no choice but to sell back the stolen lands to the people. It is not out of grace but out of fear of the people's power that the ruling circles are giving way to land distribution. It is the long years of revolutionary struggle, shaping the people into a political force, which are bearing fruit today. It is from the soil fertilised by the blood of Evangelista, Balgos, Capadocia, Feleo, del Castillo, Mamangon, and other revolutionary heroes who died and sacrificed before and after them, that the working people today are reaping their economic and social rights that have been forced from the ruling classes. It is therefore by the action of the masses themselves that they are on the way to land reform and ultimately to their class emancipation.[183]

The lies and twisted political language the PKP was compelled to employ to justify ties with Marcos are extraordinary. US imperialism, through a fascist government, was carrying out the "class emancipation" of the peasants. The "progressive" yet "fascist" Marcos administration was responding to the revolutionary demands of the people and "doubling efforts" to implement reforms. The document continued, however, by arguing that these progressive reforms carried out in response to the revolutionary struggle of the working class and peasantry were in fact being implemented on behalf of "foreign monopoly capital."

> Foreign monopoly capital in the Philippines is engaged in neo-colonial industrialisation, which necessarily entails the dismantling of feudal institutions. The imperialist scheme calls for radical change in the structure of agriculture to conform to developments in the industrial requirements of the imperialist powers.
>
> In the hands of foreign monopoly capital and their Filipino partners, land reform and the co-operative movement become instruments of exploitation. They will be utilised as means by which the labour power of the peasants is released from feudal moulds to be systematically exploited for neo-colonial industrialisation. . . .
>
> The military dictatorship is also expected to speed up the implementation of reforms of the Philippine educational system demanded by the World Bank. These reforms constitute a crash programme for training Filipino workers in the skills necessary for labour-intensive industries to be set up by multi-national corporations.[184]

The PKP thus argued that there was a temporary convergence of interests between the "fascist" dictator and the people, between the World Bank and the working class, between monopoly capitalism and the proletariat. The "rising cost of labour in Japan, the US and other major capitalist countries resulting from working-class militancy" compelled "foreign capitalists to transfer their labour-intensive industries such as textile and car-part manufacturing to puppet states and neo-colonies where labour is much cheaper."[185] The PKP and CPP had always made national industrialization the centerpiece of their political platforms. Imperialist machinations to maintain the Philippine economy in a "semi-feudal" state, they claimed, had prevented the needed development of domestic capitalism. Now, however, the PKP argued that US imperialism had, in response to its weakened global position, adopted the strategy of neocolonial industrialization, which would tear down the old feudal structures and develop the country's industrial infrastructure.

These had been the long-touted tasks of the national democratic revolution. But to carry out the needed changes by means of "limited reforms" would take "200 years or more," the PKP wrote, citing a statement from Marcos's executive secretary Melchor as evidence. "The problem is compounded by the fact that the reforms necessary for the future of capitalism in the country involves [*sic*] conflicts of interest among the ruling classes," but by declaring martial law, overriding ruling-class antagonisms, and making sweeping changes, Marcos "hopes to achieve this assigned task in the next five years or so." The national democratic revolution would thus be implemented by military dictatorship, one that the PKP still occasionally labeled "fascist." The political conclusion of the PKP was clear: in the not too distant future, the struggle for socialism might become the order of the day—perhaps in five years or so—but for now, Marcos's measures to build capitalism, carried out through military dictatorship, deserved support.

Within three months of the imposition of military dictatorship in the Philippines, the leadership of the PKP had given their full endorsement to the martial law regime. Proclamation 1081 was now effectively signed: Nihil Obstat—PKP Central Committee, December 1972. Before a merger with the "fascist" administration could be carried out, however, the party leadership needed to compel their recalcitrant members to accept the endorsement of dictatorship or, failing that, silence them permanently.

The YCL had served a twisted political function. Drawing on the foco guerrilla conceptions of Régis Debray and the urban terrorist tactics of Carlos Marighella, it had both given radical cachet to the PKP among layers of urban youth and been instrumental in supplying Marcos with his pretexts.

Francisco Nemenzo, the theoretical luminary behind the YCL, its orientation, and its strategy, was an intelligent man, yet he had functioned for the party as a useful idiot. Every measure he had taken over the course of two years had assisted Marcos in his declaration of martial law and enabled the party to secure support for it; yet when Proclamation 1081 was declared, Nemenzo opposed the new dictator and instigated a split in the PKP. He had headed the youth organization responsible for promoting and participating in the terrorist attacks being carried out by men intimately tied to the Marcos administration. He knew of these ties and yet he promoted their urban guerrilla tactics in relentlessly fawning terms. Soliman—that manly, suave, paisley-clad urban terrorist—had traveled to Moscow with assistance from the Marcos government. Each bombing that Nemenzo praised in his party publications, Marcos tallied and openly ascribed to the CPP. Nemenzo had to know where this was heading. It was widely discussed that government agents worked with the party leadership to carry out the terrorist acts that Marcos cited as pretexts for military rule. The organizations of the CPP published statements denouncing the PKP for this.[186] If Nemenzo opposed dictatorship, why did he knowingly function as one of its chief facilitators? The answer rests in the foco guerrilla theories of Debray, which served as the guiding political conceptions for Nemenzo and the YCL.

The political task, according to Debray, was the building of focos, and Nemenzo and the YCL sought to do this in Manila through small urban terrorist outfits. These units, carrying out bombings throughout the city, were the embryo of a new party, they claimed. The political line of the larger PKP apparatus was irrelevant to the YCL and its focos, for the party's goals and strategy had no bearing on the destabilizing efforts of its bombing campaigns, which would eventually serve as the architecture of a new political movement. As long as the PKP continued to assist the YCL in its efforts, supplying it with arms and capable men, this support would not be spurned, for it facilitated the goals of Nemenzo's group. The YCL would even tolerate collaborating with men who were almost certainly agents of the military. Debray had written of the need to recruit the support of the state military apparatus for the foco. If it suited Marcos to assist in the construction of the fundamental units of opposition, so much the better. The complete absence of political perspective from the writings of Debray and Marighella, men of limited technique and tactic, meant that their conceptions could be brought to serve any end. As long as the PKP and the individuals tied to the state continued to fund, arm, and assist the YCL, they would be welcome. With the declaration of martial law, however, the PKP immediately ordered an end to the bombings. They had served their purpose and now must stop. Abruptly losing support for its construction of focos, the YCL angrily turned against the party it had tolerated. And thus, having ably facilitated the imposition of dictatorship, Nemenzo and the YCL now declared their opposition.

The details of the events that followed are as hazy as they are bloody.[187] Nemenzo intended to launch a redoubled campaign of terror bombings throughout the city, later claiming that his strategy was "driven by a sense of urgency. We thought (wrongly in retrospect) that the newborn dictatorship could be prevented from consolidating by scaring off the foreign investors and tourists."[188] This was the demoralized and bankrupt political perspective to which Debray and Marighella lent themselves. Gone was any agency of the working class, of even that classless Stalinist amalgam "the people." In their stead was the revolutionary power of tourists and investors. Terrorism amounted to pressure politics brought to bear on the pocketbooks of visiting foreigners. Perhaps a well-placed bomb or two would persuade several hundred foreigners to seek the sunny shores of Bali over those of Boracay, and in so doing undermine the dictatorship.

To pursue this campaign, the YCL required arms. It had lost its state supplier and needed a new source of explosives and weapons. The PKP claimed that Nemenzo attempted to secure arms from "a top executive of a foreign company" and through "a dubious 'united front' with a notorious right-wing warlord family in the North."[189] The "warlord family" was the Crisologo clan, the cousins of Joma Sison, but Nemenzo claimed that he secured the arms not through an alliance with the Crisologos but through a raid on their mansion, which was arranged by a friend of Nemenzo's who was an "executive of the company owned by the [Crisologo] family."[190]

In October the PKP held an enlarged meeting of its secretariat in Aliaga, Nueva Ecija, to which it invited Nemenzo, where the party leadership under Macapagal "severely censured" him.[191] Looking to prevent Nemenzo from continuing his bombing campaign, the party leadership disarmed him and his two companions and interrogated them regarding the location of the arms they had recently seized. Nemenzo claimed that in the wake of this meeting, in mid-October, the "MLG core group decided to secede from the PKP and form a separate organization."[192] Thus, looking to consolidate all available forces to the formation of urban terrorist focos, Nemenzo transformed the YCL into the MLG, a political group independent of the PKP that sought to recruit members from within the party. If a potential recruit remained loyal to the PKP, the MLG would "coerce him to keep his mouth shut."[193] In addition to recruiting from the PKP, Nemenzo sought to establish ties with the CPP, although it is unclear on what terms.[194]

The PKP moved quickly to physically liquidate the MLG. Ruben Torres, who had been recruited to the PKP by Nemenzo and now was chair of the urban committee, was "in charge of resolving the 'Nemenzo problem'"; the PKP supplied him with forces recruited from Bulacan, Pampanga, and Laguna.[195] Soliman, head of the PKP's urban guerrilla squad, who had worked closely with Nemenzo until the declaration of martial law, now assisted Torres in the murder of his former comrades.[196] Ken Fuller, author of a three-volume history of the PKP, writes that a "former activist whose loyalty to the party could not be questioned" acknowledged that "a number of MLG members were shot as they lay in their beds." The MLG responded by attempting to assassinate the leadership of the PKP.[197] Pastor Tabiñas (Soliman) claimed that "there was a plan to assassinate 'all these old people' [that is, veteran leaders] as they were said to be cowards. . . . All those with an assignment to assassinate the leaders were annihilated."[198] Nemenzo, a Stalinist, described the methods used by the PKP as "the familiar Stalinist technique of conflict-revolution; namely, to kidnap, torture and execute the dissenters after forcing them to sign false confessions," while the PKP denounced Nemenzo and the MLG as "Trotskyite."[199] In its nine-page document summing up the struggle with the MLG, the PKP used the word "Trotskyite" twelve times, more than "Mao," "Marighella," "Lenin," "Stalin," or any other name. Nemenzo had nothing to do with Trotskyism. He himself had denounced Sison as a Trotskyite on numerous occasions, and Sison had used the same label against Nemenzo. "Trotskyite" is the name that Stalinists use against an opponent they intend to murder.[200]

Nemenzo was arrested in December 1972. He was not a threat to the Marcos administration; he ceased political activity and was released from prison within three years to resume tenured academic life on the Diliman campus, where his father was dean of arts and sciences.[201] Nemenzo climbed the academic ladder and eventually became president of the university. The threat to the PKP's unity with Marcos came not from Nemenzo himself but from the movement he had set in motion. The PKP slaughtered the MLG. The exact death toll from this campaign of murder and assassination is unknown. Sison claimed that the PKP "tortured and murdered twenty-seven members of the MLG," and Rosca claimed that approximately seventy members of the PKP youth were executed by the leadership when they "refused to accept collaboration" with Marcos.[202] While it is difficult to estimate the body count, it is safe to say that significantly more Communists were killed by the PKP in the wake of the declaration of martial law than were killed by the dictatorship. As it carried out the physical suppression of its own ranks, the PKP leadership issued a political transmission in December that stated that the PKP should "help them [the Marcos government] to annihilate the Maoists."[203] Any opposition to the Marcos dictatorship would be drowned in blood by the Stalinist PKP.

In the midst of its campaign to murder its former cadre, the PKP called a party congress to compel its remaining membership to endorse the party's support for the martial law regime. The party acknowledged in its own publications that the core of the dispute with the MLG was the "larger issue of the Martial Law administration of President Marcos and the acute need to forge clear ideological unity within the ranks of the Party itself."[204] In February 1973, the PKP held its Sixth Congress to resolve this issue; the previous congress had been held in 1949.[205] The party spent a great deal of time preparing for its Sixth Congress, which was dedicated to the topic of support for the martial law regime. Central Committee member Romeo Dizon stated that "the preparation took more than one year. Even before martial law was declared there were discussions."[206] Before martial law had been declared, the party was actively preparing for the congress, in which the members of the party would officially embrace it.

The Sixth Congress adopted a program and a political statement and revised the constitution of the party.[207] The program embodied the party's formal abandonment of the characterization of the Philippine economy as "semi-feudal and semi-colonial," and its replacement with the characterization of the exploitation of the Philippine economy as "neo-colonial," a position in keeping with the line being articulated by Moscow since 1969 of the "non-Capitalist path of development." Imperialism was developing industrialization through dictatorships, the party argued. The results of this were progressive, should be endorsed, and channeled to the interests of Moscow. The political statement developed this theme, declaring that "the Philippines is a neocolonial country of dynamic capitalist development. Its economy is in the main backward and deformed by colonial plunder. . . . Under the hegemony of finance capital, spearheaded by US imperialism, the Philippines is vigorously being transformed from a predominantly feudal country into a modern capitalist economy. Today it is experiencing a tremendously rapid pace of capitalist buildup through the instrumentality of the martial-law dictatorship."[208]

While he was carrying it out in the service of finance capital and imperialist interests, Marcos was in fact developing capitalism in the Philippines, the party argued. The PKP repeated its claims that dictatorship accelerated this necessary process. There were barriers to the development of capitalism in the country, particularly the old feudal oligarchies, whose opposition meant that the capitalist reforms Marcos was undertaking would take two hundred years to complete.[209] Martial law, however, stripped this opposition of its power and would "pave way for a more accelerated capitalist development."[210] Dictatorship allowed the Marcos regime to undertake the sweeping implementation of capitalism in a way that could not otherwise be achieved, and the PKP again estimated that it would take five years of martial law to carry out these measures.

The line of noncapitalist development being purveyed by Moscow meant that not all autocratic or dictatorial regimes were to be opposed. It depended on their orientation: dictatorships allied to US imperialism were bad autocracies, while those with ties to Moscow could be led to build socialism and thus were good autocracies. Marcos's martial law was contradictory, the PKP argued. It was serving the interests of neocolonialism by building capitalism in the Philippines, and this was, for at least the next five years, a positive development. He was also opening ties to the Soviet Union, making it possible for him to use his dictatorial powers to build socialism in the Philippines by taking the noncapitalist path of development, a possibility the PKP included in a section of the political statement titled "The Philippine Road to Socialism."[211] According to the PKP, the "socialist states are the decisive factor in world development."[212] Moscow's support would make it possible for autocrats in Algeria, Egypt, Burma, and the Philippines to build socialism. The working class, which Marxism described as the revolutionary class for the building of socialism and the "gravediggers" of capitalism, played but a secondary role. Their task was to support Marcos so that Moscow could assist him in building socialism. To support and further the positive possibilities latent within martial law, the PKP needed a free hand to support and pressure the Marcos regime, and thus needed to be a legal organization and play a key role in his government. This was the conclusion of the PKP congress.

In keeping with its support for the dictatorship, the PKP included "the patriotic elements in the armed forces" among the progressive sectors of society. It called for an alliance with the military, holding up "Chile's shining revolutionary example."[213] Allende, with the support of the Stalinists, welcomed the military into his government, whom the Stalinist Communist Party called "the people in uniform." Allende made Pinochet head of the Chilean Armed Forces. Five months after the PKP hailed the "shining revolutionary example" of Chile, Pinochet, with the full support of Washington, seized power, systematically arresting, torturing, and murdering large sections of the Chilean working class. Beijing promptly established friendly relations with Pinochet, who had crushed the Moscow-oriented Communist Party.[214] In keeping with its call for an alliance with the military, and flowing from the ties already established during its terror campaign, the PKP spent the next year negotiating its formal surrender and union, not with Marcos directly but with the officers of military intelligence.

In the wake of the congress, the PKP demanded a renewal of party membership, and every cadre had to state agreement with the documents of the congress in order to be a member of the PKP. Allying with Marcos and endorsing martial law were now prerequisites for membership in the party.[215]

Endorsing Martial Law

Leading members of the PKP served as the connection between the Marcos government and the party as a whole, negotiating their formal surrender and entrance into his government. The process took a year and a half, both because the party was actively engaged in suppressing its dissenters and because the terms of its entrance into the martial law regime were being haggled over. What official positions would be granted the PKP leadership? Would official relations with Moscow be opened?

Jesus Lava recounted that "when Merlin Magallona . . . was arrested, he was given the offer to negotiate [between the PKP and the Marcos government], which the Party accepted. Romy Dizon, a member of the PB [politburo], and a detainee in Fort Bonifacio, was released upon request of the PKP, to become part of the negotiating panel."[216] The arrests and detentions were formalities, ritualistic gestures to cover over the PKP's complicity in the martial law regime from its inception. Throughout this period, as the PKP negotiated with Marcos, Ruben Torres both headed the efforts to murder the MLG and traveled repeatedly to Moscow with the assistance of the Marcos government. Despite their later claims, the party leadership were not underground, nor were they at risk of arrest. Pomeroy recounted that advanced-stage negotiations were held between a "PKP PB delegation" and "top level army and intelligence officers" in mid-1974.[217] The PKP leadership thus carried out negotiations with military intelligence—rather than with the land reform bureau, the labor ministry, or Marcos himself—and reached a settlement in September 1974.[218] Pomeroy described the September 1974 agreement as follows: The substance of the September 1974 agreement was: "On the part of the PKP: (1) an expression of support for specific features of the Marcos program, including agrarian reform as far as it went . . . , industrialization . . . , establishment of industrial unions that would unite the fragmented and disputing trade unions, and the development of diplomatic and all-round relations with the socialist countries; and (2) disbanding the PKP-led armed force, the HMB, and its disarming."[219]

A land reform program drawn up by Washington, capitalist industry, state-run unions under a nationwide strike ban, and ties with the Soviet bureaucracy—the PKP proclaimed this the national democratic revolution and surrendered its arms. The Marcos government pledged the "(1) recognition of the PKP as a legal organization able to organize and propagandise freely; (2) the extension of amnesty to members of the PKP and the HMB; and (3) the release of all PKP and HMB political prisoners."[220]

On 11 October, in a widely publicized meeting between Marcos and twenty-seven members of the PKP leadership, Felicisimo Macapagal, the secretary general of the party, declared the PKP's support for Marcos: "For the first time in the political history of our country, genuine reforms are being directed and carried out in a determined manner by no less than the President; reforms that are meant to advance the frontiers of social justice and open opportunities for a better life for all our people."[221] They staged a symbolic turning over of firearms to the president, and Marcos instructed the military and the PKP "to prepare a joint study of areas in which the PKP could participate in the various programs of the government."[222] Five days later the PKP held a joint press conference at Camp Crame with top military officials, and both Macapagal and Merlin Magallona spoke, again declaring the party's support for Marcos. Marcos issued a press release that the PKP had "surrendered," Pomeroy claimed, in order to "cover himself from US and bourgeois opposition accusations that he had 'gone soft' on Communists and had made concessions to them."[223] Pomeroy concluded that Marcos "adhered to [the agreement] and never went back on the terms enabling the PKP to exist and to function legally."

In November and December 1974 a series of public ceremonies were staged in which PKP members turned over arms and received amnesty—arms supplied to them by the military—"in order to impress the newspaper photographers."[224] The ceremonies included not only the formal members of the PKP but also the membership of MASAKA, as the PKP instructed thousands of workers and peasants to attend the ceremonies in November and December, where they were photographed and fingerprinted by the PC.[225]

In April 1975, Nicolae Ceaușescu, general secretary of the Romanian Communist Party, visited Manila and signed a joint declaration with Marcos, and on 2 June 1976, the Philippines established formal diplomatic relations with the USSR.[226] Manila and Bucharest concluded a series of trade deals in which the Philippines agreed to supply Romania with twenty-eight million pounds of nickel, as well as sugar, copra, abaca, and other raw materials.[227] The PKP, now functioning in a semiofficial capacity in the Marcos government, issued warm greetings to "Comrade Ceaușescu," who arrived "at a most opportune time when the Philippines is vigorously transforming the American imperialist dictated foreign policy into one of normalizing relations with the socialist countries."[228] The PKP also issued a public statement on the significance of the visit, writing that "President Ceaușescu himself has shown them [the Filipino people] that communists are not ruthless, power-hungry men out to enrich and aggrandize themselves." This was, albeit in the negative, a rather precise description of the brutal Stalinist dictator of Romania.[229] Having lied about Ceaușescu, the PKP turned to Marcos, praising him for his "renunciation of violence as an instrument of international and domestic policy." Marcos's military intelligence forces—into which some of the leading members of the PKP had been integrated—were carrying out torture and murder on an industrial scale, and yet the PKP claimed that violence was no longer an instrument of domestic policy.[230]

Mao Embraces Marcos

Just as the CPP lost its ties to a section of the ruling class in the Philippines, it lost its connection to Beijing as well. At the beginning of 1974, Marcos succeeded in blocking Radio Beijing on AM bands, forcing listeners to use shortwave in order to hear China's broadcasts; by April, shortwave transmissions had been blocked as well.[231] The party made at least one more attempt after the *Karagatan* debacle to import arms from China, in a plot to "drop watertight tubes packed with arms off the coast of La Union province. NPA scuba teams would retrieve the weapons and ferry them ashore in small fishing boats."[232] A small passenger ship named *Doña Andrea* sailed in January 1974 from the Philippines for Hainan with a crew of twelve, intending to collect the arms. They ran aground on Pratas Reef in the middle of the South China

Sea, and a salvage ship from Hong Kong picked up the crew.[233] Beijing wanted nothing more to do with the CPP and ended the possibility of any further arms deals.[234] For the party, founded on the notion that China was the Yan'an of world revolution, the foundering of the *Andrea* signified the end of an epoch. The CPP was completely isolated.

Beijing's consternation with the incompetence of the CPP was a manifestation of the former's concern that any continued ties with the latter might undermine its advanced-stage negotiations with the Marcos administration. In September 1974, Imelda Marcos led a diplomatic mission to China to open formal ties between Beijing and Manila. She was feted throughout the country, meeting on several occasions with Zhou Enlai and once with Mao Zedong (figure 5.3). *Peking Review*, which five years earlier was running the news clippings of the CPP, now headlined China's "warm welcome" for its "distinguished guest," Madame Imelda Romualdez Marcos.[235] She secured a deal for the purchase of Chinese oil, which in the midst of the crisis of the Organization of Petroleum Exporting Countries was desperately sought, and China committed to purchase Philippine exports. Arrangements were made for a state visit by Ferdinand Marcos the next year.

In an article published in *Ang Bayan* on 20 October 1974—"A Diplomatic Victory of the People's Republic of China, a Victory of the Philippine Revolutionary Struggle"—Sison hailed Imelda Marcos's visit to China.[236] In a labored and

FIGURE 5.3. Mao Zedong greets Imelda Marcos in Beijing, September 1974.

dishonest argument, he depicted the ties between Beijing and Manila as a brilliant strategic maneuver on the part of China. Beijing was exploiting contradictions between the United States and the Soviet Union by opening up ties with Marcos, he claimed, and he held up Stalin's pact with Hitler as a positive example of such strategic diplomacy, claiming that Stalin had "defeated the maneuver of the other imperialist powers" through his deal with Nazi Germany.[237] Beijing had struck a bargain with Marcos, opening trade and diplomatic relations with the dictatorship, and Mao had agreed that China would not interfere with the martial law regime, which was an internal matter. Sison heralded this betrayal as a victory. The CPP was now completely isolated, and the Philippine revolution, Sison stated, needed to be conducted "according to Philippine conditions."

It was this proposition that Sison elaborated in the beginning of December 1974, in the document *Specific Characteristics of People's War in the Philippines*, published in mimeographed form and circulated throughout the party leadership. The isolation of the party meant that it needed to conduct its operations in a "self-sufficient" manner. This, he argued, required a central leadership but decentralized operations that would be conducted by self-sustaining units spread throughout the archipelago. As aid was not forthcoming from China, it was all the more imperative that the party secure support from sections of the elite in the Philippines. Sison broadened the party's appeal beyond the national bourgeoisie to sections of the hated landlord class, whom he now termed "the enlightened gentry," promising to "give special consideration, as the masses and circumstances may permit, to the enlightened gentry who endorse and follow our policies and who support our revolutionary war."[238]

The critical question that Sison needed to answer for the party's members and supporters was why China, long the promised ally of the Philippine revolution, had embraced Marcos's dictatorship. Sison argued that China would "fulfill its internationalist obligations" not by arming revolutions in surrounding countries but through what he called the "Leninist policy of Peaceful Coexistence, specifically the Five Principles." These principles, first articulated in the treaty between India and China in 1954, included as their third point, "Mutual non-interference in each other's internal affairs." This meant that Beijing, in concluding diplomatic and trade deals with Marcos, the shah, Pinochet, and others, agreed that it would not support armed insurgency or opposition within these countries. These principles, Sison argued, were "an important weapon in the service of the world revolution because by it the broadest possible united front can be created against the two superpowers and contradictions even in the ranks of our enemies can be taken advantage of. It fully accords with Marxism-Leninism to make use of contradictions, win over the many, oppose the few and crush our enemies one by one."[239] In other words, while the CPP was engaged in an armed struggle against the Marcos regime as the embodiment of US imperialism in the country, the CCP would enter the "broadest possible united front" with Marcos as a means of exploiting alleged "contradictions" between Marcos and Washington.

Sison justified Mao's betrayal. Capitalist restoration in China had been launched not by Deng Xiaoping but by Mao himself, who opened relations with Washington and supported its dictator allies around the globe. It was "entirely correct," Sison declared, for China to "rely on their own proletariat and people and upon such a basis carry out an external policy that would foster unity with Asia, Africa and Latin America and take advantage of inter-capitalist contradictions as well as contradictions between the two superpowers themselves."[240] The unity that China was concluding with "Asia, Africa and Latin America" was not with the working class and peasantry of these countries but with the dictators who were oppressing them. This, then, was the reason that the CPP needed to be self-sufficient. Aid from Beijing to the party was not coming; from this point forward, any aid from China to the Philippines would be sent to Marcos.

From 7 to 11 June 1975, Ferdinand and Imelda Marcos traveled throughout China. Throngs were assembled to welcome the family of the visiting dictator. The *Peking Review* reported that "huge streamers trailing from tall buildings read 'Warmly welcome President and Madame Marcos!' . . . 'Firmly support the people of the Philippines in their struggle to safeguard national independence and state sovereignty!'"[241] On 8 June, as a demonstration of Beijing's severing of ties with the CPP and support for the martial law regime, Marcos issued a statement to the press in China that his hard-line policy on rebels (that is, CPP-NPA) would continue. On 9 June, Zhou Enlai and Marcos issued a joint communiqué, which was published in the Philippines the next day, explicitly affirming the principle of noninterference in each other's internal affairs. Following Nixon's lead, Marcos affirmed the One China policy and agreed that Taiwan was an integral part of Chinese territory, and Zhou recognized the legitimacy of the Marcos government.[242] In the face of Marcos's open declaration that he would continue to suppress the CPP, Beijing signed a document affirming the legitimacy of his government and agreeing not to support the CPP in any way. Marcos returned to the Philippines on 12 June—Independence Day—and held a press conference in which he announced

> China's leaders are aware and appreciate our commitment to liquidate any insurgency or subversion that threatens our government. . . .
>
> In my five days in China, I had one long meeting with Chairman Mao, two meetings with Premier Zhou Enlai, three meetings with vice Premier Deng Xiaoping. . . .

In all these conversations of about nine hours, I pointedly asked the Chinese leaders questions about the differences in our systems, about the role that China might play, covertly, in any political struggle that might take place in the Philippines.

Consistently, I obtained the assurance that the choice of our social system is our own sovereign business in which no intervention ought to be permitted, and that we should be free to deal with any insurgency, subversion or rebellion in accordance with the security and well-being of our government and people.[243]

Neither the CPP nor the CCP made any effort to gainsay Marcos. The CCP was perfectly content to ally with Marcos as he employed the entirety of his dictatorial powers to crack down on the Filipino working class and peasantry; the party had publicly committed itself to remaining silent on these "internal matters." The CPP, founded on a nationalist program in the service of the foreign policy interests of the Stalinist bureaucracy in Beijing, was by 1975 something of an embarrassment to the CCP, and Mao Zedong severed all ties with the Philippine party. Joma Sison, who for years had heralded the CCP as the leadership of world revolution, publicly celebrated this betrayal, proclaiming it "a glorious victory" for the "proletarian foreign policy" of Beijing. He pointed the way forward for the CPP, doubling down on the party's nationalism and politics of class collaboration, insisting that the revolutionary struggle in the Philippines needed to be "self-sufficient."

The Filipino working class and peasantry, Sison argued, had no international allies on whom they could rely. The international solidarity of the working class was nothing but a rhetorical flourish for Sison. He erected nationalist barriers to this solidarity, and within the boundaries of the nation-state sought to bind workers politically to the ruling class. Thus, while Sison claimed that Filipino workers no longer had any international allies, within the country he expanded the field to include any section of the ruling class willing to work with the party. Sison openly proclaimed the party's eagerness to collaborate with landlords and capitalists alike, with anyone who expressed interest in joining the CPP's struggle against Ferdinand Marcos.

Exeunt

Ang Bayan in its earliest years stands in striking contrast to the tone and outlook adopted by the CPP's flagship publication beginning in the mid-1970s. During this early period, *Ang Bayan* dedicated much of its space to international developments, particularly focusing on the contest between the Soviet Union and China. Anyone familiar with the later tenor of the writing of the CPP immediately notices the difference. Beginning in the mid-1970s *Ang Bayan* adopted an increasingly parochial perspective. Headlines were occupied almost exclusively with reports of local armed encounters and the number of arms the party claimed to have won or the enemy combatants killed or wounded. The broadest perspective that the CPP achieved was to report on national developments. To the extent that they were reported at all, international events entered the pages of *Ang Bayan* only through the lens of Filipino nationalism and were interpreted in terms of the impact they would have on Filipinos. In the period of its founding, the CPP conceived of its nationalism as a component part of a broader international whole—the expansion of revolutionary struggles centered in China. The program of Stalinism led ineluctably toward the restoration of capitalism in China and the complete isolation of the CPP. The party turned in upon itself.

The strategy of decentralized operations, put forward by Sison in *Specific Characteristics of People's War in the Philippines* in response to the CPP's isolation from China, accelerated this involution. The nationalism of the CPP metastasized from a necessary stage in the revolution to the end in itself. The most grotesque expression of the involution of the CPP was the purges the party conducted within its own ranks from the late 1970s to the early 1990s. Over a thousand cadre were killed in witch-hunting campaigns against alleged infiltration by agents. Comrades were tortured for confessions and then executed in mass graves. The roots of the purges are complex and require detailed study, but they can only be understood in the context of demoralization and disorientation caused by the utter geopolitical isolation of the party.[244]

The ruling-class opponents of Marcos largely moved into exile. They lost political power, and some lost their family holdings as Marcos seized many of their businesses and placed them under his loyal cronies. From the vantage point of the elite, this was the worst of Marcos's crimes, and in their denunciations, Marcos's corruption, crony capitalism, and profligacy acquired near-mythic proportions. The crimes of military rule faded into the background. Last of all to depart was Ninoy Aquino, who was imprisoned the longest and only departed the country to the United States for heart surgery in 1980. In the United States he joined a group of exiles who were plotting the overthrow of Marcos. Aquino, Lopez, and Osmeña funded bombing campaigns and assassination attempts against Marcos. When Aquino returned to the country, on 21 August 1983, he was shot down on the Manila Airport tarmac, twelve years to the day after the Plaza Miranda bombing. Edgar Jopson, most prominent of the SocDem leaders, joined the CPP, becoming a leading member before being killed by the military in 1982.

The leadership of the PKP was incorporated into the Marcos government apparatus. Some took up positions in the Ministries of Land Reform or of Labor; others were given high-ranking positions within military intelligence and were responsible for the direct enforcing of dictatorial rule. Ernesto Macahiya was made a colonel in the military and then an executive of the Development Bank of the Philippines. Ruben Torres was given a high position in the Labor Ministry, which allowed him to travel throughout the world. He later ran for Senate on the Ramos and Estrada slates, before becoming a congressman in 2001. Merlin Magallona later became undersecretary of foreign affairs. Jesus Lava and Tonypet Araneta began channeling spirit guides together in prison in the immediate wake of the declaration of martial law. Upon his release from prison, Lava continued to pursue his "psychic research."

In 1975 the CPP issued instructions to both the KM and the SDK to disband. They had served their purpose, and all youth dissent would now be channeled directly into the NPA. The most dedicated youth members of the KM and SDK took to the hills when martial law was declared, and one by one they were killed. Antonio Hilario was shot in the back of the head in 1974; Antonio Tagamolila was shot on the same day; Ma. Lorena Barros was shot at close range in the neck in 1976.

Many members of the front organizations, however, and even of the party itself, simply resumed civilian life. Their future trajectories were an expression of their class ties and the character of their nationalist politics. Sonny Coloma became spokesperson for the Benigno Aquino III administration; Jerry Barican did the same for Joseph Estrada's administration. Rey Vea became president of Mapua Institute of Technology. Gary Olivar became an executive at Sumitomo Bank in New York before becoming spokesperson for President Arroyo. Rigoberto Tiglao, head of the Manila-Rizal Regional Command, became chief of staff for Arroyo and then ambassador to Greece. Chito Sta. Romana became Duterte's ambassador to China. Nilo Tayag declared his support for Marcos while in prison and on his release became a priest in the Aglipayan Church, rising to the rank of bishop.

Victor Corpus surrendered in January 1976. On his release he was promoted and drew up the military plans of the Corazon Aquino government for suppressing the CPP. Renato Casipe, also a Central Committee member, surrendered in the same year, providing evidence to the military against his comrades. Ruben Guevarra, long the party's leading executioner, left the party to become a high-ranking military intelligence officer in the Intelligence Service of the Armed Forces of the Philippines.

Dante was arrested in August 1976. He later told *Asiaweek* in an interview, "Socialism is a goal only in the very far future, if ever. Our immediate aim is a national democratic revolution. The vestiges of feudalism must be wiped out, peasants must be truly free, and the Philippines must be freed from the economic, military, political and cultural stranglehold of US imperialism. After that, the socialist revolution could come next. Maybe we will never need to have communism."[245] He set up an agricultural cooperative in central Luzon under the Corazon Aquino administration.

Joma Sison was arrested in 1977. He was released from prison in 1986 and shortly afterward took up life in exile in the Netherlands, where he resumed his role as ideological leader of the CPP. Sison died in Utrecht on 16 December 2022. He never returned home to the Philippines.

Epilogue

Shades of the present haunt every work of history, but in few instances is their presence as palpable as it is in this one. The drama is being restaged.

This narrative has been one of defeat. Over the course of a decade of intense archival work uncovering its vicissitudes, I lived with this defeat, felt its ineluctable onset each time I rewrote my way toward 1972. It was a pained account to write, but a political defeat is every bit as substantive a lesson as a victory.

I began writing the core ideas of this work in 2016, as Rodrigo Duterte took office in the Philippines. I signed the conclusion the week Ferdinand Marcos Jr. was elected president. Over the course of six years of unstinting reaction, with one eye on the page and the other on the world, I wrote this book.

In my hometown of Paniqui, on the northern edge of Tarlac province in the rice-farming valley of Central Luzon, a statue of Ferdinand Marcos was erected in the plaza. There he stands, between the church and the marketplace, the town hall and the elementary school, in the center of civic life, his arms outstretched in victory.

The election of US president Donald Trump followed that of Duterte. Jair Bolsonaro, Narendra Modi, Marine Le Pen, the Alternative für Deutschland, the United Kingdom Independence Party and Brexit, Jobbik—the springtide of authoritarianism and reaction rose around the globe. On 6 January 2021 the outgoing US president attempted to remain in power by means of a coup carried out by fascistic forces. Openly authoritarian forms of rule and the politics of the Far Right—"all the old filthy business," in Marx's phrase—recrudescent, stalk the stage. Bertolt Brecht's final lines on Arturo Ui, that mock Hitler, resonate the world over: "Do not rejoice in his defeat, you men. For though the world has stood up and stopped the bastard, the bitch that bore him is in heat again."[1]

The Marcos dictatorship ended in ignominy. In February 1986, millions of Filipinos gathered on Edsa, the main thoroughfare of Manila, in open defiance of the brutal conjugal rule of Ferdinand and Imelda. With immense courage, they stood their ground in the face of tanks and the military might of the regime, which had in recent memory opened fire on demonstrators. They demanded that the democratically elected Corazon Aquino, widow of the assassinated Ninoy, be installed as president and that the hated Marcoses be ousted. A section of the military had withdrawn its support from the president, and Washington at long last rescinded its backing. The Marcoses fled the country. The Edsa event became known as People Power and was the source of immense pride.

As the Marcoses took up exile in Hawaii, Corazon Aquino took office, the recipient of unprecedented levels of mass hope. After a decade and a half of repression, everything would be different now. Little changed. Her People Power government, which spoke incessantly of "democracy," proved to be the rule of a rival set of oligarchs.

Looking to stabilize her hold over the military, she incorporated leading figures of the Marcos regime—among them Fidel Ramos and Juan Ponce Enrile—into her cabinet and responded to a series of military coup attempts by adapting to these layers. In 1987, police forces outside the presidential palace opened fire on a peaceful march of farmers requesting land reform and killed over a dozen.

It was this political climate, in which everything changed but nothing was different, that shaped education about the martial law regime. To detail the crimes of the dictatorship would have exposed many of the allies and policies of the Aquino government. Textbooks spoke of the corruption and personal excesses of Ferdinand Sr. and Imelda, reaching almost mythical levels of theft, but not of the repressive apparatus of military rule. Imelda was remembered not for her brutality but for her thousands of shoes. The injunction "Never Again" was widely repeated, but the predicate to which it was attached became hazy and ill remembered.

The cronies of the Marcoses were rehabilitated and then the Marcoses themselves. They played a useful role in elite politics, able to mobilize a significant geographic and linguistic constituency. Her husband now dead, Imelda

Marcos returned from exile with her family. She ran for president in 1992 with the promise that she would "make the Philippines great again." Ferdinand Sr. returned as well, his waxy, embalmed corpse on display in an Ilocos Norte mausoleum awaiting the day he could be buried with national honors.

Political rot spread beneath the paraffin of post-Marcos illusions. Each successive administration inherited diminishing popular hopes that the hard-won forms of democracy would produce meaningful reforms. Living conditions for the majority of the population worsened. The working people of the country became dependent on a vast labor diaspora to sustain their families. Fully 10 percent of the country's population sought work overseas. Families were riven—mothers, fathers, sons, and daughters abroad, domestic workers, construction workers, health-care workers, home for two weeks every two years. It is the longing of this diaspora to remain connected that fuels social media use in the Philippines at one of the highest rates in the world. The propaganda of a Marcosian "golden age" found wide circulation through these networks, as Ferdinand Jr. mounted a campaign of anti-intellectualism and conspiracy theories.

No political force was as instrumental in producing the noxious political atmosphere that hangs over the Philippines today as the Communist Party of the Philippines (CPP). The party, and the various national democratic organizations that follow its political line, cultivated and sustained the illusions of the working population that one or another section of the elite would at long last use the forms of democracy to carry out substantive reforms.

In each election cycle the party mustered the support of the oppressed masses behind yet another faction of the elite. The past thirty years are a cemetery of political illusions, littered with headstones bearing the names of those the party endorsed as progressive representatives of the capitalist class: Gloria Macapagal-Arroyo, Joseph Estrada, Manny Villar, Rodrigo Duterte. Preaching that reactionary, and even racist, nationalism was the solution to the poverty and oppression of the Filipino masses, the CPP repeatedly spent the moral energy and independent initiative of the working class to purchase ties with a section of the elite.

Under conditions of global capitalist crisis, the bourgeoisie moved further to the right and their supporters in the CPP followed suit. When the national democratic organizations backed real estate billionaire Manny Villar for president in 2010, they campaigned on a shared platform with Ferdinand Marcos Jr., who launched his national political career by running for Senate on Villar's slate. Satur Ocampo, who as a leading member of the CPP was a victim of martial law torture, ran for Senate alongside Ferdinand Jr. and posed for photos with him.

The foundations of post-Marcos democracy shook with the election of Rodrigo Duterte in 2016. A vulgar, authoritarian populist, he oversaw mass murder by the police and paramilitary death squads in the name of a war on drugs that killed tens of thousands of impoverished Filipinos. The Liberal Party (LP) transformed the mayor of Davao from a regional figure—long known to be the orchestrator of dead-squad vigilantism—into a politician of national prominence. Benigno Aquino III was elected president in 2010 with the support of Duterte, and they campaigned together in the 2013 midterm election. The LP mulled running Duterte as its vice presidential candidate in 2016 before he split with the party and ran for president.

The CPP, which had long-standing ties to Duterte, touted Duterte's claim that he would be the country's first "socialist" president. "Long live President Duterte!" wrote Sison from his home in Utrecht. The Kabataang Makabayan (Nationalist Youth, KM), now but a name, announced that it was awarding its highest-ever honor—the Gawad Supremo award—to two men, in honor of their lifetime struggle for justice: Jose Maria Sison and Rodrigo Duterte. The CPP selected people to serve in Duterte's cabinet and announced its support for his drug war. Among Duterte's first presidential acts was to arrange the burial of Ferdinand Sr., with state honors, in the National Heroes Cemetery. A year later, under intense pressure from the military, Duterte had an acrimonious falling out with the CPP. The engine of state violence, chugging mercilessly, bore down on all forms of political dissent with the murderous McCarthyism of the National Task Force to End Local Communist Armed Conflict (NTF-ELCAC).

It is in the epilogue that the distinction between player and part, between author and actor—we shadows—collapses. I delivered a lecture at Nanyang Technological University in August 2020, "First as Tragedy, Second as Farce," tracing the striking parallels between the CPP's support for Duterte and the Partido Komunista ng Pilipinas's backing of Marcos in the 1970s. The pandemic, at once fragmenting and interconnecting the world, compelled the lecture to be delivered online, and it found substantial interest from the Philippines. Thousands attended. Sison responded with fury. Before I had delivered my lecture, he took the unprecedented step of publishing a special issue of *Ang Bayan* dedicated to attacking me. He declared that I was a CIA agent and a "paid informant" of Duterte's death squads. The CPP circulated images of Leon Trotsky and me as rats being killed by an outraged Filipino peasant. Death threats, in the hundreds, followed. In 2021, as Marcos Jr. publicly announced that he was running for president, his online supporters began attacking me as well, adding to the death threats and slander. This strange and unintended alignment of hatred rests on the mutual commitment of Marcos and the CPP to the falsification of history.

The Corazon Aquino government and several subsequent administrations cultivated in popular consciousness a dichotomy: Marcos, corrupt and rapacious, responsible for the country's economic destitution; and liberal democracy, the solution to the country's ills. The passage of time weakened the content, but the formal dichotomy remained, waiting for the day its polarity was reversed. This was the thrust of Ferdinand Jr.'s campaign: martial law was a golden age, all that came after a fall from grace. He stood the People Power dichotomy on its head.

Louis Napoleon to his father's Bonaparte, Marcos Jr. is an unimpressive man possessed, at best, of an artful stupidity. The child of unfathomable privilege—college dropout, business school dropout, pampered and predatory—he struggles to complete a coherent sentence, and he avoids public debates to cover this up. Every word of the opening of Marx's *Eighteenth Brumaire* is so powerfully, painfully relevant that one must fend off the impulse to quote. The dead of history conjured up, the ghost of the father stalking the battlements, serve here not to glorify new struggles but to signal the staging of a repeat performance by a lesser cast.

The Philippine elite is highly attuned, with a sensitivity honed over a century, to the tremors of working-class unrest. Their sprawling mansions are but kilometers from vast shantytowns, and the proximity invests their politics with a nervous and jealous energy. Marcos Jr.'s platform expressed the advanced preparations in these layers to scrap the institutions of democracy. His claim that martial law was a golden age was not just a lying attempt to use his family name to secure votes; it was a promise as well. He was the candidate of dictatorship.

Conjoined with this has been the rotting away of democratic liberalism. In the final years of the Duterte administration, the CPP expressed the sentiment of liberal layers when Sison appealed to the "patriotic and progressive military officers" to withdraw support from Duterte and install Vice President Leni Robredo as president. This is similar to the impulse to see Generals Jim Mattis and Mark Milley as the "adults in the room" of the Trump White House. Unwilling to issue a social appeal to the masses of the population, liberalism prays for rain. Robredo ran as the leading opponent of Marcos Jr. Her campaign persuasively presented her as the moderate, the civil, alternative. She quietly pledged to continue the war on drugs, but it would no longer be "just kill, kill, kill"; she committed to continuing the mandate of NTF-ELCAC. The fundamental social ills—poverty, wages, prices—were left without solution, without hope.

It is this irreversible and world historic abdication that ceded to Marcos Jr., like his counterparts around the globe, an objective social basis: the cultivated mass despair at the possibility of a democratic solution to the country's immense social ills. None of the basic problems confronting Philippine society have been resolved. Peasant farmers labor bent double beneath loads of cane on vast sugar estates. Millions live in shantytowns that crowd the interstices of Metro Manila. Poverty wages and inhuman conditions confront the working class. Families are torn apart by the global diaspora of labor.

There is an enthusiasm of despair, and this has fueled popular support for the Bongbong Marcos Jr. campaign. At each rally, thousands danced to "Bagong Pagsilang" (New Birth), the anthem of martial law, moving with the frenzied desperation of imperiled members of the lower middle class and remittance-dependent poor. The pageantry of nihilism brought this despair to the ballot box. Marx's assessment of 1852 echoes terribly. "Universal suffrage seems to have survived only for the moment, so that with its own hand it may make its last will and testament before the eyes of all the world and declare in the name of the people itself: 'All that exists deserves to perish.'"[2]

We are witnessing the death rattle of democracy. Social inequality has so hollowed it out that formal equality can no longer sustain itself. The election of Marcos Jr. is a milestone in this global process. He represents the naked rule of reaction, promising dictatorship and drawing in his wake fascists and political scum.

Democratic rights can only be viably defended by a movement that is dedicated to curing the social cancers that have eaten away at their foundations. That which is now constrained in despair can turn to hope if it is given such orientation. Leon Trotsky argued at the opening of the twentieth century that the fight to achieve democracy could succeed only if it became the fight for socialism. It seems that the same is true today of democracy's defense.

A new 22 September 1972 has not yet arrived, but it looms ominously. Now as then, the crisis that confronts us reduces itself to one of revolutionary leadership.

Abbreviations

A6LM	April 6 Liberation Movement
ABLPPL	Alyansa ng Bayan Laban sa Pagtaas ng Presyo ng Langis (People's Alliance against Oil Price Hikes)
ACT	Association of Concerned Teachers
AFP	Armed Forces of the Philippines
AG	Artists' Group
AIM	Anti-Imperialism Movement
AKSIUN	Ang Kapatiran sa Ika-Unlad Natin (The Brotherhood for Our Progress)
AMA	Aniban ng mga Manggagawa sa Agrikultura (Federation of Agricultural Workers)
AS	Arts & Sciences
BRPF	Bertrand Russell Peace Foundation
CCN	Chinese Commercial News
CCP	Chinese Communist Party
CEGP	College Editors Guild of the Philippines
CIA	Central Intelligence Agency
CIU	Counterintelligence Unit
CMPDR	Citizens Movement for the Protection of Our Democratic Rights
CNL	Christians for National Liberation
COMELEC	Commission on Elections
CPP	Communist Party of the Philippines
CPUSA	Communist Party of the USA
FEATI	Far Eastern Transport Inc.
FEU	Far Eastern University
FOITAF	Federacion Obrera de la Industria Tabaquera de Filipinas
FQS	First Quarter Storm
GM	General Motors
GMD	Guomindang
HLP	Humanist League of the Philippines

HMB	Hukbo Mapagpalaya ng Bayan (People's Liberation Army)
KAMI	Kesatuan Aksi Mahasiswa Indonesia (Indonesian Students Action Front)
KAMMAPA	Kaisahan ng mga Makabayang Manggagawa sa Pamahalaan (Unity of Nationalist Government Workers)
KASAMA	Katipunan ng mga Samahan ng mga Manggagawa (Federation of Workers Associations)
KASAPI	Kapulungan ng mga Sandigan ng Pilipinas (Gathering of the Pillars of the Philippines)
KBLBM	Kilusan ng Bayan Laban sa Batas Medicare (People's Movement against the Medicare Law)
KILUSAN	Pambansang Kilusan ng Paggawa (National Labor Movement)
KKD	Katipunan ng Kabataang Demokratiko (Union of Democratic Youth)
KKKP	Kilusang Kristiyano ng Kabataang Pilipino (The Tagalog name of SCMP)
KM	Kabataang Makabayan (Nationalist Youth)
KMP	Katipunan ng Malayang Pagkakaisa (Federation of Free Unity; often known as KAMP)
KONTRES	Konsehong Tagapag-Ugnay ng Rebolusyonaryong Sining (Coordinating Council of Revolutionary Art)
LAKASDIWA	Lakas ng Diwang Kayumanggi (Strength of the Brown Spirit)
LDA	Ligang Demokratiko ng Ateneo (Democratic League of Ateneo)
LEADS	League of Editors for a Democratic Society
LM	Lapiang Manggagawa (Workers' Party)
LP	Liberal Party
MAKAMASA	Malayang Kapulungan ng Makabayang Samahan (Free Assembly of Nationalist Federations)
MAKIBAKA	Malayang Kilusan ng Bagong Kababaihan (Free Movement of New Women). In 1971, it changed its name to Makabayang Kilusan ng Bagong Kababaihan (Nationalist Movement of Free Women) but kept the acronym, MAKIBAKA.
MAN	Movement for the Advancement of Nationalism
MAPAGSAT	Malayang Pagkakaisa ng mga Samahan ng Tsuper (Free Unity of Driver Federations)
MASAKA	Malayang Samahan ng Magsasaka (Free Federation of Peasants)
MCCCL	Movement of Concerned Citizens for Civil Liberties
MDP	Movement for a Democratic Philippines

MIT	Mapua Institute of Technology
MLG	Marxist-Leninist Group
MLQU	Manuel L. Quezon University
MNLF	Moro National Liberation Front
MPD	Manila Police Department
MPKP	Malayang Pagkakaisa ng Kabataang Pilipino (Free Unity of Filipino Youth)
MTT	Makabayang Tagapag-ugnay ng Tondo (Nationalist Coordinator of Tondo)
NatDem	National Democrat
NATU	National Association of Trade Unions
NBA	Nationalist Businessmen's Association
NDF	National Democratic Front
NP	Nacionalista Party
NPA	New People's Army
NPAA	Nagkakaisang Progresibong Artista-Arkitekto (United Progressive Artists-Architects)
NSL	National Students League
NTF-ELCAC	National Task Force to End Local Communist Armed Conflict
NUSP	National Union of Students of the Philippines
OPEC	Organization of Petroleum Exporting Countries
PAKSA	Panulat para sa kaunlaran ng bayan (Writing for the progress of the nation)
PC	Philippine Constabulary
PCB	Partido Comunista Brasileiro
PCC	Philippine College of Commerce
PDS	Prente para sa Demokrasyang Sosyal (Front for Social Democracy)
PKI	Partai Komunis Indonesia
PKP	Partido Komunista ng Pilipinas
PLA	People's Liberation Army
PMA	Philippine Military Academy
POKA	Pederasyon ng mga Organisasyon sa Kalookan (Federation of Organizations in Caloocan)
PRC	People's Republic of China
PRF	People's Revolutionary Front
PSMT	Pambansang Samahan ng Makabayang Tsuper (National Federation of Nationalist Drivers)
PTGWO	Philippine Transportation and General Workers Organization

QCPD	Quezon City Police Department
RA	Republic Act
RAM	Reform the Armed Forces Movement
ROTC	Reserve Officers' Training Corps
SAGUPA	Samahan ng mga Guro sa Pamantasan (Federation of University Teachers)
SCA	Student Catholic Action
SCAUP	Student Cultural Association of the University of the Philippines
SCMP	Student Christian Movement of the Philippines
SDK	Samahan ng Demokratikong Kabataan (Federation of Democratic Youth). In late 1970, SDK changed its name to Samahang Demokratiko ng Kabataan (Democratic Federation of Youth), but kept the acronym.
SDKM	Samahang Demokratiko ng Kabataan—Mendiola
SKUP	Samahan ng Kababaihan ng UP (Federation of Women of UP)
SM	Sandigang Makabansa (Patriotic Pillars)
SMS	Samahan ng Makabayan Siyentipiko (Federation of Nationalist Scientists)
SocDem	Social Democrat
SPK	Samahan Pangkaunlaran ng Kaisipan (Federation for the Development of Consciousness). In 1971, it changed its name to Samahan ng Progresibong Kabataan (Federation of Progressive Youth), but kept the acronym SPK.
SPP	Socialist Party of the Philippines
SRC	Student Revolutionary Committee
STAND	Student Alliance for National Democracy
SWP	Socialist Workers Party
TRM	Thomasians for Reforms Movement
UIF	Union de Impresores de Filipinas
UKP	Ugnayan ng Kilusang Progresibo (Progressive Movement Association)
UP	University of the Philippines
UPCA	UP College of Agriculture
UPCACS	UP College of Agriculture Cultural Society
UPCF	UP College of Forestry
UPLB	UP Los Baños
UPSC	UP Student Council
UPSCA	UP Student Catholic Action

USIS   US Information Service
UST   University of Santo Tomas
USTC   US Tobacco Corporation
USTCLU   US Tobacco Corporation Labor Union
YCL   Young Communist League

NOTES

Abbreviations

AB	*Ang Bayan*
AK	*Ang Komunista*
AM	*Ang Masa*
APL	*Asia Philippines Leader*
BP	*Bandilang Pula*
DSUMC	David Sullivan US Maoism Collection
FRUS	*Foreign Relations of the United States*, various volumes
GW	*Graphic Weekly*
JHP	Joseph Hansen Papers
JSAP	James S. Allen Papers
Kal	*Kalayaan*
LCW	Lenin, *Collected Works*
Mal	*Ang Malaya*
MB	*Manila Bulletin*
MC	*Manila Chronicle*
MECW	Marx—Engels, *Collected Works*
MT	*Manila Times*
NYT	*New York Times*
PC	*Philippine Collegian*
PekRev	*Peking Review*
PFP	*Philippines Free Press*
PH	*The Philippines Herald*
PR	*Progressive Review*
PRP	Philippine Radical Papers Archive
PSR	*Philippine Society and Revolution*
SCPW	*Specific Characteristics of People's War in the Philippines*
SND1967	*Struggle for National Democracy*
STM	*Sunday Times Magazine*
TnB	*Taliba ng Bayan*
WSWS	*World Socialist Web Site*

Note on Translation and Orthography

1. Leon Trotsky, *The Permanent Revolution and Results and Prospects* (Seattle: Red Letter Press, 2010), 178.

Introduction

1. Alfred W. McCoy, *Policing America's Empire: The United States, the Philippines, and the Rise of the Surveillance State* (Quezon City: Ateneo de Manila University Press, 2011), 372.

2. Donald L. Berlin, *Before Gringo: History of the Philippine Military, 1830–1972* (Pasig: Anvil Publishing, 2008), xx, xxi.

3. On the currency and financial crises of the late 1960s and early 1970s and the ending of Bretton Woods, see R. Roy, "The Battle for Bretton Woods: America, Britain and the International Financial Crisis of October 1967–March 1968," *Cold War History* 2, no. 2 (2002): 33–60; Jeffrey E. Garten, *Three Days at Camp David: How a Secret Meeting in 1971 Transformed the Global Economy* (New York: HarperCollins, 2021).

4. Around the world "the early 1970s witnessed the highest food prices on record." Cullen S. Hendrix and Stephan Haggard, "Global Food Prices, Regime Type, and Urban Unrest in the Developing World," *Journal of Peace Research* 52, no. 2 (2015): 147, https://doi.org/10.1177/0022343314561599.

5. The growing anger at the Vietnam War found expression in repeated demonstrations, the first of which was staged on 24 October 1966. Joseph Scalice, "The Geopolitical Alignments of Diverging Social Interests: The Sino-Soviet Split and the Partido Komunista ng Pilipinas," *Critical Asian Studies* 53, no. 1 (2021): 45–70, https://doi.org/10.1080/14672715.2020.1870867.

6. Marshall Wright, "Memorandum from Marshall Wright of the National Security Council Staff to the President's Special Assistant (Rostow)," Document 353 in *FRUS, 1964–1968*, vol. 26, *Indonesia; Malaysia-Singapore; Philippines* (Washington, DC: US Government Printing Office, 2000).

7. Mattias Fibiger, "The Nixon Doctrine and the Making of Authoritarianism in Island Southeast Asia," *Diplomatic History* 45, no. 5 (2021): 956, https://doi.org/10.1093/dh/dhab065.

8. Washington's extensive backing of the Marcos dictatorship is ably detailed in Raymond Bonner, *Waltzing with a Dictator: The Marcoses and the Making of American Policy* (New York: Vintage Books, 1987).

9. In the following I rely particularly on Trotsky's development of this question in his August 1939 work, *Three Conceptions of the Russian Revolution*, in Leon Trotsky, *Writings of Leon Trotsky*, 14 vols., 1939–40 (New York: Pathfinder Press, 1975–79), 55–73.

10. Plekhanov developed these ideas in opposition to the voluntarism and utopianism of the Narodniks. On this, see Samuel H. Baron, *Plekhanov: The Father of Russian Marxism* (Stanford, CA: Stanford University Press, 1963), 89–116.

11. Baron, 263–264.

12. This perspective was elaborated in a number of documents, most famously V. I. Lenin, "Two Tactics of Social-Democracy in the Democratic Revolution," in *Collected Works* (Moscow: Progress Publishers, 1972), 9:15–140.

13. Leon Trotsky, *The Permanent Revolution and Results and Prospects* (Seattle: Red Letter Press, 2010), 33–136.

14. Trotsky, 313. While Trotsky's theory of permanent revolution was new, it was based on a synthesis of earlier developments in Marxist thought, a fact extensively demonstrated in Richard B. Day and Daniel Gaido, eds., *Witnesses to Permanent Revolution: The Documentary Record* (Chicago: Haymarket Books, 2009).

15. Edmund Wilson, *To the Finland Station: A Study in the Writing and Acting of History* (New York: Farrar, Straus and Giroux, 1972), 553.

16. This shift was famously put forward in Lenin's *April Theses*, LCW, 24:21–26.

17. On the Russian Revolution, see Alexander Rabinowitch, *The Bolsheviks Come to Power: The Revolution of 1917 in Petrograd* (Chicago: Haymarket Books, 2004); Alexander Rabinowitch, *The Bolsheviks in Power: The First Year of Soviet Rule in Petrograd* (Bloomington: Indiana University Press, 2007); Leon Trotsky, *History of the Russian Revolution* (Chicago: Haymarket Books, 2010).

18. Leon Trotsky, *The Revolution Betrayed: What Is the Soviet Union and Where Is It Going?* (Detroit, MI: Labor Publications, 1991), 48–51.

19. David North, "Introduction," in Trotsky, *Revolution Betrayed*, xxi.

20. Vadim Z. Rogovin, *Was There an Alternative? 1923–1927: Trotskyism: A Look Back through the Years*, trans. Frederick S. Choate (Oak Park, MI: Mehring Books, 2021), 367–378.

21. Vadim Z. Rogovin, *Stalin's Terror of 1937–1938: Political Genocide in the USSR*, trans. Frederick S. Choate (Oak Park, MI: Mehring Books, 2009), documents how the drive to destroy the ideas of Trotsky was the center of the Stalinist political genocide of 1937–38.

22. This was best embodied in the manner in which the Beijing-aligned PKI established close ties with the Sukarno administration in the first half of the decade.

23. Lin Biao, *Long Live the Victory of People's War!* (Peking: Foreign Languages Press, 1967). Beijing promoted Lin Biao's people's war from 1965 through the Cultural Revolution of 1966–69, until Mao turned on Lin, removing him from power. Mao established direct ties with Washington through "ping-pong diplomacy" in 1971, at which point the CCP's official line became the "Three Worlds Theory" and "People's War" was quietly buried.

24. *The Polemic on the General Line of the International Communist Movement* (Peking: Foreign Languages Press, 1965), 15.

25. "Diplomatic Ties with Russia?," *PFP*, 15 January 1966, 65.

26. The conservative character of MASAKA is evident in its founding program (MASAKA, *Alintuntunin at Saligang-Batas ng Malayang Samahang Magsasaka (MASAKA)*, 7 November 1964) and demonstrated by its early history, as I examine in Joseph Scalice, "Crisis of Revolutionary Leadership: Martial Law and the Communist Parties of the Philippines, 1957–1974" (PhD diss., University of California, Berkeley, 2017), 201–203.

27. Patricio N. Abinales, "Jose Ma. Sison and the Philippine Revolution: A Critique of an Interface," in *Fellow Traveler: Essays on Filipino Communism* (Quezon City: University of the Philippines Press, 2001), 19–20.

28. Jose Ma Sison, "Social Revolution through National Determination," *PC*, 29 August 1961, 3. I examine Sison's earliest publications in Joseph Scalice, "'We Are Siding with Filipino Capitalists': Nationalism and the Political Maturation of Jose Ma. Sison, 1959–61," *Sojourn: Journal of Social Issues in Southeast Asia* 36, no. 1 (2021): 1–39, https://doi.org/10.1355/sj36-1a.

29. Teodoro M. Locsin, "Meeting the Dragon: Who Really Wants Government FOR the People?," *PFP*, 5 August 1967, 18–19.

30. "Dare to struggle, dare to win" was a widely quoted Maoist slogan drawn from a section of the Mao's Red Book.

31. By the beginning of 1971, the SDK had completed a "rectification" process that brought them fully into the camp of Sison and the CPP. They changed their name from Samahan ng Demokratikong Kabataan (Federation of Democratic Youth) to Samah-ang Demokratiko ng Kabataan (Democratic Federation of Youth), highlighting their political shift from a focus on the individual to a focus on the organization. The acronym SDK remained unchanged. This fact provides a useful means for dating material. Anything signed S ng DK was published before late November 1970, anything signed SD ng K, after.

32. Benedict R. O'G Anderson, *Imagined Communities: Reflections on the Origin and Spread of Nationalism* (London: Verso, 1991), 1.

33. Anderson, 3.

34. Preeminent among these works are Kathleen Weekley, *The Communist Party of the Philippines, 1968–1993: A Story of Its Theory and Practice* (Quezon City: University of the Philippines Press, 2001); Dominique Caouette, "Persevering Revolutionaries: Armed Struggle in the 21st Century, Exploring the Revolution of the Communist Party of the Philippines" (PhD diss., Cornell University, 2004).

35. Two stand out: Gregg Jones, *Red Revolution: Inside the Philippine Guerrilla Movement* (Boulder, CO: Westview Press, 1989); William Chapman, *Inside the Philippine Revolution* (New York: W. W. Norton, 1987). Jones's account is by far the better historical work.

36. This new orientation to Moscow was openly expressed by Sison in Jose Ma Sison and Rainer Werning, *The Philippine Revolution: The Leader's View* (New York: Taylor & Francis, 1989), a work never published in full in the Philippines.

1. A Storm on the Horizon

1. Joseph B. Smith, *Portrait of a Cold Warrior* (New York: Ballantine Books, 1976), 98.

2. Raul Rodrigo, *Phoenix: The Saga of the Lopez Family, Volume 1, 1800–1972* (Manila: Eugenio López Foundation, 2000), 180. On the significance of sugar holdings in the development of the Philippine ruling class, see John A. Larkin, *Sugar and the Origins of Modern Philippine Society* (Berkeley: University of California Press, 1993).

3. For an overview of internal migration patterns in the postwar period, see Wilhelm Flieger, "Internal Migration in the Philippines during the 1960s," *Philippine Quarterly of Culture and Society* 5, no. 4 (1977): 199–231.

4. Alfred W. McCoy, *Policing America's Empire: The United States, the Philippines, and the Rise of the Surveillance State* (Quezon City: Ateneo de Manila University Press, 2011), 384.

5. Mark Richard Thompson, "Searching for a Strategy: The Traditional Opposition to Marcos and the Transition to Democracy in the Philippines," vols. 1 and 2 (PhD diss., Yale University, 1991), 44–52.

6. Jose Lacaba, "We will not follow Marcos to the precipice!" *APL*, 23 April 1971, 7.

7. Carmen Navarro Pedrosa, *Imelda Romualdez Marcos: The Verdict* (Ukraine: Flipside Digital Content, 2017), chapter 1; Mina Roces, *Kinship Politics in the Postwar Philippines: The Lopez Family, 1946–2000* (Quezon City: De La Salle University Press, 2001), 124.

8. People of the Philippines v. Mariano Marcos et al., G.R. No. 47388 (1940); Raymond Bonner, *Waltzing with a Dictator: The Marcoses and the Making of American Policy* (New York: Vintage Books, 1987), 11–14.

9. Bonner, 10; Douglas Martin, "Hartzell Spence, 93, Dies; Pinup Pioneer," *NYT*, 25 May 2001, B-8.

10. Rommel A. Curaming, *Power and Knowledge in Southeast Asia: State and Scholars in Indonesia and the Philippines* (London: Taylor & Francis, 2019), chapter 2.

11. William C. Rempel, *Delusions of a Dictator: The Mind of Marcos as Revealed in His Secret Diaries* (Boston: Little, Brown, 1993).

12. Primitivo Mijares, *The Conjugal Dictatorship of Ferdinand and Imelda Marcos* (San Francisco: Union Square Publications, 1976).

13. Carmen Navarro Pedrosa, *Imelda Marcos* (New York: St. Martin's Press, 1987), 16–80.

14. Nick Joaquin, *The Aquinos of Tarlac: An Essay on History as Three Generations* (Manila: Cacho Hermanos, 1983).

15. Lewis E. Gleeck Jr., *Dissolving the Colonial Bond: American Ambassadors to the Philippines, 1946–1984* (Quezon City: New Day Publishers, 1988), 171.

16. Leon Trotsky, *History of the Russian Revolution* (Chicago: Haymarket Books, 2010), xvi.

17. For a representative example of the repeated use of these phrases, see the July 1969 issue of *Ang Bayan*.

18. Jose Ma Sison and Rainer Werning, *The Philippine Revolution: The Leader's View* (New York: Taylor & Francis, 1989), 1, 3.

19. D. R. Crisologo, "Florentina Sison: Mother to a Young Revolutionary," *GW*, 8 July 1970, 12.

20. Daniel F. Doeppers, *Feeding Manila in Peace and War, 1850–1945* (Madison: University of Wisconsin Press, 2016), 78–82.

21. Sison and Werning, *Philippine Revolution*, 9.

22. Leonard Davis, *Revolutionary Struggle in the Philippines* (New York: Palgrave Macmillan, 1989), 127; Renato Constantino, *The Making of a Filipino: A Story of Philippine Colonial Politics* (Quezon City: Malaya Books, 1971), 2–4; Smith, *Portrait of a Cold Warrior*, 286.

23. Claro M. Recto, *Political and Legal Works, 1954–1955*, vol. 8 of *The Complete Works of Claro M. Recto*, ed. Isagani R. Medina and Myrna S Feliciano (Pasay: Claro M. Recto Foundation, 1990), 360, 362.

24. Recto, 365.

25. Claro M. Recto, *Political and Legal Works, 1959–1960*, vol. 9 of *The Complete Works of Claro M. Recto*, ed. Isagani R. Medina and Myrna S. Feliciano (Pasay: Claro M. Recto Foundation, 1990), 148.

26. Emerenciana Yuvienco Arcellana, *The Life and Times of Claro M. Recto* (Pasay: Claro M. Recto Foundation, 1990), 318–343.

27. It was precisely this perspective that Sison articulated in his last public speech before going underground in February 1969. Jose Ma Sison, *Recto and the National Democratic Struggle* (Manila: Progressive Publications, 1969). A month later he oversaw the founding of the New People's Army (NPA).

28. Eduardo Lachica, *The Huks: Philippine Agrarian Society in Revolt* (Quezon City: Solidaridad Publishing House, 1971), 156.

29. Lachica, 157.

30. Lachica, 157.

31. I detail this arrangement in Joseph Scalice, "Crisis of Revolutionary Leadership: Martial Law and the Communist Parties of the Philippines, 1957–1974" (PhD diss., University of California, Berkeley, 2017), 240–45.

32. Thompson, "Searching for a Strategy," 110–111. The source for this statement was an interview with Sison himself.

33. The term "united front" was routinely used by Stalinist parties around the globe to justify their alliances with sections of the capitalist class. The tactic of the united front has an important history. It was discussed in considerable detail in 1922, prior to Stalin's rise to power, at the Fourth Congress of the Comintern. The Congress explained that "The united-front tactic is an initiative for united struggle of the Communists with all workers who belong to other parties and groups, with all unaligned workers, to defend the most basic interests of the working class against the bourgeoisie." "On the Tactics of the Comintern," Appendix 7 in John Riddell, ed, *Toward the United Front: Proceedings of the Fourth Congress of the Communist International, 1922* (Leiden: Brill, 2012), 1158. Trotsky urged the formation of a united front of the German working class in the early 1930s, calling for the unity of the Social Democratic and Communist workers against the imminent danger of Nazism. The workers' organizations would preserve their political and organizational independence, as there should be "no common platform with the Social Democracy . . . no common publications, banners, or placards," but the entire working class needed to wage a common fight. They should, he wrote, "march separately, but strike together!" Leon Trotsky, *The Struggle Against Fascism in Germany* (New York: Pathfinder Press, 1971), 138–139. The German Communist Party, under Stalinist leadership, rejected Trotsky's call for a united front. They attacked the Social Democrats as "social fascists," divided the German working class, and made possible Hitler's rise to power in 1933. In 1934, Stalin led the Comintern to drastically reverse course, calling for the formation of "popular front" alliances with capitalist parties against fascism. It was this latter policy of alliance with the bourgeoisie that Stalinism came to refer to as the tactic of the "united front." Throughout this book, the references made by the CPP and PKP to a "united front" are calls to carry out a class collaborationist, popular front policy.

34. Gregg Jones, *Red Revolution: Inside the Philippine Guerrilla Movement* (Boulder, CO: Westview Press, 1989), 27, 29. Sison claimed that he first met Dante in December 1968 in Capas, that the January meeting was their second meeting, and that he returned to live with Dante beginning in February (Sison and Werning, *Philippine Revolution*, 59).

35. *MB*, 1 August 1969.

36. "Dive, dive, dive," *MB*, 18 August 1969.

37. Amado Hernandez, "Biglang Taas ng mga Presyo," *AM*, 6 December 1969. The banner article carried the byline Mando Plaridel. This was almost certainly Amado Hernandez's pen name, as Mando Plaridel was the protagonist in Amado V. Hernandez, *Mga Ibong Mandaragit* (Quezon City: International Graphic Service, 1969). Hernandez focused his ire not on capitalism but on the Chinese, arguing that the coming demonstrations needed to demand that the government compel the "Chinese grocery and bodega owners" to release the goods they had hoarded. Bread prices, he stated, had risen precipitously. "And remember," he wrote, "almost all bakeries [*panaderia*] are monopolized by the Chinese [*intsik*] just like the groceries and clothing

stores" ("Biglang Taas," 3). Hernandez detailed a number of rising prices: vegetable prices had doubled, the prices of bread and eggs had gone up by 20 percent, and the price of the fish *dalagang bukid* had risen from ₱1.60 to ₱2.60 per kilogram ("Biglang Taas," 3).

38. Rodrigo, *Phoenix*, 351.

39. Henry Kissinger, "Memorandum to President Nixon," Document 222 in *FRUS, 1969–1976*, vol. 20, Southeast Asia (Washington, DC: US Government Printing Office, 2006).

40. "Memorandum of Conversation," Document 233 in *FRUS, 1969–1976*, vol. 20.

41. This was Lopez's third term as vice president; the first was in 1949–53, under Quirino.

42. Quoted in Raul Rodrigo, *The Power and the Glory: The Story of the Manila Chronicle, 1945–1998* (Pasig: Eugenio Lopez Foundation, 2007), 227.

43. Quijano de Manila, "Why Did Ninoy Throw That Bomb?," *APL*, 7 May 1971, 52.

44. Rodrigo, *Power and the Glory*, 226. The rising oil prices, for which both the Lopez brothers and the CPP denounced Marcos, were in large part the result of the formation of the Organization of Petroleum Exporting Countries (OPEC) in 1969.

45. Rodrigo, 236.

46. Rodrigo, 232.

47. Patricio N. Abinales and Donna J. Amoroso, *State and Society in the Philippines* (Pasig: Anvil Publishing, 2005), 202.

48. "The Students and the Press," *MC*, 8 January 1970.

49. Hermie Rotea, *I Saw Them Aim and Fire* (Manila: Daily News, 1970), 23.

50. A significant new voice in this chorus was a savagely anti-Marcos weekly launched in April 1971, the *Asia-Philippines Leader*, which during its first year of publication demonstrated its ties to the student radicals by publishing the polemics of the Partido Komunista ng Pilipinas (PKP) and CPP. The *APL* was operated by Jose Ma. Jacinto, scion of the Jacinto family, which had interests in steel production and, like the Lopez brothers, was in a bitter economic dispute with Marcos, who had demanded shares of the corporation in return for continued government subsidies to their steel mill (Thompson, "Searching for a Strategy," 115).

51. "Tondo Players to Stage Drama," *PC*, 5 August 1970, 6. The play had initially been staged at the Philam Life Auditorium on 18 and 19 April by Tanghalang Bayan.

52. Soliman M. Santos and Paz Verdades M. Santos, eds., *SDK: Militant but Groovy: Stories of Samahang Demokratiko ng Kabataan* (Manila: Anvil Publishing, 2008), 113.

53. Thompson, "Searching for a Strategy," 116.

54. Thompson, 52.

55. Thompson, 151.

56. Thompson, 118.

57. Thompson, 117.

58. Thompson, 148. The hitmen were August McCormick Lehman, Robert Pincus (both of whom had mafia ties), Larry Trachtman, Sam Cummins, and Brian Bothwick (Thompson, 149).

59. Thompson, 109 fn. 51. The mole was Jose Maristella.

60. Vizmanos's involvement can be reconstructed from snippets and stray details scattered throughout his three books: Danilo P. Vizmanos, *Through the Eye of the Storm*

(Quezon City: KEN, 2000); Danilo P. Vizmanos, *Martial Law Diary and Other Papers* (Quezon City: KEN, 2003); Danilo P. Vizmanos, *A Matter of Conviction* (Quezon City: Ibon Books, 2006).

61. Vizmanos, *Through the Eye*, 169.

62. Thompson, "Searching for a Strategy," 155.

63. Benjamin T. Tolosa Jr., ed., *Socdem: Filipino Social Democracy in a Time of Turmoil and Transition, 1965–1995* (Manila: Friedrich-Ebert-Stiftung, 2011), 11.

64. On the role of KAMI, see John Hughes, *The End of Sukarno: A Coup That Misfired, a Purge That Ran Wild* (Singapore: Archipelago, 2002); Justus M. Van Der Kroef, *Indonesia after Sukarno* (Vancouver: University of British Columbia Press, 1971).

65. Tolosa, *Socdem*, 13.

66. Loosely translated as the Gathering of the Pillars of the Philippines.

67. Many of the SocDem organizations received support through the Friedrich Ebert Stiftung offices in Manila, demonstrating their deep ties to the Second International (Tolosa, *Socdem*, 51).

68. Jennifer Conroy Franco, *Elections and Democratization in the Philippines*, Comparative Studies in Democratization (New York: Routledge, 2001), 88–89.

69. In an interview with Pat Robertson on the *700 Club*, Aquino, by this point in political exile in the United States, hailed one such group that called itself the April 6 Liberation Movement (A6LM). Aquino had deep ties to the A6LM, which was attempting through terrorist bombings to overthrow Marcos. Talitha Espiritu, *Passionate Revolutions: The Media and the Rise and Fall of the Marcos Regime* (Athens: Ohio University Press, 2017), 149. In 1980 another SocDem group, working in conjunction with the Moro National Liberation Front, launched Operation June Bride, a bombing campaign waged throughout Manila that was prepared and staged from Sabah (Tolosa, *Socdem*).

70. Franco, *Elections and Democratization*, 90.

71. KM, *Brief History of Kabataang Makabayan (1964–1972)*, 1 November 1984, 7, PRP 08/15.01.

72. KASAPI, *Bukas na Liham sa mga Kawal ng Gobyerno*, [January 1971], PRP 08/32.01.

73. "Rebolusyon ng Kabataan Sinang-ayunan ni Ferrer," *AM*, 15 May–15 June 1971, 2.

74. Ina Alleco R. Silverio, *Ka Bel: The Life and Struggle of Crispin Beltran* (Quezon City: Southern Voices, 2010), 77. With funding and support from Ninoy Aquino, Gillego later carried out a series of bombings in Manila in the late 1970s. This was known as Project Mactan and was separate from A6LM. Alfred W. McCoy, *Closer Than Brothers: Manhood at the Philippine Military Academy* (Manila: Anvil Publishing, 1999), 156.

75. I examine this event and its significance in Joseph Scalice, "The Geopolitical Alignments of Diverging Social Interests: The Sino-Soviet Split and the Partido Komunista ng Pilipinas," *Critical Asian Studies* 53, no. 1 (2021): 45–70, https://doi.org/10.1080/14672715.2020.1870867.

76. Teddy Owen, "Marcos Warns on Social Scars," *MB*, 6 February 1967.

77. While it had been renamed, Azcarraga had not yet become Recto in popular terminology, a fact best evidenced by Lacaba's insistent use of the older street name throughout his *Days of Disquiet*.

78. David Conde, "Students in the Philippines," *Eastern Horizon* 8, no. 2 (1969): 57; Student Power Assembly of the Philippines, *The Diliman Declaration*, 9 March 1969, PRP 17/12.01.

79. "By the mid-1960s, UP's student population was about 15,000, which included Los Baños and other campuses, but the densely packed U-belt area teemed with some 200,000 students." Nelson A. Navarro, *Doc Prudente: Nationalist Educator* (Mandaluyong City: Anvil Publishing, 2011), 74–75. By 1970, the numerical and class gap had grown substantially wider.

80. My account of the developments at the Lyceum is based on Jose F. Lacaba, *Days of Disquiet, Nights of Rage: The First Quarter Storm & Related Events* (Pasig: Anvil Publishing, 2003), 23–37.

81. Lacaba, 32.

82. Corazon Damo-Santiago, *A Century of Activism* (Manila: Rex Bookstore, 1972), 151.

83. Lacaba, *Days of Disquiet*, 35.

84. Damo-Santiago, *Century of Activism*, 152.

85. Damo-Santiago, 151.

86. Lacaba, *Days of Disquiet*, 23.

87. Damo-Santiago, *Century of Activism*, 156.

88. Damo-Santiago, 153.

89. Damo-Santiago, 157.

90. Damo-Santiago, 158.

91. Among those leading the TRM was Noli Collantes (Damo-Santiago, 159).

92. Damo-Santiago, 164–168.

93. Jose Ma Sison, "Student Power," *Eastern Horizon* 8, no. 2 (1969): 52–56.

94. Sison, 52.

95. Christine Ebro, "Political Action and the UP Coed," *PC*, 4 September 1968, 3.

96. Progresibong Kabataan ng MLQU, *Nasa Atin ang Tagumpay*, 17 September 1969, PRP 14/15.01.

97. Emphasis added.

98. Sison, "Student Power," 55.

99. Sison, 56.

100. Elias T. Ramos, "Labor Conflict and Recent Trends in Philippine Industrial Relations," *Philippine Quarterly of Culture and Society* 15, no. 3 (1987): 181. The data for 1972 were cut off by the declaration of martial law in September, but by the end of August over a million worker-days had been lost.

101. Ninotchka Rosca, "Anatomy of a Strike," *GW*, 23 July 1969, 6–8; "Laganap na pasismo, inihayag, tinutuligsa," *PC*, 6 November 1969.

102. Ninotchka Rosca, "Protest '69," *GW*, 24 September 1969, 6–9.

103. Ninotchka Rosca, "Teacher Went Out," *GW*, 19 November 1969, 4–5.

104. This incident served as the basis for the 1976 film *Minsa'y isang Gamu-gamo*, in which Nora Aunor delivered one of the more renowned lines in Philippine cinema: "My brother is not a pig!"

105. Amadis Ma. Guerrero, "Deaths in US Bases: Who Will Heal the Wounds," *GW*, 15 October 1969, 4–5, 71.

106. Monico M. Atienza, "Pangkalahatang Ulat sa 1969—Kabataang Makabayan sa Lahat ng Larangan," *AM*, 6 December 1969, 6.

107. Manuel Almario, "The Threat from Magsaysay," *GW*, 4 June 1969, 9.

108. *PFP*, 6 January 1969, 3.

109. "Memorandum from the Acting Executive Secretary of the Department of State (Walsh) to the President's Assistant for National Security Affairs" (2 July 1969), Document 190 in *FRUS, 1969–1976*, vol. 20, Southeast Asia (Washington, DC: US Government Printing Office, 2006).

110. *MB*, 8 July 1969, 1.

111. *MB*, 11 July 1969, 19. Osmeña's claim that Marcos was "flirting with Red China" was baseless.

112. *MB*, 11 July 1969, 20.

113. *MB*, 29 July 1969, 17.

114. *MB*, 29 July 1969.

115. Linda McFarland, *Cold War Strategist: Stuart Symington and the Search for National Security* (Westport, CT: Praeger, 2001), 148.

116. "Telegram from the Embassy in the Philippines to the Department of State," Document 196 fn. 4 in *FRUS, 1969–1976*, vol. 20, Southeast Asia.

117. US Senate Committee on Foreign Relations, *Hearings before the Subcommittee on United States Security Agreements and Commitments Abroad (SACA) of the Committee on Foreign Relations, US Senate, Ninety-First Congress, First Session, Part 1* (Washington, DC: US Government Printing Office, 1969), 245–246.

118. Scalice, "Crisis of Revolutionary Leadership," 240–245.

119. Lachica, *Huks*, 217.

120. Lachica, 209, 219.

121. Lachica, 220. In January 1970, the KM hailed Llorente as "a progressive element" and denounced the PC for his attempted "assassination." *First Quarter Storm of 1970* (Manila: Silangan Publishers, 1970), 161.

122. McCoy, *Policing America's Empire*, 391.

123. The evidence for the PKP's Manila bombing campaign under Soliman from 1969 to 1972 is based on the accounts written up in *their own* publications, particularly in the issues of *Ang Mandirigma*.

124. Nick Joaquin, *A Kadre's Road to Damascus: The Ruben Torres Story* (Quezon City: Milflores, 2003), 79, 81.

125. *Ang Mandirigma* 1, no. 3 (1972): 13, PRP 36/06.04.

126. Lualhati Milan Abreu, *Agaw-dilim, Agaw-liwanag* (Quezon City: University of the Philippines Press, 2009), 45.

127. *MB*, 24 July 1969.

128. *MB*, 25 July 1969.

129. Ken Fuller, *A Movement Divided: Philippine Communism, 1957–1986* (Quezon City: University of the Philippines Press, 2011), 135. Within two weeks of the bombings, three delegates from the PKP—Ruben Torres, Haydee Yorac, and Soliman—traveled to Moscow via Tokyo. Yorac and Soliman remained there until 1970 and, upon returning to Manila, reported to Torres (Joaquin, *Kadre's Road to Damascus*, 80).

130. "Seeing through the Tricks of Nixon the Master and Marcos the Puppet," *AB*, August 1969, 1.

131. "New People's Army Annihilates More U.S. Imperialists," *AB*, September 1969, 11.

132. "Diokno Tackles Poll Issues at AS," *PC*, 17 September 1969, 3.

133. *PC*, 3 November 1969.

134. Hernando J. Abaya, *The Making of a Subversive: A Memoir* (Quezon City: New Day Publishers, 1984), 194.

135. I have not been able to locate a copy of this document. Its substance, however, was summarized by Jose Lava in an article published in November 1971. See Jose Lava [Francisco Balagtas, pseud.], "The Philippines at the Crossroads," *World Marxist Review* 14, no. 11 (1971): 42.

136. MAN, *M.A.N's Goal: The Democratic Filipino Society* ([Manila]: Malaya Books, 1969), 58–60.

137. "Reformist Organizations Beg for Land Reform from Reactionary Government," *AB*, October 1969, 10.

138. A good deal of the election data is drawn from Jose Veloso Abueva, "The Philippines: Tradition and Change," *Asian Survey* 10, no. 1 (1970): 56–64.

139. Rotea, *I Saw Them Aim and Fire*, 6.

140. Manuel F. Almario, "Where Lies the Opposition," *GW*, 18 February 1970, 13.

2. The First Quarter Storm

1. UP Council of Leaders, *UP Council of Leaders Denounces Election Terrorism*, 1969, PRP 17/47.01. On 19 November, the student council, in an effort at "elevating the political consciousness of our people," who "despite the seeming meaninglessness of our democracy . . . still cling to it," called for a boycott of classes to "express alarm over the indications of a moribund society." UP Student Council (UPSC), *Boycott Our Classes and Join the Show of Protest against the Fraudulent Elections!!*, 29 November 1969, PRP 18/02.04. They created a steering committee to coordinate a nationwide rally with all schools and sectors against election fraud. *Leaders Denounce Nov. 11 Terrorism*, 19 November 1969, PRP 37/18.01. An additional resolution by the Arts & Sciences Student Council on the same day noted that *both* political parties were guilty of cheating and violence. The UPSC issued a similar resolution stating that "both political parties are merely two faces of the same dirty coin, two factions of the same exploitative alliance of hacendero, comprador and American imperialist classes." UPSC and UP Council of Leaders, *Manifesto*, 19 November 1969, PRP 18/02.25.

2. "An Interview with Mindo and Gary," *Breakthrough* 3, nos. 3–4 (November 1971): 4, PRP 29/11.02. The MDP was also occasionally, but rarely, referred to by the Tagalog Kilusan Para sa Pambansang Demokrasya (Movement for National Democracy).

3. MDP, "Declaration of Principles," *PC*, 27 November 1969, 2.

4. MDP, *Manifesto of the Movement for a Democratic Philippines*, 11 December 1969, PRP 11/18.12.

5. Jose F. Lacaba, *Days of Disquiet, Nights of Rage: The First Quarter Storm & Related Events* (Pasig: Anvil Publishing, 2003), xiii.

6. Gary Olivar, "Notes on the Press," *PC*, 5 January 1970, 4.

7. An open faculty letter published in the *Collegian* estimated that 150 people attended. Cesar Majul et al., "Declaration of Concern," *PC*, 8 January 1970, 7.

8. Eduardo T. Gonzales, "A Chronicle of Protests," *Dare to Struggle, Dare to Win*, January 1971, 2, PRP 30/03.01.

9. KM, *Uphold People's Democratic Rights, Fight the Fascistic State*, 7 January 1970, PRP 08/19.18. The same leaflet identified the protesters who had been suppressed on 29 December as part of "student reform movements."

10. "UP, Others Hit 'Rise of Fascism,'" *PC*, 8 January 1970.

11. *"Demonstrasyon Ngayon,"* 1896 1, no. 1 (1970), PRP 30/07.01.

12. *1896* 1, no. 1. The periodical *1896* reports that this rally took place on the fifteenth, but comparing the various press accounts leads to the conclusion that the rally was in fact held on Friday, 16 January. The *Collegian* reported that "close to 3,000 students and workers" participated. "Students Rally with NMI Strikers," *PC*, 22 January 1970.

13. "Students Rally with NMI Strikers," *PC*, 22 January 1970. Details of the protest on the twenty-second are scant, other than the fact that it was headed by the National Students League (NSL).

14. There are a number of firsthand accounts of the FQS. Three stand out: Ceres S. C. Alabado, *I See Red in a Circle . . .* (Manila, 1972); Hermie Rotea, *I Saw Them Aim and Fire* (Manila: Daily News, 1970); Lacaba, *Days of Disquiet*. Rotea's and Lacaba's accounts are compilations of articles written at the time of the events. Alabado's work is a first-person account of participation in the FQS through the eyes of Alabado's daughter. Lacaba's account is by far the most memorable. *Days of Disquiet* was written for the *Philippines Free Press*, but it transcends reportage and embodies in its prose both the shock and the anger of the storm. It ranks among the better works of Philippine literature in English.

15. Rotea reported that "as early as Jan. 19 [law enforcement] started mapping out security measures for the Jan. 26 public appearance of President Marcos in Congress. . . . Col. Cezar C. Jasmin of the Metrocom served as the over-all task force commander. In effect, Manila was placed under Metrocom control. The city police merely provided the sub-task force. But it was the Metrocom which called the shots" (Rotea, *I Saw Them Aim and Fire*, 43).

16. Antonio Tagamolila, "The Strike that Never Was," *PC*, 22 January 1970, 12.

17. Lacaba, *Days of Disquiet*, xvii; Rotea, *I Saw Them Aim and Fire*, 36, 38.

18. Jose Carreon, Rogelio Razon, and Roberto Ordoñez, "Riot Cops Battle Demonstrators," *PH*, 27 January 1970, 11. The protesters dispatched a representative who met with Senator Aquino to request that Marcos's speakers be taken down, but they were not removed. Benigno S. Aquino Jr., *When Law and Order Went Amok*, 27 January 1970, 29, PRP 01/28.01.

19. Carreon, Razon, and Ordoñez, "Riot Cops," *PH*, 27 January 1970, 10.

20. Rotea, *I Saw Them Aim and Fire*, 46.

21. MPKP, *The Sad State of the Nation*, 26 January 1970, PRP 10/29.19.

22. Rotea, *I Saw Them Aim and Fire*, 48.

23. Reprinted in *First Quarter Storm of 1970* (Manila: Silangan Publishers, 1970), 155–168, 156 (hereafter cited parenthetically in the text as *FQS*).

24. Among those who spoke were Portia Ilagan of the NSL; Crispin Aranda, Philippine College of Commerce (PCC); Luis Taruc; Renato Constantino; Roger Arienda; Father Navarro, a seminarian of San Carlos; and Edgar Jopson of the NUSP (Rotea, *I Saw Them Aim and Fire*, 46–47).

25. Rotea, 48.

26. Lacaba, *Days of Disquiet*, 44. J26M stood for January 26 Movement.

27. Lacaba, 46–47.

28. Rotea, *I Saw Them Aim and Fire*, 50.

29. Lacaba, *Days of Disquiet*, 48.

30. Rotea, *I Saw Them Aim and Fire*, 53.

31. Lacaba, *Days of Disquiet*, 48.

32. Lacaba, 50.

33. Lacaba, 51–52.

34. Lacaba, 55.

35. Rotea, *I Saw Them Aim and Fire*, 59.

36. Rotea, 60.

37. Rotea, 61.

38. Lacaba, *Days of Disquiet*, 58.

39. Carreon, Razon, and Ordoñez, "Riot Cops," *PH*, 27 January 1970, 10.

40. MPKP, *Police Riots Again!*, 27 January 1970, PRP 10/29.18.

41. Rotea, *I Saw Them Aim and Fire*, 62.

42. Rotea, 64.

43. Lacaba, *Days of Disquiet*, 57, 176 fn. 57.

44. Lacaba, xviii; *PC*, 28 January 1970.

45. Perfecto Tera Jr. [Rodrigo Rojas, pseud.], "The State of the Nation," *Eastern Horizon* 9, no. 1 (1970): 46; Rotea, *I Saw Them Aim and Fire*, 74.

46. Lacaba, *Days of Disquiet*, xviii.

47. Faculty of the University of the Philippines (UP), *UP Faculty Protests Repression of Civil Liberties!*, 27 January 1970, PRP 17/13.01. The UP faculty, including President Salvador Lopez, marched to Malacañang on Thursday and held a rally. They met with Marcos and presented him their declaration.

48. *AB*, "On the January 26th Demonstration," January 1970. It denounced the attempts to subordinate the demonstration to the demand for a nonpartisan constitutional convention, as well as the House-Senate investigation, which it termed "a worn-out device of the reactionaries to conduct a witch-hunt under the guise of helping the students. The 'nationalist' prestige of Tañada is now being conveniently used for this purpose."

49. "Reactionary UPSCA Elements Faked *The Partisan*," *The Partisan* 3, no. 5 (1970): 6, PRP 37/15.02. UPSCA disputed this, stating that to circulate fake leaflets would be "unchristian." UPSCA Committee on Mass Media, *So That the People May Know*, 1 June 1970, PRP 18/20.01. The fake leaflet is "NUSP Leadership Censured," *The Partisan* [counterfeit issue], 30 January 1970, PRP 37/18.02.

50. MPKP, *For a People's Constitution*, 30 January 1970, PRP 10/29.04.

51. Lacaba, *Days of Disquiet*, xix.

52. Benjamin V. Afuang, "Special Report: The Students vs the State, 1970," *STM*, 22 February 1970, 23.

53. Gary Oliver, "Venceremos Counters," *PC*, 23 July 1970, 6.

54. Nelson A. Navarro, *The Half-Remembered Past: A Memoir* (Quezon City: Alphan Publishers, 2013), 70.

55. Navarro, 69.

56. Alabado, *I See Red in a Circle*, 101. Information on Felicisimo Singh Roldan varies. Lacaba has "Feliciano Roldan of FEU" (Lacaba, *Days of Disquiet*, 69). Aquino has

Felicismo Singh Roldan of FEU. Benigno S. Aquino Jr., *Black Friday, January 30*, 2 February 1970, 6, PRP 01/28.01. Of those killed, we know the most about Alcantara, who was not an activist but was memorialized in *Sinag* as "an ordinary fellow about campus. His classmates remembered him mostly as an habitue of the Basement very much preoccupied over his part in 'Hair.'" "The University of the Philippines and the Unfinished Revolution," *Sinag*, August 1972, 5. In early March, the UPSC passed a resolution renaming the town hall, on the second floor of Vinzons Hall, "Alcantara," in honor of the "martyr" Ricardo Alcantara (Alabado, *I See Red in a Circle*, 387).

57. Alabado, *I See Red in a Circle*, 151; *Pingkian*, February 1970, 6, PRP 38/02.

58. Aquino, *Black Friday*, 11. Marcos promoted the commander of the Metrocom, Col. Ordoñez, who had directly overseen the assault on the students, to general on the spot (Aquino, 7). In 1972, the Armed Forces of the Philippines (AFP) admitted that a number of "government penetration agents" had participated in the "violent demonstration," including Sgt. Elnora Estrada. *So the People May Know* (Quezon City: General Headquarters, Armed Forces of the Philippines, 1972), 7:18.

59. Lacaba, *Days of Disquiet*, 71. Classes were suspended on the orders of Education Secretary Onofre Corpuz (Gonzales, "Chronicle of Protests," 2).

60. Aquino, *Black Friday*, 12. In an attempt to shore up the claim that Communists were behind the violence of the demonstrations, the military published a selection from the documents captured in Sta. Rita in June 1969. The first volume of the series, *So the People May Know*, was released on 5 February, and AFP chief of staff Manuel Yan wrote the foreword. "The violence which accompanied the student demonstrations in Manila last 26 and 30 January 1970 was instigated by subversive elements and provocateurs who subscribe to Mao Zedong's dictum of armed revolution. . . . In the light of these developments, I fell [*sic*] that we must takes [*sic*] steps to inform the general public about the intentions of the local Communist movement." *So the People May Know* (Quezon City: General Headquarters, Armed Forces of the Philippines, 1970), 1:152. The copious typographical and spelling errors throughout the foreword reveal the haste with which this publication was produced.

61. KM, *Be Resolute! Unite and Oppose the Murder, Maiming and Mass Arrest of Fellow Students and Countrymen!*, 2 February 1970, PRP 08/13.03.

62. *First Quarter Storm of 1970*, 36–45 (hereafter cited parenthetically in the text as *FQS*).

63. This statement was later published in *AB*, 28 February 1970. I have not located an extant original and am using the reprinted version in Jose Ma Sison, *Foundation for Resuming the Philippine Revolution: Selected Writings, 1969 to 1972*, ed. Julieta de Lima, vol. 1 of *Continuing the Philippine Revolution* (Quezon City: Aklat ng Bayan, 2013), 153–68.

64. Sison, 157.

65. Sison, 159–60.

66. Sison, 155.

67. Sison, 165.

68. Sison, 166.

69. Gonzales, "Chronicle of Protests," 2.

70. Representing the MDP and NATU were Ignacio Lacsina, PCC president Nemesio Prudente, Teodosio Lansang, Felixberto Olalia, Carlos del Rosario, Jerry Barican,

and Ramon Sanchez, "among others" (Rotea, *I Saw Them Aim and Fire*, 287). The SDK had at least two representatives in the room; the KM at least one.

71. "Demonstration Goes on Tomorrow in UP," *PC*, 11 February 1970, 1, 6.

72. Rotea, *I Saw Them Aim and Fire*, 288.

73. Lacaba, *Days of Disquiet*, 72–73.

74. "Demonstration Goes on Tomorrow in UP," *PC*, 11 February 1970, 6.

75. Sison later stated, "I consider as my most important contribution to the First Quarter Storm of 1970 the reversal and undoing of the agreement entered into with Marcos by leaders of major mass organizations calling off the mass action scheduled for February 12 in protest against the outrageous killing of six students and other barbarities on January 30–31, 1970." Jose Ma Sison and Rainer Werning, *The Philippine Revolution: The Leader's View* (New York: Taylor & Francis, 1989), 39. The KM leaflet published on Sison's instructions was KM, *Fight Fascism: Join the February 12 Demonstration*, 12 February 1970, PRP 08/13.07.

76. *PC*, 11 February 1970.

77. Lacaba, *Days of Disquiet*, 73.

78. Gonzales, "Chronicle of Protests," 2.

79. Lacaba, *Days of Disquiet*, 77. It is significant that the "hatchetmen" of the LP were known to be present at the FQS rallies and were suspected of attempting to instigate violent protest. The fact that Lopez and the LP benefited from these rallies was a poorly kept secret.

80. The article, "The February 12 Demonstration," appeared in *AB*, 28 February 1970, and was reprinted in Sison, *Foundation for Resuming*, 175–183.

81. Sison, 179.

82. Sison, 179.

83. Jose Ma Sison, *Defeating Revisionism, Reformism and Opportunism: Selected Writings, 1969 to 1974*, ed. Julieta de Lima, vol. 2 of *Continuing the Philippine Revolution* (Quezon City: Aklat ng Bayan, 2013), 177–178.

84. KM, *Pasidhiin ang Pakikibaka Laban sa Pasistang Papet na Pamahalaan ni Marcos*, 14 February 1970, PRP 08/13.23.

85. The remaining conservative layers of the MDP were being edged out and were looking to pull the umbrella group back from the clutches of the KM. On the same day that the majority of the organization's members agreed to hold a Second People's Congress, the spokesperson of the MDP, Nelson Navarro, met with Justice Secretary Juan Ponce Enrile, at the Butterfly Restaurant where he was celebrating his forty-sixth birthday. Student leaders Miriam Defensor and Violeta Calvo were both now employed in his office and had arranged his meeting with the MDP spokesperson (Navarro, *Half-Remembered Past*, 54).

86. Gonzales, "Chronicle of Protests," 2. Among the organizations gathered there were the KM, SDK, MPKP, Socialist Party of the Philippines, NATU, and the NSL.

87. MPKP, *The People's Congress and the National Democratic Struggle*, 18 February 1970, PRP 10/29.15. On "parliament in the streets," see page 8.

88. MPKP, *The Neocolonial System and the "Purely Anti-Marcos Line,"* 18 February 1970, PRP 10/29.09. One wonders what resort to "slanderous phrase-mongering" would be warranted.

89. Lacaba, *Days of Disquiet*, 86.

90. Sison, *Foundation for Resuming*, 185–186.

91. "Issues explained at Miranda rally," *PC*, 19 February 1970; Lewis E. Gleeck Jr., *Dissolving the Colonial Bond: American Ambassadors to the Philippines, 1946–1984* (Quezon City: New Day Publishers, 1988), 240.

92. Sison, *Foundation for Resuming*, 186.

93. Lacaba, *Days of Disquiet*, 100.

94. Lacaba, 102.

95. Lacaba, 102. On 1 March, the MPKP published a leaflet denouncing the Supreme Court decision and calling for a "struggle against bourgeois legalism." MPKP, *Philippine Judiciary Is an Inseparable Part of the Neocolonial System*, 1 March 1970, PRP 10/29.17.

96. Gonzales, "Chronicle of Protests," 2.

97. Lacaba, *Days of Disquiet*, 110; "The PCC Raid Puts the Academe in Crisis," *STM*, 22 March 1970, 14; Simeon G. Del Rosario, *Surfacing the Underground Part II, Volume One: The Involvements of Benigno S. Aquino, Jr., with 29 Perpetuated Testimonies Appended* (Quezon City: Manlapaz, 1977), 43.

98. Alabado, *I See Red in a Circle*, 259.

99. MDP, *Pagibayuhin ang Pakikibaka Tungo sa Pambansang Demokrasya!*, 2 March 1970, PRP 11/18.15. The leaflet's insistence on the continuation of the struggle suggests that there may have been discussion or opposition on this point.

100. "Calendar," *PC*, 9 March 1970, 2–3.

101. Alabado, *I See Red in a Circle*, 357–358, 391. The KM and SDK were provided with their own separate radio broadcasts as well.

102. Recah Trinidad, "The Long March," *STM*, 22 March 1970, 19, 20, 22.

103. MPKP, *People's Violence against State Violence*, 3 March 1970, PRP 10/29.16.

104. KM, *Ipagpatuloy ang Pakikibaka Laban sa Imperyalismong Amerikano, Katutubong Piyudalismo at Pasismo!*, 3 March 1970, PRP 08/13.12.

105. *PC*, 9 March 1970, 2; Trinidad, "Long March," *STM*, 22 March 1970, 22.

106. Trinidad, "Long March," *STM*, 22 March 1970, 23.

107. Gonzales, "Chronicle of Protests," 2.

108. Trinidad, "Long March," *STM*, 22 March 1970, 24; Mila Astorga-Garcia, "To Carry On," 5 April 1970, 7. On 10 March, three thousand students marched from Lyceum to South Cemetery in a funeral procession for Sta. Brigida that was at the same time a protest rally. "Plans for 'March' Finalized on Sat.," *PC*, 12 March 1970.

109. "On the March 3 People's March," *AB*, 1 June 1970, 26.

110. "Plans for 'March' Finalized on Sat.," *PC*, 12 March 1970.

111. Gonzales, "Chronicle of Protests," 2.

112. KM, *Ibunsod ang Malawakang Pakikibaka Laban sa Imperyalismong Amerikano, Katutubong Piyudalismo at Burokrata-Kapitalismo!*, 17 March 1970, PRP 08/13.10.

113. MDP, *Magkaisa at Makibaka para sa Pambansang Demokrasya*, 17 March 1970, PRP 11/18.10.

114. MPKP, *Paghihirap ng Bayan at ang Imperyalismo*, 17 March 1970, PRP 10/29.13. Where the KM and MDP blamed Marcos, however, the MPKP declared that "because the prevailing system is bad, it needs to be changed and not merely the people. Even if we get good leaders if the system itself is rotten, they will still not succeed because they themselves will become its victims." The MPKP made no reference to Marcos or to any specific person or political event. The logic of their leaflet, however, could eas-

ily be interpreted as arguing that Marcos himself was a good leader but the rotten system was corrupting him. It was not a stretch of logic to assume that if the system could be repaired, Marcos could be rescued to be the good leader that he had always intended to be.

115. MDP, *Magkaisa at Makibaka para sa Pambansang Demokrasya*, 17 March 1970, PRP 11/18.10.

116. Recah Trinidad, "The Case against Poverty," *STM*, 5 April 1970, 15.

117. *Labandera* are "washerwomen," individual women who earn a living laundering people's clothes.

118. One is reminded of what Karl Marx wrote in 1847: "The proletariat, which will not permit itself to be treated as rabble, needs its courage, its self-confidence, its pride and its sense of independence even more than its bread" (MECW, 6:231).

119. Trinidad, "Case Against Poverty," *STM*, 5 April 1970, 15

120. Ninotchka Rosca, "Anatomy of a Strike," *GW*, 23 July 1969, 6–8.

121. Trinidad, "Case Against Poverty," *STM*, 5 April 1970, 15.

122. Ninotchka Rosca, "The Opposing Culture," *GW*, 8 April 1970, 7; Lacaba, *Days of Disquiet*, 136.

123. Mercedes Tira, "The Anti-Poverty March and the People's Tribunal," *GW*, 1 April 1970, 5; Trinidad, "Case Against Poverty," *STM*, 5 April 1970, 22.

124. Lachica quoted in Leon Ty, "Why the Marchers Failed," *Examiner*, 21 March 1970, 2.

125. "On the March 3 People's March," *AB*, 1 June 1970, 28.

126. On Good Friday, 27 March, the MDP returned to Plaza Moriones, where they staged a passion play. No longer appealing to Sigue-Sigue, they sought to recruit with the crucifix instead. Fascists crucified Juan de la Cruz, and from his cross he uttered a modified set of the Seven Last Words—telling the crowd, "My country . . . my country . . . prosecute them for they know what they do," and "I say unto you from this day on you will be with me in freedom" (Gonzales, "Chronicle of Protests," 3; Mila Astorga-Garcia, "The Cross of Juan de la Cruz," *STM*, 19 April 1970, 21).

127. Crispin Aranda spoke on behalf of the MDP, denouncing imperialist control of oil as the cause of the rising price of transit. Alfredo Paras of the Crusaders condemned the "fascism" of Marcos. "Fascism, High Prices Hit at Miranda Meeting," *PC*, 10 April 1970, 2.

128. Norberto Boceta, "Northern Motors Strike," *Molabe Monthly* 1, no. 3 (1969): 62–65. While this news item appeared in the September–October issue of *Molabe Monthly*, the article itself is dated 15 November.

129. "Pickets, Demonstrations, Riots—An Assessment," *GW*, 8 April 1970, 1; "Vital News of the Week," *Examiner*, 7 March 1970, 15; "Without Jeepneys, Manilans Walked," *GW*, 18 March 1970, 14.

130. Mercedes Tira, "Traffic Anarchy," *GW*, 1 April 1970, 8.

131. Rodolfo Tupas, "The Decline of Buying Power," *STM*, 19 April 1970, 12.

132. Tira, "Traffic Anarchy," *GW*, 1 April 1970, 9.

133. Raul Rodrigo, *The Power and the Glory: The Story of the Manila Chronicle, 1945–1998* (Pasig: Eugenio Lopez Foundation, 2007), 224.

134. MDP, *Manifesto*, 11 April 1970, PRP 11/19.01.

135. "A Reminder and a Warning," *GW*, 22 April 1970, 1.

136. Leon Ty, "Are We Moving Toward Military Dictatorship?" *Examiner*, 28 March 1970, 4.

137. Gonzales, "Chronicle of Protests," 3.

138. Rizal Yuyitung, ed., *The Case of the Yuyitung Brothers: Philippine Press Freedom under Siege* (Binondo: Yuyitung Foundation, 2000), i.

139. In the 1950s and onward, Go was closely tied to Edward Lansdale.

140. Caroline S. Hau, *The Chinese Question: Ethnicity, Nation, and Region in and beyond the Philippines* (Kyoto: Kyoto University Press, 2014), 91; Yuyitung, *Case of the Yuyitung Brothers*, iii.

141. Yuyitung, *Case of the Yuyitung Brothers*, v.

142. Yuyitung, x.

143. While Marcos was focused on attacking the press by deporting the Yuyitung brothers, it is important to note that the roots of their deportation were more complex than this. Hau documents that the Yuyitungs had "run afoul of certain Chinese community leaders and the GMD and the Embassy of the Republic of China for refusing to toe the Taipei line." This was in part the result of the Yuyitungs' "campaign for citizenship by jus soli and mass naturalization by administrative process" (Hau, *Chinese Question*, 93–94). Chien-Wen Kung's recent book examining the diasporic anticommunism of the Guomindang in the Philippines is essential for understanding the Yuyitung affair. Kung, *Diasporic Cold Warriors: Nationalist China, Anticommunism, and the Philippine Chinese, 1930s–1970s* (Ithaca, NY: Cornell University Press, 2022).

144. Teodoro Locsin, "A Philippine Dreyfus Case," *PFP*, 30 May 1970.

145. Quote is from Zola's "J'Accuse . . . !" in Alain Pagès, ed., *The Dreyfus Affair: J'accuse and Other Writings* (New Haven, CT: Yale University Press, 1996), 43–52.

146. Alfredo B. Saulo, *Communism in the Philippines*, enlarged ed. (Quezon City: Ateneo de Manila University Press, 1990), 113; UPSCA Committee on Public and National Affairs, *Tayag!*, 10 July 1970, PRP 18/21.01; Free Nilo Tayag Movement, *Manifesto*, 1 September 1970, PRP 07/19.01. RA1700 was enacted in 1957 by the McCarthyite House Committee on Anti-Filipino Activities. The law declared the Communist Party illegal and made being a ranking member of the organization a capital offense. Vigilance Committee of Catholic Action of the Philippines, *Philippine Anthology on Communism I* (n.p.: n.p., 1962), 93; Jose Ma Sison and Julieta de Lima Sison, "Foundation for Sustained Development of the National Democratic Movement in the University of the Philippines," in *Serve the People: Ang Kasaysayan ng Radikal na Kilusan sa Unibersidad ng Pilipinas*, ed. Bienvenido Lumbera et al. (Quezon City: Ibon Books, 2008), 45; Saulo, *Communism in the Philippines*, 1.

147. SDK, *Free Nilo Tayag!*, 16 June 1970, PRP 15/22.02.

148. SDK. Casipe was a member of the Central Committee of the CPP.

149. Rodrigo, *Power and the Glory*, 204. By late 1973, Portem was working as the highest-ranking NPA member in Bicol. "Portem, Buhay Pa," *TnB*, 21 October 1973, 3.

150. "Tayag Arraignment on New Charges Set," *PC*, 8 July 1970.

151. SDK, *Free Nilo Tayag!*; Pi Omicron, *Palayain si Nilo Tayag!*, 18 June 1970, PRP 13/35.01.

152. SDK, *Free Nilo Tayag!*

153. "Martial Law: Marcos Type," *The Partisan*, Summer 1970, 4, 37/15.01.

154. The details of Estrada's infiltration of the KM can be found in Quijano de Manila, "Love Me, Love My War; or L'Amour among the Activists," in *Reportage on Lovers* (Quezon City: National Bookstore, 1977), 92–102.

155. de Manila, 95.

156. Elnora Estrada and Ruben C. Guevarra, "The Parting of Ways," *Weekly Nation*, 31 August 1970, 90.

157. "Ang Kilusan," *PC*, 11 September 1970, 2.

158. de Manila, "Love Me, Love My War," 99.

159. de Manila, 95.

160. SDK, [*Letter to the Editor*], 13 September 1970, PRP 15/18.12. The MTT was a member organization of the MDP, closely allied with the KM and SDK. By 1972 it had merged with the KM. See the signature line of Alfonso Sabilano in "Mula sa mga Bilanggong Pulitikal," *Mal*, 17 March 1972, 4.

161. Jose Rimon II, "The Case for KM," *PC*, 17 September 1970, 7.

162. Ma. Lorena Barros, "Prison Visit," *PC*, 27 August 1970, 5.

163. Lualhati Abreu confirms the party execution of Dasmariñas in her memoirs, referring to two comrades who were executed by the CPP on the basis of suspicions in the early years of the party: Danny Cordero, in connection with the Plaza Miranda bombing of 1971, and Eddie Dasmariñas. Lualhati Milan Abreu, *Agaw-dilim, Agaw-liwanag* (Quezon City: University of the Philippines Press, 2009), 67–68. Guevarra chaired the party trial condemning Cordero to execution. Guevarra later became an intelligence officer for the military.

164. Jose Ma Sison, "[Open Letter]," *PC*, 8 July 1970, 3.

165. The timeline in Sison's 1989 book claims that *PSR* was published in January 1970, but this is incorrect (Sison and Werning, *Philippine Revolution*, 205).

166. Susan F. Quimpo and Nathan Gilbert Quimpo, *Subversive Lives: A Family Memoir of the Marcos Years* (Pasig: Anvil Publishing, 2012), 35.

167. "Editors note," *PC*, 23 July 1970, 4. Valencia claimed in 2008 that he wrote the first chapter of *PSR* on instructions from SDK head Tony Hilario and that Sison appropriated it. I have seen no evidence to support this claim. Soliman M. Santos and Paz Verdades M. Santos, eds., *SDK: Militant but Groovy: Stories of Samahang Demokratiko ng Kabataan* (Manila: Anvil Publishing, 2008), 7.

168. Jose Ma. Sison [Amado Guerrero, pseud], "The Philippine Crisis," *Mal*, 21 September 1970, 6–7, 9.

169. These chapters then began to be published in other newspapers as well. David Ryan Quimpo recounted that he arranged the publication of selections of *The Philippine Crisis* in the San Beda High School paper, the *Cub Recorder* (Quimpo and Quimpo, *Subversive Lives*, 65).

170. Sison and Sison, "Foundation for Sustained Development," 57.

171. *PSR*, iii.

172. Mao Zedong, *Selected Works of Mao Tse-Tung*, 5 vols. (Peking: Foreign Languages Press, 1975), 2:305–331.

173. Mao Zedong, 2:313.

174. Mao Zedong, 2:318.

175. Mao Zedong, 2:320–321.

176. Mao Zedong, 2:330.

177. D. N. Aidit, *Indonesian Society and Indonesian Revolution* (Djakarta: Jajasan "Pembaruan," 1958).

178. The section on Macapagal runs from page 86 to page 96. Hereafter, citations to *PSR* appear parenthetically in the text.

179. Nick Beams, *The Way Forward for the Philippine Revolution* (Sydney: Socialist Labour League, 1987), 22.

180. Jesus Lava, *Paglilinaw sa "Philippine Crisis,"* 1970, PRP 09/36.01.

181. On 27 January *Ang Bayan* published a special issue in which Sison offered an additional response to Lava's *Paglilinaw*, titled "Against the Wishful Thinking of a Revisionist Puppet of US Imperialism" (Sison, *Defeating Revisionism*, 59–76). This edition of *Ang Bayan* is no longer extant. The text of Sison's response can be reconstructed from Jose Ma. Sison [Amado Guerrero, pseud.], "Against the Wishful Thinking of a Revisionist Puppet of US Imperialism," *PC*, 18 February, 4–5; and 25 February 1971, 4–5. Sison's response contained a great deal more vitriol than Lava's. Where Lava suggested that Sison might be lying, Sison denounced Lava's *Paglilinaw* as a "brazen act of treason" and "unmitigated treason" (Sison, *Defeating Revisionism*, 61, 62). Lava's response, while not conciliatory in tone, lacked the bile of Sison's diatribes. "Against the Wishful Thinking" added essentially nothing to what had already been said.

182. LCW, 25:418.

183. Sison, *Foundation for Resuming*, 282.

184. For cadre, it was assigned along with "Guide for Party Cadres and Members of the CPP," "On People's War," "Organs of Political Power," and the current political report of the Central Committee (Sison, 289). For mass educational work, *PSR* was assigned along with *Quotations from Mao Zedong* and three articles: "Serve the People," "The Foolish Old Man Who Removed the Mountains," and "In Memory of Norman Bethune" (Sison, 290).

185. Gregg Jones, *Red Revolution: Inside the Philippine Guerrilla Movement* (Boulder, CO: Westview Press, 1989), 48.

186. Ortega styled himself a "democratic socialist." fpnej&r [dear fellow student], 1970, PRP 07/17.01. Abbas stated that his party had "no disagreement" with the "necessity of fighting . . . the trilogy of evil [imperialism, fascism, and feudalism]." Kalayaan [*UP Election Platform*], 1970, PRP 08/24.01.

187. SM, "Party Platform of Sandigang Makabansa for 1970–71," 1970, PRP 16/10.13.

188. MPKP, *On the Correct View of the Campus Elections*, [1970], PRP 10/29.12.

189. KM, "Strip the Handful of Reactionaries of Their Revolutionary Pretensions," *Kal*, 24 July 1970, PRP 32/01.02.

190. Popoy Valencia, "Lessons from the Diliman Commune," *BP* 1, no. 1 (February 1971): 2. Among the other victories were the elections of Crispin Aranda as student council chair at PCC; Ely Bañares, of the Ligang Makabansa, as student council chair at Lyceum; and Roberto Corrales, of the Samahang Kaisahan at Mapua Institute of Technology (MIT). "Ang Kilusan," *PC*, 4 September, 2; "Ang Kilusan," 11 September, 2; "Ang Kilusan," 17 September 1970, 2. The significance accorded by the CPP to the UP campus elections is made clear by the fact that Sison published a special issue of *Ang Bayan* with a statement he had written on issues arising out of the campus

election, titled "On the Counterrevolutionary Line of the Lava Revisionist Renegades," which was reprinted in Sison, *Defeating Revisionism*, 43–50.

191. The conference was sponsored by the student councils of UP Diliman, UP College of Agriculture, UP College of Forestry, Far Eastern Transport Inc. (FEATI), PCC, Araneta University, Mapua, La Salle, and Lyceum. "STAND Organized," *AGG* 46, no. 3 (1970): 2, PRP 19/03. Crispin Aranda, chair of the PCC Student Council and member of the MDP Secretariat, was made chair of STAND, but this was declared to be an interim appointment until the official founding congress of the organization, which was slated to be held in January. Charo Nabong-Carbado, "Ang Sandigan sa Kilusan," *Ang Sandigang Makabansa*, 25 January 1971, 4, PRP 40/08.01; "Samahan ng mga SC Binuo," *PC*, 3 December 1970, 3).

192. "Samahan ng mga SC Binuo," *PC*, 3 December 1970.

193. *Second National Conference on the Nationalist Student Movement* (Quezon City: University of the Philippines, Diliman, 6 November 1970), PRP 12/05.01.

194. Quimpo and Quimpo, *Subversive Lives*, 144.

195. Work to organize LEADS began in the second half of 1970, and it was officially founded on 10 January 1971. Jaime Florcruz, editor of *Ang Malaya*, headed an interim secretariat.

196. "LEADS, Itinatag ng mga Patnugot," *PC*, 21 January 1971, 3; "Progresibong Editor, Binuo ang LEADS," *BP* 1, no. 1 (February 1971): 3, PRP 22/02.

197. Jose Ma Sison, "Pierce the Enemies with Your Pens," *Dare to Struggle, Dare to Win*, January 1971, 6, PRP 30/03.01.

198. LEADS not only promoted the political line of the CPP but also followed the party's lead in attacking the PKP and its front organizations. Aranda wrote that campus newspapers must expose "the groups whose political line is taken from the co-conspirators of Imperialist America—the social-Imperialist Revisionist Soviet Union." Crispin Aranda, "Ang Pambansang Demokratikong Kilusan ng mga Estudyante sa Susunod na Dekada," *Dare to Struggle, Dare to Win*, January 1971, 8.

199. Corazon Santana, "Women's Lib in the Philippines," *APL*, 23 April 1971, 39.

200. It was founded in the final stages of the formal rectification of the political line of the SDK to that of the CPP. MAKIBAKA followed suit, changing its name to Makabayang Kilusan ng Bagong Kababaihan (Nationalist Movement of New Women) and retaining the acronym MAKIBAKA.

201. Lorna M. Kalaw, "And What Are the Women Up To?," *APL*, 9 April 1971, 14-b; Maita Gomez, "Maria Lorena Barros: Gentle Warrior," in *Six Filipino Martyrs*, ed. Asuncion David Maramaba (Pasig: Anvil Publishing, 1997), 63.

202. Pat Dimagiba, "Makibaka, Gabriela Style," *APL*, 10 December 1971, 3.

203. Judy Taguiwalo, "Developments in the Women's Front," *PC*, 1 April 1971, 3.

204. "Ang Kilusan," *PC*, 3 December 1970, 2.

205. "MDP Holds Press Confab on Fascism," *PC*, 13 August 1970; "The Movement," *PC*, 13 August 1970, 2.

206. "The Movement," *PC*, 5 August 1970, 2; Beth Cunanan, "Ang MDP sa Patuloy na Pakikibaka," 17 September 1970, 4.

207. "USSR Offers Grads Three Scholarships," *PC*, 29 July 1970, 2.

208. See the correspondence in JSAP, box 9, folder Auerbach, Isabelle re: Philippines 1951–1972.

209. "Rusong Eskolar sa UP," *PC*, 3 December 1970. In 1972 Barbero assisted Marcos in the implementation of martial law and was made undersecretary of defense.

210. NPA, *Expose and Oppose the Vicious Crimes of the Monkees-Armeng Bayan-MASAKA (Lava) Gang*, May 1970, PRP 11/15.01. This leaflet was then reprinted in *AB*, 1 June 1970.

211. They published the names of four "bureaucrats": Francisco Nemenzo, Haydee Yorac, Ruben Torres, and Francisco Lava Jr.; three "surrenderees": Domingo Castro, Felicisimo Macapagal, and Danny Pascual; and two "intelligence agents": Godofredo Mallari and Antonio Santos.

212. Ken Fuller, *A Movement Divided: Philippine Communism, 1957–1986* (Quezon City: University of the Philippines Press, 2011), 108. A year later the PKP would reciprocate, naming Sison and others as members of the CPP, and Sison would denounce them for "red-baiting."

213. MPKP, "Ang Pambasang Demokratikong Pakikibaka at ang Taksil na Kabataang Makabayan," *Kilusan* 3, no. 4 (1970): 7–8, 13–14, 19. This article was apparently originally published in English in the 28 September issue of *Struggle*, an issue that is no longer extant, as it was this text to which the KM responded on 9 October. I have relied on the Tagalog translation of the MPKP article in *Kilusan*, which was published on 4 October.

214. KM, "Bombard the Headquarters of the Proven Renegades, Traitors and Scabs," *Kal*, 9 October 1970, PRP 32/01.03. A Tagalog translation was published in the December 1970 edition of *Kalayaan*. See KM, "Durugin ang himpilan ng mga napatunayang taksil, traydor at iskirol," *Kal* 6, no. 12 (December 1970): 4, 7, 9, 11.

215. KM, "Bombard the Headquarters," 3. While the PKP at this point kept silent on details, the CPP had no such compunction. The KM wrote that Francisco Lava Jr. "calls the shots" through Romeo Dizon, the MPKP general secretary, who was also the son-in-law of Jose Lava, and Lava's "principal pawn in this dirty game of betraying the national democratic movement" was Francisco Nemenzo (3).

216. KM, "Bombard the Headquarters," 5.

3. Barricades

1. David S. Painter, "Oil and Geopolitics: The Oil Crises of the 1970s and the Cold War," *Historical Social Research / Historiche Sozialforschung* 39, no. 4 (2014): 190.

2. Alfredo Salanga, "The Economics of Exploitation and the Politics of Frustration," *NOW*, 13 March 1971, 8.

3. Salanga, "Economics of Exploitation," *NOW*, 13 March 1971, 9.

4. Samahan ng Makabayan Siyentipiko (Federation of Scientific Nationalists, SMS), "The Recent Price Increase Petitions of the Oil Companies in the Philippines," *Ang Makabayang Siyentipiko*, no. 7 (1972), 8, PRP 36/02.03.

5. Bong Montes, "Jan. 25, 1971," *NOW*, 27 February 1971, 11.

6. Raul Rodrigo, *The Power and the Glory: The Story of the Manila Chronicle, 1945–1998* (Pasig: Eugenio Lopez Foundation, 2007), 228; Napoleon Rama, "Will There Be Martial Law?," *PFP*, 30 January 1971.

7. "Marcos Accepts Lopez's Resignation," *NOW*, 30 January 1971, 48.

8. Eduardo T. Gonzales, "A Chronicle of Protests," *Dare to Struggle, Dare to Win*, January 1971, 3, PRP 30/03.01.

9. Ninotchka Rosca, introduction to *Jose Maria Sison: At Home in the World—Portrait of a Revolutionary*, by Jose Ma Sison and Ninotchka Rosca (Manila: Ibon Books, 2004), 22.

10. Alfred W. McCoy, *Closer Than Brothers: Manhood at the Philippine Military Academy* (Manila: Anvil Publishing, 1999), 197.

11. *SND1967*, 139.

12. Gregg Jones, *Red Revolution: Inside the Philippine Guerrilla Movement* (Boulder, CO: Westview Press, 1989), 46.

13. J. Santiago Sta. Romana, "Genesis of a Revolutionary," *PC*, 7 January 1971, 8.

14. McCoy, *Closer Than Brothers*, 197.

15. McCoy, 197.

16. McCoy, 197.

17. McCoy, 197.

18. McCoy, 204.

19. Antonio Lopez, "Running Revolution: The Life and Times of the Philippines Most Formidable Guerrilla Chief," *Asiaweek*, 9 March 1994, 35.

20. The plans, originally circulated in mimeographed form, were reprinted in Jose Ma Sison, *Foundation for Resuming the Philippine Revolution: Selected Writings, 1969 to 1972*, ed. Julieta de Lima, vol. 1 of *Continuing the Philippine Revolution* (Quezon City: Aklat ng Bayan, 2013).

21. Lopez, "Running Revolution," 35.

22. Jose Ma Sison and Rainer Werning, *The Philippine Revolution: The Leader's View* (New York: Taylor & Francis, 1989), 90. Like a good deal of the opposition, Dy made peace with Marcos after the declaration of martial law. He remained governor of Isabela until 1992, the dominant warlord of the region, and his family continues to rule much of the province.

23. Jones, *Red Revolution*, 47.

24. Dabet Castañeda, "Armed Struggle Still Relevant—CPP Founding Member," *Bulatlat*, 8 May 2006, https://www.bulatlat.com/2006/05/08/armed-struggle-still-relevant-%E2%80%93-cpp-founding-member/.

25. Jones, *Red Revolution*, 47. Jones errs on one point, claiming the raid took place on 30 December. Contemporary newspaper accounts report the raid took place on 29 December. Two members of the NPA team, Benjamin Sanguyo and Ernesto Mayuyu, later testified in a military court that Aquino personally supplied one of the vehicles used in the raid. Lualhati Milan Abreu, *Agaw-dilim, Agaw-liwanag* (Quezon City: University of the Philippines Press, 2009), 61; Simeon G. Del Rosario, *Surfacing the Underground Part II, Volume One: The Involvements of Benigno S. Aquino, Jr., with 29 Perpetuated Testimonies Appended* (Quezon City: Manlapaz Publishing Company, 1977), 496–508; Simeon G. Del Rosario, *Surfacing the Underground Part II, Volume Two: The Involvements of Benigno S. Aquino, Jr., with 29 Perpetuated Testimonies Appended* (Quezon City: Manlapaz Publishing Company, 1977), 940–964.

26. Rodrigo, *Power and the Glory*, 205.

27. "Colleague Follows Corpus to NPA," *APL*, 16 April 1971, 58.

28. Antonio Tagamolila, "My Brother, the Defector," *APL*, 14 May 1971, 16. William Pomeroy wrote of his imprisonment here in 1953, "The detention cells of Camp Panopio are for persuading revolutionaries to cooperate. Cooperation, a decent word for laudable relationships, is here made indecent." William J. Pomeroy, *Bilanggo: Life*

as a Political Prisoner in the Philippines, 1952–1962 (Quezon City: University of the Philippines Press, 2009), 111.

29. Tagamolila, "My Brother, the Defector," 18.

30. "Marso 29: Pulang Araw," *Kal* 7, no. 13 (May 1971): 12, PRP 32/03.02. The letter was published on 1 April 1971. Crispin Tagamolila, *Statement on the Corruption and Thievery in the Mercenary Puppet Armed Forces of the Philippines (AFP)*, 1 April 1971, PRP 17/23.01.

31. Jones, *Red Revolution*, 47; McCoy, *Closer Than Brothers*, 198.

32. Sanggunian ng Mag-aaral ng UPCA, "Nabigong Pagsalakay," *Sanggunian* 1, no. 1 (7 January 1971): 5, PRP 40/09.01.

33. The report was then reprinted in the *Collegian* in December 1970. *PC*, 9 December 1970, 4).

34. "Political Report to the Second Plenum of the First Central Committee of the Communist Party of the Philippines," *AB*, 15 October 1970, 13.

35. "Political Report," *AB*, 15 October 1970, 14.

36. The CPP held the Second Plenum of the Central Committee, for which this report was prepared, in early 1971. The dating of the plenum is somewhat problematic. Caouette reports at one point that it took place in mid-1971 and elsewhere that it was in April 1971. Dominique Caouette, "Persevering Revolutionaries: Armed Struggle in the 21st Century, Exploring the Revolution of the Communist Party of the Philippines" (PhD diss., Cornell University, 2004), 129, 193. Kintanar claims that the plenum was held between January and February 1971 in "the forest near Dipugo, between the towns of Jones and Echague in Isabela." Galileo C. Kintanar and Pacifico V. Militante, *Lost in Time: From Birth to Obsolescence, the Communist Party of the Philippines, Book One: 1930–1972* (Quezon City: Truth/Justice Foundation, 1999), 127. Guevarra confirms this date and location. Ruben Guevarra, *The Story behind the Plaza Miranda Bombing* (Quezon City: Katotohanan at Katarungan Foundation Inc., 1998), 27. One of the documents to come out of the discussions of this plenum, "Patnubay sa pagtayo ng mga organo ng kapangyarihan pampulitika" (Guide to building organs of political power), was signed 20 April 1971. CPP, *Mga Kaukulang Probisyon sa Saligang Batas ng Partido Komunista ng Pilipinas*, n.d., 16, PRP 04/02.02.

37. KM, *Resist the Fascist Suppression*, 1 December 1970, PRP 08/13.26.

38. KM—Philippine College of Commerce (PCC), *Pumupula ang Landas ng Pakikibaka*, December 1970, PRP 08/13.24; SDK-UP College of Agriculture Cultural Society (UPCACS), *Bombard the Headquarters of Fascist School Administrators*, 2 December 1970, PRP 15/23.02; Bong Montes, "Vanguard of Nationalist Youth," *NOW*, 30 January 1971, 15.

39. "On the Expulsion of Campus Activists," *PC*, 3 December 1970, 8.

40. KM, *Resist the Fascist Suppression*.

41. SDK-UPCACS, *Bombard the Headquarters*. Two days later, the SDK denounced the "fascism" of Dean Dioscoro Umali at UP Los Baños (UPLB), using the word "fascism" fifteen times in the single-sided leaflet. SDK-UPCACS, *Smash Fascism in UP Los Baños*, 4 December 1970, PRP 15/23.04.

42. The march was initiated by the Student Alliance for National Democracy (STAND) and was intended to proceed through the university belt and culminate in front of the Department of Education building. UP Student Council (UPSC), *Patiba-*

yin ang Lakas ng Nagkakaisang-Hanay na Siyang Nagtataguyod ng Pambansang Demokra-tikong Pangkulturang Rebolusyon Laban sa mga Mapang-Aping Kapitalista Administrador ng mga Paaralang Nagpipilit na Ituro ang Kolonyal na Uri ng Edukasyon!!!, 4 December 1970, PRP 18/02.34; "Magdaraos ng Demo Ukol sa Kaso ng 300 Aktibista," *PC*, 3 Decem-ber 1970; SDK, *Avenge the Death of Sontillano!!! Crush Fascism!!!*, December 1970, PRP 15/22.01.

43. Nine others were injured, among them Clarence Agarao, head of the Malay-ang Katipunan ng Kabataan (Free Federation of Youth).

44. The demonstrators claimed that the pillbox had been thrown from the fourth floor of FEATI, but Metrocom did not go upstairs in the building to attempt to deter-mine who threw the explosive. KM—UP, *Bakit Namatay si Francis Sontillano?*, Decem-ber 1970, PRP 08/19.01; Samahan ng Kababaihan ng UP (Federation of Women of UP, SKUP) and Bagong Pilipina, *We Must Not Forget Our Heroes*, 8 December 1970, PRP 15/27.05; Samahan ng Progresibong Propagandista (Federation of Progressive Propa-gandists, SPP), [*Hinggil sa kamatayan ni Francis Sontillano*], 7 December 1970, PRP 15/36.01; UPSC, *Ipaghiganti si Sontillano!*, 7 December 1970, PRP 18/02.15. The Ma-nila Police Department eventually arrested a FEATI security guard.

45. UPSC, *Ipaghiganti si Sontillano!*

46. "Martsa at Rally sa Lawton Ngayon," *PC*, 9 December 1970; Sangguniang Mag-aaral ng Sining at Agham, *Durugin ang Pasismo ng mga Mapang-Aping Paaralan!!!*, 6 De-cember 1970, PRP 17/44.02.

47. "Baril, Batuta Ginamit sa Dis. 9 Rally," *PC*, 17 December 1970.

48. KM-PCC, *Pumupula ang Landas*.

49. D. B. Mirasol, "Lagot na Tanikala sa Harap ng Manibela," *APL*, 14 May 1971, 35; Gonzales, "Chronicle of Protests," 3; "Ang Kilusan," *PC*, 21 January 1971, 2.

50. Jose Dalisay Jr. and Marvin Benaning, "4 Namatay sa Rally," *PC*, 14 January 1971.

51. Rene Guioguio, "Isang Araw sa Buhay ng Isang Aktibista," *PC*, 14 January 1971, 2.

52. "Ang Kilusan," *PC*, 21 January 1971, 2.

53. Dalisay and Benaning, "4 Namatay," *PC*, 14 January 1971; Sandigang Makabansa (Patriotic Pillars, SM), "Ang Maghimagsik ay Makatarungan," *Ang Sandigang Maka-bansa*, 25 January 1971, PRP 40/08.01; Ted O. Lopez, "A Bridge from the Past: From CLO to FQS," in *Tibak Rising: Activism in the Days of Martial Law*, ed. Ferdinand C. Llanes (Mandaluyong: Anvil Publishing, 2012), 8. Bolano was shot at close range in the forehead by a police officer when he cursed the police. Emmanuel Osorio, "Guns for Anarchists and Revolutionists," *NOW*, 13 February 1971, 16. The brutal police sup-pression of the 13 January protest was headlined as the "Plaza Miranda Massacre." Seven months later it became known as the "First Plaza Miranda Massacre," for three grenades exploded in the crowded plaza had become the "Second." Within a year or two the violence of 13 January had been largely forgotten, and the Plaza Miranda Mas-sacre today refers exclusively to the events of August 1971.

54. "Ang Kilusan," *PC*, 21 January 1971, 2.

55. "Ang Kilusan," *PC*, 21 January 1971, 2.

56. Quoted in Rama, "Will There Be Martial Law?"

57. By the beginning of 1971, every inch of column space in every issue of the eight-page weekly UP student paper was given over to the perspective of the CPP. Its headlines

denounced fascism and martial law while its editorial pages called for armed struggle in the countryside.

58. "The State of the Nation," *PC*, 21 January 1971, 8.

59. "Ang Kilusan," *PC*, 21 January 1971, 2.

60. KASAPI, *Bukas na Liham sa mga Kawal ng Gobyerno*, [January 1971], PRP 08/32.01.

61. Jack Teotico, "Ano ang Kleriko-Pasismo," *BP* 1, no. 1 (February 1971): 2. The *Asia-Philippines Leader* wrote that the PDS was "hastily assembled" for the purpose of shifting the rally to 23 January and existed "only on paper." Lorna Kalaw, "And What are the Women Up To?" *APL*, 9 April 1971, 15.

62. Stephen Henry S. Totanes, "Student Activism in the Pre-martial Law Era: A Historical Overview," in *Down from the Hill: Ateneo de Manila in the First Ten Years under Martial Law, 1972–1982*, ed. Christina J. Montiel and Susan Evangelista (Quezon City: Ateneo de Manila University Press, 2005), 26; Mila D. Aguilar, "The Diliman 'Commune': Two Views," *GW*, 24 February 1971, 8.

63. Totanes, "Student Activism," 26.

64. Deborah Ruiz, "Krisis at Militarisasyon Tatalakayin," *PC*, 21 January 1971, 7.

65. MDP, *Ang Tunay na Kalagayan ng Bansa*, 25 January 1971, PRP 11/18.23; MDP, *The True State of the Nation*, 25 January 1971, PRP 11/18.21. Working closely with the MDP, the UP Student Council issued a statement on 24 January calling on *"all* UP students to be brave. . . . The threat of martial law shall ultimately be exposed of its yellow character if we answer with revolutionary courage. . . . MAKIBAKA, HUWAG MATAKOT!" UPSC, *January 25th Is Our Day*, 25 January 1971, PRP 18/02.16.

66. Malayang Pagkakaisa ng Kabataang Pilipino (Free Unity of Filipino Youth, MPKP) et al., *US Imperialist Schemes in the Present Crisis*, 23 January 1971, PRP 11/01.09; Pambansang Kilusan ng Paggawa (National Labor Movement, KILUSAN) et al., *Ang mga Pakana ng Imperyalismong Amerikano sa Kasalukuyang Krisis*, 23 January 1971.

67. Antonio Tagamolila, "A Perspective for Mass Actions," *PC*, 21 January 1971, 8.

68. Eduardo Gonzales, "Some Reminders for January 25," *PC*, 21 January 1971, 8.

69. "A Chance for Greatness: The Manila Chronicle–Manila Times–Daily Mirror Pooled Editorial," *PFP*, 23 January 1971, 45.

70. *PFP*, 6 February 1971, 45; McCoy, *Closer Than Brothers*, 129; Ken Fuller, *A Movement Divided: Philippine Communism, 1957–1986* (Quezon City: University of the Philippines Press, 2011), 123.

71. Quijano de Manila, "Why Did Ninoy Throw That Bomb?," *APL*, 7 May 1971, 53. The words are those of Aquino from an interview with Nick Joaquin.

72. Aristeo Celeste and Efren Cabrera, "Kongreso ng Bayan, Malaking Tagumpay," *PC*, 27 January 1971.

73. Celeste and Cabrera, "Kongreso ng Bayan," *PC*, 27 January 1971, 5.

74. Celeste and Cabrera, "Kongreso ng Bayan," *PC*, 27 January 1971, 1, 5.

75. SM, "Ang Maghimagsik ay Makatarungan."

76. Ferdinand Marcos, "Sixth State of the Nation Address, January 25 1971: The Democratic Revolution," Official Gazette, https://www.officialgazette.gov.ph/1971/01/25/ferdinand-e-marcos-sixth-state-of-the-nation-address-january-25-1971-2/.

77. Antonio Tagamolila, "Peace Was Not the Issue," *PC*, 6 January 1971, 6.

78. "Ballet, Movie Draw Mixed Reactions," *The Partisan* 2, no. 2 (1969): 2.

79. Susan F. Quimpo and Nathan Gilbert Quimpo, *Subversive Lives: A Family Memoir of the Marcos Years* (Pasig: Anvil Publishing, 2012), 88; Totanes, "Student Activism," 33.

80. Soliman M. Santos and Paz Verdades M. Santos, eds., *SDK: Militant but Groovy: Stories of Samahang Demokratiko ng Kabataan* (Manila: Anvil Publishing, 2008), 11. During the two-day event, Dulaang Sadeka, the theatrical arm of the SDK, staged a performance of Bertolt Brecht's *Mother*, translated by Rolando Peña and Ma. Lorena Barros, and titled "Bandilang Pula," after the red flag carried by Palagea at the end of the play (SM, "Ang Maghimagsik ay Makatarungan," 4; Santos and Santos, *SDK: Militant but Groovy*, 34).

81. SDK-UPCACS, *Crush Puppet Umali's Reactionary Ploy! On with the Struggle for National Democracy!*, 5 January 1971, PRP 15/23.03.

82. "57 Kahilingan Sinagot ng Pangako," *PC*, 21 January 1971, 2. An examination of the fifty-seven demands reveals that they either were so vague as to be unenforceable (e.g., "revision of the bar exam") or were subject to easy promises (e.g., "liberal attitude in the selection of professors and books") or were outside the power of the university president (e.g., "increase of the UP budget by Congress"). "57 Demands Set for SP," *Kalatas* 3, no. 1 (1970), PRP 31/08.

83. Liza Go, "57 Hiling, Iniharap kay SP," *PC*, 8 October 1970, 7.

84. Mong Palatino, "Pagbabalik-tanaw sa Diliman Commune," in *Serve the People: Ang Kasaysayan ng Radikal na Kilusan sa Unibersidad ng Pilipinas*, ed. Bienvenido Lumbera et al. (Quezon City: Ibon Books, 2008), 103; "Pamantasan, Pinasok ng Metrocom," *PC*, 14 January 1971, 2.

85. Popoy Valencia, "Lessons from the Diliman Commune," *BP* 1, no. 1 (February 1971): 3; SDK, *Ika-4 ng Pebrero, 1971*, 4 February 1971, PRP 15/18.15. The following account is based largely on Ric Umali, "Pasismo sa Los Baños," *PC*, 21 January 1971, 4.

86. Constantino Atos, "Martial Law na sa Los Baños," *PC*, 21 January 1971.

87. Within a week the PC had filed charges before the Los Baños Municipal Court against sixty-five protesters at the barricades for "grave coercion" and "disturbance of peace and order." "Inihabla, 65 Aktibista," *PC*, 27 January 1971. In July 1971, Vic Ladlad, chair of the UPLB Student Council, was arrested on the charge of grave coercion as a result of the events of 13–15 January in Los Baños. "Ladlad, Inaresto sa Los Baños," *PC*, 9 July 1971.

88. Quimpo and Quimpo, *Subversive Lives*, 90.

89. These were the primary barricade sites, but according to the *Collegian*, students also erected barricades, at least briefly, in Laguna, Baguio, Rizal, Cavite, and other locations. "Ang Kilusan," *PC*, 10 February 1971, 2. Because of the prominence given to the Diliman Commune in contemporary accounts, records of the barricades erected elsewhere are partial and sporadic.

90. "Ang Kilusan," *PC*, 4 February 1971, 2; Eric S. Giron, "A Dialogue of Bullets, Tear Gas versus Stones, Bombs," *Mirror*, 20 February 1971, 1; SDK, *Sa mga kasamang tsuper mag-aaral at mamamayan*, 1 February 1971, PRP 15/18.13.

91. Giron, "Dialogue of Bullets." My account of the barricades in the university belt is based on Giron.

92. SDK, *Ika-4 ng Pebrero, 1971*.

93. "Nagbarikada rin sa Los Baños," *PC*, 10 February 1971, 3, 8.

94. Constantino Atos, "The Masses are Behind the Barricades," *PC*, 10 February 1971, 8.

95. *Report of the Committee of Inquiry on the Events and Occurrences at the Diliman Commune from February 1 to 9, 1971* [Quezon City]: [University of the Philippines, Diliman], 1971, 1.

96. Mario Taguiwalo and Rey Vea, "II. The University as Base for the Cultural Revolution," *PC*, 10 February 1971, 10, 9.

97. "Pagsalakay Binigo!" *BP*, 5 February 1971, 2.

98. SDK, *Statement of the Samahang Demokratiko ng Kabataan*, 1 February 1971, PRP 15/18.22.

99. *Report of the Committee of Inquiry*, 1–2.

100. *Report of the Committee of Inquiry*, 2.

101. Oscar L. Evangelista, *Icons and Institutions: Essays on the History of the University of the Philippines, 1952–2000* (Quezon City: University of the Philippines Press, 2008), 44.

102. Rey Vea, "'5' at ang Baril," *PC*, 11 September 1970, 3.

103. *Report of the Committee of Inquiry*, 3.

104. Enrico Manzano, "Tungo sa Barikada ng Lipunan," *PC*, 10 February 1971, 4.

105. Palatino, "Pagbabalik-tanaw," 103; *BP*, 5 February 1971, 2.

106. *Report of the Committee of Inquiry*, 3; "Pagsalakay Binigo!," *BP*, 5 February 1971; Santos and Santos, *SDK: Militant but Groovy*, 83.

107. Mario Taguiwalo, "Sonny," *PC*, 10 February 1971, 9.

108. *Report of the Committee of Inquiry*, 3.

109. Baculinao's argument seems highly suspect. Campos drove to the barricades in body armor and armed with multiple weapons. His assault on the students was clearly premeditated.

110. *Report of the Committee of Inquiry*, 5–6.

111. "Quezon City–U.P. Police Cooperation," *University of the Philippines (UP) Gazette*, 28 February 1971, 20.

112. The arrested students were released after four hours. "Pagsalakay Binigo!," *BP*, 5 February 1971, 2. This account states that Baculinao was among those arrested. The Committee of Inquiry's report, however, claimed that Baculinao was not arrested but went to Quezon City Hall to protest the arrests and that he found Lopez there. This version corresponds with Armando Malay's account.

113. Armando J. Malay, "The UP Barricades: In Retrospect," *We Forum*, 29 September 1982, 6.

114. UPSC, *Oppose Student Fascism! Down with Violent Student Activism*, 2 February 1971, PRP 18/02.30.

115. SMS, *Support the Strike and Oppose Campus Fascism*, 2 February 1971, PRP 15/32.03. On 3 February the various front organizations of the PKP—the MPKP, Bertrand Russell Peace Foundation (BRPF), Ang Kapatiran sa Ika-Uunlad Natin (The Brotherhood for Our Progress, AKSIUN), Kilusan—issued a joint statement on the strike signed by a number of drivers and operators associations. They called for the continuation of the struggle against US oil monopolies and called on "drivers, militant students, and the Filipino masses" to "expose and oppose the phony revolutionaries and paid agents and provocateurs who are carrying out needless violence that confuses the masses and ruins the national democratic movement while covering up the true issue against imperialism." MPKP, *Kabakahin ang Pasismo, Ipagpatuloy ang Pakikibaka Laban sa*

mga Monopolyong Kompanya ng Langis, at Isulong ang Pakikipaglaban sa Imperyalismo, 3 February 1971, PRP 13/28.01. These groups, however, were now operating entirely off campus, and no further mention of the strike was made in the "Commune." Palatino correctly noted that after the first day, "the issue was no longer the oil price hike but the interference of the military [*panghihimasok ng militar*] on campus" (Palatino, "Pagbabalik-tanaw," 104).

116. "Sinalakay ang UP!," *PC*, 4 February 1971; "Pagsalakay Binigo!," *BP*, 5 February 1971, 2.

117. MPKP, *Oppose Militarization of the UP Campus*, 2 February 1971, PRP 10/31.04. The leaflet cited the March 1970 MPKP statement, "People's Violence against State Violence," as the correct political line, a statement that denounced both the state and the KM. MPKP, *People's Violence against State Violence*, 3 March 1970, PRP 10/29.16.

118. Giron, "Dialogue of Bullets," 6.

119. "Ang Depensa ng Diliman: Pananaw Militar," *BP*, 12 February 1971, 5.

120. Giron, "Dialogue of Bullets," 6.

121. "Ang Depensa ng Diliman," *BP*, 12 February 1971, 5.

122. Petronilo Bn Daroy, "Commune and Communards," *GW*, 10 March 1971, 9.

123. Daroy, 8.

124. Malay, "UP Barricades," 4 October 1982, 8.

125. Malay, "UP Barricades," 4 October 1982; Daroy, "Commune and Commu-nards," 9.

126. Aguilar, "Diliman 'Commune.'"

127. Daroy, "Commune and Communards," 9.

128. Daroy, 9. Delfin was not a supporter of the commune guarding the barricades. He was a member of the Vanguard Fraternity, a right-wing organization opposed to the KM and SDK. Delfin later claimed that he was caught in the crossfire and that the trajectory of the bullet revealed that he was shot in the back. *Convocation Sabotaged*, 5 August 1971, PRP 20/15.01. For a brief time after the events, Delfin was hailed by the KM and SDK as a hero; but when he revealed that he was a Vanguard member who had been shot in the back, he was denounced. In mid-1972 he wrote a bitter public letter:

> *A year and half after, I'm still confined to a wheel chair, unable to walk or stand by my-self. The doctors say that in a year or two, I might finally be able to walk. I don't know.*
>
> *Last year, right after the barricades and during the early part of the campus cam-paign, some groups on campus, specifically those who set up the barricades, were prais-ing me as Kumander Delfin, one of the heroes and martyrs of the barricades. Until I told the truth during the AS confrontation [in July 1971]. Since then I have been con-sistently denounced as a propagandist for Malacañang. In a wheel chair?* (Danilo Del-fin, *An Open Letter from a Victim*, 1972, PRP 06/16.01)

129. "Radyo Diliman Libre," *BP*, 12 February 1971, 6.

130. "3 Nabaril, 60 Nasugatan," *PC*, 4 February 1971, 5.

131. Malay, "UP Barricades," 6 October 1982, 7.

132. Daroy, "Commune and Communards," 9; "Ang Depensa ng Diliman," *BP*, 12 February 1971, B.

133. "Commune 'Normalized' to Consolidate Gains," *BP*, 12 February 1971, 7.

134. Salvador Lopez, *Press Statement*, February 1971, PRP 10/12.04.

135. Eduardo Gonzales, "Radio Diliman: A New Style of Protest," *PC*, 4 February 1971, 3.

136. Reuben R. Canoy, *The Counterfeit Revolution: Martial Law in the Philippines* (Manila: n.p., 1980), 2; Ninotchka Rosca, "View from the Left: Word War I," *APL*, 16 April 1971, 10.

137. Aguilar, "Diliman 'Commune.'" Aguilar's account was fiercely supportive of the commune but still notes that by 4 February it did not have significant student support. Prominent among those who joined the barricades was the explicitly anarchist Samahan ng Demokratikong Kabataan—Mendiola (SDKM) under Jerry Araos, who later stated that an SDKM member was present at every barricade.

138. Malay, "UP Barricades," 1 October 1982, 6.

139. Gonzales, "Radio Diliman," *PC*, 4 February 1971, 3; Aguilar, "Diliman 'Commune,'" 8; Ericson M. Baculinao, Jeunne Pagaduan, and Herminio B. Coloma, *Resolution Commending the Revolutionary Courage of the Heroic Defenders of the Diliman Commune against the Fascist State and Its Campus Collaborators*, 13 February 1971, PRP 18/02.36.

140. *Bagong Pilipina* 1, no. 4 (February 1971): 3, PRP 22/01, PRP 22/01.

141. Malay, "UP Barricades," 11 October 1982.

142. Malay, "UP Barricades," 11 October 1982; "Radyo Diliman Libre," *BP*, 12 February 1971, 6.

143. The story of Marcos's affair with Beams and the scandal that followed are detailed in Hermie Rotea, *Marcos' Lovey Dovie* (Los Angeles: Liberty Publishing, 1984).

144. Hermie Rotea, *I Saw Them Aim and Fire* (Manila: Daily News, 1970), 132; Raul Rodrigo, *Kapitan: Geny Lopez and the Making of ABS-CBN* (Quezon City: ABS-CBN Publishing, 2006), 210.

145. Malay, "UP Barricades," 8 October 1982, 7.

146. In the aftermath of the barricades, *Bandilang Pula* became the title of the SDK paper, and much later, the name of the official paper of the NPA.

147. Antonio Tagamolila, "The Moment of Truth," *PC*, 4 February 1971, 6.

148. Daroy, "Commune and Communards," 10.

149. Babes Almario, "A Ladies' Dorm Resident Writes on the Barricades," *PC*, 5 August 1971, 4.

150. Ronaldo Reyes, [*Memorandum*], 8 February 1971, PRP 15/05.01.

151. UPSCA Law Chapter, *Panawagan*, 5 February 1971, PRP 18/22.01.

152. AS Rooftop Junta, *Manifesto for a New Order*, 7 February 1971, PRP 02/03.01.

153. Jose Ma Sison and Julieta de Lima Sison, "Foundation for Sustained Development of the National Democratic Movement in the University of the Philippines," in Lumbera et al., *Serve the People*, 58.

154. The demands partially granted were that students be given control of programming on DZUP and access to the university press.

155. Santos and Santos, *SDK: Militant but Groovy*, 77.

156. "Barikada, ayaw pa ring alisin," *Tinig ng Mamamayan*, no. 2 (10 February 1971), PRP 43/05.01.

157. "Bayan, Laban sa Presyo ng Langis," *PC*, 10 February 1971, 9.

158. "Barikada, ayaw pa ring alisin"; *PC*, 18 February 1971, 2.

159. "Commune 'Normalized,'" *BP*, 12 February 1971, 7.

160. "Bayan, Laban sa Presyo ng Langis," *PC*, 10 February 1971, 9. The commandeering of taxis, "without much regard for the political significance," was among the errors listed by Rey Vea, one of the leaders of the commune, in his assessment of the barricades (Taguiwalo and Vea, "University as Base").

161. Malay, "UP Barricades," 13 October 1982, 6.

162. Reyes [*Memorandum*].

163. Malay, "UP Barricades," 13 October 1982, 6; Palatino, "Pagbabalik-tanaw," 104; Rey Vea, "'Normalcy,'" *PC*, 18 February 1971, 10. Taguiwalo and Vea wrote on 10 February that "the slogans and caricatures that decorate the buildings were the product" of the "revolutionary artists" of the Nagkakaisang Progresibong Artista-Arkitekto (United Progressive Artists-Architects, NPAA) and the SDK-Artists' Group (AG) (Taguiwalo and Vea, "University as Base," 10).

164. Ericson M. Baculinao, Jeunne Pagaduan, and Rey Vea, *"Barricades Are Fine": Resolution Endorsing the Barricades as a Form of Protest*, 13 February 1971, PRP 18/02.01; Baculinao, Pagaduan, and Coloma, *Resolution Commending the Revolutionary Courage*. Twenty-four students voted for and five against the resolution endorsing the barricades. Baculinao circulated a letter to the student body identifying the voters. Ericson M. Baculinao, [*Letter to Students on Barricade Resolution*], 18 February 1971, PRP 18/02.18.

165. "Nakatatak sa Kasaysayan: Durog na ang Barkadang MPKP-BRPF," *Kal* 2, no. 2 (1971): 7, PRP 32/02.02; MPKP—UP, *On the KM-SDK "Occupation" of UP*, 10 February 1971, PRP 10/31.03.

166. "Ang Leksiyon ng Pakikibaka," *BP*, 12 February 1971, A.

167. The SDK began directly blaming the MPKP for the vandalism and theft that had occurred during the commune, arguing that if the MPKP had manned the barricades with them there would have been sufficient forces to prevent such crimes. "Ibunyag at Tuluyang Itakwil ang Kontra Rebolusyonaryong MPKP-Ahente ng Reaksyon sa Hanay ng Kabataan!," *BP* 1, no. 4 (July 1971): 10, PRP 22/02.

168. Salvador Lopez initiated a Committee of Inquiry into the causes of the barricades. The committee's final report, issued on 17 March, was based on interviews with seventy-eight participants, including students, faculty, police, and university officials. Ericson Baculinao and many of the leaders of the commune refused to be interviewed. The UPSC made Sonny Coloma, one of the spokesmen of the barricades, head of the Diliman Historical Committee, which was charged with commemorating the commune. "Diliman Historical Commission, Binuo," *PC*, 4 Marchober1971.

169. Gintong Silahis, *Barikada: Isang Makasaysayang Pagtatanghal*, 15 September 1971, PRP 17/14.01.

170. SDK, "On the Style of Work of Malacañang's Most Loyal Agent in Vinzons," *The Partisan*, 30 September 1971, 2, PRP 37/17.03.

171. Santos and Santos, *SDK: Militant but Groovy*, 119.

172. "CFI Acquits Campos," *PC*, 14 September 1972.

173. CPP, *Mga Kaukulang Probisyon*, 14.

174. "Political Report," *AB*, 15 October 1970, 18.

175. Jose Ma Sison, *Ka Felixberto 'Bert' Olalia: Hero and Martyr of the Working Class and the Filipino People*, 13 August 2003, https://www.josemariasison.org/inps/talpara kayKaBertOlalia.html.

176. Ninotchka Rosca, "Where's Charlie?," *APL*, 7 May 1971, 47. Several sources list del Rosario's birth year as 1943, but all affirm that he was twenty-seven at the time of his death in March 1971.

177. Corazon Damo-Santiago, *A Century of Activism* (Manila: Rex Bookstore, 1972), 71.

178. The KM would incorrectly claim in its obituary for del Rosario that he was the first secretary general of the KM. Jose Ma Sison, "Greetings to the Movement for a Democratic Philippines," *Anak-Pawis*, 1971, 2, PRP 19/09.01.

179. "Assembly ng MDP Itinakda sa Marso 29–30," *PC*, 18 March 1971, 7.

180. Rosca, "Where's Charlie?"

181. He secretly served as an informant for the CIA, a fact that I document in Joseph Scalice, "A Deliberately Forgotten Battle: The Lapiang Manggagawa and the Manila Port Strike of 1963," *Journal of Southeast Asian Studies* 53, no. 1-2 (2022): 226–251.

182. Rodolfo del Rosario was the vice president of NATU in September 1963. "Letters to the Editor," *MC*, 20 September 1963, 4.

183. Jose Ma Sison, "Cast Away the Labor Aristocrats," *AB*, 18 February 1971.

184. Ceres S. C. Alabado, *I See Red in a Circle . . .* (Manila, 1972), 389–390.

185. Ernesto Valencia, "Our Summer of Discontent," *PC*, 4 September 1970, 6.

186. Valencia, "Our Summer of Discontent," *PC*, 4 September 1970, 6.

187. "Mga Liham," *PC*, 30 September 1970, 6.

188. "The Movement," *PC*, 15 July 1970.

189. This did not deter the party from referring to the events of the twenty-fifth as the "first general strike." "All Blows Against US Imperialism and its Running Dogs Are Fine," *AB*, 24 February 1971.

190. "All Blows," *AB*, 24 February 1971.

191. *PFP*, 6 March 1971, 6, 46.

192. Lacsina responded by filing a libel suit against two KM leaders. Ignacio P. Lacsina, "The View from the Left: What Is the KM's Game?," *APL*, 30 April 1971, 44; Teodosio A. Lansang, "One More View from the Left," *APL*, 14 May 1971, 46.

193. Jess Rivera and NATU, *Mag-ingat sa mga Itimang Propagandista ng mga Laban sa Paggawa*, n.d., PRP 15/06.01; *PFP*, 6 March 1971, 6.

194. "NMI, Tumiwalag sa NATU," *AM*, 28 February 1971, 8. The unions represented workers at L. K. Guarin, Gentex, Goya, Interwood Lumber, C. Valdez Accounting, J. S. Zulueta Accounting, Liberty Flour Mills, Union Pipes, Sulo Hotel, and many other department store (*bazar*) unions (Rivera and NATU, *Mag-ingat sa mga Itimang Propagandista*).

195. Rivera and NATU.

196. "Ang Kilusan," *PC*, 18 February 1971, 2.

197. Rivera and NATU, *Mag-ingat sa mga Itimang Propagandista*.

198. The CPP's failed attempt to take over NATU pushed Lacsina back toward the PKP. By late May, Sison wrote of Lacsina's having been brought together with the "Soviet modern revisionists." Jose Ma Sison, *Defeating Revisionism, Reformism and Opportunism: Selected Writings, 1969 to 1974*, ed. Julieta de Lima, vol. 2 of *Continuing the Philippine Revolution* (Quezon City: Aklat ng Bayan, 2013), 87. Lacsina's reunion with the PKP was not without difficulty, and NATU and the PKP unions fought each other to be represented in the Moscow-oriented international trade union federation, World Federation of Trade Unions. SDK, "Ilantad at Durugin ang mga Huwad na Lider Obrero," *Talang*

Ginto, 1971, PRP 43/01.01; Juan J. Cruz, "The July 4 Incident," *APL*, 21 July 1972, 4. The dispute for supremacy within the PKP-NATU alliance was resolved in favor of the PKP, and Lacsina accepted a subordinate role within the renewed relationship.

199. *PFP*, 6 March 1971, 6.

200. *PFP*, 6 March 1971, 6.

201. *PFP*, 6 March 1971, 6.

202. SDK, *Expose the Lazaro-Gervero Gang*, 1971, PRP 15/18.04. Gervero and MAPAG-SAT published an open letter denouncing the student activists and announcing their expulsion from the drivers organizations, claiming that KM, SDK, and MDP had solicited funds ostensibly on behalf of the drivers but had given them none of it—"kahit isang sentimo" (not even one cent). The activists had published statements in the names of the drivers organizations but did not seek the organizations' permission or knowledge, he claimed. They had raised barricades at the university and distracted everyone's attention from the drivers' struggles, and, "worst of all," they had deliberately stoked confusion and dissension among the strikers in the attempt to incite violence. MAPAGSAT and Glicerio G. Gervero, [*Open Letter*], 1971, PRP 07/26.01.

203. "Strike ng Tsuper, Itinakda sa Peb. 25," *PC*, 18 February 1971; A. B. Colayco, "The Making of an Activist," *APL*, 9 April 1971, 15.

204. These were Northern Motors, US Tobacco (which had lost the support of the USTC workers), American Manufacturer and Parts, Bee Guan T-Shirt, Manila Cordage, PRTI and J. S. Zulueta and Co., and CPAs and Bankers Club. SDK, "Paggunita sa Mayo Uno," *BP*, 1 May 1972, PRP 22/02. The group initially called itself the Workers' Federation, but by 18 February it had adopted the name KASAMA. Virgilio San Pedro of Northern Motors was made president of KASAMA. Mauro Samonte, "The Gathering Storm Over Oil," *APL*, 21 January 1972, 44; Lopez, "Running Revolution," 30.

205. "Atake nina Lazaro, Jopson—Nakabuti pa?," *BP* 1, no. 2 (March 1971): 3, PRP 22/02; "Makabayang Pederasyon ng Tsuper Itinatag," *PC*, 18 March 1971, 2.

206. PSMT held its official founding congress in April at PCC, and Villar was elected president (Mirasol, "Lagot na Tanikala"). The speakers at the congress stressed that PSMT must work to build "a national united front allied with the nationalist bourgeoisie." "Manggagawang Tsuper Nagdaos ng Unang Pambansang Kongreso," *Kal* 7, no. 13 (May 1971): 2, PRP 32/03.02.

207. *PFP*, 6 March 1971, 6, 46.

208. Sison, *Defeating Revisionism*, 86.

209. *PFP*, 6 March 1971, 6, 46.

210. Rosca, "Where's Charlie?," 10.

211. Antonio Tagamolila, "Waiting for Charlie," *PC*, 25 March 1971, 8; Sison, "Greetings to the MDP"; SDK, "Ilantad at Durugin." In May, Victor Corpus and Crispin Tagamolila published a statement with the same claim, citing inside sources in the military. Victor N. Corpus and Crispin Tagamolila, *Expose the Criminal Hand of the Marcos Fascist Puppet Clique in the Kidnapping and Murder of Carlos B. del Rosario*, 22 May 1971, PRP 06/09.01.

212. Sison, *Defeating Revisionism*, 86.

213. Vic Felipe, "Plaza Miranda—First Anniversary," *APL*, 25 August 1972, 17.

214. SDK, "Ilantad at Durugin," 2; KASAMA, *Unang Pambansang Kongreso*, 27 February 1972, PRP 09/10.02.

215. The CPP and KASAMA used the word "intsik" only negatively. They avoided it when writing about Mao or the Chinese revolution or the Chinese Communist Party. They knew it was a racial slur and used it as such.

216. "The Chinese Kumintang in the Philippines and US Imperialism," *The Partisan*, March 1971, 6, PRP 37/15.05. Accompanying the article was a caricature of a scowling slant-eyed Chinese man with a queue side by side with a snarling Uncle Sam.

217. "Labanan ang Mapanghuthot na Komprador-Burgesya—Mga Ayudante ng mga Imperyalistang Amerikano sa Pagpapanatiling Alipin ang Bayang Pilipinas!," *BP* 1, no. 4 (July 1971): 2, PRP 22/02.

218. "Labanan ang Mapanghuthot na Komprador-Burgesya," *BP* 1, no. 4 (July 1971): 5, PRP 22/02.

219. "Labanan ang Mapanghuthot na Komprador-Burgesya," *BP* 1, no. 4 (July 1971): 13, PRP 22/02.

220. MDP, "11 People's Demands," *Breakthrough* 3, nos. 3–4 (November 1971): 16, PRP 29/11.02.

221. KASAMA, *Unang Pambansang Kongreso*, 38 (emphasis added).

222. Ricardo Lee, "Dugo sa Agua de Mayo," *APL*, 14 May 1971, 55–58.

223. Ninotchka Rosca, "May Day Grief," *APL*, 14 May 1971, 52; Commission on the Churches' Participation in Development (CCPD), World Council of Churches, and Philippine Ecumenical Writing Group, *Moving Heaven and Earth: An Account of Filipinos Struggling to Change Their Lives and Society* (Manila: CCPD, 1982), 74.

224. "Gory Labor Day," *APL*, 7 May 1971, 4.

225. Rosca, "May Day Grief," 51.

226. Lee, "Dugo sa Agua de Mayo," 56.

227. SDK, "Ilantad at Durugin"; Rosca, "May Day Grief," 51; STAND, "Ang Mayo Uno sa Kasaysayan ng Pilipinas," *Ang Estudyante* 1, no. 2 (1 May 1972): 2, PRP 30/08.01; Lee, "Dugo sa Agua de Mayo."

228. Jose F. Lacaba, *Days of Disquiet, Nights of Rage: The First Quarter Storm & Related Events* (Pasig: Anvil Publishing, 2003), 155; Lee, "Dugo sa Agua de Mayo"; Friends of the Philippines, *Makibaka, Join Us in Struggle!* (London: Friends of the Philippines, 1978), 35.

229. SDK, "Ilantad at Durugin"; Rosca, "May Day Grief," 51; STAND, "Mayo Uno sa Kasaysayan," 2; Lee, "Dugo sa Agua de Mayo."

230. "Gory Labor Day," *APL*, 7 May 1971, 4; Rosca, "May Day Grief," 52.

231. Rosca, "May Day Grief," 52.

232. Rosca, "May Day Grief," 52; Lee, "Dugo sa Agua de Mayo."

233. Lee, "Dugo sa Agua de Mayo," 58.

234. Rosca, "View from the Left," 45.

235. Ninotchka Rosca, "Word War II: Lava versus Guerrero," *APL*, 23 April 1971, 12, 42, 44–45.

236. Lacsina, "View from the Left"; KM, "And What Is Lacsina's Racket?," *APL*, 30 April 1971, 11, 50–51.

237. Lansang, "One More View from the Left"; Vicente Wenceslao, "On the KM-Lacsina Feud," *APL*, 21 May 1971, 14, 48.

238. Alfredo B. Saulo, *Communism in the Philippines*, enlarged ed. (Quezon City: Ateneo de Manila University Press, 1990), 64. They were "Antonio Santos, Francisco

Lava, Jr., Romeo Dizon, Aida Lava, Godofredo Mallari, Domingo Castro, Danny Pascual, Bartolome Pasion, Felicisimo Macapagal, Alejandro Briones, Haydee Yorac, Ching Maramag, Maximo Lacanilao, Merlin Magallona, Ruben Torres, Francisco Baltazar, Leonor Magtolis, Connie (a pseudonym), Egmidio of Union de Impresores de Filipinas (UIF), Ana Maria Nemenzo, and [Francisco] Nemenzo himself." Trinidad P. Calma, "What Is Lansang (and His Likes) up To?," *APL*, 11 June 1971, 14. The list is accurate. Lansang attempted to dismiss Calma's revelations with sexism, calling her a "slip of a girl" and a "skirt behind which these poseurs hide." Teodosio A. Lansang, "Lansang Is (and His Likes Are) out to Unmask Poseurs," *APL*, 2 July 1971, 12, 47.

239. Reyes's memo was later published in full in the *Collegian* on 2 July. Liwayway T. Reyes, "Memorandum to the Movement for a Democratic Philippines and Its Allied Organizations: Facts That Should Be Known by the Leaders and Organizations of the National Democratic Movement," *PC*, 6 July 1971, 6. An original circulating copy of the memo, to which the *Collegian* article corresponds exactly, is available at Hoover. Liwayway T. Reyes, *Memorandum to the Movement for a Democratic Philippines and Its Allied Organizations: Facts That Should Be Known by the Leaders and Organizations of the National Democratic Movement*, 18 May 1971, JHP. Nemenzo denounced Reyes for her "McCarthyite tactics" but did not respond to the substance of her claims. Francisco Nemenzo Jr., "Nemenzo Answers," *PC*, 9 July 1971, 6.

240. I have been unable to locate a copy of this document. The front page of the January 1971 issue of *Struggle* was reproduced in *PFP* 6, no. 3 (April 1971). That the BRPF made this claim is attested in numerous sources, including the articles by Lansang in *APL* and by the KM in *PC*. The BRPF did not dispute the fact that it published this issue or that it named Sison's brother.

241. Hoover Domine, "Malacañang Aide Missing," *MT*, 12 June 1971.

242. Aurora Javate, "Sison Disappearance—Another Fascist Crime?," *PC*, 13 August 1971, 6.

243. Joma Sison later claimed that the PKP and the AFP Counterintelligence Unit (CIU) were responsible for his brother's murder, specifically accusing "Lavaite CIU double agents" Danilo Pascual and Sid Robielos (Sison and Werning, *Philippine Revolution*, 63). We know from Jesus Lava's own account that Sid Robielos, a party member and brother of Central Committee member Cipriano Robielos, was closely tied to the military, was sufficiently integrated into its upper ranks, and was in personal contact with Macario Peralta, the head of the Armed Forces under Macapagal. Jesus Lava, *Memoirs of a Communist* (Pasig: Anvil Publishing, 2002), 289.

244. Jose Ma Sison, "A Brief Comment to My Detractors," *APL*, 11 June 1971, 3.

245. Jose Ma Sison, "Jose Ma. Sison's Statement on His Brother's Disappearance," *PC*, 9 July 1971, 6.

246. *AK*, July 1971, PRP 33/13.01. This attack was soon repeated by the MPKP in a leaflet dated 9 August. MPKP, *Will the Parrots of Peking Also Change Their Tune?*, 9 August 1971, PRP 10/29.21.

247. "Nixon, Sumuko kay Mao!," *AM*, July 1971.

248. I have not been able to locate a copy of this issue of *Ang Bayan*. The text of the statement was reprinted in Sison, *Defeating Revisionism*, 273–287, as well as in the *Collegian* in October 1971. I have checked the 2013 reprint against this contemporary edition. "On the Lavaite Misrepresentation of the Proletarian Foreign Policy of China,"

PC, 8 October 1971, 4; 13 October 1971, 6–7. A Tagalog version of the text was published in *Mal*, 4 November 1971, 4–5, 7, under the title "Ang Proletaryong Patakarang Panlabas ng Republikang Bayan ng Tsina" (The proletarian foreign policy of People's Republic of China). In January 1972, the PKP would allege that this response had been written later and then backdated, declaring that "the local Maoists under the traitor Amado Guerrero were forced to take a very long, embarrassed pause before coming out with a position on ping-pong diplomacy. After months of silence, the 'Central Committee' of the Mao Thought Party has finally come up with a miserable piece of apologetic blabber. . . . In this *backdated* reply to a stinging attack from the official organ of Partido Komunista ng Pilipinas . . . the Filipino Maoists could hardly conceal their consternation at the invitation China extended to Nixon and the implicit repudiation of what they had been taught to regard as 'the correct line' in international affairs." PKP, "Ideological Dispute between Maoism and the International Communist Movement," *AK* 3, no. 1 (January 1972), PRP 33/13.03. The PKP did not go on to specify or substantiate when the "backdated" CPP article had actually been written, but it could not have been later than the beginning of October.

249. "Facts Which Ought to Be Known About a Proven Warrior of Counter-Revolution," *Struggle* 3, no. 2 (1971), PRP 42/03.02. It published a Tagalog version as well: "Mga bagay-bagay na dapat malaman hinggil sa isang subok na kawal ng kontra-rebolusyon" (PRP 42/04).

250. "Facts Which Ought to Be Known," *Struggle* 3, no. 2 (1971), 3, PRP 42/02. One feels a sense of vicarious chagrin reading these words printed in the name of Bertrand Russell, now over a year dead.

251. "Ibunyag at Tuluyang Itakwil ang Kontra Rebolusyonaryong MPKP—Ahente ng Reaksyon sa Hanay ng Kabataan," *BP* 1, no. 4 (July 1971): 10, PRP 22/02.

252. KM, "Palisin ang Lahat ng Pesteng Maka-Lava!," *Kal* 7, no. 6 (23 July 1971), PRP 32/01.04 [Tagalog 32/03.03].

253. CPP, *Report to the Central Committee on Lavaite Propaganda for Revisionism and Fascism*, November 1971. The report was reprinted in Sison, *Defeating Revisionism*, 145–272.

254. Sison, *Defeating Revisionism*, 145.

255. Sison, 169, 207.

256. *Deception and Murder Is the Meaning of the Lavaite 'Theory of Physical Affinity' and 'Armed Struggle as Secondary Form,'* 1971, PRP 12/13.01.

257. "Letters," *APL*, 6 August 1971, 3.

258. Fred Panizales, "Nahalal sa Los Baños sina Lantin at Acosta," *PC*, 30 July 1971. The KM-SDK student party at Ateneo, LDA, also saw its candidate, Alex Aquino, elected president of the Ateneo Student Council by a substantial majority (Santos and Santos, *SDK: Militant but Groovy*, 102; Quimpo and Quimpo, *Subversive Lives*, 92).

259. "Maikling Balita," *PC*, 16 July 1971, 3.

260. Gilbert Lozada, "70 Mag-Aaral Tatakbo sa Halalan ng Council," *PC*, 23 July 1971.

261. Wilfrido Nepomuceno, "Fraternities in Revolution," *PC*, 30 July 1971, 7.

262. Over the course of the next school year, the rumbles between what the KM called "progressive fraternities" and "reactionary fraternities" worsened, as the political maneuvers of the KM and SDK produced a fraternity war on the Diliman campus. Beginning in

October 1971, a series of fraternity "rumbles" were staged on campus, each increasingly more violent. Mon Lagman, "Alitan ng Beta Sigma at Sigma Rho, Ayos na," *PC*, 15 October 1971. The rumbles were politically motivated events, staged between SM-affiliated fraternities and their rivals. By February and March the SM fraternities were holding bare-fisted brawls against the "reactionary" fraternities. SM, *Ituloy ang Boykoteo*, 28 February 1972, PRP 36/01.02. The SM itself stated that the "progressive" fraternities agreed to fights because the "provocations had reached its saturation point" (SM, 2). A number of students were severely injured in the violent altercations as the brawls continued and grew. Weapons were being brought to the fights, and at least one student was shot. The fraternity violence provided a pretext to finally end the ban on outside police forces entering the campus. Salvador Lopez and Manny Ortega met with Col. Tomas Karingal and Mayor Amoranto to arrange unlimited access for the police, granting them authorization to station men, carry out searches, and make arrests on campus. Diego Geronimo et al., *Declaration of Grave Concern*, 1972, PRP 07/25.01; SM, *Ituloy ang Boykoteo*.

263. SDK, *Tuluyang Itakwil ang Mga Napatunayang Ahente sa Campus at Mapangahas na Ibandila ang Watawat ng Pambansang Demokrasya*, 2 August 1971, PRP 15/22.11; "Nagbatuhan, Nagkagulo sa University Theater," *PC*, 5 August 1971; SM, *All Lies and Intrigues of Reactionaries Fail in the Face of Reality!! Trust the Masses!! Onward with the National Democratic Struggle!!*, 9 August 1971, PRP 16/10.01; SPP, "On the Serious Man-handling of Several Members of the Samahan ng Progresibong Propagandista (SPP) by the Vanguard-SDS Fascist Thugs," *Alab*, 27 September 1971, PRP 19/05.03.

264. *Convocation Sabotaged*.

265. In the final week of the election, a group calling itself the Secret Victor Corpus Movement issued a leaflet on the Diliman campus that opened with the question "Was last Monday's incident at the University Convocation the start of Operation Good Friday?" Secret Victor Corpus Movement, *What Is Operation Good Friday?*, [August 1971], PRP 16/17.02. It went on to explain that Operation Good Friday was the "code-name of a highly confidential project being undertaken by Malacañang and the Armed Forces of the Philippines and being executed under the command of top psy-war expert and undersecretary of home defense Jose Crisol," of which the "immediate goal" was to "muzzle the militancy of UP as a preparatory step for the silencing of the national student movement."

266. "Pahayag," *PC*, 13 August 1971.

267. SM, *All Lies and Intrigues*, 2; SM, *From Sandigang Makabansa: A Summing-Up of the Campaign, a Final Word of Warning!*, 5 August 1971, PRP 16/10.07; "This Will Be a Fine Year!," *PC*, 13 August 1971, 5.

268. *Convocation Sabotaged*; "This Will Be a Fine Year!," *PC*, 13 August 1971, 5.

269. "Walang Kinalabasan ang Imbistigasyon," *PC*, 3 September 1971, 3.

270. A. B. Colayco, "Good Friday at State U," *APL*, 20 August 1971, 10.

271. Santos and Santos, *SDK: Militant but Groovy*, 84.

272. KM—UP, *Sharpen Vigilance against Persistent Fifth Column Tactics of Reactionary Die-Hards!!*, 17 August 1971, PRP 08/19.16.

273. SM, *All Lies and Intrigues*, 4.

274. SM, 1. The SM routinely referred to Katipunan ng Malayang Pagkakaisa (Federation of Free Unity (KMP) as KAMP to associate the organization with Hitler's *Mein Kampf*.

275. Ann Clemente, "Initiation to Campus Intrigues," *PC*, 13 August 1971, 3; SM, *All Lies and Intrigues*.

276. A separate SM leaflet explained, "The national democratic movement has always made it a point to be precise and clear-cut in its pronouncements, never attempting to confuse the masses. Thus, if the tactical slogan is COMBAT LIBERALISM! it is written as COMBAT LIBERALISM! An investigation of the slogans painted in the upper floors revealed that the slogan on liberalism was FIGHT LIBERALISM!" SM, *Who Is the Clever Culprit?*, 9 August 1971, PRP 16/10.20. This assessment of fake graffiti as "black propaganda" became the official account of the election defeat. The historical retrospective published in the *Collegian* in September 1972 declared that the defeat was caused by malicious forces from Malacañang who "painted Moist [*sic*] slogans at the AS building." Laverne Peralta, "Thank You, Mr. President," *PC*, 21 September 1972, 11.

277. "This Will Be a Fine Year!," *PC*, 13 August 1971, 5.

278. Quoted in Ramon V. Puno, *The Suppression of Individual Rights and the Right to Dissent: The Emerging Fascism of the Baculinao-Sta. Romana Clique*, 13 December 1970, 2, PRP 14/24.02.

279. "Patuloy ang Pakikibaka," *PC*, 24 September 1971, 2; Jose Dalisay, "Cooking the Collegian," 13 October 1971, 12; SDK, "On the Style of Work."

280. Santos and Santos, *SDK: Militant but Groovy*, 84.

281. "Ipangibabaw ang Kapangahasan at Buong Tapang na Pukawin ang Masa," *Talang Ginto* 1, no. 5 (September 1971), PRP 43/01.02.

282. "Isaayos ang Gawaing Pang-Organisasyon," *Talang Ginto* 1, no. 5 (September 1971), 3, PRP 43/01.02.

283. "Huwag Kailanman Lilimutin ang Tunggalian ng mga Uri at ang Pagsasabuhay ng Linyang Pangmasa!!," *Talang Ginto* 1, no. 5 (September 1971), 12, PRP 43/01.02.

284. It is noteworthy that Hilario used this formulation in the same year that the KM and SDK had founded several labor federations, including KASAMA, which they had publicly hailed as great victories. When writing privately, however, they admitted these were but crumbs.

285. Santos and Santos, *SDK: Militant but Groovy*, 67.

286. Santos and Santos, 68.

287. Sonny Coloma, "'Good Friday': 1," *PC*, 20 August 1971, 6.

288. SM, *Statement of Sandigang Makabansa*, 23 August 1971, PRP 16/10.19.

289. Santos and Santos, *SDK: Militant but Groovy*, 84.

290. The reorientation of the KM and SDK was implemented simultaneously throughout the country and throughout their allied organizations. On 23 August, for example, a new group calling itself the August 23 Movement was founded in Tarlac. August 23rd Movement, *Long Live the Anti-Imperialist United Front of Tarlac Citizens!*, 23 August 1971, PRP 02/11.01. The August 23 Movement was not formed in opposition to the suspension of the writ of habeas corpus, which had not yet been announced, and its founding statement focused almost exclusively on rising prices. The signatories to the founding of the August 23 Movement were the SDK, KM, Kilusang Kristiyano ng Kabataang Pilipino (The Tagalog name of SCMP, KKKP), and UPSCA, a union of conservative religious groups with the erstwhile communards.

291. KKKP, *July 4th Message to Filipino Christians*, 4 July 1971, PRP 17/09.01.

292. Gary Olivar, "An Open Letter to the Congregation," *The Herald* 1, no. 1 (January 1972), PRP 30/19.01.

293. Ma. Socorro S. Garcia, "Protest by Candlelight," *NOW*, September 1972, 36–38, PRP 44/36.01; "'Prusisyon' Caps Two-Day CNL Assembly," *Breakthrough* 4, no. 4 (August 1972): 7, PRP 29/11.04.

294. Bonifacio was the founder and head of the Katipunan, a secret society that organized the Philippine revolution against Spain. Damaso was a character in Jose Rizal's anticolonial novel, *Noli me Tangere*, who came to represent in popular consciousness the brutality and obscurantism of the Catholic religious orders.

4. The Writ Suspended

1. Quijano de Manila, *Language of the Street and Other Essays* (Metro Manila: National Book Store, 1980), 157.

2. Ninotchka Rosca, "The Plaza Miranda Tragedy and its Repercussions," *APL*, 3 September 1971, 6; Edel Garcellano, "The Plaza Miranda Tragedy as the *Leader* Photographers Saw It," 7; Gregg Jones, *Red Revolution: Inside the Philippine Guerrilla Movement* (Boulder, CO: Westview Press, 1989), 59.

3. Manuel Salak Jr., "FM Suspends Habeas Corpus," *MT*, 24 August 1971, 5.

4. A. B. Colayco, "Plaza Miranda: Questions Without Answers," *APL*, 25 August 1972, 6.

5. Rosca, "Plaza Miranda," *APL*, 3 September 1971, 6.

6. "Night of Violence at Plaza Miranda," *MT*, 22 August 1971, 8; Manuel Festin Martinez, *More Assassinations & Conspiracies* (Pasig: Anvil Publishing, 2004), 190.

7. "Pagsalakay sa Arca: Tagumpay ng Armadong Propaganda!," *Ang Mandirigma*, April–May 1972, 36/06.04.

8. Alfred W. McCoy, *Policing America's Empire: The United States, the Philippines, and the Rise of the Surveillance State* (Quezon City: Ateneo de Manila University Press, 2011), 372.

9. Seth Mydans, "2 Key Military Leaders Quit and Urge Marcos to Resign; He Calls on Them to Submit," *NYT*, 23 February 1986.

10. Jones, *Red Revolution*, 321, n. 21.

11. Jones, 320 fn 11. Jones based this on interviews with Guevarra himself and with a senior military officer who claimed to have read Guevarra's statement.

12. Victor N. Corpus, *Silent War* (Quezon City: VNC Enterprises, 1989), 11.

13. Corpus, 12.

14. Corpus, 13.

15. Jones, *Red Revolution*, 66.

16. Jones, 59–70.

17. Ruben Guevarra, *The Story behind the Plaza Miranda Bombing* (Quezon City: Katotohanan at Katarungan Foundation, 1998), 17.

18. Guevarra, *Story*, 13; "How Ninoy Evaded the Blast," *MC*, 24 August 1989, 1, 8; Jose Dalisay, Jr. and Marvin Benaning, "4 Namatay sa Rally!," *PC*, 14 January 1971, 2; Simeon G. Del Rosario, *Surfacing the Underground Part II, Volume Two: The Involvements of Benigno S. Aquino, Jr., with 29 Perpetuated Testimonies Appended* (Quezon City: Manlapaz, 1977), 707.

19. Guevarra, *Story*, 22.

20. I do not examine the deeply problematic evidence that Aquino was aware of the bombing in advance, which was presented during his trial. It is a fraught question worthy of investigation, but in this work I will reserve judgment on the matter.

21. Victor Corpus was a named source. Jones's next source was a "former NPA officer in Isabela, January 28 and February 3, 1988." Elsewhere, Jones (318 fn 13; 317 fn 3) claimed that he interviewed Ariel Almendral on those dates. Almendral fits Jones's description exactly. In a similar fashion it was possible to identify each of Jones's other sources.

22. Jones, *Red Revolution*, 67.

23. Corpus, *Silent War*.

24. Guevarra, *Story*. I am citing from the 1998 edition. Guevarra's book was printed by a publishing firm known for producing pro-Marcos, anti-Communist literature.

25. Jones, *Red Revolution*, 61. Jones's source for this claim was Ricardo Malay, who he claimed had been briefed on the plot by Tubianosa.

26. Jones, 62.

27. Jones, 62; Corpus, *Silent War*, 15.

28. Jones, *Red Revolution*, 320 fn 10.

29. Rogelio Ordoñez, "Ang Kalookan at mga Aktibista Kontra Asistio," *APL*, 21 May 1971, 55.

30. Conrado de Quiros, *Dead Aim: How Marcos Ambushed Philippine Democracy* (Pasig City: Foundation for Worldwide People's Power, 1997), 99.

31. I have reconstructed Guevarra's account using Jones, *Red Revolution*, 63; Guevarra, *Story*, 33, 34; Galileo C. Kintanar and Pacifico V. Militante, *Lost in Time: From Birth to Obsolescence, the Communist Party of the Philippines, Book One: 1930-1972* (Quezon City: Truth/Justice Foundation, 1999), 144; de Quiros, *Dead Aim*, 166. As for the identity of Cordero's two companions, this is again based on Guevarra's testimony. These details can be reconstructed using Guevarra, *Story*, 45; Kintanar and Militante, *Lost in Time, Book One*, 154. Guevarra identifies the second accomplice as Ka Daniel. This individual can be identified as Danilo Valero, who was present at Cordero's trial, using the account of Ruth Firmeza. Ruth Firmeza, *Gera* (Manila: Linang at Mainstream, People's Art, Literature, and Education Resource Center, 1991).

32. Jovito R. Salonga, *A Journey of Struggle and Hope* (Quezon City: UP Center for Leadership, Citizenship, and Democracy, 2001), 177ff.

33. The source for this claim is again Guevarra, but the fact that Guevarra and Cordero were in Isabela from the second half of 1971 through mid-1972 is not disputed by anyone.

34. Jones, *Red Revolution*, 321 fn 21. Although Aquino did on occasion offer Sison and his companions the use of his helicopter, Abadilla's claim is highly suspect and adds nothing substantive to the narrative of Miranda.

35. Guevarra is the main source for these details, and his account is decidedly self-serving. However, the trial of Cordero on the basic charges that Guevarra mentions is beyond dispute, so in its broad outlines—that there was a dispute over the lie-low policy of the NPA, which Cordero opposed—this account is correct.

36. Kintanar and Militante, *Lost in Time, Book One*, 169.

37. Jones, *Red Revolution*, 64.

38. de Quiros, *Dead Aim*, 150.

39. de Quiros, 162. Corpus later cited a similar complaint for his disillusionment with the party. He wrote that ordinary cadre were starved of resources and going hungry in the countryside while Joma and the entire Central Committee used party funds to buy cars and were living in the city in air-conditioned underground houses (Corpus, *Silent War*, 13).

40. Guevarra, *Story*, 46; Kintanar and Militante, *Lost in Time, Book One*, 170. The participation of Principe, who carried out the sentence of execution, can be independently confirmed in a number of sources. Among the many sources documenting the Cordero execution is an interview in the Philippine *Daily Globe* from 25 August 1989, in which Rodolfo Salas, head of the CPP from 1977 to 1986, confirmed that Cordero had accused Sison of ordering the bombing of Plaza Miranda.

41. de Quiros, *Dead Aim*, 150.

42. The details of the trial can be reconstructed from the accounts of Guevarra; Almendral, who detailed them to both Jones and Jovito Salonga; and Pablo Araneta. These separate accounts are in complete agreement on the details of what transpired.

43. Guevarra, *Story*, 48.

44. Guevarra, 49.

45. Jones, *Red Revolution*, 64. Principe had been a UP student of nursing before joining the NPA (Jones, 53).

46. Guevarra, *Story*, 52.

47. de Quiros, *Dead Aim*, 171.

48. Guevarra, *Story*, 30; Jones, *Red Revolution*, 72.

49. Jones, *Red Revolution*, 322 fn 6.

50. Jose Lacaba, "A Benedictine in People's China," *APL*, 24 December 1971, 5.

51. Jones, *Red Revolution*, 73.

52. Mario Miclat, *Secrets of the Eighteen Mansions: A Novel* (Pasig: Anvil Publishing, 2010). Miclat wrote the book as a novel, but the claim is nonetheless clear.

53. The delegation wound up being stranded in China. They arrived but a few weeks after Henry Kissinger's secret negotiations to open up relations between Washington and Beijing. Ties between China and the Marcos administration followed, and as we will see, the Chinese Communist Party (CCP) cut all ties with the CPP in early 1974. The delegation was sent to Hunan province for reeducation among the peasantry (Jones, *Red Revolution*, 80, 82). They were subsequently allowed to return to Beijing, and in the 1980s, Baculinao, Sta. Romana, and Florcruz all took up journalism. They became known as the "gang of three," serving as Beijing bureau chiefs for CNN, NBC, and ABC news. The majority of US news coverage on China coursed through the editorial oversight of these three former members of the front organizations of the CPP.

54. One could alternatively assume that Jones fabricated the interviews with the four former Central Committee members. But the problem with this hypothesis is that they were alive long after his publication, yet they made no effort to gainsay the accounts attributed to them even after their testimony in Jones's account was on the front page of the major dailies in the Philippines.

55. Mauro Gia Samonte, "In the Eye of the Storm," 2014, http://maoblooms.blogspot.com/2014/02/normal-0-false-false-false-en-us-x-none.html. I base the date for the event on the fact that this was the rally in which Barbers was injured with a pillbox to the face.

56. Jose Ma Sison and Rainer Werning, *The Philippine Revolution: The Leader's View* (New York: Taylor & Francis, 1989), 71; Ninotchka Rosca, introduction to *Jose Maria Sison: At Home in the World—Portrait of a Revolutionary*, by Jose Ma Sison and Ninotchka Rosca (Manila: Ibon Books, 2004), 28–29.

57. Seth Mydans, "2 Key Military Leaders Urge Marcos to Resign, He Calls on Them to Submit," *NYT*, 23 February 1986.

58. Raymond Bonner, *Waltzing with a Dictator: The Marcoses and the Making of American Policy* (New York: Vintage Books, 1987), 80.

59. Taomo Zhou, *Migration in the Time of Revolution: China, Indonesia, and the Cold War* (Ithaca, NY: Cornell University Press, 2019), 161–162.

60. Enrile had already outlined the legal architecture for the suspension of the writ as early as 1952. Juan Ponce Enrile, "The Effect of the Suspension of Habeas Corpus on the Right to Bail in Cases of Rebellion, Insurrection and Sedition," *Philippine Law Journal* 27 (1952): 48–61.

61. A. B. Colayco, "The Plaza Miranda Tragedy and its Repercussions," *APL*, 3 September 1971, 6; Members of the Faculty University of the Philippines (UP) Tarlac, *A Message to President Marcos*, 26 August 1971, PRP 18/08.01.

62. "Presidential Proclamation 889," *APL*, 3 September 1971, 7.

63. Vic Felipe, "Plaza Miranda—First Anniversary," *APL*, 25 August 1972, 17; Dante Simbulan, "Continuing Trend Towards Militarization," *Breakthrough* 3, nos. 3–4 (November 1971): 4, PRP 29/11.02.

64. "Pag-iibayuhin, Gawain ng Propagandista," *PC*, 25 August 1971, 2; "Palayain ang mga Bilanggong Politikal!," 3 September 1971.

65. Jones, *Red Revolution*, 49. Among those arrested were radio commentator Roger Arienda, KM secretary general Luzvimindo David, and PCC president Nemesio Prudente. Simeon G. Del Rosario, *Surfacing the Underground Part II, Volume One: The Involvements of Benigno S. Aquino, Jr., with 29 Perpetuated Testimonies Appended* (Quezon City: Manlapaz, 1977), 43; Citizens Movement for the Protection of Our Democratic Rights (CMPDR), *An Open Letter*, 20 August 1971, PRP 03/10.01. On 1 September, E. Voltaire Garcia filed a petition before the Supreme Court on behalf of Luzvimindo David for habeas corpus. E. Voltaire Garcia, *In Defense of Personal Liberty*, 1 September 1971, PRP 07/24.01. The Supreme Court denied the petition, upholding the legality of Marcos's proclamation.

66. MPKP, *Ibayong Katatagan Laban sa Ibayong Karahasan!*, 6 September 1971, PRP 10/29.05.

67. Jose Ma Sison, "Clarifying Tales," *PC*, 30 August 1971, 2.

68. Federico Angel, "The Philippine Crisis," *Eastern Horizon* 10, no. 5 (1971): 58.

69. This statement appeared in a special issue of *Ang Bayan* on 22 August, which is no longer extant. It was reprinted in *Welga!* 1, no. 1 (1971): 3, PRP 43/17.01.

70. "Expose and Oppose Military Takeover," *PC*, 30 August 1971.

71. The *Asia Philippines Leader* described the MCCCL as "a broad front of organizations ranging from the Kabataang Makabayan to the Adoracion Nocturna." Colayco, "Plaza Miranda," *APL*, 25 August 1972, 26.

72. The founding membership of the MCCCL can be found in MCCCL, *People's Demands*, September 1971, PRP 11/26.03.

73. CEGP, *Labanan Ang Pasismong EU-Marcos!!*, 13 September 1971, PRP 03/17.02.

74. Makamasa, "Expose the Marcos-US-Imperialist Plot of Counter-Revolution," *Sinag* 1, no. 2 (September 1971): 10, PRP 42/02.02.

75. KM et al., *Sasalakayin ang Pamantasan ng Pilipinas!!!*, 24 August 1971, PRP 08/19.14; Stefani Saño, "Ipagpatuloy ang Pakikibaka," *PC*, 30 August 1971.

76. The *Collegian* wrote that, again, five thousand participated in this protest. Saño, "Ipagpatuloy ang Pakikibaka," *PC*, 30 August 1971.

77. CMPDR, *An Open Letter*. The statement was then published in the *Collegian*. *PC*, 30 August 1971, 5.

78. Samahan ng mga Guro sa Pamantasan (Federation of University Teachers, SA-GUPA) et al., *Fearlessly Expose the Facts about the Fascist-Marcos US-Imperialist Plot of Counter-Revolution*, 26 August 1971, 2, PRP 15/30.01.

79. Sandigan Makabansa (Patriotic Pillars, SM), *Militantly Oppose Fascist Suppression*, 30 August 1971, PRP 16/10.16.

80. Rosca, introduction, 23; CEGP, *Labanan Ang Pasismong EU-Marcos!!*; MDP, *Suporta ng MDP sa MCCCL: Tungo sa Isang Malawak na Nagkakaisang Hanay Laban sa Teroristang Sabwatan Ng Rehimeng Estados Unidos-Marcos*, August 1971, PRP 11/18.24.

81. "Kailangan Kumilos ang Masa—Gillego," *PC*, 29 September 1971, 2.

82. The growth of protests brought university life to a stop. The KM and SDK called for an indefinite boycott of classes in protest of the suspension of the writ, and the UP Faculty in Arts and Sciences passed a resolution calling for a shift from normal classes to faculty-student tutorial and consultative work as a means of dealing with the academic problems created by student nonattendance. Ester Albano et al., *Faculty Position on Some Academic Problems Caused by the Suspension of the Privilege of the Writ of Habeas Corpus*, 9 September 1971, PRP 10/03.01.

83. Valentino Abelgas, "Komunidad, Nagkaisa at Kumilos," *PC*, 9 September 1971.

84. "Ibalik ang Writ!," *Welga!* 1, no. 1 (1971): 1, PRP 43/17.01. The *Collegian* also reported that fifty thousand participated.

85. SM, "The Anti-Fascist United Front," *Ang Sandigan*, 13 September 1971, PRP 40/07.01.

86. The features of the rightward reorientation of the party were examined at the end of the previous chapter.

87. Mila De Guzman, *Women against Marcos* (San Francisco: Carayan Press, 2016), 9.

88. SM, "Anti-Fascist United Front," 2.

89. SM.

90. Rogelio Ordoñez, "Order ni Garcia: Pasismo Oil!," *APL*, 4 June 1971, 58.

91. Resil B. Mojares, "Letter from Cebu," *APL*, 2 July 1971, 16.

92. *GW*, 7 July 1971, 6.

93. *GW*, 13 October 1971, 6.

94. SDK, "On the Style of Work of Malacañang's Most Loyal Agent in Vinzons," *The Partisan*, 30 September 1971, 2, PRP 37/17.03. The UKP was the community organization created by the KM and SDK in Caloocan. Sonny Melencio described the UKP as "the coalition of all the radical organizations in the clustered areas of Caloocan, Malabon, and Navotas or Camana. . . . In reality, the UKP also housed the district communist party, which was the underground formation leading the radical movement in Camana." Cesar Melencio, *Full Quarter Storms: Memoirs and Writings on the Philippine Left (1970–2010)* (Quezon City: Transform Asia, 2010), 30–31.

95. UKP, "Sandata ng mga Asistio," *PC*, 8 October 1971, 3; Humanist League of the Philippines (HLP), *Caloocan, October First*, 1 October 1971, PRP 07/37.02; HLP, *Asistio, et al.*, October 1971, PRP 07/37.01.

96. Bobby Coles, "5 Wounded as Goons, Cops Stop Rally," *MT*, 2 October 1971.

97. SDK, "On the Style of Work," 2; MDP, *Crush the Warlord-Bureaucrat Asistio, Fascist Puppet of the US-Marcos Regime!!*, 12 October 1971, PRP 11/18.03.

98. Jose F. Lacaba, *Days of Disquiet, Nights of Rage: The First Quarter Storm & Related Events* (Pasig: Anvil Publishing, 2003), 155. The *Collegian* had slightly different names, reporting that the dead included Ernesto Santos and Romeo Antonio, both of whom were ten years old. In addition to the four listed above, two more were "confirmed dead but their bodies could not be seen [*hindi makita ang bangkay*]" because they "were carried away by policemen." "Sa mga Nasawi," *PC*, 8 October 1971, 8. Onofre Tibar was murdered. His death was not a direct result of the violent altercation in Caloocan but was timed, it seems, to coincide with the deaths of the protesters, perhaps so that it would be buried in the day's news. Tibar was shot nine times as he was leaving the workplace and was subsequently taken to a hospital, where he died (MDP, *Crush the Warlord-Bureaucrat*; "Kay Kasamang Fred," *PC*, 15 October 1971, 7.

99. MDP, *Crush the Warlord-Bureaucrat*.

100. "Biktima sa Kalookan Rally Nawawala pa," *PC*, 8 October 1971.

101. See, for example, the denunciation of the Chinese in Nationalist Businessmen's Association (NBA), "Ilantad ang Sabwatang Asistio at Kumintang na Intsik!," *Ang Kalakal*, 8 October 1971, PRP 31/07.01.

102. "Long March Successful," *National Liberation Fortnightly*, 26 November 1971, 3, PRP 37/01.01.

103. "8000 March to Caloocan," *Kalayaan International* 1, no. 4 (1971): 10, TLBNP, box 32, folder Kalayaan; Serve the People Brigade, "Caloocan Masaker—Tanda ng Pasismo at Burukrata-Kapitalismo," *Ang Pamantasan* 1, no. 2 (October 1971), PRP 37/13.01.

104. Filemon Lagman, "Rally sa Kaloookan Hindi Napatigil ng Ulan at Goons," *PC*, 13 October 1971. This article in the *Collegian* was the first to carry the byline of Filemon "Popoy" Lagman. Lagman would later become a central figure in the leadership of the CPP based in Manila.

105. Lagman, "Rally sa Kalookan," *PC*, 13 October 1971.

106. They succeeded in securing an upset election victory for Samson, who ousted Asistio in November. A. B. Colayco, "The Perils of Performance," *APL*, 19 November 1971, 49.

107. Alejandro R. Roces, *A Stupid TV Ad*, 15 October 1971, PRP 15/07.01.

108. "On the Anti-Youth Smear Campaign," *Breakthrough* 3, nos. 3–4 (November 1971): 3, PRP 29/11.02.

109. "Martsa sa Luson, Laban sa Pasismo," *PC*, 8 October 1971, 2; Jose Dalisay Jr., "Four Days on the Road," *APL*, 19 November 1971, 16.

110. MDP, *Wakasan ang Pagdarahop at Pasismo, Ibukod at Durugin ang mga Kaaway ng Bayan, Magkaisa at Makibaka Para sa Pambansang Demokrasya!*, 20 October 1971, PRP 11/18.26.

111. NBA, "Ipaglaban ang Pambansang Industrialisasyon!," *Ang Kalakal*, 19 October 1971, PRP 31/07.02.

112. NBA.

113. Ricardo Lee, "Oktubre ng Isang Mahabang Martsa," *APL*, 19 November 1971, 34; "Long March Successful," *National Liberation Fortnightly*, 26 November 1971. Sison had established close ties with Lichauco in the early 1960s. In his glowing obituary for Lichauco, written in 2015, Sison spoke repeatedly of their "close friendship," their work together in founding the Movement for the Advancement of Nationalism and meeting with Marcos, and the funds that Lichauco raised for rallies staged by the front organizations of the CPP. Jose Ma Sison, *Alejandro Lichauco: A Great Filipino Patriot, Advocate of Full National Independence and Genuine Economic Development*, 22 May 2015.

114. BRPF—UP, *UP Students! Expose, Oppose, and Isolate the Fascist Agents within Our Ranks!*, 13 September 1971, PRP 02/25.03. The disputed leaflet is BRPF—UP, *Parliamentary Struggle Is the Answer*, 10 September 1971, PRP 02/25.01.

115. BRPF—UP, *The Tyranny of the Vanguard Fraternity*, 24 September 1971, PRP 02/25.02.

116. The PKP kept silent for the rest of the campaign. They reemerged during the week of the election just long enough to issue an obligatory final statement, instructing their readers not to "become a tool of the stingy [*hidhid*] candidates—NP, LP, or independents who have been leashed by the imperialists. . . . We must unite and shout our *complete and universal boycott* in the coming elections!" MPKP and BRPF, *Itakwil ang Panloloko—Huwag Bumoto!*, November 1971, PRP 10/29.07.

117. Colayco, "Perils of Performance," *APL*, 19 November 1971, 6.

118. SDK and Rey Vea, [*Letter regarding the arrest of Gary Olivar*], November 1971, PRP 15/21.01; "On the Anti-Youth Smear Campaign," *Breakthrough* 3, nos. 3–4 (November 1971): 3, PRP 29/11.02.

119. Maximo Soliven, "In Moment of Victory, LP Offers FM Cooperation," *MT*, 11 November 1971, 5.

120. Manuel Salak Jr., "FM Sounds Call for National Unity," *MT*, 11 November 1971, 8.

121. "People Reject US-Marcos Rule," *National Liberation Fortnightly*, 26 November 1971.

122. "MDP on the Elections," *National Liberation Fortnightly*, 26 November 1971, 5.

123. MCCCL, *Laban sa Paniniil at Militarismo*, 3 December 1971, PRP 11/26.02; Kaisahan ng mga Makabayang Manggagawa sa Pamahalaan (Unity of Nationalist Government Workers, KAMMAPA), [*Leaflet on Suspension of the Writ of Habeas Corpus*], 1971, PRP 08/22.02.

5. Martial Law

1. The restoration was the culmination of an incremental process, as Marcos had been lifting the suspension on a piecemeal, regional basis for the past few months until finally restoring the writ entirely at the beginning of 1972. *So the People May Know, Volume VII* (Quezon City: General Headquarters, Armed Forces of the Philippines, 1972), 27–28. The Movement for a Democratic Philippines (MDP) declared that the lifting of the suspension of the writ was "a fascist bluff designed to deodorize a tottering regime with an aura of restraint and benevolence." MDP, *Press Statement*, 17 January 1972, PRP 11/18.13. One does not know exactly what to do with such a collection of metaphors.

2. Jose Carreon, "A House Divided," *APL*, 14 April 1972, 8.

3. Quijano de Manila, "Breakfast with Ninoy," *APL*, 21 April 1972, 51.

4. Carreon, "A House Divided," *APL*, 14 April 1972, 56.

5. Carreon, "A House Divided," *APL*, 14 April 1972, 56.

6. Kabataang Makabayan (Nationalist Youth, KM), *Ang Suliranin ng Langis sa Pilipinas*, [1972], 8, PRP 08/13.32; ABLPPL, *Tutulan Ang Muling Pagtataas ng Presyo ng Langis at Gasolina! Ipaghiganti ang mga Martir sa Masaker ng Enero 13, 1971*, 13 January 1972, PRP 01/15.02.

7. Movement for Democratic Reforms, *Reform the University*, 24 February 1972, PRP 11/18.18; Movement for the Retention of the University of the Philippines at Tarlac, "Matatag na Ipagtanggol ang Ating Baseng Pangkultura!," *Ilaw ng Masa* 1, no. 2 (12 February 1972), PRP 31/01.01.

8. AIM, [*Manifesto*], [1972], PRP 01/24.02.

9. Conrado de Quiros, "KASAMA and the Case against Medicare," *APL*, 5 May 1972, 41.

10. Committee on External Affairs Student Council of the Institute of Social Work and Community Development University of the Philippines (UP), *The Filipino People vs Marcos on the True State of the Nation*, 24 January 1972, PRP 17/50.01.

11. "Peaceful Rally at Congress," *PC*, 26 January 1972.

12. "SM Sportsfest Ends, Beta Sigma, SPP Win," *PC*, 2 March 1972, 2.

13. KM, *Alay Kay Kasamang Arsenio Rienda*, 16 March 1972, PRP 08/13.01.

14. At some point during the May Day rally, a fight broke out between members of the Malayang Pagkakaisa ng Kabataang Pilipino (Free Unity of Filipino Youth, MPKP) and the MDP, leaving several wounded. Billy F. Lacaba, "May Day 1972," *APL*, 19 May 1972, 15, 43–44.

15. SDK, "Paggunita sa Mayo Uno," *BP*, 1 May 1972, 2, PRP 22/02. A leaflet circulated by the Student Alliance for National Democracy (STAND) stated that "at least nine workers and students" were killed in the Guarin massacre. STAND, "Ang Mayo Uno sa Kasaysayan ng Pilipinas," *Ang Estudyante* 1, no. 2 (1 May 1972): 3, PRP 30/08.01.

16. Lacaba, "May Day 1972," 43.

17. A sense of the emerging tensions can be found in SDK, "On the Merger Question," in *SDK: Militant but Groovy: Stories of Samahang Demokratiko ng Kabataan*, ed. Soliman M. Santos and Paz Verdades M. Santos (Manila: Anvil Publishing, 2008), 159–176.

18. UN resolution 2758, which admitted China to the United Nations, had been introduced by Albania on 15 July, as Kissinger concluded his meetings with Zhou. Manila voted against China's admission.

19. "Joint Communique," *PekRev*, 3 March 1972, 5.

20. "First Lady Returns from USSR Trip," *APL*, 7 April 1972, 61.

21. E. P. Patanñe, "Imelda in Moscow," *APL*, 14 April 1972, 58. On her return from Moscow she stopped in Spain to attend the wedding of Franco's granddaughter.

22. Alfredo Salanga Jr., "Doy in Peking," *APL*, 14 April 1972, 53.

23. The Aquino and Laurel families had long-standing ties dating back to the Japanese occupation, when Salvador Laurel's father had served as president and Ninoy Aquino's as vice president of the puppet government. Salvador and Ninoy spent the final months of the war together in Japan, where their fathers were received by the emperor.

24. PKP, "Ideological Dispute between Maoism and the International Communist Movement," in "Issues in the Ideological Dispute between Maoism and the International Communist Movement," special issue, *AK* 3, no. 1 (January 1972), PRP 33/13.03.

25. MPKP—UP, "Strengthen Revolutionary Unity and Combat Maoist Counter-Revolution!," *Siklab*, January 1972, PRP 42/06.02.

26. PKP, "Nixon-Mao Collusion against the International Communist Movement," *AK*, 27 March 1972, 9, PRP 33/13.04; PKP, "China under Mao: On the Road to Capitalist Integration," *AK* 3 (April 1972), PRP 33/13.05.

27. PKP, "The Moscow Summit: A Victory for Peace and Socialist Foreign Policy," *AK* 4, no. 4 (June 1972), PRP 33/13.07.

28. "Castillo's Murder: Another Maoist Crime against the Masses," *Struggle* 1, no. 2 (December 1971): 1, PRP 42/03.01. This issue of *Struggle* was published out of Cebu and is numbered differently from the editions published at UP Diliman.

29. "Castillo's Murder," *Struggle*, 1, no. 2 (December 1971): 1, PRP 42/03.01.

30. "Castillo's Murder," *Struggle*, 1, no. 2 (December 1971): 4, PRP 42/03.01.

31. "Marcos and Osmeña are both Representatives of Exploiting Classes," *AB*, July 1969, 12.

32. For an extended political critique of Castroism, see Bill Van Auken, "Castroism and the Politics of Petty-Bourgeois Nationalism," *WSWS*, 7 January 1998, accessed 27 June 2017, https://www.wsws.org/en/articles/1998/01/cast-j07.html.

33. Régis Debray, *Revolution in the Revolution? Armed Struggle and Political Struggle in Latin America*, trans. Bobbye Ortiz (New York: Grove Press, 1967) (hereafter cited parenthetically in the text as *RR*).

34. Debray's book took the Left intelligentsia of the world by storm. *Monthly Review* published a book of articles on Debray's thesis in 1969, featuring contributions praising Debray from Perry Anderson, Robin Blackburn, Leo Huberman, Paul Sweezy, and Andre Gunder Frank. Debray wrote the concluding note to the volume, in which he dismissed his own thesis, but two years old, as "a utopian notion" and "not a coherent revolutionary line." Régis Debray, "A Reply," in *Regis Debray and the Latin American Revolution*, ed. Leo Huberman and Paul Sweezy, trans. Mary Klopper (New York: Modern Reader, 1969), 146.

35. The work was published in English in 1970 by a Berkeley counterculture magazine, *Berkeley Tribe*, and was disseminated in countless mimeographed editions around the world. Its underground character means that there is no reliable first edition in English to which reference can be made. The edition of Marighella's manual published on the *Marxist Internet Archive* is a generally accurate transcription. Carlos Marighella, "Minimanual of the Urban Guerrilla," 1969, https://www.marxists.org/archive/marighella-carlos/1969/06/minimanual-urban-guerrilla/index.htm.

36. Marighella founded an urban guerrilla group that in 1969 distinguished itself by kidnapping the US ambassador to Brazil, whom they released in exchange for fifteen political prisoners. Marighella was killed by the police in late 1969.

37. Ken Fuller, *A Movement Divided: Philippine Communism, 1957–1986* (Quezon City: University of the Philippines Press, 2011), 129.

38. Fuller, 104; "Komite Sentral Itinatag; Mandela Tagapangulo ng YCL," *Ang Mandirigma* 1, no. 2 (March 1972), PRP 36/06.02.

39. YCL, *Don't Be Cowed by Red Baiters*, July 1971, PRP 18/39.01; *Ang Mandirigma* 1, no. 1 (December 1971), PRP 36/06.01. In keeping with the orientation of the Nemenzo

group, *Ang Mandirigma* occasionally republished statements from *Granma*, the journal of the Cuban Communist Party, but never from the Soviet *Pravda*.

40. "At the Vanguard of the Revolutionary Youth Movement," *Ang Mandirigma* 1, no. 1 (December 1971), 2, PRP 36/06.01.

41. In addition to attacking agents of the state, the first issue heralded the killing of three members of the NPA. ("Durugin ang mga Taksil sa Masa!," *Ang Mandirigma* 1 no. 3 (May 1972), 11 PRP 36/06.04.)

42. "Durugin ang mga Taksil sa Masa!," *Ang Mandirigma* 1, no. 3 (May 1972): 11, PRP 36/06.04.

43. *Ang Mandirigma* 1, no. 2 (March 1972), PRP 36/06.02.

44. "Kumander Angela," *Ang Mandirigma* 1, no. 3 (May 1972): 10, PRP 36/06.04.

45. This claim was in error; the bombings occurred in January 1971. The April-May issue of *Ang Mandirigma* corrected this error.

46. "Maikling Kasaysayan ng Hukbong Mapagpalaya ng Bayan," *Ang Mandirigma* 1, no. 3 (May 1972): 13, PRP 36/06.04; Soliman, "Pahayag ng HMB Ukol sa Pagbomba ng Arca," *Ang Mandirigma* 1 no. 3 (May 1972): 15, PRP 36/06.04.

47. KM, *Labanan ang mga Tunay na Subersibo!*, 13 March 1972, PRP 08/13.19.

48. "Pagsalakay sa Arca: Tagumpay sa Armadong Pakikibaka," *Ang Mandirigma* 1, no. 3 (May 1972), PRP 36/06.04. The building was owned by Antonio Roxas Chua, head of Arca sugar, whom the PKP denounced as a "notorious comprador, financial swindler and Guomindang agent who purchased 'Filipino citizenship' from the corrupt neocolonial government by fraudulent means" (Soliman, "Military Communique on the Bombing of Arca," *Ang Mandirigma* 1, no. 3 (May 1972): 15).

49. Soliman, "Military Communique," *Ang Mandirigma* 1, no. 3 (May 1972): 15, PRP 36/06.04. It was not only the YCL and *Ang Mandirigma* hailing these bombings. On 29 March, *Ang Komunista*, the flagship publication of the PKP—equivalent to the CPP's *Ang Bayan*—published the "Manifesto of the HMB," which took credit for numerous bombings carried out under the name People's Revolutionary Front (Fuller, *A Movement Divided*, 122–124).

50. Raul Rodrigo, *The Power and the Glory: The Story of the Manila Chronicle, 1945–1998* (Pasig: Eugenio Lopez Foundation, 2007), 248.

51. Rodrigo, 248.

52. Forces inside the military regularly leaked information to Aquino regarding Marcos's plan for military dictatorship. This culminated in Aquino's speech in September 1972 exposing the details of the secret Oplan Sagittarius. Nelson A. Navarro, *Doc Prudente: Nationalist Educator* (Mandaluyong City: Anvil Publishing, 2011), 107.

53. Jose F. Lacaba, *Days of Disquiet, Nights of Rage: The First Quarter Storm & Related Events* (Pasig: Anvil Publishing, 2003), 161; Mila De Guzman, *Women against Marcos* (San Francisco: Carayan Press, 2016), 10–11.

54. Lacaba, *Days of Disquiet*, 164.

55. Jurgette Honculada, "May 20 and Militarization," *Breakthrough* 4, no. 3 (June 1972): 7, PRP 29/11.03.

56. Makabayang Kilusan ng Bagong Kababaihan (Nationalist Movement of New Women, MAKIBAKA), *Labanan at Ibagsak ang Imperyalismong Amerikano, Makibaka para sa Pambansang Kalayaan!*, 7 June 1972, PRP 10/21.01; "Long March," *Medical Partisan* 1, no. 1 (July 1972): 2, PRP 36/09.01; "Long March," *National Liberation Forum* 1, nos.

5–6 (July 1972): 5, TLBNP box 31, folder National Liberation Forum. The KM 1984 anniversary statement incorrectly claims that the march took place in 1971. KM, *Brief History of Kabataang Makabayan (1964–1972)*, 1 November 1984, 6, PRP 08/15.01.

57. MPKP—UP, *Who Are Using Fascist Tactics to Justify the Fascist Programme of Mr. Marcos?*, 11 July 1972, PRP 10/31.07.

58. *On the July 4 Ambuscade: Weed Out the Agents of Fascism and Reaction Hiding behind the Mask of Revolutionism!*, 1972, PRP 14/22.02.

59. Nick Joaquin, *A Kadre's Road to Damascus: The Ruben Torres Story* (Quezon City: Milflores Publishing, 2003), 82.

60. Conrado de Quiros, *Dead Aim: How Marcos Ambushed Philippine Democracy* (Pasig City: Foundation for Worldwide People's Power, 1997), 312; Gregg Jones, *Red Revolution: Inside the Philippine Guerrilla Movement* (Boulder, CO: Westview Press, 1989), 75.

61. Jones, *Red Revolution*, 75; Jose Lacaba, "The Palanan Puzzle," *APL*, 28 July 1972, 24.

62. Jones, *Red Revolution*, 75; Galileo C. Kintanar and Pacifico V. Militante, *Lost in Time: From Birth to Obsolescence, the Communist Party of the Philippines, Book One: 1930–1972* (Quezon City: Truth/Justice Foundation, 1999), 181; Rolando Peña, "*Liberation*: Early Days," in *Tibak Rising: Activism in the Days of Martial Law*, ed. Ferdinand C. Llanes (Mandaluyong: Anvil Publishing, 2012), 186.

63. de Quiros, *Dead Aim*, 313; Jones, *Red Revolution*, 51; Kintanar and Militante, *Lost in Time, Book One*, 181.

64. Jones, *Red Revolution*, 51.

65. *APL*, 28 July 1972, 6; *The Palanan Incident*, 1972, PRP 13/08.01.

66. Jones, *Red Revolution*, 76. Mitra delivered a speech in the legislature to this effect. Lacaba, "Palanan Puzzle," *APL*, 28 July 1972, 25.

67. "Ship Ahoy!," *APL*, 28 July 1972, 5.

68. This was the account given, for example, by Dante Simbulan, "The Continuing Trend Toward Militarization," *Breakthrough* 4, no. 4 (August 1972): 9, PRP 29/11.04.

69. "PC Nagnakaw ng Relief Goods," *BP* 2, no. 1 (August 1972), PRP 22/02; Samahan ng Makabayan Siyentipiko (Federation of Scientific Nationalists, SMS), *Devastating Floods and Calamities: By-product of a Semi-feudal, Semi-colonial Society*, 18 August 1972, PRP 36/02.05.

70. Reuben R. Canoy, *The Counterfeit Revolution: Martial Law in the Philippines* (Manila: n.p., 1980), 2–3.

71. MDP, *Baha at Hirap: Dulot ng Rehimeng US-Marcos!*, 1972, PRP 11/18.01.

72. Joselito Ruaya, *Operasyon tulong, Patuloy*, August 1972, PRP 42/01.05; MDP and Nagkakaisang Progresibong Artista-Arkitekto (United Progressive Artists-Architects, NPAA), *Ang Bayan at ang Baha*, August 1972, 11/18.02.

73. The arrests and interrogations were overseen by Commander Melody, a former Central Committee member of the CPP, who was now working with the military. "Operation Tulong Relief Center, Ni-Raid," *BP* 1, no. 2 (18 August 1972), PRP 22/03.

74. "Airgram from the Embassy in the Philippines to the Department of State," Document 257 in *FRUS, 1969–1976*, vol. 10, *Southeast Asia, 1969–1972* (Washington, DC: US Government Printing Office, 2006).

75. This summary is contained in a separate confidential embassy memorandum to the State Department, A-245, 21 September 1972. A digital copy of the memorandum is available in Lisandro Claudio, "Ninoy Networked with Everyone, Reds Included," *GMA*

News, 18 August 2010, http://www.gmanetwork.com/news/story/198820/news/specialreports/ninoy-networked-with-everyone-reds-included.

76. The US embassy used this name to distinguish the CPP from the Moscow section.

77. Confidential embassy memorandum to the State Department, A-245, 21 September 1972. Sison disputed that he personally met with Aquino on this occasion, claiming that Julius Fortuna acted as his emissary, a claim that Fortuna confirmed. The meeting took place on 7 September (Fuller, *Movement Divided*, 96; de Quiros, *Dead Aim*, 347).

78. CPP, *Programme for a People's Democratic Revolution*, 26 December 1968, DSUMC; CPP, *Programa sa Demokratikong Rebolusyong Bayan sa Pilipinas*, 26 December 1968, PRP 04/02.13.

79. A. B. Colayco, "Times Which Try Men's Souls," *APL*, 22 September 1972, 6, 46.

80. SAGUPA, *Vigorously Oppose Military Rule!*, 18 September 1972, PRP 15/31.08.

81. Canoy, *Counterfeit Revolution*, 3.

82. The text of Aquino's speech is available in Benigno S. Aquino Jr., *A Garrison State in the Make and Other Speeches* (n.p.: Benigno S. Aquino Jr. Foundation, 1985), 345–351.

83. de Quiros, *Dead Aim*, 391.

84. KM—UP, *Terrorist Bombings—Prelude to Martial Law*, 11 September 1972, PRP 08/19.17; Arts & Sciences (AS) Student Council, *Oppose Terrorist Bombings as a Prelude to the Imposition of Martial Law!!!*, 11 September 1972, PRP 17/44.05.

85. *Kal*, September 1972, 32/01.05. An issue of *Bandilang Pula*, meanwhile, accused Commander Melody, now a key agent of Marcos, of being behind the Plaza Miranda bombing under instructions from the US-Marcos regime. "PC Nagnakaw ng Relief Goods," *BP* 2, no. 1 (August 1972):, 2, PRP 22/02.

86. SDK, *Expose and Oppose the US-Marcos Scheme to Militarize the Country*, 19 September 1972, PRP 36/06.05. This was a two-page issue of *Bandilang Pula*, but it was misfiled in the *Ang Mandirigma* folder of the PRP (36/06).

87. Both Alfredo Montoya, head of the Metrocom, and Gen. Ignacio Paz, head of military intelligence, had been stationed as military attachés in Indonesia during Suharto's seizure of power (de Quiros, *Dead Aim*, 360–361, 398; Raymond Bonner, *Waltzing with a Dictator: The Marcoses and the Making of American Policy* [New York: Vintage Books, 1987], 96).

88. Bernardino Ronquillo, "The Guerilla Mystery," *Far Eastern Economic Review*, 16 September 1972, 25. This bill had been drawn up by "four pro-Marcos congressmen (Barbero, Yñiguez, Navarro, and Natividad)." *UPCLL Bulletin*, no. 7 (June 1972), PRP 43/15.01.

89. The first was almost certainly Nonie Villanueva.

90. These arrests are documented in a number of publications of the front organizations of the CPP. On the same day, the Humanist League of the Philippines (HLP) published a statement claiming that "48 activists within the national liberation ranks were arrested." The haste with which the leaflet was produced is indicated by the fact that it was originally intended to be a statement on art. The notification of the arrests abruptly turned in its second paragraph to the distinction between the writings of Jose Garcia Villa and Amado Hernandez, criticizing Villa and Andy Warhol as bourgeois art-

ists and concluding "art is political! Artists, unite and fight fascism and militarism!" HLP, *Fascist Tactics by Government Troopers Again Led to the Arrest of 48 Activists within the National Liberation Ranks Last 17 September 1972*, September 1972, PRP 07/37.03. The same figure of forty-eight student activists arrested was included in a leaflet issued by the Association of Concerned Teachers (ACT). ACT—UP, *The Politics of Terror*, [1972], PRP 02/04.01. The MDP claimed that over fifty activists had been arrested and that thirteen headquarters had been shut down. MDP, *Pag-isahin ang Sambayanan at Gapiin ang Diktadurang EU-Marcos*, 19 September 1972, PRP 11/18.16. The UP Women's Club also wrote on the raids, and Panulat para sa kaunlaran ng bayan (Writing for the progress of the nation, PAKSA) claimed that fourteen headquarters were shut down. Samahan ng Kababaihan ng UP (Federation of Women of UP, SKUP), *[Untitled]*, [18 September 1972], PRP 15/27.03; PAKSA, *Mga Katanungan ng Bayan*, 18 September 1972, PRP 13/17.03.

91. SM, *The Situation Is Critical—What Is to Be Done?*, 19 September 1972, PRP 16/10.18.

92. "Diokno Says: Reforms, Not Martial Law," *PC*, 21 September 1972.

93. Simeon G. Del Rosario, *Surfacing the Underground Part II, Volume One: The Involvements of Benigno S. Aquino, Jr., with 29 Perpetuated Testimonies Appended* (Quezon City: Manlapaz Publishing Company, 1977), 121.

94. Aquino's speech can be found in Del Rosario, 121–124.

95. Simeon G. Del Rosario, *Surfacing the Underground Part II, Volume Two: The Involvements of Benigno S. Aquino, Jr., with 29 Perpetuated Testimonies Appended* (Quezon City: Manlapaz Publishing Company, 1977), 121.

96. Dante L. Ambrosio, "Pangangapa sa simula ng Martial Law," in *Serve the People: Ang Kasaysayan ng Radikal na Kilusan sa Unibersidad ng Pilipinas*, ed. Bienvenido Lumbera et al. (Quezon City: Ibon Books, 2008), 114.

97. Bonner, *Waltzing with a Dictator*, 101.

98. F. D. Pinpin, ed., *Proclamation No. 1081 and Related Documents, Volumes 1 to 4* (Mandaluyong: Cacho Hermanos, 1972).

99. Alfred W. McCoy, *Closer Than Brothers: Manhood at the Philippine Military Academy* (Manila: Anvil Publishing, 1999), 193.

100. Canoy, *Counterfeit Revolution*, 21; Hernando J. Abaya, *The CLU Story: 50 Years of Struggle for Civil Liberties* (Quezon City: New Day Publishers, 1987), 125.

101. de Quiros, *Dead Aim*, 419; Abaya, *CLU Story*, 125.

102. de Quiros, *Dead Aim*, 422.

103. Hernando J. Abaya, *The Making of a Subversive: A Memoir* (Quezon City: New Day Publishers, 1984), 6–7.

104. Abaya, 7.

105. Abaya, 9.

106. Mark Richard Thompson, "Searching for a Strategy: The Traditional Opposition to Marcos and the Transition to Democracy in the Philippines," vols. 1 and 2 (PhD diss., Yale University, 1991), vol. 1, 186.

107. Mijares, *Conjugal Dictatorship*, 69.

108. Lewis E. Gleeck Jr., *President Marcos and the Philippine Political Culture* (Manila: Loyal Printing, 1987), 120.

109. Augusto Caesar Espiritu, *How Democracy Was Lost: A Political Diary of the Constitutional Convention of 1971–1972* (Quezon City: New Day Publishers, 1993), 22.

110. Filemon Rodriguez, *The Marcos Regime: Rape of the Nation* (New York: Vantage Press, 1985), 95–96.

111. Espiritu, *How Democracy Was Lost*, 50.

112. Espiritu, 129. Espiritu, himself the head of an opposition bloc in the convention, recounts in his diary that he responded to Roco, "'We are dissenting, because we have to be true to ourselves.' Raul Roco straightened up and looked straight into our eyes. 'The time to be true to ourselves has passed'" (130).

113. Jovito Salonga, *The Lives and Times of Gerry Roxas and Ninoy Aquino* (Mandaluyong City: Regina Publishing, 2010), 7.

114. Thompson, "Searching for a Strategy," 205.

115. Canoy, *Counterfeit Revolution*, 30; Simeon G. Del Rosario, *An Integrated Course on Communism and Democracy: A Self-Study Reader* (Quezon City: SGR Research & Publishing, 1973), 25.

116. Abaya, *CLU Story*, 124.

117. William H. Sullivan, *Obbligato 1939–1979: Notes on a Foreign Service Career* (New York: W.W. Norton, 1984).

118. Arturo Tolentino, *Voice of Dissent* (Quezon City: Phoenix Publishing House, 1990), 467.

119. *APL*, 2 June 1972, 54. It was Marcos's cronies who profited from the trade relations with the Soviet Union made possible by martial law. Marcos established the National Export Trade Corporation, known as NETRACOR, a private corporation under government control to exercise a monopoly on all trade established with the Soviet bloc. NETRACOR was run by the crony capitalists of the Marcos administration, including Roberto Benedicto and Alfredo Montelibano. Ben Javier, "Tapping Markets Among the Reds," *Examiner* (6–13 May 1972), 4–5. Enrile was made chairman. Ricardo Manapat, *Some are Smarter than Others: The History of Marcos' Crony Capitalism* (New York: Aletheia Publications, 1991), 171. Danding Cojuangco, one of the Rolex Twelve, headed up Filsov Shipping Company, a joint venture with Soviet freight for shipping to the Soviet bloc. Manapat, *Some are Smarter*, 245.

120. Civil Liberties Brigade UP Student Council, [*Untitled*], 23 September 1972, PRP 18/04.01.

121. It referred to Marcos as a "paper tiger" and enjoined the masses to "dare to struggle, dare to win!!!" This was the stock vocabulary of the Maoists, and the Maoists alone.

122. Nagkakaisang Mamayan ng Pilipinas Laban sa Taksil at Pasistang Pangkating Estados Unidos-Marcos, *The Defeat of the US-Marcos Clique Is the Victory of the Filipino People*, 1972, PRP 12/01.01.

123. Jose Ma Sison and Rainer Werning, *The Philippine Revolution: The Leader's View* (New York: Taylor & Francis, 1989), 61; Jones, *Red Revolution*, 6.

124. Cesar Melencio, *Full Quarter Storms: Memoirs and Writings on the Philippine Left (1970–2010)* (Quezon City: Transform Asia, 2010), 47.

125. Student Revolutionary Movement, *A Call to the Filipino Student Youth*, 9 October 1972, PRP 17/15.01 (hereafter cited parenthetically in the text as *FSY*).

126. KM, *Brief History of KM*, 7.

127. A useful book on revolutionary work under conditions of repression is Victor Serge, *What Everyone Should Know about State Repression*, trans. Judith White (New York:

New Park Publications, 1979), which Serge wrote on the basis of his study of the archives of the Okhrana, the czarist secret police, which the Bolsheviks captured in October 1917.

128. "Lights Out!," *Dissent* 1, no. 1 (6 December 1972), 6, PRP 30/06.01.

129. "Editorial," *Dissent* 1, no. 1 (6 December 1972), 8, PRP 30/06.01.

130. "Protest Actions Intensify," *Dissent* 1, no. 1 (6 December 1972), 5, PRP 30/06.01.

131. Kapit Bisig—UP, *UPGA Prison*, 1972, PRP 08/30.01.

132. Susan F. Quimpo and Nathan Gilbert Quimpo, *Subversive Lives: A Family Memoir of the Marcos Years* (Pasig: Anvil Publishing, 2012), 124.

133. Quimpo and Quimpo, 124.

134. Ambrosio, "Pangangapa sa simula ng Martial Law," 117; Arnel De Guzman, "UP after the 'Storm,'" in Llanes, *Tibak Rising*, 25.

135. Ambrosio, "Pangangapa sa simula ng Martial Law," 120.

136. SDK—UP, "Crush the US-Marcos Fascist Bunch and Their Campus Marionettes!," *BP* 1, no. 2 (17 November 1972), PRP 22/03.

137. UP SRC, *Free the University!!*, 1972, PRP 18/24.01.

138. Patricio N. Abinales, "Fragments of History, Silhouettes of Resurgence: Student Radicalism in the Early Years of the Marcos Dictatorship," *Southeast Asian Studies* 46, no. 2 (2008): 179.

139. There is some confusion in dating the initial issues of *Taliba ng Bayan*. The issue published as volume 1, no. 1, is not dated but can be placed after 23 October, as it refers to an event that transpired on this date. The first issue is labeled "edition of the Katipunan ng Kabataang Demokratiko (Katipunan ng Kabataang Demokratiko [Union of Democratic Youth] [KKD])." Issue 2, however, is dated 9 October. It is possible that this is a misprint and that it was published on 9 November, but no events occurring after 30 September are mentioned. It is also possible that there were multiple local versions of the first issues of *TnB*, which would explain the variant dating.

140. "Tuloy ang Kilusang Propaganda ng Pambansang Demokratikong Kilusan," *TnB* 1, no. 1, 3.

141. A nonsensical word and part of the original rhyme

142. "Ipinagbawal pa rin ang Mini-Skirt!," *TnB*, 3 November 1972, 6.

143. Satur Ocampo, *Tala-Gabay sa Pagtalakay ng*, Ang Alternative Press sa Panahon ng Batas Militar, 10 October 2014; Lourdes Gordolan, "Butch Dalisay, Ricky Lee, and Other Writers Remember Prison Life in Martial Law Era," *Rogue*, April 2012.

144. "Editorial: The Truth about Martial Law," *Bangon!* 1, no. 1 (5 October 1972): 3, PRP 22/04.

145. "Military in the 'New Society,'" *Bangon!* 1, no. 2 (11 October 1972): 1, PRP 22/04.

146. "Mabuti pang Mamatay nang Marangal—Aquino," *TnB*, 9 September 1973, 2.

147. "'Soc' Condemns Martial Law," *Liberation* 1, no. 7 (7 December 1972), 5, PRP 34/01.05. In November the NDF reported that "freedom fighters" in Marawi City killed 519 AFP soldiers and wounded 236. NDF, "Oppose the Con-Con Plot to Legalize Dictatorship," *Liberation* 1, no. 4 (7 November 1972), PRP 34/01.03.

148. NDF, "The Cultural Revolution Gains New Heights as the US-Marcos Dictatorship Is Encircled from the Countrysides," *Liberation* 1, no. 2 (19 October 1972), PRP 34/01.01.

149. NDF, "'Vote No' Movement Snowballs," *Liberation* 1, no. 8 (15 December 1972), PRP 34/01.06. It further reported that the NPA had begun deploying "sparrow units" for carrying out urban assassination and that a squad had opened fire in the movie theater in Tarlac, killing three PC and one Barrio Self-Defense Unit man.

150. "A Report: When Marcos Became Dictator," *Bangon!* 1, no. 1 (5 October 1972): 3, PRP 22/04.

151. Konsehong Tagapag-Ugnay ng Rebolusyonaryong Sining (Coordinating Council of Revolutionary Art, KONTRES), "Ibagsak ang Diktadurang EU-Marcos upang Makamit ang Pambansang Kalayaan at Demokrasya," *Kontres* 1, no. 4 (November 1972): 15, PRP 33/15.03.

152. Quoted in Ambrosio, "Pangangapa sa simula ng Martial Law," 121 fn 8.

153. The formulation is Trotsky's. In his book on the 1905 Russian revolution, he wrote, "Opportunism . . . needs allies. It rushes from place to place, grabbing possible allies by the coattails. It harangues its own adherents, admonishing them to be more considerate towards all potential allies. 'Tact, more tact, still more tact!' It is gripped by a special disease, the mania of caution in respect to liberalism, the sickness of tact; and, driven berserk by its sickness, it attacks and wounds its own party." Leon Trotsky, *1905* (Chicago: Haymarket Books, 2016), 252.

154. Antonio Hilario, *Hinggil sa Legal na Pakikibaka*, 4 January 1974, PRP 15/18.05 (hereafter cited parenthetically in the text as *Hinggil*). I base Hilario's authorship of this document on Abinales, "Fragments of History." While Abinales dates the document to the last months of 1973, the *PRP* copy is signed 4 January. This would be in 1974. I have dated it accordingly.

155. Benjamin Pimentel, *Rebolusyon! A Generation of Struggle in the Philippines* (New York: Monthly Review Press, 1991), 166–167.

156. Jose Ma Sison, *Defeating Revisionism, Reformism and Opportunism: Selected Writings, 1969 to 1974*, ed. Julieta de Lima, vol. 2 of *Continuing the Philippine Revolution* (Quezon City: Aklat ng Bayan, 2013), 5–39 (hereafter cited parenthetically in the text as *DR*).

157. Sison and Werning, *Philippine Revolution*, 87; Del Rosario, *Surfacing II, One*, 220; Pimentel, *Rebolusyon!*, 138.

158. Sison, *Defeating Revisionism*, 36.

159. Sison, 109.

160. Sison, 271.

161. MASAKA was founded with funding from the Macapagal administration in keeping with the charter of his land reform program, which the new organization promoted. I examine this in detail in Joseph Scalice, "Crisis of Revolutionary Leadership: Martial Law and the Communist Parties of the Philippines, 1957–1974" (PhD diss., University of California, Berkeley, 2017), 182–187, 201–203.

162. MECW, 11:187–188.

163. Fuller, *Movement Divided*, 45; Alfredo B. Saulo, *Communism in the Philippines*, enlarged ed. (Quezon City: Ateneo de Manila University Press, 1990), 84.

164. de Quiros, *Dead Aim*, 40.

165. de Quiros, *Dead Aim*, 330; Ferdinand E. Marcos, *Today's Revolution: Democracy* (n.p.: n.p., 1971).

166. Marcos, *Today's Revolution*, 60 (hereafter cited parenthetically in the text as *TR*).

167. Jesus Lava, *Memoirs of a Communist* (Pasig: Anvil Publishing, 2002), 333.

168. Fuller, *Movement Divided*, 120–121 fn 32. How Moscow became aware of this and how the Pomeroys prevented its transmission are both unclear.

169. The Pomeroys spent the summers of 1972 and 1973 in Moscow, and William referenced this travel in letters to James S. Allen, 3 December 1972 and 15 August 1973 in JSAP, box 1, folder 20 (Correspondence 1972).

170. William J. Pomeroy to James S. Allen, 1 October 1972 in JSAP, box 1, folder 20 (Correspondence 1972).

171. Joaquin, *Kadre's Road to Damascus*, 79, 88; *Deception and Murder Is the Meaning of the Lavaite 'Theory of Physical Affinity' and 'Armed Struggle as Secondary Form,'* 1971, PRP 12/13.01; Ernesto Macahiya, "Hands Off," *PC*, 21 January 1971, 6.

172. James S. Allen to William J. Pomeroy, 6 October 1972 in JSAP, box 1, folder 20 (Correspondence 1972).

173. James P. Cannon, *Socialism on Trial* (New York: Pioneer Publishers, 1965), 3; David North, *The Heritage We Defend: A Contribution to the History of the Fourth International* (Detroit: Labor Publications, 1988), 47.

174. Quoted in North, *Heritage We Defend*, 47.

175. William J. Pomeroy to James S. Allen, 3 December 1972 in JSAP, box 1, folder 20 (Correspondence 1972).

176. David Wurfel, "The Development of Post-war Philippine Land Reform: Political and Sociological Explanations," in *Second View from the Paddy: More Empirical Studies on Philippine Rice Farming and Tenancy*, ed. Antonio J. Ledesma, Perla Q. Makpil, and Virginia A. Miralao (Quezon City: Ateneo de Manila University Press, 1983), 8.

177. James Putzel, *A Captive Land: The Politics of Agrarian Reform in the Philippines* (New York: Monthly Review Press, 1992), 15.

178. Wurfel, "Development of Post-war Philippine Land Reform," 8.

179. Jennifer Conroy Franco, *Elections and Democratization in the Philippines*, ed. Andrew Appleton, Comparative Studies in Democratization (New York: Routledge, 2001), 110–111.

180. PKP, "The Philippines: What Is Behind Dictatorship?," *Comment: Communist Fortnightly Review* 10, no. 26 (1972): 409. The editorial introduction continued, "The full statement makes detailed examination, amongst other questions, of the provocative role played by Maoist groups in creating a situation which Marcos was able to exploit in establishing his military dictatorship, and discusses the new tactics of US imperialism contained within the concepts of the Nixon doctrine and the process known as 'neo-colonial industrialisation.'" I have been unable to locate the entire PKP statement, but it almost certainly was the Political Transmission titled *New Situation, New Tasks*, published in December, which declared that the PKP would be assisting the Marcos regime. This work was referenced in Fuller, *Movement Divided*, 128. However, it seems that Fuller himself had not seen the document, as he did not directly cite it but included a reference to Nemenzo.

181. PKP, "Philippines," 409.

182. PKP, "Philippines," 409.

183. PKP, 410.

184. PKP, 410.

185. PKP, 410.

186. KM, *Labanan ang mga Tunay na Subersibo!*

187. My account of this affair is based almost entirely on Nemenzo's and the PKP's own versions of events.

188. Fuller, *Movement Divided*, 135.

189. Fuller, 129; PKP, "The Party's Struggle against Ultra-'leftism' under Martial Law," *Ang Buklod* 1, no. 1 (1973): 25, PRP 29/08.01.

190. Fuller, *Movement Divided*, 130.

191. Fuller, 131.

192. Fuller, 132.

193. Fuller, 134.

194. Francisco Nemenzo Jr., "Rectification Process in the Philippine Communist Movement," in *Armed Communist Movements in Southeast Asia*, ed. Lim Joo-Jock (Singapore: Institute of Southeast Asian Studies, 1984), 84.

195. Joaquin, *Kadre's Road to Damascus*, 104.

196. Joaquin, 104.

197. Fuller, *Movement Divided*, 136.

198. Fuller, 137.

199. PKP, "Struggle against Ultra-'leftism,'" 21.

200. The use of "'Trotskyite" as a political label to justify execution finds its roots in the systematic murder of the old Bolsheviks carried out under Stalin's orders.

201. On his release he faced a renewed threat from the party, but when he warned that he would orchestrate a hit against the family members of party leaders, the threat disappeared. Jose Y. Dalisay and Josef T. Yap, *Lessons from the Nationalist Struggle: The Life of Emmanuel Quiason Yap* (Mandaluyong City: Anvil Publishing, 2016), 56.

202. Sison and Werning, *Philippine Revolution*, 79; Ninotchka Rosca, introduction to *Jose Maria Sison: At Home in the World—Portrait of a Revolutionary*, by Jose Ma Sison and Ninotchka Rosca (Manila: Ibon Books, 2004), 24.

203. Fuller, *Movement Divided*, 128.

204. PKP, "Struggle against Ultra-'leftism,'" 26.

205. It had, in fact, been so long since the party had held a congress that the PKP was uncertain whether this was its fifth or sixth congress. In the *PRP* the materials from the congress are labeled as "Sixth," but when the documents were published in New Delhi later in the year, they were labeled "Fifth." In 1977 the party held its seventh congress (Fuller, *Movement Divided*, 138, 158 fn 3).

206. Fuller, 141.

207. PKP, *Ang Saligang Batas ng Partido Komunista ng Pilipinas*, 12 February 1973, PRP 04/02.16; PKP, *Program of the Partido Komunista ng Pilipinas (PKP), 6th Congress*, 11 February 1973, PRP 04/02.12; PKP, *Political Resolution, 6th Congress*, February 1973, PRP 04/02.11.

208. PKP, *Political Resolution, 6th Congress*, 29.

209. PKP, 42.

210. PKP, 43.

211. PKP, *Program, 6th Congress*, 15–16.

212. PKP, *Political Resolution, 6th Congress*, 6.

213. PKP, *Program, 6th Congress*, 5; PKP, *Political Resolution, 6th Congress*, 9.

214. Matthew D. Rothwell, *Transpacific Revolutionaries: The Chinese Revolution in Latin America* (London: Routledge, 2013), 25.

215. PKP, "Struggle against Ultra-'leftism,'" 27.

216. Lava, *Memoirs of a Communist*, 334.

217. William J. Pomeroy, "Negotiation as a Form of Struggle: The PKP Experience," *Debate: Philippine Left Review*, no. 6 (1993): 73.

218. Col. Thomas Halim, working out of the offices of Gen. Fabian Ver, played a critical role in these discussions (Dalisay and Yap, *Lessons from the Nationalist Struggle*, 65–67).

219. Pomeroy, "Negotiation as a Form of Struggle," 74.

220. Pomeroy, 74.

221. Fuller, *Movement Divided*, 186.

222. Fuller, 186.

223. Pomeroy, "Negotiation as a Form of Struggle," 75.

224. Fuller, *Movement Divided*, 189.

225. Fuller, 189.

226. Simeon G. Del Rosario, *Surfacing the Underground: The Church and State Today* (Quezon City: Manlapaz, 1975), 131–136; Del Rosario, *Surfacing II, Two*, Appendix EE, 1261.

227. PKP, *The Significance of the State Visit of President Ceaușescu*, April 1975, 3, PRP 03/03.01.

228. Felicisimo C. Macapagal, *To Comrade Nicolae Ceaușescu*, 9 April 1975, PRP 10/16.02.

229. PKP, *State Visit of President Ceaușescu*, 1.

230. PKP, 2.

231. Danilo P. Vizmanos, *Martial Law Diary and Other Papers* (Quezon City: KEN, 2003), 174, 224.

232. Jones, *Red Revolution*, 78.

233. Jones, 78; Quimpo and Quimpo, *Subversive Lives*, 176.

234. Quimpo and Quimpo, *Subversive Lives*, 176–190.

235. "Madame Imelda Marcos' Visit to China Welcomed," *PekRev*, 27 September 1974, 3.

236. Jose Ma Sison, *Building Strength through Struggle: Selected Writings, 1972 to 1977*, ed. Julieta de Lima, vol. 3 of *Continuing the Philippine Revolution* (Quezon City: Aklat ng Bayan, 2013), 149–172.

237. Sison, 152.

238. *SCPW*, 5.

239. *SCPW*, 36.

240. *SCPW*, 37.

241. "President and Madame Marcos in China," *PekRev*, 13 June 1975, 4.

242. The full text of the communiqué was printed in *PekRev*, 7–8.

243. Del Rosario, *Surfacing II, One*, 144.

244. Robert Francis Garcia, *To Suffer thy Comrades: How the Revolution Decimated Its Own* (Manila: Anvil Publishing, 2001) is a vivid personal account and examination of the purges.

245. "A Talk with Dante," *Asiaweek*, 11 September 1981, 27.

Epilogue

1. Bertolt Brecht's *The Resistible Rise of Arturo Ui* is a parable play of the political ascent of Adolf Hitler.

2. MECW, 11:108.

BIBLIOGRAPHY

Archives

Hoover Institution Archives, Stanford University

Arthur Leroy Carson Collection
Charles T. R. Bohannan Papers
Edward Geary Lansdale Papers
Joseph Hansen Papers
Library of Social History Collection
Socialist Workers Party Records

Tamiment Archives, Bobst Library, New York University

Communist Party of the United States of America (CPUSA) Papers
David Sullivan US Maoism Collection: TAM 527
James S. Allen Papers

Other

Ira Gollobin Papers. New York Public Library
Philippine Radical Papers Archive. University of the Philippines, Diliman. The numbering system in the PRP corresponds to the box/folder.item of the collection housed at UP Diliman (e.g., 40/02.01 is box 40, folder 2, item 1).

Periodicals

1896, 1970. PRP 30/07
AGG, 1970. PRP 19/03
Alab, 1970–72. PRP 19/05
Asia Philippines Leader, 1971–72
Bagong Pilipina, 1970–71. PRP 22/01
Bandilang Pula, 1971–73. PRP 22/02–03
Bangon!, 1972. PRP 22/04
Ang Bayan, 1969–75
Breakthrough, 1970–72. PRP 29/11
Ang Buklod, 1973
Dare to Struggle, Dare to Win, 1971–73. PRP 33/03
Dissent, 1972. PRP 30/06
Examiner, 1970–72

Graphic Weekly, 1966–72

Kalatas, 1969–72. PRP 31/08

Kalayaan, 1965–72. PRP 32

Kalayaan International, 1971. TLBNP, box 32, folder Kalayaan

Kilusan, 1967–70. PRP 33/12.01 (1967)

Ang Komunista, 1971–72. PRP 33/13

Liberation, 1972–73. PRP 34/01

Ang Makabayang Siyentipiko, 1971–72. PRP 36/02

Ang Malaya, 1970–72. PRP 36/04

Ang Mandirigma, 1971–72. PRP 36/06

Manila Bulletin, 1959–72

Manila Chronicle, 1959–72

Manila Times, 1959–72

Ang Masa, 1969–72

Medical Partisan, 1972. PRP 36/09.01

Molabe Monthly, 1969

National Liberation Fortnightly, 1971. PRP 37/01.01

National Liberation Forum, 1972. PRP 36/16.01; TLBNP, box 31, folder NLF

New York Times

NOW, 1969–72

The Partisan, 1969–72

Peking Review, 1959–74

Philippine Collegian, 1959–72

Philippine Socialist Review, 1971–72

Philippines Free Press, 1959–72

Philippines Herald, 1970–71

Pingkian, 1969–70. PRP 38/02

Progressive Review, 1963–70

Ang Sandigang Makabansa, 1971. PRP 40/08

Sinag, 1969–72

Struggle, 1970–71. PRP 42/03–04

Sunday Times Magazine, 1969–72

Talang Ginto, 1971. PRP 43/01

Taliba ng Bayan, 1972–75. PRP 42/12

UPCLL Bulletin, 1972. PRP 43/15

Welga!, 1971–72. PRP 43/17

World Socialist Web Site, 1998–2021. https://www.wsws.org.

Books and Articles

Abaya, Hernando J. *The CLU Story: 50 Years of Struggle for Civil Liberties*. Quezon City: New Day Publishers, 1987.

Abaya, Hernando J. *The Making of a Subversive: A Memoir*. Quezon City: New Day Publishers, 1984.

Abinales, Patricio N. "Fragments of History, Silhouettes of Resurgence: Student Radicalism in the Early Years of the Marcos Dictatorship." *Southeast Asian Studies* 46, no. 2 (2008): 175–199.

Abinales, Patricio N. "Jose Ma. Sison and the Philippine Revolution: A Critique of an Interface." In *Fellow Traveler: Essays on Filipino Communism*, 9–101. Quezon City: University of the Philippines Press, 2001.

Abinales, Patricio N., and Donna J. Amoroso. *State and Society in the Philippines*. Pasig: Anvil Publishing, 2005.

Abreu, Lualhati Milan. *Agaw-dilim, Agaw-liwanag*. Quezon City: University of the Philippines Press, 2009.

Abueva, Jose Veloso. "The Philippines: Tradition and Change." *Asian Survey* 10, no. 1 (1970): 56–64.

Afuang, Benjamin V. "Special Report: The Students vs the State, 1970." *STM*, 22 February 1970, 12–34.

Aguilar, Mila D. "The Diliman 'Commune': Two Views." *GW*, 24 February 1971.

Aidit, D. N. *Indonesian Society and Indonesian Revolution*. Djakarta: Jajasan "Pembaruan," 1958.

"Airgram from the Embassy in the Philippines to the Department of State." Document 257 in *FRUS, 1969–1976*, vol. 20, *Southeast Asia, 1969–1972*. Washington, DC: US Government Printing Office, 2006.

Alabado, Ceres S. C. *I See Red in a Circle . . .* Manila, 1972.

Albano, Ester, Leslie Bauzon, Manuel Bonifacio, Ernesto Constantino, and Roger Posadas. *Faculty Position on Some Academic Problems Caused by the Suspension of the Privilege of the Writ of Habeas Corpus*, 9 September 1971. PRP 10/03.01.

Almario, Manuel F. "Where Lies the Opposition." *GW*, 18 February 1970.

Alyansa ng Bayan Laban sa Pagtataas ng Presyo ng Langis (ABLPPL). *Tutulan Ang Muling Pagtataas ng Presyo ng Langis at Gasolina! Ipaghiganti ang mga Martir sa Masaker ng Enero 13, 1971*, 13 January 1972. PRP 01/15.02.

Ambrosio, Dante L. "Pangangapa sa simula ng Martial Law." In Lumbera, Taguiwalo, Tolentino, Guillermo, and Alamon, *Serve the People*, 114–121.

Anderson, Benedict R. O'G. *Imagined Communities: Reflections on the Origin and Spread of Nationalism*. London: Verso, 1991.

Ang Bayan—Microfilm. University of California, Berkeley. Microfilm 77965.

Angel, Federico. "The Philippine Crisis." *Eastern Horizon* 10, no. 5 (1971): 58–61.

Anti-Imperialist Movement of the Philippines (AIM Philippines). [*Manifesto*], [1972]. PRP 01/24.02.

Aquino, Benigno S., Jr. *Black Friday, January 30*, 2 February 1970. PRP 01/28.01.

Aquino, Benigno S., Jr. *A Garrison State in the Make and Other Speeches*. N.p.: Benigno S. Aquino Jr. Foundation, 1985

Aquino, Benigno S., Jr. *When Law and Order Went Amok*, 27 January 1970. PRP 01/28.01.

Arcellana, Emerenciana Yuvienco. *The Life and Times of Claro M. Recto*. Pasay: Claro M. Recto Foundation, 1990.

Arts and Sciences Student Council. *Oppose Terrorist Bombings as a Prelude to the Imposition of Martial Law!!!*, 11 September 1972. PRP 17/44.05.

AS Rooftop Junta. *Manifesto for a New Order*, 7 February 1971. PRP 02/03.01.

Association of Concerned Teachers (ACT)—UP. *The Politics of Terror*, [1972]. PRP 02/04.01.

Atienza, Monico M. "Pangkalahatang Ulat sa 1969—Kabataang Makabayan sa Lahat ng Larangan." *AM*, 6 December 1969, 6–8.

August 23rd Movement. *Long Live the Anti-Imperialist United Front of Tarlac Citizens!*, 23 August 1971. PRP 02/11.01.

Baculinao, Ericson M. [*Letter to Students on Barricade Resolution*], 18 February 1971. PRP 18/02.18.

Baculinao, Ericson M., Jeunne Pagaduan, and Herminio B. Coloma. *Resolution Commending the Revolutionary Courage of the Heroic Defenders of the Diliman Commune against the Fascist State and Its Campus Collaborators, 13 February 1971.* PRP 18/02.36.

Baculinao, Ericson M., Jeunne Pagaduan, and Rey Vea. *"Barricades Are Fine": Resolution Endorsing the Barricades as a Form of Protest*, 13 February 1971. PRP 18/02.01.

Balagtas, Francisco. *See* Lava, Jose.

"Barikada, ayaw pa ring alisin." *Tinig ng Mamamayan*, no. 2 (10 February 1971). PRP 43/05.01.

Baron, Samuel H. *Plekhanov: The Father of Russian Marxism.* Stanford, CA: Stanford University Press, 1963.

Barros, Ma. Lorena. "Prison Visit." *PC*, 27 August 1970, 5.

Beams, Nick. *The Way Forward for the Philippine Revolution.* Sydney: Socialist Labour League, 1987.

Berlin, Donald L. *Before Gringo: History of the Philippine Military, 1830–1972.* Pasig: Anvil Publishing, 2008.

Bertrand Russell Peace Foundation (BRPF)—UP. *Parliamentary Struggle Is the Answer,* 10 September 1971. PRP 02/25.01 [authenticity disputed].

Bertrand Russell Peace Foundation (BRPF)—UP. *The Tyranny of the Vanguard Fraternity*, 24 September 1971. PRP 02/25.02.

Bertrand Russell Peace Foundation (BRPF)—UP. *UP Students! Expose, Oppose, and Isolate the Fascist Agents within Our Ranks!*, 13 September 1971. PRP 02/25.03.

Bonner, Raymond. *Waltzing with a Dictator: The Marcoses and the Making of American Policy.* New York: Vintage Books, 1987.

Calma, Trinidad P. "What Is Lansang (and His Likes) up To?" *APL*, 11 June 1971, 12, 14.

Cannon, James P. *Socialism on Trial.* New York: Pioneer Publishers, 1965.

Canoy, Reuben R. *The Counterfeit Revolution: Martial Law in the Philippines.* Manila: n.p., 1980.

Caouette, Dominique. "Persevering Revolutionaries: Armed Struggle in the 21st Century, Exploring the Revolution of the Communist Party of the Philippines." PhD diss., Cornell University, 2004.

Castañeda, Dabet. "Armed Struggle Still Relevant—CPP Founding Member." *Bulatlat*, 8 May 2006. https://www.bulatlat.com/2006/05/08/armed-struggle-still-relevant-%E2%80%93-cpp-founding-member/.

"A Chance for Greatness: The Manila Chronicle–Manila Times–Daily Mirror Pooled Editorial." *PFP*, 23 January 1971, 45.

Chapman, William. *Inside the Philippine Revolution.* New York: W.W. Norton, 1987.

Citizens Movement for the Protection of Our Democratic Rights (CMPDR). *An Open Letter*, 20 August 1971. PRP 03/10.01.

Civil Liberties Brigade UP Student Council. [*Untitled*], 23 September 1972. PRP 18/04.01.

Claudio, Lisandro. "Ninoy Networked with Everyone, Reds Included." *GMA News*, 18 August 2010. http://www.gmanetwork.com/news/story/198820/news/specialreports/ninoy-networked-with-.

College Editors Guild of the Philippines (CEGP). *Labanan Ang Pasismong EU-Marcos!!*, 13 September 1971. PRP 03/17.02.

Commission on the Churches' Participation in Development (CCPD), World Council of Churches, and Philippine Ecumenical Writing Group. *Moving Heaven and Earth: An Account of Filipinos Struggling to Change Their Lives and Society*. Manila: CCPD, 1982.

Committee on External Affairs Student Council of the Institute of Social Work and Community Development University of the Philippines (UP). *The Filipino People vs Marcos on the True State of the Nation*, 24 January 1972. PRP 17/50.01.

Communist Party of the Philippines (CPP). *Drowing: Tulong sa Pagtuturo*, n.d. PRP 06/25.01.

Communist Party of the Philippines (CPP). *Mga Kaukulang Probisyon sa Saligang Batas ng Partido Komunista ng Pilipinas*, n.d. PRP 04/02.02.

Communist Party of the Philippines (CPP). *Programa sa Demokratikong Rebolusyong Bayan sa Pilipinas*, 26 December 1968. PRP 04/02.13.

Communist Party of the Philippines (CPP). *Programme for a People's Democratic Revolution*, 26 December 1968. DSUMC.

Communist Party of the Philippines (CPP). *Report to the Central Committee on Lavaite Propaganda for Revisionism and Fascism*, November 1971.

Conde, David. "Students in the Philippines." *Eastern Horizon* 8, no. 2 (1969): 57–62.

Constantino, Renato. *The Making of a Filipino: A Story of Philippine Colonial Politics*. Quezon City: Malaya Books, 1971.

Convocation Sabotaged, 5 August 1971. PRP 20/15.01.

Corpus, Victor N. *Silent War*. Quezon City: VNC Enterprises, 1989.

Corpus, Victor N., and Crispin Tagamolila. *Expose the Criminal Hand of the Marcos Fascist Puppet Clique in the Kidnapping and Murder of Carlos B. del Rosario*, 22 May 1971. PRP 06/09.01.

Crisologo, D. R. "Florentina Sison: Mother to a Young Revolutionary." *GW*, 8 July 1970, 12–13, 43.

Curaming, Rommel A. *Power and Knowledge in Southeast Asia: State and Scholars in Indonesia and the Philippines*. London: Taylor & Francis, 2019.

Dalisay, Jose Y., and Josef T. Yap. *Lessons from the Nationalist Struggle: The Life of Emmanuel Quiason Yap*. Mandaluyong City: Anvil Publishing, 2016.

Damo-Santiago, Corazon. *A Century of Activism*. Manila: Rex Bookstore, 1972.

Daroy, Petronilo Bn. "Commune and Communards." *GW*, 10 March 1971, 8–10.

Davis, Leonard. *Revolutionary Struggle in the Philippines*. New York: Palgrave MacMillan, 1989.

Day, Richard B., and Daniel Gaido, eds. *Witnesses to Permanent Revolution: The Documentary Record*. Chicago: Haymarket Books, 2009.

De Guzman, Arnel. "UP after the 'Storm.'" In Llanes, *Tibak Rising*, 24–25.

De Guzman, Mila. *Women against Marcos*. San Francisco: Carayan Press, 2016.

de Manila, Quijano. *Language of the Street and Other Essays*. Metro Manila: National Book Store, 1980.

de Manila, Quijano. "Love Me, Love My War; or L'Amour among the Activists." In *Reportage on Lovers*, 92–102. Quezon City: National Bookstore, 1977.

de Manila, Quijano. "Why Did Ninoy Throw That Bomb?" *APL*, 7 May 1971, 11–13, 51–54.

de Quiros, Conrado. *Dead Aim: How Marcos Ambushed Philippine Democracy*. Pasig City: Foundation for Worldwide People's Power, 1997.

Debray, Régis. "A Reply." In *Regis Debray and the Latin American Revolution*, edited by Leo Huberman and Paul Sweezy, translated by Mary Klopper, 139–147. New York: Modern Reader, 1969.

Debray, Régis. *Revolution in the Revolution? Armed Struggle and Political Struggle in Latin America*. Translated by Bobbye Ortiz. New York: Grove Press, 1967.

Deception and Murder Is the Meaning of the Lavaite 'Theory of Physical Affinity' and 'Armed Struggle as Secondary Form,' 1971. PRP 12/13.01.

Del Rosario, Simeon G. *An Integrated Course on Communism and Democracy: A Self-Study Reader*. Quezon City: SGR Research & Publishing, 1973.

Del Rosario, Simeon G. *Surfacing the Underground: The Church and State Today*. Quezon City: Manlapaz, 1975.

Del Rosario, Simeon G. *Surfacing the Underground Part II, Volume One: The Involvements of Benigno S. Aquino, Jr., with 29 Perpetuated Testimonies Appended*. Quezon City: Manlapaz, 1977.

Del Rosario, Simeon G. *Surfacing the Underground Part II, Volume Two: The Involvements of Benigno S. Aquino, Jr., with 29 Perpetuated Testimonies Appended*. Quezon City: Manlapaz, 1977.

Delfin, Danilo. *An Open Letter from a Victim*, 1972. PRP 06/16.01.

Doeppers, Daniel F. *Feeding Manila in Peace and War, 1850–1945*. Madison: University of Wisconsin Press, 2016.

Enrile, Juan Ponce. "The Effect of the Suspension of Habeas Corpus on the Right to Bail in Cases of Rebellion, Insurrection and Sedition." *Philippine Law Journal* 27 (1952): 48–61.

Espiritu, Augusto Caesar. *How Democracy Was Lost: A Political Diary of the Constitutional Convention of 1971–1972*. Quezon City: New Day Publishers, 1993.

Espiritu, Talitha. *Passionate Revolutions: The Media and the Rise and Fall of the Marcos Regime*. Athens: Ohio University Press, 2017.

Estrada, Elnora, and Ruben C. Guevarra. "The Parting of Ways." *Weekly Nation*, 31 August 1970, 90.

Evangelista, Oscar L. *Icons and Institutions: Essays on the History of the University of the Philippines, 1952–2000*. Quezon City: University of the Philippines Press, 2008.

Faculty of the University of the Philippines (UP). *UP Faculty Protests Repression of Civil Liberties!*, 27 January 1970. PRP 17/13.01.

Fibiger, Mattias. "The Nixon Doctrine and the Making of Authoritarianism in Island Southeast Asia." *Diplomatic History* 45, no. 5 (2021): 954–982. https://doi.org/10.1093/dh/dhab065.

Firmeza, Ruth. *Gera*. Manila: Linang at Mainstream, People's Art, Literature, and Education Resource Center, 1991.

First Quarter Storm of 1970. Manila: Silangan Publishers, 1970.

Flieger, Wilhelm. "Internal Migration in the Philippines during the 1960s." *Philippine Quarterly of Culture and Society* 5, no. 4 (1977): 199–231.

Foreign Relations of the United States, various volumes. Washington, DC: US Government Printing Office, 1958–76.

fpnej&r. [*dear fellow student*], 1970. PRP 07/17.01.

Franco, Jennifer Conroy. *Elections and Democratization in the Philippines*. Comparative Studies in Democratization. New York: Routledge, 2001.

Free Nilo Tayag Movement. *Manifesto*, 1 September 1970. PRP 07/19.01.

Friends of the Philippines. *Makibaka, Join Us in Struggle!* London: Friends of the Philippines, 1978.

Fuller, Ken. *The Lost Vision: The Philippine Left, 1986–2010*. Quezon City: University of the Philippines Press, 2015.

Fuller, Ken. *A Movement Divided: Philippine Communism, 1957–1986*. Quezon City: University of the Philippines Press, 2011.

Garcia, E. Voltaire. *In Defense of Personal Liberty*, 1 September 1971. PRP 07/24.01.

Garcia, Ma. Socorro S. "Protest by Candlelight." *NOW*, September 1972, 36–38. PRP 44/36.01.

Garcia, Robert Francis. *To Suffer thy Comrades: How the Revolution Decimated Its Own*. Manila: Anvil Publishing, 2001.

Garten, Jeffrey E. *Three Days at Camp David: How a Secret Meeting in 1971 Transformed the Global Economy*. New York: HarperCollins, 2021.

Geronimo, Diego, Herbert Li, Alexander King, Lucio Calungcagin, Mario Santos, and Nicandro Falcis. *Declaration of Grave Concern*, 1972. PRP 07/25.01.

Gintong Silahis. *Barikada: Isang Makasaysayang Pagtatanghal*, 15 September 1971. PRP 17/14.01.

Giron, Eric S. "A Dialogue of Bullets, Tear Gas versus Stones, Bombs." *Mirror*, 20 February 1971.

Gleeck, Lewis E., Jr. *Dissolving the Colonial Bond: American Ambassadors to the Philippines, 1946–1984*. Quezon City: New Day Publishers, 1988.

Gleeck, Lewis E., Jr. *President Marcos and the Philippine Political Culture*. Manila: Loyal Printing, 1987.

Gomez, Maita. "Maria Lorena Barros: Gentle Warrior." In *Six Filipino Martyrs*, edited by Asuncion David Maramaba, 43–87. Pasig: Anvil Publishing, 1997.

Gonzales, Eduardo T. "A Chronicle of Protests." *Dare to Struggle, Dare to Win*, January 1971, 2–3. PRP 30/03.01.

Gordolan, Lourdes. "Butch Dalisay, Ricky Lee, and Other Writers Remember Prison Life in Martial Law Era." *Rogue*, April 2012.

Gregorio, Andres N. *See* Sison, Jose Ma.

Guerrero, Amado. *See* Sison, Jose Ma.

Guevarra, Ruben. *The Story behind the Plaza Miranda Bombing*. Quezon City: Katotohanan at Katarungan Foundation, 1998.

Hau, Caroline S. *The Chinese Question: Ethnicity, Nation, and Region in and beyond the Philippines*. Kyoto: Kyoto University Press, 2014.

Hendrix, Cullen S., and Stephan Haggard. "Global Food Prices, Regime Type, and Urban Unrest in the Developing World." *Journal of Peace Research* 52, no. 2 (2015): 143–157. https://doi.org/10.1177/0022343314561599.

Hernandez, Amado V. *Mga Ibong Mandaragit*. Quezon City: International Graphic Service, 1969.

Hilario, Antonio. *Hinggil sa Legal na Pakikibaka*, 4 January 1974. PRP 15/18.05.

Hughes, John. *The End of Sukarno: A Coup That Misfired, a Purge That Ran Wild*. Singapore: Archipelago, 2002.

Humanist League of the Philippines (HLP). *Asistio, et al.*, October 1971. PRP 07/37.01.

Humanist League of the Philippines (HLP). *Caloocan, October First*, 1 October 1971. PRP 07/37.02.

Humanist League of the Philippines (HLP). *Fascist Tactics by Government Troopers Again Led to the Arrest of 48 Activists within the National Liberation Ranks Last 17 September 1972*, September 1972. PRP 07/37.03.

Joaquin, Nick. *The Aquinos of Tarlac: An Essay on History as Three Generations*. Manila: Cacho Hermanos, 1983.

Joaquin, Nick. *A Kadre's Road to Damascus: The Ruben Torres Story*. Quezon City: Milflores, 2003.

Jones, Gregg. *Red Revolution: Inside the Philippine Guerrilla Movement*. Boulder, CO: Westview Press, 1989.

Kabataang Makabayan (KM). *Alay Kay Kasamang Arsenio Rienda*, 16 March 1972. PRP 08/13.01.

Kabataang Makabayan (KM). "And What Is Lacsina's Racket?" *APL*, 30 April 1971, 11, 50–51.

Kabataang Makabayan (KM). *Be Resolute! Unite and Oppose the Murder, Maiming and Mass Arrest of Fellow Students and Countrymen!*, 2 February 1970. PRP 08/13.03.

Kabataang Makabayan (KM). "Bombard the Headquarters of the Proven Renegades, Traitors and Scabs." *Kal*, 9 October 1970. PRP 32/01.03.

Kabataang Makabayan (KM). *Brief History of Kabataang Makabayan (1964–1972)*, 1 November 1984. PRP 08/15.01.

Kabataang Makabayan (KM). "Durugin ang himpilan ng mga napatunayang taksil, traydor at iskirol." *Kal* 6, no. 12 (December 1970): 4, 7, 9, 11.

Kabataang Makabayan (KM). *Fight Fascism: Join the February 12 Demonstration*, 12 February 1970. PRP 08/13.07.

Kabataang Makabayan (KM). *Ibunsod ang Malawakang Pakikibaka Laban sa Imperyalismong Amerikano, Katutubong Piyudalismo at Burokrata-Kapitalismo!*, 17 March 1970. PRP 08/13.10.

Kabataang Makabayan (KM). *Ipagpatuloy ang Pakikibaka Laban sa Imperyalismong Amerikano, Katutubong Piyudalismo at Pasismo!*, 3 March 1970. PRP 08/13.12.

Kabataang Makabayan (KM). *Labanan ang mga Tunay na Subersibo!*, 13 March 1972. PRP 08/13.19.

Kabataang Makabayan (KM). "Palisin ang Lahat ng Pesteng Maka-Lava!" *Kal* 7, no. 6 (23 July 1971). PRP 32/01.04 [Tagalog 32/03.03].

Kabataang Makabayan (KM). *Pasidhiin ang Pakikibaka Laban sa Pasistang Papet na Pamahalaan ni Marcos*, 14 February 1970. PRP 08/13.23.

Kabataang Makabayan (KM). *Resist the Fascist Suppression*, 1 December 1970. PRP 08/13.26.

Kabataang Makabayan (KM). "Strip the Handful of Reactionaries of Their Revolutionary Pretensions." *Kal*, 24 July 1970. PRP 32/01.02.

Kabataang Makabayan (KM). *Ang Suliranin ng Langis sa Pilipinas*, [1972]. PRP 08/13.32.

Kabataang Makabayan (KM). *Uphold People's Democratic Rights, Fight the Fascistic State*, 7 January 1970. PRP 08/19.18.

Kabataang Makabayan (KM), Samahang Demokratiko ng Kabataan (SDK), Sandigang Makabansa (SM), Student Cultural Association of the University of the Philippines (SCAUP), Progresibong Samahan sa Inhinyeriya at Agham (PSIA), Nationalist Businessmen's Association (NBA), and Samahan ng Progresibong Propagandista (SPP). *Sasalakayin ang Pamantasan ng Pilipinas!!!*, 24 August 1971. PRP 08/19.14.

Kabataang Makabayan (KM)—PCC. *Pumupula ang Landas ng Pakikibaka*, December 1970. PRP 08/13.24.

Kabataang Makabayan (KM)—UP. *Bakit Namatay si Francis Sontillano?*, December 1970. PRP 08/19.01.

Kabataang Makabayan (KM)—UP. *Sharpen Vigilance against Persistent Fifth Column Tactics of Reactionary Die-Hards!!*, 17 August 1971. PRP 08/19.16.

Kabataang Makabayan (KM)—UP. *Terrorist Bombings—Prelude to Martial Law*, 11 September 1972. PRP 08/19.17.

Kaisahan ng mga Makabayang Manggagawa sa Pamahalaan (KAMMAPA). [*Leaflet on Suspension of the Writ of Habeas Corpus*], 1971. PRP 08/22.02.

Kalayaan. [*UP Election Platform*], 1970. PRP 08/24.01.

Kapit Bisig—UP. *UPGA Prison*, 1972. PRP 08/30.01.

Kapulungan ng mga Sandigan ng Pilipinas (KASAPI). *Bukas na Liham sa mga Kawal ng Gobyerno*, [January 1971]. PRP 08/32.01.

Katipunan ng mga Samahan ng mga Manggagawa (KASAMA). *Unang Pambansang Kongreso*, 27 February 1972. PRP 09/10.02.

Kilusang Kristiyano ng Kabataang Pilipino (KKKP). *July 4th Message to Filipino Christians*, 4 July 1971. PRP 17/09.01.

Kintanar, Galileo C., and Pacifico V. Militante. *Lost in Time: From Birth to Obsolescence, the Communist Party of the Philippines, Book One: 1930–1972*. Quezon City: Truth / Justice Foundation, 1999.

Konsehong Tagapag-Ugnay ng Rebolusyonaryong Sining (KONTRES). "Ibagsak ang Diktadurang EU-Marcos upang Makamit ang Pambansang Kalayaan at Demokrasya." *Kontres* 1, no. 4 (November 1972). PRP 33/15.03.

Kung, Chien-Wen. *Diasporic Cold Warriors: Nationalist China, Anticommunism, and the Philippine Chinese, 1930s–1970s*. Ithaca, NY: Cornell University Press, 2022.

Lacaba, Jose F. *Days of Disquiet, Nights of Rage: The First Quarter Storm & Related Events*. Pasig: Anvil Publishing, 2003.

Lachica, Eduardo. *The Huks: Philippine Agrarian Society in Revolt*. Quezon City: Solidaridad Publishing House, 1971.

Lacsina, Ignacio P. "The View from the Left: What Is the KM's Game?" *APL*, 30 April 1971, 10, 44.

Lansang, Teodosio A. "Lansang Is (and His Likes Are) out to Unmask Poseurs." *APL*, 2 July 1971, 12, 47.

Lansang, Teodosio A. "One More View from the Left." *APL*, 14 May 1971.

Larkin, John A. *Sugar and the Origins of Modern Philippine Society.* Berkeley: University of California Press, 1993.

Lava, Jesus. *Memoirs of a Communist.* Pasig: Anvil Publishing, 2002.

Lava, Jesus. *Paglilinaw sa "Philippine Crisis,"* 1970. PRP 09/36.01.

Lava, Jose [Francisco Balagtas, pseud.]. "The Philippines at the Crossroads." *World Marxist Review* 14, no. 11 (1971): 40–43.

Leaders Denounce Nov. 11 Terrorism, 19 November 1969. PRP 37/18.01.

Lenin, V. I. *Collected Works.* 45 vols. Moscow: Progress Publishers, 1972–76.

Lenin, V. I. "Two Tactics of Social-Democracy in the Democratic Revolution." In *Collected Works,* 9:15–140.

Lin Biao. *Long Live the Victory of People's War!* Peking: Foreign Languages Press, 1967.

Llanes, Ferdinand C., ed. *Tibak Rising: Activism in the Days of Martial Law.* Mandaluyong: Anvil Publishing, 2012.

Lopez, Antonio. "Running Revolution: The Life and Times of the Philippines Most Formidable Guerrilla Chief." *Asiaweek,* 9 March 1994, 28–41.

Lopez, Salvador. *Press Statement,* February 1971. PRP 10/12.04.

Lopez, Ted O. "A Bridge from the Past: From CLO to FQS." In Llanes, *Tibak Rising,* 8–11.

Lumbera, Bienvenido, Judy M. Taguiwalo, Rolando B. Tolentino, Ramon G. Guillermo, and Arnold Alamon, eds. *Serve the People: Ang Kasaysayan ng Radikal na Kilusan sa Unibersidad ng Pilipinas.* Quezon City: Ibon Books, 2008.

Macapagal, Felicisimo C. *To Comrade Nicolae Ceaușescu,* 9 April 1975. PRP 10/16.02.

Makabayang Kilusan ng Bagong Kababaihan (MAKIBAKA). *Labanan at Ibagsak ang Imperyalismong Amerikano, Makibaka para sa Pambansang Kalayaan!,* 7 June 1972. PRP 10/21.01.

Malay, Armando J. "The UP Barricades: In Retrospect." *We Forum,* 22 September–17 November 1982.

Malayang Pagkakaisa ng Kabataang Pilipino (MPKP). *For a People's Constitution,* 30 January 1970. PRP 10/29.04.

Malayang Pagkakaisa ng Kabataang Pilipino (MPKP). *Ibayong Katatagan Laban sa Ibayong Karahasan!,* 6 September 1971. PRP 10/29.05.

Malayang Pagkakaisa ng Kabataang Pilipino (MPKP). *Kabakahin ang Pasismo, Ipagpatuloy ang Pakikibaka Laban sa mga Monopolyong Kompanya ng Langis, at Isulong ang Pakikipaglaban sa Imperyalismo,* 3 February 1971. PRP 13/28.01.

Malayang Pagkakaisa ng Kabataang Pilipino (MPKP). *The Neocolonial System and the "Purely Anti-Marcos Line,"* 18 February 1970. PRP 10/29.09.

Malayang Pagkakaisa ng Kabataang Pilipino (MPKP). *On the Correct View of the Campus Elections,* [1970]. PRP 10/29.12.

Malayang Pagkakaisa ng Kabataang Pilipino (MPKP). *Oppose Militarization of the UP Campus,* 2 February 1971. PRP 10/31.04.

Malayang Pagkakaisa ng Kabataang Pilipino (MPKP). *Paghihirap ng Bayan at ang Imperyalismo,* 17 March 1970. PRP 10/29.13.

Malayang Pagkakaisa ng Kabataang Pilipino (MPKP). "Ang Pambasang Demokratikong Pakikibaka at ang Taksil na Kabataang Makabayan." *Kilusan* 3, no. 4 (1970): 7–8, 13–14, 19.

Malayang Pagkakaisa ng Kabataang Pilipino (MPKP). *The People's Congress and the National Democratic Struggle*, 18 February 1970. PRP 10/29.15.

Malayang Pagkakaisa ng Kabataang Pilipino (MPKP). *People's Violence against State Violence*, 3 March 1970. PRP 10/29.16.

Malayang Pagkakaisa ng Kabataang Pilipino (MPKP). *Philippine Judiciary Is an Inseparable Part of the Neocolonial System*, 1 March 1970. PRP 10/29.17.

Malayang Pagkakaisa ng Kabataang Pilipino (MPKP). *Police Riots Again!*, 27 January 1970. PRP 10/29.18.

Malayang Pagkakaisa ng Kabataang Pilipino (MPKP). *The Sad State of the Nation*, 26 January 1970. PRP 10/29.19.

Malayang Pagkakaisa ng Kabataang Pilipino (MPKP). *Will the Parrots of Peking Also Change Their Tune?*, 9 August 1971. PRP 10/29.21.

Malayang Pagkakaisa ng Kabataang Pilipino (MPKP) and Bertrand Russell Peace Foundation (BRPF). *Itakwil ang Panloloko—Huwag Bumoto!*, November 1971. PRP 10/29.07.

Malayang Pagkakaisa ng Kabataang Pilipino (MPKP), Malayang Samahan ng Magsasaka (MASAKA), Pambansang Kilusan ng Paggawa (KILUSAN), Ang Kapatiran sa Ika-Uunlad Natin (AKSIUN), Bertrand Russell Peace Foundation (BRPF), and Samahang Progresibo ng Kababaihang Pilipino (SPKP). *US Imperialist Schemes in the Present Crisis*, 23 January 1971. PRP 11/01.09.

Malayang Pagkakaisa ng Kabataang Pilipino (MPKP)—UP. *On the KM-SDK "Occupation" of UP*, 10 February 1971. PRP 10/31.03.

Malayang Pagkakaisa ng Kabataang Pilipino (MPKP)—UP. *"Strengthen Revolutionary Unity and Combat Maoist Counter-Revolution!" Siklab*, January 1972. PRP 42/06.02.

Malayang Pagkakaisa ng Kabataang Pilipino (MPKP)—UP. *Who Are Using Fascist Tactics to Justify the Fascist Programme of Mr. Marcos?*, 11 July 1972. PRP 10/31.07.

Malayang Pagkakaisa ng mga Samahan ng Tsuper (MAPAGSAT) and Glicerio G. Gervero. *[Open Letter]*, 1971. PRP 07/26.01.

Malayang Samahan ng Magsasaka (MASAKA). *Alintuntunin at Saligang-Batas ng Malayang Samahang Magsasaka (MASAKA)*, 7 November 1964.

Manapat, Ricardo. *Some Are Smarter than Others: The History of Marcos' Crony Capitalism*. New York: Aletheia Publications, 1991.

Mao Zedong. *Selected Works of Mao Tse-Tung*. 5 vols. Peking: Foreign Languages Press, 1975.

Marcos, Ferdinand E. *Today's Revolution: Democracy*. n.p.: n.p., 1971.

Marighella, Carlos. "Minimanual of the Urban Guerrilla," 1969. https://www.marxists.org/archive/marighella-carlos/1969/06/minimanual-urban-guerrilla/.

Martinez, Manuel Festin. *More Assassinations & Conspiracies*. Pasig: Anvil Publishing, 2004.

Marx, Karl, and Frederick Engels. *Marx–Engels Collected Works*. 50 vols. Moscow: Progress Publishers, 1975–89.

McCoy, Alfred W. *Closer Than Brothers: Manhood at the Philippine Military Academy*. Manila: Anvil Publishing, 1999.

McCoy, Alfred W. *Policing America's Empire: The United States, the Philippines, and the Rise of the Surveillance State.* Quezon City: Ateneo de Manila University Press, 2011.

McFarland, Linda. *Cold War Strategist: Stuart Symington and the Search for National Security.* Westport, CT: Praeger, 2001.

Melencio, Cesar. *Full Quarter Storms: Memoirs and Writings on the Philippine Left (1970–2010).* Quezon City: Transform Asia, 2010.

Members of the Faculty University of the Philippines (UP) Tarlac. *A Message to President Marcos,* 26 August 1971. PRP 18/08.01.

Miclat, Mario. *Secrets of the Eighteen Mansions: A Novel.* Pasig: Anvil Publishing, 2010.

Mijares, Primitivo. *The Conjugal Dictatorship of Ferdinand and Imelda Marcos.* San Francisco: Union Square Publications, 1976.

Mojares, Resil B. "Letter from Cebu." *APL,* 2 July 1971, 15–16.

Movement for a Democratic Philippines (MDP). *Baha at Hirap: Dulot ng Rehimeng US-Marcos!,* 1972. PRP 11/18.01.

Movement for a Democratic Philippines (MDP). *Crush the Warlord-Bureaucrat Asistio, Fascist Puppet of the US-Marcos Regime!!,* 12 October 1971. PRP 11/18.03.

Movement for a Democratic Philippines (MDP). *Magkaisa at Makibaka para sa Pambansang Demokrasya,* 17 March 1970. PRP 11/18.10.

Movement for a Democratic Philippines (MDP). *Manifesto,* 11 April 1970. PRP 11/19.01.

Movement for a Democratic Philippines (MDP). *Manifesto of the Movement for a Democratic Philippines,* 11 December 1969. PRP 11/18.12.

Movement for a Democratic Philippines (MDP). *Pagibayuhin ang Pakikibaka Tungo sa Pambansang Demokrasya!,* 2 March 1970. PRP 11/18.15.

Movement for a Democratic Philippines (MDP). *Pag-isahin ang Sambayanan at Gapiin ang Diktadurang EU-Marcos,* 19 September 1972. PRP 11/18.16.

Movement for a Democratic Philippines (MDP). *Press Statement,* 17 January 1972. PRP 11/18.13.

Movement for a Democratic Philippines (MDP). *Suporta ng MDP sa MCCCL: Tungo sa Isang Malawak na Nagkakaisang Hanay Laban sa Teroristang Sabwatan Ng Rehimeng Estados Unidos-Marcos,* August 1971. PRP 11/18.24.

Movement for a Democratic Philippines (MDP). *The True State of the Nation,* 25 January 1971. PRP 11/18.21.

Movement for a Democratic Philippines (MDP). *Ang Tunay na Kalagayan ng Bansa,* 25 January 1971. PRP 11/18.23.

Movement for a Democratic Philippines (MDP). *Wakasan ang Pagdarahop at Pasismo, Ibukod at Durugin ang mga Kaaway ng Bayan, Magkaisa at Makibaka Para sa Pambansang Demokrasya!,* 20 October 1971. PRP 11/18.26.

Movement for a Democratic Philippines (MDP) and Nagkakaisang Progresibong Artista-Arkitekto (NPAA). *Ang Bayan at ang Baha,* August 1972. PRP 11/18.02.

Movement for Democratic Reforms. *Reform the University,* 24 February 1972. PRP 11/18.18.

Movement for the Advancement of Nationalism (MAN). *M.A.N's Goal: The Democratic Filipino Society.* [Manila]: Malaya Books, 1969.

Movement for the Retention of the University of the Philippines at Tarlac. "Matatag na Ipagtanggol ang Ating Baseng Pangkultura!" *Ilaw ng Masa* 1, no. 2 (12 February 1972). PRP 31/01.01.

Movement of Concerned Citizens for Civil Liberties (MCCCL). *People's Demands*, September 1971. PRP 11/26.03.

Movement of Concerned Citizens for Civil Liberties (MCCCL). *Laban sa Paniniil at Militarismo*, 3 December 1971. PRP 11/26.02.

Nagkakaisang Mamayan ng Pilipinas Laban sa Taksil at Pasistang Pangkating Estados Unidos-Marcos. *The Defeat of the US-Marcos Clique Is the Victory of the Filipino People*, 1972. PRP 12/01.01.

National Democratic Front (NDF). "The Cultural Revolution Gains New Heights as the US-Marcos Dictatorship Is Encircled from the Countrysides." *Liberation* 1, no. 2 (19 October 1972). PRP 34/01.01.

National Democratic Front (NDF). "Oppose the Con-Con Plot to Legalize Dictatorship." *Liberation* 1, no. 4 (7 November 1972). PRP 34/01.03.

National Democratic Front (NDF). "Reject the Marcos Constitution." *Liberation* 1, no. 7 (7 December 1972). PRP 34/01.05.

National Democratic Front (NDF). "'Vote No' Movement Snowballs." *Liberation* 1, no. 8 (15 December 1972). PRP 34/01.06.

Nationalist Businessmen's Association (NBA). "Ilantad ang Sabwatang Asistio at Kumintang na Intsik!" *Ang Kalakal*, 8 October 1971. PRP 31/07.01.

Nationalist Businessmen's Association (NBA). "Ipaglaban ang Pambansang Industrialisasyon!" *Ang Kalakal*, 19 October 1971. PRP 31/07.02.

Navarro, Nelson A. *Doc Prudente: Nationalist Educator*. Mandaluyong City: Anvil Publishing, 2011.

Navarro, Nelson A. *The Half-Remembered Past: A Memoir*. Quezon City: Alphan Publishers, 2013.

Nemenzo, Francisco, Jr. "Rectification Process in the Philippine Communist Movement." In *Armed Communist Movements in Southeast Asia*, edited by Lim Joo-Jock, 71–105. Singapore: Institute of Southeast Asian Studies, 1984.

New People's Army (NPA). *Expose and Oppose the Vicious Crimes of the Monkees-Armeng Bayan-MASAKA (Lava) Gang*, May 1970. PRP 11/15.01.

North, David. *The Heritage We Defend: A Contribution to the History of the Fourth International*. Detroit, MI: Labor Publications, 1988.

North, David. "Introduction." In Trotsky, *Revolution Betrayed*, ix–lv.

"NUSP Leadership Censured." *The Partisan* [counterfeit issue], 30 January 1970. PRP 37/18.02.

Ocampo, Satur. *Tala-Gabay sa Pagtalakay ng*. Ang Alternative Press sa Panahon ng Batas Militar, 10 October 2014.

Olivar, Gary. "An Open Letter to the Congregation." *The Herald* 1, no. 1 (January 1972). PRP 30/19.01.

On the July 4 Ambuscade: Weed Out the Agents of Fascism and Reaction Hiding behind the Mask of Revolutionism!, 1972. PRP 14/22.02.

Painter, David S. "Oil and Geopolitics: The Oil Crises of the 1970s and the Cold War." *Historical Social Research / Historiche Sozialforschung* 39, no. 4 (2014): 186–208.

The Palanan Incident, 1972. PRP 13/08.01.

Palatino, Mong. "Pagbabalik-tanaw sa Diliman Commune." In Lumbera, Taguiwalo, Tolentino, Guillermo, and Alamon, *Serve the People,* 103–105.

Pambansang Kilusan ng Paggawa (KILUSAN), Malayang Samahan ng Magsasaka (MASAKA), Malayang Pagkakaisa ng Kabataang Pilipino (MPKP), Bertrand Russell Peace Foundation (BRPF), and Samahang Progresibo ng Kababaihang Pilipino (SPKP). *Ang mga Pakana ng Imperyalismong Amerikano sa Kasalukuyang Krisis,* 23 January 1971.

Panulat para sa Kaunlaran ng Sambayan (PAKSA). *Mga Katanungan ng Bayan,* 18 September 1972. PRP 13/17.03.

Partido Komunista ng Pilipinas (PKP). "China under Mao: On the Road to Capitalist Integration." *AK* 3 (April 1972). PRP 33/13.05.

Partido Komunista ng Pilipinas (PKP). "Ideological Dispute between Maoism and the International Communist Movement." In "Issues in the Ideological Dispute between Maoism and the International Communist Movement," special issue. *AK* 3, no. 1 (January 1972). PRP 33/13.03.

Partido Komunista ng Pilipinas (PKP). "The Moscow Summit: A Victory for Peace and Socialist Foreign Policy." *AK* 4, no. 4 (June 1972). PRP 33/13.07.

Partido Komunista ng Pilipinas (PKP). "Nixon-Mao Collusion against the International Communist Movement." *AK,* 27 March 1972. PRP 33/13.04.

Partido Komunista ng Pilipinas (PKP). "The Party's Struggle against Ultra-'leftism' under Martial Law." *Ang Buklod,* no. 1 (1973): 21–30. PRP 29/08.01.

Partido Komunista ng Pilipinas (PKP). "The Philippines: What Is behind Dictatorship?" *Comment: Communist Fortnightly Review* 10, no. 26 (1972): 409–411.

Partido Komunista ng Pilipinas (PKP). *Political Resolution, 6th Congress,* February 1973. PRP 04/02.11.

Partido Komunista ng Pilipinas (PKP). *Program of the Partido Komunista ng Pilipinas (PKP), 6th Congress,* 11 February 1973. PRP 04/02.12.

Partido Komunista ng Pilipinas (PKP). *Ang Saligang Batas ng Partido Komunista ng Pilipinas,* 12 February 1973. PRP 04/02.16.

Partido Komunista ng Pilipinas (PKP). *The Significance of the State Visit of President Ceauşescu,* April 1975. PRP 03/03.01.

Pedrosa, Carmen Navarro. *Imelda Marcos.* New York: St. Martin's Press, 1987.

Pedrosa, Carmen Navarro. *Imelda Romualdez Marcos: The Verdict.* Ukraine: Flipside Digital Content, 2017.

Peña, Rolando. "*Liberation*: Early Days." In Llanes, *Tibak Rising,* 186–190.

Pi Omicron. *Palayain si Nilo Tayag!,* 18 June 1970. PRP 13/35.01.

Pimentel, Benjamin. *Rebolusyon! A Generation of Struggle in the Philippines.* New York: Monthly Review Press, 1991.

Pinpin, F.D., ed. *Proclamation No. 1081 and Related Documents, Volumes 1 to 4.* Mandaluyong: Cacho Hermanos, 1972.

The Polemic on the General Line of the International Communist Movement. Peking: Foreign Languages Press, 1965.

Pomeroy, William J. *Bilanggo: Life as a Political Prisoner in the Philippines, 1952–1962.* Quezon City: University of the Philippines Press, 2009.

Pomeroy, William J. "Negotiation as a Form of Struggle: The PKP Experience." *Debate: Philippine Left Review,* no. 6 (1993): 61–76.

Progresibong Kabataan ng MLQU. *Nasa Atin ang Tagumpay,* 17 September 1969. PRP 14/15.01.

Puno, Ramon V. *The Suppression of Individual Rights and the Right to Dissent: The Emerging Fascism of the Baculinao-Sta. Romana Clique,* 13 December 1970. PRP 14/24.02.

Putzel, James. *A Captive Land: The Politics of Agrarian Reform in the Philippines.* New York: Monthly Review Press, 1992.

"Quezon City–U.P. Police Cooperation." *University of the Philippines (UP) Gazette,* 28 February 1971, 20–21.

Quimpo, Susan F., and Nathan Gilbert Quimpo. *Subversive Lives: A Family Memoir of the Marcos Years.* Pasig: Anvil Publishing, 2012.

Rabinowitch, Alexander. *The Bolsheviks Come to Power: The Revolution of 1917 in Petrograd.* Chicago: Haymarket Books, 2004.

Rabinowitch, Alexander. *The Bolsheviks in Power: The First Year of Soviet Rule in Petrograd.* Bloomington: Indiana University Press, 2007.

Rama, Napoleon. "Will There Be Martial Law?" *PFP,* 30 January 1971.

Ramos, Elias T. "Labor Conflict and Recent Trends in Philippine Industrial Relations." *Philippine Quarterly of Culture and Society* 15, no. 3 (1987): 173–197.

Recto, Claro M. *Political and Legal Works, 1954–1955.* Vol. 8 of *The Complete Works of Claro M. Recto,* edited by Isagani R Medina and Myrna S. Feliciano. Pasay: Claro M. Recto Foundation, 1990.

Recto, Claro M. *Political and Legal Works, 1959–1960.* Vol. 9 of *The Complete Works of Claro M. Recto,* edited by Isagani R. Medina and Myrna S. Feliciano. Pasay: Claro M. Recto Foundation, 1990.

Rempel, William C. *Delusions of a Dictator: The Mind of Marcos as Revealed in His Secret Diaries.* Boston: Little, Brown, 1993.

Report of the Committee of Inquiry on the Events and Occurrences at the Diliman Commune from February 1 to 9, 1971, [Quezon City]: [University of the Philippines, Diliman], 1971.

Reyes, Liwayway T. *Memorandum to the Movement for a Democratic Philippines and Its Allied Organizations: Facts That Should Be Known by the Leaders and Organizations of the National Democratic Movement,* 18 May 1971. JHP, box 92, folder 12.

Reyes, Liwayway T. "Memorandum to the Movement for a Democratic Philippines and Its Allied Organizations: Facts That Should Be Known by the Leaders and Organizations of the National Democratic Movement." *PC,* 6 July 1971, 6.

Reyes, Ronaldo. [*Memorandum*], 8 February 1971. PRP 15/05.01.

Riddell, John, ed. *Toward the United Front: Proceedings of the Fourth Congress of the Communist International, 1922.* Leiden: Brill, 2012.

Rivera, Jess, and National Association of Trade Unions (NATU). *Mag-ingat sa mga Itimang Propagandista ng mga Laban sa Paggawa,* n.d. PRP 15/06.01.

Roces, Alejandro R. *A Stupid TV Ad,* 15 October 1971. PRP 15/07.01.

Roces, Mina. *Kinship Politics in the Postwar Philippines: The Lopez Family, 1946–2000.* Quezon City: De La Salle University Press, 2001.

Rodrigo, Raul. *Kapitan: Geny Lopez and the Making of ABS-CBN.* Quezon City: ABS-CBN Publishing, 2006.

Rodrigo, Raul. *Phoenix: The Saga of the Lopez Family,* Vol. 1, *1800–1972.* Manila: Eugenio López Foundation, 2000.

Rodrigo, Raul. *The Power and the Glory: The Story of the Manila Chronicle, 1945–1998.* Pasig: Eugenio Lopez Foundation, 2007.

Rodriguez, Filemon. *The Marcos Regime: Rape of the Nation.* New York: Vantage Press, 1985.

Rogovin, Vadim Z. *Stalin's Terror of 1937–1938: Political Genocide in the USSR.* Translated by Frederick S. Choate. Oak Park, MI: Mehring Books, 2009.

Rogovin, Vadim Z. *Was There an Alternative? 1923–1927: Trotskyism: A Look Back through the Years.* Translated by Frederick S. Choate. Oak Park, MI: Mehring Books, 2021.

Rojas, Rodrigo. *See* Tera Jr., Perfecto.

Ronquillo, Bernardino. "The Guerilla Mystery." *Far Eastern Economic Review,* 16 September 1972, 25.

Rosca, Ninotchka. "Anatomy of a Strike." *GW,* 23 July 1969, 6–8.

Rosca, Ninotchka. Introduction to *Jose Maria Sison: At Home in the World—Portrait of a Revolutionary,* by Jose Ma Sison and Ninotchka Rosca, 1–35. Manila: Ibon Books, 2004.

Rosca, Ninotchka. "View from the Left: Word War I." *APL,* 16 April 1971, 10–11, 44–45.

Rosca, Ninotchka. "Word War II: Lava versus Guerrero." *APL,* 23 April 1971, 12, 42, 44–45.

Rotea, Hermie. *I Saw Them Aim and Fire.* Manila: Daily News, 1970.

Rotea, Hermie. *Marcos' Lovey Dovie.* Los Angeles: Liberty Publishing, 1984.

Rothwell, Matthew D. *Transpacific Revolutionaries: The Chinese Revolution in Latin America.* London: Routledge, 2013.

Roy, R. "The Battle for Bretton Woods: America, Britain and the International Financial Crisis of October 1967–March 1968." *Cold War History* 2, no. 2 (2002): 33–60.

Ruaya, Joselito. *Operasyon tulong, Patuloy,* August 1972. PRP 42/01.05.

Salonga, Jovito R. *A Journey of Struggle and Hope.* Quezon City: UP Center for Leadership, Citizenship, and Democracy, 2001.

Salonga, Jovito R. *The Lives and Times of Gerry Roxas and Ninoy Aquino.* Mandaluyong City: Regina Publishing, 2010.

Samahan ng Demokratikong Kabataan (SDK). *Free Nilo Tayag!,* 16 June 1970. PRP 15/22.02.

Samahan ng Demokratikong Kabataan (SDK). [*Letter to the Editor*], 13 September 1970. PRP 15/18.12.

Samahan ng Kababaihan ng UP (SKUP). [*Untitled*], [18 September 1972]. PRP 15/27.03.

Samahan ng Kababaihan ng UP (SKUP) and Bagong Pilipina. *We Must Not Forget Our Heroes,* 8 December 1970. PRP 15/27.05.

Samahan ng Makabayang Siyentipiko (SMS). *Devastating Floods and Calamities: By-product of a Semi-feudal, Semi-colonial Society,* 18 August 1972. PRP 36/02.05.

Samahan ng Makabayang Siyentipiko (SMS). *Support the Strike and Oppose Campus Fascism*, 2 February 1971. PRP 15/32.03.

Samahan ng mga Guro sa Pamantasan (SAGUPA). *Vigorously Oppose Military Rule!*, 18 September 1972. PRP 15/31.08.

Samahan ng mga Guro sa Pamantasan (SAGUPA), Katipunan ng mga Gurong Makabayan (KAGUMA), Malayang Kapulungan ng Makabayang Samahan (MAKAMASA), and Makabayang Kilusan ng mga Mag-aaral sa Sining at Agham (MAKIMASA). *Fearlessly Expose the Facts about the Fascist-Marcos US-Imperialist Plot of Counter-Revolution*, 26 August 1971. PRP 15/30.01.

Samahan ng mga Makabayang Siyentipiko (SMS). "The Recent Price Increase Petitions of the Oil Companies in the Philippines." *Ang Makabayang Siyentipiko*, 1 August 1972, 2–17. PRP 36/02.03.

Samahan ng Progresibong Propagandista (SPP). [*Hinggil sa kamatayan ni Francis Sontillano*], 7 December 1970. PRP 15/36.01.

Samahan ng Progresibong Propagandista (SPP). "On the Serious Manhandling of Several Members of the Samahan ng Progresibong Propagandista (SPP) by the Vanguard-SDS Fascist Thugs." *Alab*, 27 September 1971. PRP 19/05.03.

Samahang Demokratiko ng Kabataan (SDK). *Avenge the Death of Sontillano!!! Crush Fascism!!!*, December 1970. PRP 15/22.01.

Samahang Demokratiko ng Kabataan (SDK). *Expose and Oppose the US-Marcos Scheme to Militarize the Country*, 19 September 1972. PRP 36/06.05.

Samahang Demokratiko ng Kabataan (SDK). *Expose the Lazaro-Gervero Gang*, 1971. PRP 15/18.04.

Samahang Demokratiko ng Kabataan (SDK). *Ika-4 ng Pebrero, 1971*, 4 February 1971. PRP 15/18.15.

Samahang Demokratiko ng Kabataan (SDK). "Ilantad at Durugin ang mga Huwad na Lider Obrero." *Talang Ginto*, 1971. PRP 43/01.01.

Samahang Demokratiko ng Kabataan (SDK). "On the Merger Question." In Santos and Santos, *SDK: Militant but Groovy*, 159–176.

Samahang Demokratiko ng Kabataan (SDK). "On the Style of Work of Malacañang's Most Loyal Agent in Vinzons." *The Partisan*, 30 September 1971. PRP 37/17.03.

Samahang Demokratiko ng Kabataan (SDK). "Paggunita sa Mayo Uno." *BP*, 1 May 1972. PRP 22/02.

Samahang Demokratiko ng Kabataan (SDK). *Sa mga kasamang tsuper mag-aaral at mamamayan*, 1 February 1971. PRP 15/18.13.

Samahang Demokratiko ng Kabataan (SDK). *Statement of the Samahang Demokratiko ng Kabataan*, 1 February 1971. PRP 15/18.22.

Samahang Demokratiko ng Kabataan (SDK). *Tuluyang Itakwil ang Mga Napatunayang Ahente sa Campus at Mapangahas na Ibandila ang Watawat ng Pambansang Demokrasya*, 2 August 1971. PRP 15/22.11.

Samahang Demokratiko ng Kabataan (SDK) and Rey Vea. [*Letter regarding the arrest of Gary Olivar*], November 1971. PRP 15/21.01.

Samahang Demokratiko ng Kabataan (SDK)—UP. "Crush the US-Marcos Fascist Bunch and Their Campus Marionettes!" *BP* 1, no. 2 (17 November 1972). PRP 22/03.

Samahang Demokratiko ng Kabataan UPCA Cultural Society (SDK-UPCACS). *Bombard the Headquarters of Fascist School Administrators*, 2 December 1970. PRP 15/23.02.

Samahang Demokratiko ng Kabataan UPCA Cultural Society (SDK-UPCACS). *Crush Puppet Umali's Reactionary Ploy! On with the Struggle for National Democracy!*, 5 January 1971. PRP 15/23.03.

Samahang Demokratiko ng Kabataan UPCA Cultural Society (SDK-UPCACS). *Smash Fascism in UP Los Baños*, 4 December 1970. PRP 15/23.04.

Samonte, Mauro Gia. "In the Eye of the Storm," 2014. http://maoblooms.blogspot .com/2014/02/normal-0-false-false-false-en-.

Sandigang Makabansa (SM). *All Lies and Intrigues of Reactionaries Fail in the Face of Reality!! Trust the Masses!! Onward with the National Democratic Struggle!!*, 9 August 1971. PRP 16/10.01.

Sandigang Makabansa (SM). "The Anti-Fascist United Front." *Ang Sandigan*, 13 September 1971. PRP 40/07.01.

Sandigang Makabansa (SM). *From Sandigang Makabansa: A Summing-Up of the Campaign, a Final Word of Warning!*, 5 August 1971. PRP 16/10.07.

Sandigang Makabansa (SM). *Ituloy ang Boykoteo*, 28 February 1972. PRP 36/01.02.

Sandigang Makabansa (SM). "Ang Maghimagsik ay Makatarungan." *Ang Sandigang Makabansa*, 25 January 1971. PRP 40/08.01.

Sandigang Makabansa (SM). *Militantly Oppose Fascist Suppression*, 30 August 1971. PRP 16/10.16.

Sandigang Makabansa (SM). *Party Platform of Sandigang Makabansa for 1970–71*. 1970. PRP 16/10.13.

Sandigang Makabansa (SM). *The Situation Is Critical—What Is to Be Done?*, 19 September 1972. PRP 16/10.18.

Sandigang Makabansa (SM). *Statement of Sandigang Makabansa*, 23 August 1971. PRP 16/10.19.

Sandigang Makabansa (SM). *Who Is the Clever Culprit?*, 9 August 1971. PRP 16/10.20.

Sanggunian ng Mag-aaral ng UPCA. "Nabigong Pagsalakay." *Sanggunian* 1, no. 1 (7 January 1971). PRP 40/09.01.

Sangguniang Mag-aaral ng Sining at Agham. *Durugin ang Pasismo ng mga Mapang-Aping Paaralan!!!*, 6 December 1970. PRP 17/44.02.

Santos, Soliman M., and Paz Verdades M. Santos, eds. *SDK: Militant but Groovy: Stories of Samahang Demokratiko ng Kabataan*. Manila: Anvil Publishing, 2008.

Saulo, Alfredo B. *Communism in the Philippines*. Enlarged ed. Quezon City: Ateneo de Manila University Press, 1990.

Scalice, Joseph. "Crisis of Revolutionary Leadership: Martial Law and the Communist Parties of the Philippines, 1957–1974." PhD, University of California, Berkeley, 2017.

Scalice, Joseph. "A Deliberately Forgotten Battle: The Lapiang Manggagawa and the Manila Port Strike of 1963." *Journal of Southeast Asian Studies* 53, nos. 1–2 (2022): 226–251.

Scalice, Joseph. "The Geopolitical Alignments of Diverging Social Interests: The Sino-Soviet Split and the Partido Komunista ng Pilipinas, 1966–1967." *Critical*

Asian Studies 53, no. 1 (2021): 45–70. https://doi.org/10.1080/14672715.2020 .1870867.

Scalice, Joseph. "'We Are Siding with Filipino Capitalists': Nationalism and the Political Maturation of Jose Ma. Sison, 1959–61." *Sojourn: Journal of Social Issues in Southeast Asia* 36, no. 1 (2021): 1–39. https://doi.org/10.1355/sj36-1a.

Second National Conference on the Nationalist Student Movement. Quezon City: University of the Philippines, Diliman, 6 November 1970. PRP 12/05.01.

Secret Victor Corpus Movement. *What Is Operation Good Friday?*, [August 1971]. PRP 16/17.02.

Serge, Victor. *What Everyone Should Know about State Repression.* Translated by Judith White. New York: New Park Publications, 1979.

Serve the People Brigade. "Caloocan Masaker—Tanda ng Pasismo at Burukrata-Kapitalismo." *Ang Pamantasan* 1, no. 2 (October 1971). PRP 37/13.01.

Silverio, Ina Alleco R. *Ka Bel: The Life and Struggle of Crispin Beltran.* Quezon City: Southern Voices, 2010.

Sison, Jose Ma. *Alejandro Lichauco: A Great Filipino Patriot, Advocate of Full National Independence and Genuine Economic Development,* 22 May 2015. https://josemariasison.org/alejandro-lichauco-a-great-filipino-patriot-advocate-of-full-national-independence-and-genuine-economic-development/.

Sison, Jose Ma. "A Brief Comment to My Detractors." *APL,* 11 June 1971, 4, 56.

Sison, Jose Ma. *Building Strength through Struggle: Selected Writings, 1972 to 1977.* Edited by Julieta de Lima. Vol. 3 of *Continuing the Philippine Revolution.* Quezon City: Aklat ng Bayan, 2013.

Sison, Jose Ma. "Clarifying Tales." *PC,* 30 August 1971, 2.

Sison, Jose Ma. *Defeating Revisionism, Reformism and Opportunism: Selected Writings, 1969 to 1974.* Edited by Julieta de Lima. Vol. 2 of *Continuing the Philippine Revolution.* Quezon City: Aklat ng Bayan, 2013.

Sison, Jose Ma. *Foundation for Resuming the Philippine Revolution: Selected Writings, 1969 to 1972.* Edited by Julieta de Lima. Vol. 1 of *Continuing the Philippine Revolution.* Quezon City: Aklat ng Bayan, 2013.

Sison, Jose Ma. "Greetings to the Movement for a Democratic Philippines." *Anak-Pawis,* 1971. PRP 19/09.01.

Sison, Jose Ma. "Jose Ma. Sison's Statement on His Brother's Disappearance." *PC,* 9 July 1971, 6.

Sison, Jose Ma. *Ka Felixberto 'Bert' Olalia: Hero and Martyr of the Working Class and the Filipino People,* 13 August 2003. https://www.josemariasison.org/inps/talparakayKaBertOlalia.htm.

Sison, Jose Ma. "[Open Letter]." *PC,* 8 July 1970, 3.

Sison, Jose Ma. [Amado Guerrero, pseud.]. *Philippine Society and Revolution.* Hong Kong: Ta Kung Pao, 1971.

Sison, Jose Ma. "Pierce the Enemies with Your Pens." *Dare to Struggle, Dare to Win,* January 1971, 6. PRP 30/03.01.

Sison, Jose Ma. *Recto and the National Democratic Struggle.* Manila: Progressive Publications, 1969.

Sison, Jose Ma. "Social Revolution through National Determination." *PC,* 29 August 1961, 3.

Sison, Jose Ma. [Amado Guerrero, pseud.]. *Specific Characteristics of People's War in the Philippines*. Oakland, CA: International Association of Filipino Patriots (IAFP), 1979.

Sison, Jose Ma. *Struggle for National Democracy*. Quezon City: Progressive Publishers, 1967.

Sison, Jose Ma. "Student Power." *Eastern Horizon* 8, no. 2 (1969): 52–56.

Sison, Jose Ma, and Julieta de Lima Sison. "Foundation for Sustained Development of the National Democratic Movement in the University of the Philippines." In Lumbera, Taguiwalo, Tolentino, Guillermo, and Alamon, *Serve the People*, 43–62.

Sison, Jose Ma, and Rainer Werning. *The Philippine Revolution: The Leader's View*. New York: Taylor & Francis, 1989.

Smith, Joseph B. *Portrait of a Cold Warrior*. New York: Ballantine Books, 1976.

So the People May Know. Vol. 1. Quezon City: General Headquarters, Armed Forces of the Philippines, 1970.

So the People May Know. Vol. 7. Quezon City: General Headquarters, Armed Forces of the Philippines, 1972.

Student Power Assembly of the Philippines. *The Diliman Declaration*, 9 March 1969. PRP 17/12.01.

Student Revolutionary Movement. *A Call to the Filipino Student Youth*, 9 October 1972. PRP 17/15.01.

Students' Alliance for National Democracy (STAND). "Ang Mayo Uno sa Kasaysayan ng Pilipinas." *Ang Estudyante* 1, no. 2 (1 May 1972). PRP 30/08.01.

Sullivan, William H. *Obbligato 1939–1979: Notes on a Foreign Service Career*. New York: W. W. Norton, 1984.

Tagamolila, Antonio. "My Brother, the Defector." *APL*, 14 May 1971, 16, 18.

Tagamolila, Crispin. *Statement on the Corruption and Thievery in the Mercenary Puppet Armed Forces of the Philippines (AFP)*, 1 April 1971. PRP 17/23.01.

Taguiwalo, Mario, and Rey Vea. "II. The University as Base for the Cultural Revolution." *PC*, 10 February 1971, 10, 9.

"A Talk with Dante." *Asiaweek*, 11 September 1981, 27.

Tera, Perfecto, Jr. [Rodrigo Rojas, pseud.]. "The State of the Nation." *Eastern Horizon* 9, no. 1 (1970): 44–50.

Thompson, Mark Richard. "Searching for a Strategy: The Traditional Opposition to Marcos and the Transition to Democracy in the Philippines." Vols. 1 and 2. PhD diss., Yale University, 1991.

Tolentino, Arturo. *Voice of Dissent*. Quezon City: Phoenix Publishing House, 1990.

Tolosa, Benjamin T., Jr., ed. *Socdem: Filipino Social Democracy in a Time of Turmoil and Transition, 1965–1995*. Manila: Friedrich-Ebert-Stiftung, 2011.

Totanes, Stephen Henry S. "Student Activism in the Pre-martial Law Era: A Historical Overview." In *Down from the Hill: Ateneo de Manila in the First Ten Years under Martial Law, 1972–1982*, edited by Christina J. Montiel and Susan Evangelista, 1–54. Quezon City: Ateneo de Manila University Press, 2005.

Trotsky, Leon. *1905*. Translated by Anya Bostock. Chicago: Haymarket Books, 2016.

Trotsky, Leon. *History of the Russian Revolution*. Chicago: Haymarket Books, 2010.

Trotsky, Leon. *The Permanent Revolution and Results and Prospects.* Seattle: Red Letter Press, 2010.

Trotsky, Leon. *The Revolution Betrayed: What Is the Soviet Union and Where Is It Going?* Detroit, MI: Labor Publications, 1991.

Trotsky, Leon. *The Struggle Against Fascism in Germany.* New York: Pathfinder Press, 1971.

Trotsky, Leon. *Writings of Leon Trotsky.* 14 vols. New York: Pathfinder Press, 1975–79.

UP Council of Leaders. *UP Council of Leaders Denounces Election Terrorism,* 1969. PRP 17/47.01.

UP Student Catholic Action (UPSCA) Committee on Mass Media. *So That the People May Know,* 1 June 1970. PRP 18/20.01.

UP Student Catholic Action (UPSCA) Committee on Public and National Affairs. *Tayag!,* 10 July 1970. PRP 18/21.01.

UP Student Catholic Action (UPSCA) Law Chapter. *Panawagan,* 5 February 1971. PRP 18/22.01.

UP Student Council (UPSC). *Boycott Our Classes and Join the Show of Protest against the Fraudulent Elections!!,* 29 November 1969. PRP 18/02.04.

UP Student Council (UPSC). *Ipaghiganti si Sontillano!,* 7 December 1970. PRP 18/02.15.

UP Student Council (UPSC). *January 25th Is Our Day,* 25 January 1971. PRP 18/02.16.

UP Student Council (UPSC). *Oppose Student Fascism! Down with Violent Student Activism,* 2 February 1971. PRP 18/02.30.

UP Student Council (UPSC). *Patibayin ang Lakas ng Nagkakaisang-Hanay na Siyang Nagtataguyod ng Pambansang Demokratikong Pangkulturang Rebolusyon Laban sa mga Mapang-Aping Kapitalista Administrador ng mga Paaralang Nagpipilit na Ituro ang Kolonyal na Uri ng Edukasyon!!!,* 4 December 1970. PRP 18/02.34.

UP Student Council (UPSC) and UP Council of Leaders. *Manifesto,* 19 November 1969. PRP 18/02.25.

UP Student Revolutionary Committee (UP SRC). *Free the University!!,* 1972. PRP 18/24.01.

US Senate Committee on Foreign Relations. *Hearings before the Subcommittee on United States Security Agreements and Commitments Abroad (SACA) of the Committee on Foreign Relations, US Senate, Ninety-First Congress, First Session, Part 1.* Washington, DC: US Government Printing Office, 1969.

Van Auken, Bill. "Castroism and the Politics of Petty-Bourgeois Nationalism." *WSWS,* 7 January 1998. https://www.wsws.org/en/articles/1998/01/cast-j07.html.

Van Der Kroef, Justus M. *Indonesia after Sukarno.* Vancouver: University of British Columbia Press, 1971.

Vigilance Committee of Catholic Action of the Philippines. *Philippine Anthology on Communism I.* N.p.: n.p., 1962.

Vizmanos, Danilo P. *Martial Law Diary and Other Papers.* Quezon City: KEN, 2003.

Vizmanos, Danilo P. *A Matter of Conviction.* Quezon City: Ibon Books, 2006.

Vizmanos, Danilo P. *Through the Eye of the Storm.* Quezon City: KEN, 2000.

Weekley, Kathleen. *The Communist Party of the Philippines, 1968–1993: A Story of Its Theory and Practice.* Quezon City: University of the Philippines Press, 2001.

Wenceslao, Vicente. "On the KM-Lacsina Feud." *APL*, 21 May 1971, 14, 48.

Wilson, Edmund. *To the Finland Station: A Study in the Writing and Acting of History.* New York: Farrar, Straus and Giroux, 1972.

Wright, Marshall. "Memorandum from Marshall Wright of the National Security Council Staff to the President's Special Assistant (Rostow)." Document 353 in *FRUS, 1964–1968*, vol. 26, *Indonesia; Malaysia-Singapore; Philippines*. Washington, DC: US Government Printing Office, 2000.

Wurfel, David. "The Development of Post-war Philippine Land Reform: Political and Sociological Explanations." In *Second View from the Paddy: More Empirical Studies on Philippine Rice Farming and Tenancy*, edited by Antonio J. Ledesma, Perla Q. Makpil, and Virginia A. Miralao, 1–14. Quezon City: Ateneo de Manila University Press, 1983.Young Communist League (YCL). *Don't Be Cowed by Red Baiters*, July 1971. PRP 18/39.01.

Yuyitung, Rizal, ed. *The Case of the Yuyitung Brothers: Philippine Press Freedom under Siege*. Binondo: Yuyitung Foundation, 2000.

Zola, Emile. "J'accuse." In *The Dreyfus Affair: J'accuse and Other Writings*, edited by Alain Pagès, translated by Eleanor Levieux, 43–52. New Haven; Yale University Press, 1996.

Zhou, Taomo. *Migration in the Time of Revolution: China, Indonesia, and the Cold War.* Ithaca, NY: Cornell University Press, 2019.

INDEX

Kamanyang Players, 64
KAMI (Kesatuan Aksi Mahasiswa Indone-
  sia), 41
Karagatan. *See* arms, shipments of
Karingal, Tomas, 55, 129–131, 308–309n262
KASAMA (Katipunan ng mga Samahan ng
  mga Manggagawa), 145–147, 173,
  305n204, 306n215, 310n284
KASAPI (Kapulungan ng mga Sandigan ng
  Pilipinas), 41–42, 118, 120, 160
Katipunan-Makabansa, 104
Katipunan ng Kababaihan para sa Kalayaan,
  106
Kaunlaran, 155
KBLBM (Kilusan ng Bayan Laban sa Batas
  Medicare), 190
Khrushchev, Nikita, 234
Kissinger, Henry, 36–37, 52, 150, 152, 192,
  313n53KM
KM (Kabataang Makabayan), 10, 40, 50,
  64–67, 69–70, 73, 76, 79, 81–83, 88,
  103, 104, 112, 117, 125–138, 147–150,
  155–159, 166, 169, 175, 190, 220, 224,
  236, 259
  claims repression breeds resistance, 80,
    176, 191
  election (1969), 58
  in election (1971), 154, 179–183
  infiltration by agents, 69, 89–90
  Marcos, support for, 12
  MPKP-BRPF, fight with, 108–109,
    150–155, 193–194, 201–202
  SDK, relations with, 61, 63, 75, 78, 191–192
  working class, role in, 139–147, 191
KMP (Katipunan ng Malayang Pagkakaisa),
  155–159, 309n274
Kosygin, Alexei, 192

Lacaba, Jose, 26, 46, 61, 66, 67, 69, 72, 76,
  166, 201, 225, 280n77, 284n14
Lachica, Eduardo, 54, 84
Lacsamana, Jimmy, 148
Lacsina, Ignacio, 15, 141–143, 145, 151, 236,
  304n181, 304–305n198
Ladlad, Vic, 104, 299n87
LAKASDIWA (Lakas ng Diwang Kayumanggi), 42, 120
land reform:
  1963, 94–95, 242
  1972, 236, 239, 242, 252
  See also agrarian question
Lansang, Teodosio, 151, 286n70,
  306–307n238

Lansdale, Edward, 24, 29
Lapiang Manggagawa, 12, 20
Laurel-Langley Agreement (1955), 3–4, 33
Laurel, Jose P., 24
Laurel, Salvador, 14, 25, 67, 79, 132, 188,
  192, 318n23
  support for martial law, 212
Laurel, Sotero, 45–46
Lava, Jesus, 92, 94–95, 97, 151, 238, 251, 259,
  307n243
Lazaro, Lupiño, 127, 144–145
LDA (Liga Demokratiko ng Ateneo),
  125–126
LEADS (League of Editors for a Democratic
  Society), 105, 112, 177, 293n195,
  293n198
Lee, Ricky, 148, 226
Lenin, Vladimir, 6–8, 99, 102, 140, 234, 238
  democratic dictatorship, 6
Le Pen, Marine, 261
Liberal Party. *See* LP
Lichauco, Alejandro, 184, 317n113
Lin Biao, 10, 14, 93, 275n23
Lion's Club, 190, 216
literature, of the Communist parties, 18-19
Liu Shaoqi, 93
Llorente, Max, 54
LM (Lapiang Manggagawa), 12, 20
Locsin, Teodoro, Jr., 13
Lopez family, 16, 25–26, 38–39, 41, 86, 110,
  119, 134, 188, 199–200
  See also Lopez, Eugenio; Lopez, Fernando
Lopez, Eugenio, 24, 61, 63, 110, 123, 132,
  134, 188, 199–200
  See also Lopez family
Lopez, Fernando, 14, 73, 110–111, 118–119,
  121, 138, 188, 199
  See also Lopez family
Lopez, Salvador, 62, 126, 128–133, 285n47,
  303n168, 308–309n262
LP (Liberal Party), 14, 23, 50–52, 58–59, 113,
  187–188, 233
  election (1971), 163, 164, 264
  endorses martial law, 212
  FQS, 63, 76
  relations with CPP, 176
Lumumba University, 108
Luneta, Jose, 168, 172
Lyceum, 24, 45–46, 81, 88, 89, 141, 288n108,
  292n190

Macahiya, Ernesto, 239, 259
Macalde, Benilda, 90

Index of Places

Printed in the USA
CPSIA information can be obtained
at www.ICGtesting.com
LVHW091121240923
759040LV00002B/100

9 781501 770470